April 2020

Discourse and power in
 educational organizations

Discourse and Power in Educational Organizations

UNDERSTANDING EDUCATION AND POLICY

William T. Pink and George W. Noblit, *series editors*

Discourse and Power in Educational Organizations
  David Corson, ed.

Continuity and Contradiction: The Futures of the Sociology of Education
  George W. Noblit and William T. Pink, eds.

Good Schools: The Policy Environment Perspective
  Charles A. Tesconi

forthcoming

Stepping Back: Grounded Perspectives on Interagency Collaboration
  Amee Adkins, Catherine Awsumb, George W. Noblit, and Penny Richards

The Social Construction of Urban Education
  Louis F. Miron

A General Theory for a Democratic School
  Art Pearl and Tony Knight

Accommodating Change at Parkview School
  Hilary A. Radnor

From Disabling to Enabling Schools
  Roger Slee, Mel Ainscow and Michael Hardman

For

William John Corson

Contents

PART TWO: THE DISCOURSES OF POLICY AND CURRICULUM

Foreword

This book follows the "discursive turn" in the social sciences. Linguists, sociologists, historians, and anthropologists have long discovered important differences in the discursive practices of culturally, socially, and historically remote peoples, differences that no doubt have deep implications for differences in social cognition and human interests. For many people, the "discursive turn" now occurring across the social sciences could not come soon enough. It has been delayed mainly by institutional forces to do with the boundaries between academic disciplines and with the vested interests of those tied to earlier ways of perceiving the world. Its arrival is now having an impact even on the most conservative of disciplines.

In their important book, Rom Harré and Grant Gillett (1994) signal the appearance and the rapid rise of a genuinely new psychology: "discursive psychology." Even though their focus seems to be on psychology, this new field extends to all branches of the human sciences, involving anthropology, sociology, and linguistics in a synthesis of trends that are already appearing or established. "It is both remarkable and interesting that the old psychologies continue to exist alongside the new" say the authors, and they begin their description with a critical look at "the traditional experimentalist psychology that still exists, particularly in the United States" (p. 2).

Although this edited collection is not part of the discursive psychology literature, the two have a common source. The source of discursive psychology is in the idea of the social world as a discursive construction. In psychology the work of Jerome Bruner opened the way for thinking about human cognition in other than the methods and the metaphysics of the experimentalist tradition. Discursive psychology has already gone beyond Bruner's path-breaking work by discarding the twin dogmas of cognitive science: that inner mental states and processes exist; and that they are much the same for all human beings. As a result, discursive psychology acknowledges the reality and importance of those differences that linguists, sociologists, historians, and anthropologists have long discovered in the cognitive performances and practices of people.

Wittgenstein's idea of following a rule is at the root of the new discursive revolution: Mental activity is not tied to some internal set of processes; it is a range of moves set against a background of human activity governed by informal conventions or rules, especially rules to do with the ways in which words and other symbols are used within the structures of a language (Corson, 1995). For Harré and Gillett, whatever existence the psychological world might have, it is not reducible or replaceable by explanations based on physiology, or any materialist discipline that does not get to grips with the structure of meanings in the lives of the cultural group to which a subject belongs. Getting inside those structures means getting inside the forms of life, norms, conventions, and rules, and seeing them as the subject does.

These ideas complement developments in a critical realist philosophy of the social sciences (Bhaskar, 1986; Corson, 1991a; 1991c) in which the task in understanding human behavior is one of interpretation and empathy, not prediction and control. Notably the self reports of the people under study provide the real data for investigation, but these are not falsifiable reports of mind states; they are statements of how things really are to the "subject." They are ontologically real and must be treated as true indicators of the social structures and cultural values that are important in the lives of subjects. Even the terms "observer" and "subject" become redundant in this account, to be replaced by the idea of co-participants who are making sense of the world and their experience of it.

As in discursive psychology, the subject matter of the social sciences in general is changing radically to include discourses, significations, subjectivities, and positionings because this is where mental events are really located. As Harré and Gillett conclude: "the study of the mind is a way of understanding the phenomena that arise when different sociocultural discourses are integrated within an identifiable human individual situated in relation to those discourses" (p. 22). This shift in direction alters the theoretical base of psychology. It threatens to destroy its subject matter entirely because the mind of an individual becomes a nexus or meeting point of social relations, integrating the multifaceted subjectivity that arises from this intersection of influences. Each human individual stands at a unique intersection of discourses and relationships: a "position" that largely determines mind.

If the influences that shape individual cognition are social and interpersonal, then discourse has a formative influence on the development of individual psychology: Social influences shape brain function, as Harré and Gillett argue. But it is a corollary of their argument that seems central to a critical realist account of the world set within a postmodern condition. If social influences shape brain function, which shapes social influences, then this provisionally explains the workings of many forms of groupthink such as ideology, propaganda, stereotypes, religious and political indoctrination, and the group loyalty of criminal gangs, fanatical subcultures, and many bureaucrats. Doubtless it increases the prospects of emancipation from some of these influences.

For some time, discourse analysts, ethnomethodologists, conversation analysts, and sociologists of language have been setting this new course in the social sciences. The "discursive turn" is now beginning to have a wider impact on educational studies. This book tries to show the relevance of the "discursive turn" to one area of educational studies: educational administration—which is a field of enquiry that is ripe for reform and redirection.

DISCOURSE AND POWER IN EDUCATIONAL ORGANIZATIONS

The ideas and the facts assembled in this volume are radical ones for the study of school organizations and classrooms. Every chapter adds a complex and challenging dimension to the rather monadic account of power that informs much of the work in educational administration. In that account, power in organizations is said to depend either on formal authority, or on prestige, and it is demonstrated through dominance over others.

Although the alternative to this monadic view is clearly a more provocative one, I think that it is also much more optimistic. It tends to challenge the cosy acceptance of hierarchy and formal authority that we still see almost everywhere in the management of schools: the preoccupation with manipulating or surveying the affairs of others, as those others, in their turn, control the affairs of their students. As a result, it also bypasses approaches to the study of educational administration that fill most of the pages of educational administration journals: approaches that often seem divorced from concern for the quality and relevance of curriculum, for the humanity of pedagogy, for the moral consequences of policies, and for the wishes of diverse sociocultural communities now reaching into schools from every side.

In general, this alternative view grows from critical, poststructuralist, and postpositivist conceptions of the relationship between discourse and social reality, including relations of dominance. It sees social reality and relations of dominance as constituted subjectively: social realities cannot be identified in abstraction from the discourses in which they are embedded. Language, as always, is the prime data in social research. In fact, it is the *only* data with which we can work to understand the social world because everything, including information about values, attitudes, ideologies, and preferences, has to be put into a language before we can share it with one another and work with it. More than this, as the developing field of "discursive psychology" contends, discourse is the true origin of the self, of the emotions, of consciousness, and of human freedom itself.

Although this "discursive turn" is an unsettling one for the many who are steeped in the old ways of doing things, it is becoming hard to ignore because it is consistent with almost all contemporary positions in the philosophy of the social sciences. As a result, there is a new openness in theory and practice in the human sciences. Disciplinary boundaries are crumbling, as disciplinary discourses that were once distinct begin to integrate with one another. It is likely that the study of educational administration cannot remain a remote outpost in the human sciences—a walled institution located on a backroad—and still survive as an area of study.

ACKNOWLEDGMENTS

This book about discourse, power, and educational organizations was planned as a collaborative venture by Andy Hargreaves and me—as a marriage, late in life, of the postmodernist and the critical realist perspectives. Considering our somewhat different perspectives on these issues, our decision that the book should go ahead with only me as editor might seem to arise from some conflict of perspective. But this was not the case. Rather, Andy's busy schedule of commitments meant that the book, and the important material it contains, would have been delayed by many months if its completion were to fit into that schedule. So, rather than be named as a co-editor, Andy settled for my offer of "effusive comments in the Foreword," which is what these words are conveying.

Andy's assistance with the editing and the revising of many of the submitted chapters was invaluable. I am also indebted to him for his suggestions about contributors, which add greatly to the success of the volume. Also Bob Young agreed to read the manuscript and to comment, especially on the two linking chapters. His laconic appraisal was that all seemed to be in order with the theory and the argument but that I would probably upset a few postmodernists by presenting that argument. This was music to my ears, of course. Although I find much to agree with in "postmodernism," as in critical theory, there is much to argue with in both as well. In an applied field like educational administration, in which everything has to have a remote link (at least) with mundane practice, it is best not to operate from a single campsite. As academic disciplines in the social sciences just begin to fade from view at last, it would be a shame to replace them with new paradigms of thought that are just as impermeable, if a little more fashionable. There is a quote from Foucault that I like as much as any other:

> I think I have in fact been situated in most squares on the political checkerboard, one after another and sometimes simultaneously: as anarchist, leftist, ostentatious or disguised Marxist, nihilist, explicit or secret anti-Marxist, technocrat in the service of Gaullism, new liberal, etc. . . . None of these descriptions is important by itself; taken together, on the other hand, they mean something. And I must admit that I rather like what they mean. (1984, pp. 383-384)

I inevitably fall short of Foucault as "a protean being," but I think that there is virtue in trying to maintain with him "a quasi-Nietzschean refusal to let thought coagulate into systematic dogma."

Much of the time and effort that I have put into other books was spared me in putting this book together because of the remarkable way in which Tiiu Strauss, a graduate assistant at OISE, took it all on. The list of tasks is impressive: She compiled a single set of references from diversely referenced single chapters; she followed up authors in six countries with queries and oversights; she made the many chapters consistent in their style and structure; she dealt with the nightmare of 14 chapters each one produced in a slightly different computer application; and she did it all while dodging blizzards between Toronto and St. Catharines. She likened it all to "herding cats."

David Corson
OISE
Toronto, Canada
November 1994

Series Preface

Books in this series, *Understanding Education and Policy*, will present a variety of perspectives to better understand the aims, practices, content and contexts of schooling, and the meaning of these analyses for educational policy. Our primary intent is to redirect the language used, the voices included in the conversation, and the range of issues addressed in the current debate concerning schools and policy. In doing this, books in the series will explore the differential conceptions and experiences that surface when analysis includes racial, class, gender, ethnic and other key differences. Such a perspective will span the social sciences (anthropology, history, philosophy, psychology, sociology etc.), and research paradigms.

Books in the series will be grounded in the contextualized lives of the major actors in school (students, teachers, administrators, parents, policy makers etc.) and address major theoretical issues. The challenge to authors is to fully explore life-in-schools, through the multiple lenses of various actors and within the anticipated scope that such a range of empirically sound and theoretically challenging work will contribute to a fundamental and needed rethinking of the content, process and context for school reform.

In this book edited by David Corson, *Discourse and Power in Educational Organizations*, authors from several countries take a fresh look at key organizational issues. The role of language in the exercise of power is the central focus of the book. The international perspectives, together with the use of post-modern conceptualizations and critical theory, help reframe the frequently ethnocentric ways of problematizing the forms and content of educational organizations. We are happy to present this book as the third in the series, *Understanding Education and Policy*.

List of Contributors

Jill Blackmore
Faculty of Education
Deakin University
Victoria
Australia 3217

Jo Blase
University of Georgia
College of Education
Dept. of Educational Leadership
G-10 Aderhold Hall
Athens, GA 30602-7171

Jo Roberts Blase
University of Georgia
College of Education
Dept. of Educational Leadership
G-10 Aderhold Hall
Athens, GA 30602-7171

Jan Branson
School of Education
Centre for the Study of Cultural
    and Educational Practice
La Trobe Univeristy
Bundoora Victoria
Australia

Cleo Cherryholmes
Dept. of Political Science
Michigan State University
346 South Keckzie Hall
East Lansin, MI 48824

David Corson
Dept. of Educational Administration
Ontario Institute for
    Studies in Education
252 Bloor Street West
Toronto, Ontario M5S 1V6

James Cummins
Depart of Curriculum
Ontario Institute for
    Studies in Education
252 Bloor Street West
Toronto, Ontario M5V 1V6

Favardin Daliri
School of Education
James Cook University of Queensland
Townsville Q 4811
Australia

Norman Fairclough
Dept. of Linguistics and
   Modern English Language
Lancaster University
Lancaster, LA1 4YT
United Kingdom

Tracey Hill
Macquarie University
North Ryde NSW
2109 Australia

Joan Kale
School of Education
James Cook University of Queensland
Townsville Q 4811
Australia

Jane Kenway
Faculty of Education
Deakin University
Victoria
Australia 3217

Allan Luke
School of Education
James Cook University of Queensland
Townsville Q 4811
Australia

Don Miller
School of Education
Centre for the Study of Cultural
   and Educational Practice
La Trobe University
Bundoora Victoria
Australia 3083

Andy Perry
Administration and Policy Studies
Hofstra University
Hempstead, NY 11550

Viviane Robinson
Education Department
The University of Aukland
Private Bag 92019
Aukland, New Zealand

Charol Shakeshaft
Administration and Policy Studies
Hofstra, NY 11550

Michael Garbutcheon Singh
School of Education
James Cook University of Queensland
Townsville Q 4811
Australia

Duncan Waite
University of Georgia
College of Education
Dept. of Educational Leadership
G-10 Aderhold Hall
Athens, GA 30602

Ruth Wodak
Dept. of Applied Linguistics
University of Vienna
Berggasse 11/1/8
1090 Vienna
Australia

Stanton E.F. Wortham
Department of Education
Bates College
Lewiston, ME 04240

Robert Young
Dept. of Social Policy
   Studies in Education
Sydney, NSW
Australia 2006

PART ONE

THE DISCOURSES OF ADMINISTRATION AND SUPERVISION

1

Discursive Power in Educational Organizations: An Introduction

David Corson
Ontario Institute for Studies in Education

POWER AND LANGUAGE

This books use of the term *language* is an inclusive one. In some places *language* means "a language" or "a language variety." Elsewhere it refers to "verbal repertoire," "mode of discourse," or some other elements of language as organized for use. As Dell Hymes (1966) urges, in determining the role of discourse or language in human affairs, one has to get down to cases, and cases are always a matter of specific modes of use and specific organizations of linguistic means.

There are many theories of power, but none seems to capture in full the range of meanings that individuals can reasonably attach to this difficult term (Lukes, 1974; Wrong, 1979). Rather than working from any single theory of power, the purposes here are better served by dealing directly with the link between *power* and *language*. This seems a reasonable course to follow because even including the form of power that is expressed through physical violence (in punishment, warfare, confinement or any of the other manifestations of physical violence), all kinds of power are directed, mediated or resisted through language. For most everyday human purposes, power is exerted through verbal channels: Language is the vehicle for identifying, manipulating, and changing power relations between people.

Relating Language and Power: Four Lines of Debate

This brief account gives only a few signposts to the many theorists who discuss the relationship between language and power. In this section I present four lines of debate that are far from discrete. In general, this chapter's starting ideas come from the third and the fourth lines of debate. Later I return to the second when siting my discussion in the postmodern condition that provides the context for current debates.

The oldest continuous line of debate about language and power has its roots in the surviving classical works of political and moralist orators such as Cicero and Demosthenes, who used language as an instrument for wielding power, even while reflecting themselves upon the rhetorical force of that usage. Both were very aware that oratorical language can be almost devoid of propositional content yet still have power. It is easy to see this debate continuing in the ideas of Dewey, Hegel, and Marx, who saw a connection between moral power brokering and the sophisticated human ability to wield complex vocabularies. Bourdieu (1988) extends this line of debate in his discussion of "magisterial language," especially as it is wielded by public figures and academics in universities: The language acquires a status and authority that tends to rule out any question about the genuinely informative efficiency of the communication.

A second line of debate connects the instability of discourse with structures of power and meaning. This debate can be traced back to one of the earliest Western historians, Thucydides, who wondered why it was, after the devastations of the Peloponnesian War between the Athenian and the Spartan alliances, that "many words had lost their meanings." This and the first line of debate recur in contemporary hermeneutics, especially in those disciplines in which the difficult ideas of poststructuralism are discussed. Poststructuralists argue that if human subjectivity is unstable, then anything that depends on subjectivity as a base, such as discourses about social arrangements, power distributions, and structures, is inherently unstable and potentially illusory.

A third line of debate springs from the ideas of Marx and Engels (1846/1976) linking power and language by way of ideology.[1] That influence continues through the work of key interpreters in the Marxian tradition on this topic, such as Gramsci, Habermas, Bourdieu, and Bhaskar, who see structure and agency as key concepts in addressing the issue, and who see power over discourse as a means for elevating the needs and interests of powerless groups above those of the system that is designed and controlled by elites. Modern ide-

---

[1]In trying to understand the several interpreters of Marxian ideas discussed here, there is a key distinction in the writings of Marx himself. For him *ideology* has two manifestations, and each is inseparable from language and meaning: In the one, ideology is a system of ideas that distorts reality in order to serve the interests of a dominant group (e.g., for Bhaskar *positivism* is a system of ideas that distorts reality in this way); in the other, ideology is a means of penetrating the consciousness of human actors and uncovering the real foundations of activities (i.e., the task of critical theory).

ology studies, which examine language from two vantage points, continue this line of debate. In the one approach to the study of language and ideology, questions are asked about the development of "political narratives" and their effects. These narratives seem to take on a power of their own so that structural relations of domination become represented as "legitimate" through the stories that are told to justify the exercise of power by agents who hold it. For example, Faye's study of narratives of National Socialism that were developed during the Weimar period in Germany shows how effective these "stories" were when circulated within their limited sphere of operation and structured space (cited in Thompson, 1984). Any power in the battle of words that took place under Weimar lay with the languages of German nationalism, antisemitism, and militarism. In the other approach to the study of language and ideology, questions are asked not so much about the discourse of the ideologues themselves but about the language of everyday life and the taken-for-granted semantic structures that mundane discourse distributes among men and women.

A fourth line, not unrelated to the third, can be traced through German Romantic ideas about any power that language has in shaping thought and world view. Extending these ideas, thinkers such as Herder, von Humboldt, and Fichte were outspoken in promoting notions of linguistic nationalism, eventually with the tragic human consequences already noted. These thinkers have had their own academic impact too in linguistic anthropology, especially through the Sapir-Whorf hypothesis and in the ideas of some feminist writers who see "manmade language" having an Orwellian role in "controlling" women's thought. This account of "thought control via malespeak" is difficult to support because meaning in language depends on context and is ultimately indeterminate; no group can fix meaning or exercise power over it (Cameron, 1984). Sapir's view, too, that language is a guide to social reality and even powerfully conditions all our thinking about social problems and processes, seems overstated. However, it is clear that language is an expression of a world view (Hymes, 1966): In many contexts of use it does more than just reflect social structures; it can also perpetuate existing differences in power by expressing a prejudiced view of the world.

The Immanent Power of Language

There is a key question implicit in all these debates: Does language have power of and by itself? Certainly George Orwell in his fictional *1984* seemed worried by the immanent influence of language, especially at the mass political level. His negative utopian account of totalitarianism at work found its factual parallel in many real-world regimes of the left and the right. It is true that key figures in these regimes have often operated as if they believed that language has power of and by itself. Yet, as Wrong (1979) notes, even the Orwellian use of language to control people at a distance depended on science fiction techniques to overcome the visibility problem: two-way television screens that projected the powerful into the setting of the controlled. Language alone was not enough. Indeed, even the intensity and comprehensiveness of power itself tends to vary inversely with its extensiveness. On the other hand, as mentioned, language does reflect social patterns such as sex-role stereotypes in such a way as to reinforce and disseminate those patterns, embodying a point of view of which people are unaware, and this is a form of power without any clear agency. Perhaps we have some reason for assenting to the immanent power of language if we allow that it does fashion, reflect, and reinforce structures of domination with no apparent agents at work.

Whichever way we look at language, it is hard to ignore that language is essentially powerless on its own. It is people who have the power to use language in various ways; it is people who give discourse its form and make judgments about the status of various texts; and it is the situations in which people have power and are using language to serve some potent purpose that give language a power that it lacks when it is without such precise contexts. As Bakhtin observes, by manipulating the effects of context it is "very easy to make even the most serious utterance comical" (1975/1981, p. 340). For examples of this we need look no further than the clever ironies and satires that are used in television comedies such as *Yes Minister* and *Monty Python* to parody the pretensions and the pomposity of powerful figures by putting their language into contexts that are subtly but critically removed from settings that are normally pregnant with power. Again the dissident movements in Eastern European countries from the 1950s to the 1980s used the language of theater and satirical poetry to counter power. But this power of dissident resistance came about because the powerful allowed the dissidents their theater and poetry as a political safety valve for dissent. Without that shrewd concession, made by authorities creating contexts of meaning where dissident power could be exercised while the authorities remained relentlessly totalitarian in other contexts, the language of the dissenters might have had much less influence.

Language then seems mainly an instrument of power, a claim that meshes with Michel Foucault's (1972, 1977, 1980) judgment on the matter: Rather than a privilege that is ascribed to the individual, power itself is a network of relations constantly in tension and ever-present in activity; rather than possessed and localized in individual hands, power is exercised through the production, accumulation, and functioning of various discourses; rather than the mere verbalization of conflicts of domination, power is the very object of human conflict; and rather than concerned with conscious intention or decision, the study of power is best located at the point where any intentions of the powerful are invested in real and effective practices. In short, the development of particular forms of language meets the needs of the powerful and depends on a particular exercise of power through discourse practices.

POWER AND THE POSTMODERN CONDITION

Postmodernism is not the same as poststructuralism. As mentioned earlier, post-structuralists are part of an intellectual movement that maintains that because human subjectivity is unstable, then anything that depends on subjectivity as a base, such as discourses about social arrangements, power distributions, and structures, is inherently unstable and potentially illusory. In contrast, postmodernism is neither an intellectual movement nor a philosophy; it is a condition of society said to characterize the postindustrial and postpositivist age that contemporary social institutions are a part of. Those who describe the postmodern condition often borrow poststructuralist terminology; they rely heavily on Foucault's theories of power (Skeggs, 1991). Indeed, they often seem unwilling to theorize any form of power other than the local, following Foucault's view that systems of knowledge operate within localized settings to codify techniques and social practices. As a result, postmodernity is often portrayed as having two distinct but balancing tendencies (after Hargreaves, 1994): an almost universal trend away from things such as centralization, mass production, specialization, and mass consumption, including the standardized school systems that used to be the norm almost everywhere; and an almost universal trend toward the development of flexible technologies that are developed and used in smaller and more diverse units, including a rapid increase in diversity among schools and greater devolution of educational control. A welcome result of these very real tendencies in human affairs is that more voices seem to be raised and at least heard in society these days, including the voices of those who were formerly dispossessed.

Yet there is an anachronism in Foucault's work that underlines a dilemma that confronts all those who theorize about language and power. Habermas (1985) observes that Foucault has to fall back on the linguistic tools of reason in order to argue against that same "tradition of reason" that has always been a centerpiece of the modernity that we are said to be leaving behind.[2] So in order to put froward the case that he advances, Foucault still has to marshall resources of language that are the product of the very macro and rationalistic power relationships of which he does not speak. These resources include formula expressions and robust metaphors, conventions of vocabulary, and the communicative power of an official language of rationalism that is standardized nationally and internationally. Clearly these tools of discourse are structured as much by macro forces as by the mundane discourse of individuals and small local groups.

Postmodernism as presently theorized tends to overlook the fact that whereas more diverse voices are being raised and heard, power forces beyond the local continue to ignore the messages that those voices are conveying. This

---

[2]Habermas himself advocates a devolved communicative approach to resolving the sociopolitical problems that modernism has created (see Chapter 8); yet the discourse of his own writings is hardly a model to follow in reaching the solution that he recommends.

is nowhere more the case than in education, in which often the tendency toward devolution in decision making has been accompanied by a trend toward inequity in provisions and injustice on a grand scale. Foucault's ideas are less useful for understanding the power of centralized organizations and institutions and their ideologies. Yet, like micro power, this form of power can also have a positive or a negative influence; this potential for both good and evil in a macro system is much greater than the aggregate potentials that might arise from all of that systems local devolved sites.

Adding a Critical Realist Perspective to Postmodernity

To bring questions of access, equity, and quality of provision into debates about education, we need to add into the discussion a critical realist account of discourse and power, especially one that sees the organization of contemporary education almost everywhere as intricately entwined with capitalist social relations. A major contradiction for education in settings of cultural and social diversity comes from the fact that capitalist social relations are among the most homogenizing and assimilationary forces that the world has ever seen. But in the world of affluence, privilege, and consumerism often described by theorists of postmodernity, policies and practices touching directly on these social and cultural relations often remain untheorized. Moreover, postmodern social actors are said to inhabit such a diversity of language games that their sociocultural identities and allegiances tend to mean nothing. Some critics of *postmodernism* see this as an advocacy of anarchy or nihilism, in which no one accepts responsibility for others or acknowledges their collective identity. However, this seems to be more a recipe for ultraconservatism than for anarchy: If postmodernity is a condition in which anything goes, then probably everything will remain the same.

A critical realist account is concerned with identifying the actual structures that constrain human action, structures whose modification and removal can prove emancipatory for human beings in general. I am using the notion of *structure* to refer to the intractability of the social world. Structures set limits to freedom, often in tacit ways, through a complex interplay of powers within diverse social institutions. Cultural values, for example, are structures that influence discourse norms; the very existence of the cultural values is manifested in those discursive practices (Corson, 1993b). In Roy Bhaskar's account outlined in Chapter 6, structures of power have no existence separate from the activities that they govern and from agents' reports (in language) of those activities. It is true that the discourse of individuals is heavily influenced by institutional practices: Human agents are tightly constrained by discursive structures, and the effects of these constraints often show up in stereotyped and unjust oppositions that severely disadvantage females and social or cultural minorities. But it is also true that structures in their turn are reconstructed and reinforced by acts of individual discourse in micro settings. Indeed, the very possibility of emancipation from oppressive ideologies and structures depends on this being so.

Critical realism takes into account the wider contexts of human social interaction and the power relations that both constrain and liberate that interaction. But it is more a way of theorizing society than a body of theory about society. Its critique is expressed in a healthy skepticism about things that are often taken for granted in the social world, especially those things that go unchallenged because of ideologies about disciplinary boundaries, fixed categories, and orthodoxies of all kinds. Rather than being engaged in a mission to accumulate knowledge, critical realism is more a mission of "crap detection." Its success depends on free and open discourse in every human context. For this reason, some of the ideas of Habermas (1984) about communicative action in social institutions are important for this discussion.

Habermas believes that the Western world is still largely stuck in a crisis of modernity, in which the communicatively structured interaction that is needed to move beyond modernity, has been increasingly pushed to the margins. Chapter 6 tries to outline the relevance of his solution to this crisis; and Chapter 8 relates his solution to the problems of policy and practice in schools and classrooms. In outline, his solution involves the creation of organizations and institutions in which practical questions of general interest can be submitted to public discussion and resolved on the basis of discursively achieved agreement.

A CRITICAL ACCOUNT OF LANGUAGE, EDUCATION, AND POWER

Socialization Process

The process of schooling is a form of "social and cultural reproduction" that is linked openly to other structures in society, especially economic structures, that reproduce social relations. Apple (1982b) lists some of the major social functions that schools have: They select and certify a workforce; they maintain privilege by taking the form and content of the dominant culture and defining it as legitimate knowledge to be passed on; they are agents in the creation and the re-creation of an effectively dominant culture; they legitimate new knowledge, new classes, and strata of social personnel. In short, for Apple, as part of their raison d'être, schools allocate people and legitimate knowledge, or legitimate people and allocate knowledge. As a result, formal education in many of its practices looks after the interests of some social groups better than the interests of some other social groups. As I argue later, language is the vehicle for this routine activity of power distribution through education.

Society, Language, and Control

Although an individual's language code and styles of usage are very personal possessions, there are obvious similarities between people in the codes and styles of language that they use. These commonalities in language orientation make communication possible; the degree of commonality is roughly in inverse proportion to the social distance between people. Social distance (or closeness) between individuals is maintained by aspects of social structure, by the possibilities for interaction, by constraints on social behavior, and by a myriad of other sociocultural processes and norms. All of these things combine to help shape the meaning and value of an individual's code and style of language. This means that in any context the prevailing constraints of social structure interact with the social behavior and social location of individuals in such a way as to add or subtract shades of meaning or significance, so that what is said and the way in which it is said is heavily influenced by factors external to the individual. A cornerstone of poststructuralist ideas about language is that the meaning of any item of discourse cannot be disentangled from its social context. For example, in interactions between speakers of different social, gender, or cultural backgrounds, the same fragment of discourse uttered by different individuals can be given very different meanings. More than this, a different pragmatic or cultural value may be placed on that utterance depending on the background of the utterer.

Ideology theorists are alert to the influence of these extralinguistic factors on how language is valued and used. They speak of language users having images of themselves and of their roles that make them conform in their language behavior to dominant influences in their social environment. Gramsci (1948) highlights the noncoercive aspect of domination, comparing it with the more obvious coercive forms of power. His concept of *hegemony* describes the organization of consent through invisible cultural dominance rather than through visible political power. In developed modern societies, control is exercised in a modern way that gives stability by basing power on wide-ranging consent and agreement. This noncoercive "force" is said to penetrate consciousness itself so that the dominated become accomplices in their own domination.

So it is argued that power hegemonies are reinforced from both sides of the power relationship: In their language usages the nondominant adhere to the linguistic norms created by dominant groups, while not recognizing that they are being "voluntarily coerced." This is a point about how power operates more generally, which writers such as Orwell and Dostoevsky also observe. Wrong (1979) concludes that there are psychological pressures from both sides of the power equation that help the powerful by converting coercive forms of power into what is perceived instead as legitimate authority. This phenomenon has been repeatedly evidenced in sociolinguistic studies: The classic instance is from Labov (1972) who found that stigmatized features of speech are judged most harshly by the very people whose speech most exhibits those features. In legitimating norms for language behavior, this noncoercive psychological pressure can produce conformity even among actors from different sociological categories. For example, socially powerless men use the same sorts of features of speech that women do in formal social settings (O'Barr, 1982). In this instance, speech differences correlate with lack of power rather than just with gender; social rank interacts with gender. Socialization into the role of an accomplice in one's own domination in social settings shows up in a use of linguistic norms that acknowledge the legitimacy of those imbalanced social relations.

The next two chapters in this volume take up questions of power relationships between speakers of different statuses and relate them especially to gender differences in administrative discourse. In Chapter 2, Charol Shakeshaft and Andy Perry set the "language of power" alongside the "language of empowerment." They examine the performance of women as school managers and the gender differences in communication, evaluation, and feedback that accompany that performance. Their chapter proposes that one explanation for the difference in effectiveness and style of women administrators lies in the language used by women themselves, which emphasizes power with rather than power over others.

In Chapter 3, Ruth Wodak uses a real-world context for her study of power, discourse, and styles of female leadership in school committee meetings. After considering the relationship between power, hierarchy, and interaction in public institutions, she reports on studies carried out in three schools in which statutory committees have been established to conform with a school/community partnership law. In these conventionally hierarchical institutions, female principals adopt contrasting discursive strategies to justify, legitimize, and achieve their administrative agenda.

DISCOURSE, IDEOLOGY, AND POWER IN EDUCATIONAL ADMINISTRATION

As I have argued, current debates on the nature of power link the concept intricately with the use of discourse. Again, the development of particular forms of language meets the needs of the powerful, but this development depends reciprocally on a particular exercise of power through discourse practices. These views are radical ones for the study of the administration of schools. They add a complex and challenging dimension to the rather monadic account of power that emerges from the structuralist/functionalist and logical empiricist traditions. In those traditions, power in any organization is said to depend on either formal authority or on prestige, and it is demonstrated through dominance over others (Abbott & Caracheo, 1988).

A more contemporary view grows from poststructuralist and postpositivist conceptions of the relationship between discourse and social reality, which includes relations of dominance. This view is more characteristic of the postmodern condition in which we increasingly find ourselves. It sees social reality and relations of dominance as constituted subjectively: Social realities cannot be identified in abstraction from the language in which they are embedded

(Hughes, 1990). Following this account, the reality of social organizations, or of structures and entities in the natural world, cannot be conceived of or known independent of the concepts in language; reality is constructed through the use of language. More than this, language and meanings are not private and subjective things; they are public and intersubjective things, subject to struggles and disputes that lead to the creation of new meanings and the constant evolution of language itself. Because of this, meanings receive their sense from the context in which they are located through an interpretation made by speakers who are informed by that background context and by all the intellectual baggage that they bring with them into the context. Disputes about actions and activities do not come about because of the inadequacy of natural language in saying what we mean; these disputes are characteristic features of language as a social activity and as the central part of society's nature as a moral order.

Although there has been some support for the idea that power in school organizations is in some sense relational (Muth, 1984), even in this case power is still seen in rather simple terms as a convenient manipulative tool. The ideology that power is naturalistically hierarchical has been challenged formally in the literature by Corson (1986a) and implicitly by Dunlap and Goldman (1991). The latter argue that power in schools is primarily facilitative and interactive, rather than authoritative and coercive, but that this does not necessarily exclude more determinative forms of power from a role. A point to note is that power on this more recent account is something that can hardly be portrayed in an organizational flowchart or in the feedback loops and diagrams of systems analysts, because no flowchart or diagram is sophisticated enough to represent the situational effects of language in creating the background to power. Indeed, the recent account linking discourse and power sits uncomfortably with many scholarly debates in educational administration as the field has developed alongside compulsory schooling itself.

Chapters 4 and 5 capture some of the complexities involved, both in exercising discursive power as a school administrator and in responding to that administrative power as a teacher. Jo Roberts and Joseph Blase in Chapter 4 examine the micropolitics of successful supervisor-teacher interaction in instructional conferences. They note the lack of systematic research that goes beyond the bureaucratic and technical character of the supervisory conference. Reporting interactions of novice and experienced supervisors with teachers in instructional conferences, they suggest that the key goals of supervisory conferences are often put out of reach by political factors at work in the setting. The chapter contrasts control-oriented with empowering discursive strategies and their role in the development of successful conferencing.

In response to the growing use of instructional conferences as a device of administration, Chapter 5 also examines administrator-teacher conferences. Although the teacher supervision literature conventionally presents supervision as growth inducing for teachers and as a means for the improvement of instruction, Duncan Waite tries to deal more adequately with the balance of power in these conferences, especially with the problem of teacher resistance. Using conversational analysis, he presents the tactics and resources available to teachers for asserting countercontrol in conference settings and for making them more cooperative and empowering during administrative activities.

Earlier Studies of Discourse and Educational Administration

Prior to the studies reported in this volume, the literature of educational administration presented only a few analytical studies of the actual discourse used in administrative contexts. This is not surprising given the recent developments in discourse analysis and given the fact that educational administration as a field of study has been rather isolated from many developments in the parent disciplines of the social sciences. This includes those developments in the philosophy of the social sciences that increasingly license researchers to recognize human reasons and accounts in language as priority, social scientific data. Here I mention only two sets of studies that appear in the early literature. These have their origins in the late 1970s and are linked no doubt to the quickening of interest in discourse analysis that began at that time. Gronn (1983, 1984) and Hargreaves (1981) both used transcribed analyses of administrator or teacher talk in schools as brute data for their theorizing.

Gronn's two case studies analyze extracts from transcripts of talk recorded by the researcher. The first study (1983) concentrated on informal talk by and with the principal of a school recorded in the corridor, office, and staffroom. Gronn argued that this talk that takes up so much of the principal's day is really "the work" of educational administration, and that through his use of discourse the principal relaxes and tightens his administrative control. The second study (1984) concentrated on semiformal talk, recorded at a school council meeting in which the principal and the councillors debate the allocation of money for teaching aids. In this case study, Gronn went beyond the discourse itself by consulting the participants after the council meeting and inviting their reflections on his data. He also argued that his study is useful for understanding the internal dynamics of the leader-follower relationship.

Hargreaves (1981) attended to teacher staffroom talk of two types. The first type he characterized as *contrastive rhetoric*: "the introduction into discussion of outrageous and stereotyped examples of alternative practice which, by implication, quickly serves to mark the boundaries of reasonable and acceptable decision-making" (p. 215). He compared this contrastive rhetoric with what he called forms of *extremist talk*: "which are deployed by certain junior members of staff to push the boundaries of discussion outwards" (p. 215). The main point of the study is that both these forms of talk affect staff decision-making processes and thereby the course of educational innovation, by either limiting or enlarging the range of educational practices considered "acceptable."

Although these studies may not exhaust the literature, they do suggest that this is an approach to inquiry in educational administration that is already considered rich in possibilities, given the further development of epistemologically and methodologically sophisticated techniques for examining texts. Indeed, developments of this kind have occurred quickly in the last decade. Almost every social science discipline now has its own approach to discourse analysis as a way of using texts and utterances of all kinds as the prime data of their inquiry. Other influential methods also give special attention to reports offered in language: content analysis, conversational analysis, ethnography, prosopography, and so on.

The Gronn and Hargreaves studies are of considerable value and relevance. From this distance, however, they seem less than perfect in the range, precision, and depth of their analyses. For example, in the transcriptions that Gronn and Hargreaves provided for their readers, there is very little prosodic information. By this I mean any transcribed detail related to intonation, speed of delivery, stress, timing, interruption patterns, and so on. The absence of this detail limits the quality of the message that readers can take from the transcripts and obviously makes them imperfect replicas of their originals. Now that formal linguistic studies have moved a little away from their former preoccupation with syntax and phonology, the semantic and pragmatic dimensions of human communication have assumed greater importance. As a result, the information content of prosodic features, coupled when possible and necessary with the nonverbal language of gestures, laughter, and other body language, now figures much more prominently in the analysis of texts than was the case a decade ago. At the same time, it is still important to keep distracting symbols to a minimum in transcripts, depending on the sorts of research questions being asked.

Interviews with interactants after the analysis of their discourse help confirm that their interpretations of what was said are consistent with the researcher's interpretations. This view is supported not just by discourse analysts themselves (Potter & Wetherell, 1987), but also by the very course that the philosophy of the social sciences has been taking in the last decade. As mentioned already, researchers must make allowances in both their methods and their theorizing for the distinctly human capacity for second-order monitoring. This capacity enables people to reflect on their discourse and to render an interpretation of those practices in a new discursive account that has priority as evidence over other accounts that may be offered by a researcher who is unable to perform that monitoring (Hughes, 1990). Moreover, this post-hoc interaction with participants allows the researcher to give due recognition to the context of situation of the discourse: The participants' several perceptions and interpretations of the context may be much broader or much narrower than either the researcher's or any other single one of them. This difference directly affects the meanings or *indexicality* that they place on their own words and the words of others. However, there will inevitably be spillage of context because no single discursive context can be isolated from others. Indeed, controlling the context of interaction in the open systems in which the social sciences always operate is a key problem for social scientists.

Ideology does not appear as an explicitly discussed concept in either of Gronn's studies. In Hargreaves' study there is a reference to those "psychiatric ideologies" used by practitioners in medicine that are protective of professional occupational identities in psychiatry in much the same way as the "contrastive rhetoric" used by his teachers consolidates their own views of themselves as professionals. Although Hargreaves only gives this limited attention to ideology, his study is concerned much with ideological practices, such as symbolization, distorted communication, the use of stereotypes, inexplicit messages, and so on.

Discourse, Ideology, and Power in Educational Organizations

Chapter 6 combines considerations of prosody and ideology and uses follow-up interviews to elaborate on primary data. It examines discursive bias and ideology in the administration of minority group interests. Like Ruth Wodak in Chapter 3, David Corson studies a formal school meeting. His chapter suggests how easily distorted communication can arise in formal administrative discourse when the interests of those with some stake are not represented among participants in the discourse. Using three episodes of discourse, the study generalizes from the unjust use of discursive power in the treatment of one cultural outgroup to other culturally different minorities whose views and interests are not often represented among administrators and policymakers in education. The chapter recommends how discursive power could be exercised more fairly and more generally.

Bridging Parts I and II of this volume, Chapter 7 considers the problems of identifying and evaluating power in discourse. Viviane Robinson argues the need for a normatively neutral theory of power for use in studies on the exercise and evaluation of power in administrative discourse. She also critiques the practices of discourse analysts who make normative judgments about the negative or oppressive use of power in texts. Using an administrative case study, she examines the usefulness of her normative theory of power for evaluating actual staff interaction in a school meeting.

2

The Language of Power versus the Language of Empowerment: Gender Difference in Administrative Communication

Charol Shakeshaft
Hofstra University

Andrew Perry
Westfield Public Schools

Research that examines gender issues in school administration has documented differences between males and females (Shakeshaft, 1987). This chapter argues that one explanation for the difference in effectiveness and style of women administrators can be found in the language used by women administrators, language that emphasizes power with, rather than power over, others.

FEMALE PERFORMANCE AS SCHOOL MANAGERS

Numerous studies have been published that document how well women perform in administrative positions in schools. In a synthesis of hundreds of studies comparing the administrative styles and effectiveness of male and female school managers, women were found to do as well or better than men on the variables studied (Shakeshaft, 1987). This synthesis, as well as other reviews of work from the United States and England, indicates the following gender differences for males and females in school administration (Driver, 1990; Ortiz & Marshall, 1988; Shakeshaft, 1987; for a full discussion of these differences with specific references for each, see chapter 6 of Shakeshaft, 1987):

Relationships. Women spend more time with people, communicate more, care more about individual differences, are concerned more with teachers and marginal students, and motivate more than do men. Not surprisingly, staffs of women administrators rate women higher, are more productive, and have higher morale than staffs of male administrators. Students in schools with women principals also have higher morale and are more involved in student affairs. Furthermore, parents are more favorable toward schools and districts run by women and thus are more involved in school life than are parents in schools run by men.

Teaching and Learning. Women administrators are more instrumental in instructional learning than men, and they exhibit greater knowledge of teaching methods and techniques. Women administrators are more likely to coordinate instructional programs and evaluate student progress. In these schools and districts, women administrators know their teachers, and they know the academic progress of their students. Women are more likely to help new teachers and to supervise all teachers directly more than are men. Women also create a school climate more conducive to learning, one that is more orderly, safer, and quieter. Not surprisingly, academic achievement is higher in schools and districts in which women are administrators than in those run by men.

Community. Building a community is an essential part of a woman administrator's style. From speech patterns to decision-making styles, women exhibit a more democratic participatory style that encourages inclusiveness rather than exclusiveness. Women involve themselves more with staff and students, ask for and get higher participation, and maintain more closely knit organizations than do men. Staffs of women principals have higher job satisfaction and are more engaged in their work than those of male administrators. These staffs also are more aware of and committed to the goals of learning, and the members of the staffs have more shared professional goals. These are schools and districts in which teachers receive a great deal of support from their female administrators. They are also districts and schools in which achievement is emphasized (Shakeshaft, 1987).

There are several explanations for why women and men might approach their jobs as school administrators differently. One reason might be found in the ability differences of those who have traditionally chosen teaching as a profession. Because women had fewer career choices than men, studies report that a larger proportion of women than men in teaching represent the "best and the brightest." Although these differences may not continue as women have more career options, they may account for some of past difference. Another explanation might be motivation. Women teachers are much more likely than men teachers to say they always wanted to teach. Men are more likely to describe their career in education as an accident or as a second choice. A third explanation might be that women tend to have been teachers longer than men when they become school administrators, thus giving them better insights into instruction and learning and the culture of schools.

However, there is a fourth explanation for these differences that relates most to the topic of this chapter. Because males and females are socialized differently, they learn different behaviors and responses as they grow up. Females, for instance, are more likely than males to be taught to be good listeners and to pay attention to the emotional lives of families and friends. It is this different socialization that may account for the seemingly superior—or at least more appropriate for schools—administrative skills that we have found in women. Although some of the socialization is not directly related to communication— ego and status needs, for instance—much of it is communication based. The remainder of this chapter discusses the work done by us in examining gender differences in communication patterns in school administrators.

GENDER DIFFERENCES IN ADMINISTRATIVE COMMUNICATION

Researchers who have examined gender and communication styles report inconsistent findings. Corson (1992a) reviewed research on language, gender, and education and found contradictory results. In his overall review of the literature on gender and communication he found:

> It seems that where gender differences in speech do emerge they are strongly influenced by the particular discourse context, including the gender and perceived power of the addressee. But power is mediated through language; it does not derive from it: different inequalities that exist in power, dominance, expertise and status, intersect with gender, class and cultural differences and receive expression in different forms of discourse in different discourse settings. (p. 238)

Tannen (1990) makes strong claims of gender difference in the communication patterns of males and females. Her work documents the asymmetry in male and female language as well as the tendency of females to use rapport talk, whereas males report. She also asserts that women tend to use language to make connections, whereas men use it to maintain independence. Tannen describes women as focusing on establishing connections with people and maintaining intimacy and community, whereas men tend to focus on status, and maintaining hierarchy:

[A man engages the world] as an individual in a hierarchical social order in which he [is] either one-up or one-down. In this world, conversations are negotiations in which people try to achieve and maintain the upper hand if they can, and protect themselves from others' attempts to put them down and push them around. Life, then, is a contest, a struggle to preserve independence and avoid failure.

[A woman approaches the world] as an individual in a network of connections. In this world, conversations are negotiations for closeness in which people try to seek and give confirmation and support, and to reach consensus. They try to protect themselves form others' attempts to push them away. Life, then, is a community, a struggle to preserve intimacy and avoid isolation. (pp. 24-25)

Using this general literature on gender differences in communication as a backdrop, we wondered whether or not there might be differences in the communication patterns of female and male school administrators and, if so, what the effects of these differences might be on their leadership and supervisory styles. We questioned whether or not gender and gender expectations might partially determine how supervisors interact with those they supervise. We wondered whether the same words spoken by a male supervisor might have different meanings to male and female teachers than those spoken by females. Conversely, we were interested in whether an interaction between a female principal and a male teacher was the same as an exchange between a female principal and a female teacher.

Because of some research that states that men and women communicate differently and that they listen for different information (Borisoff & Merrill, 1985; Tannen, 1990), we hypothesized that the female approach might be rapport and the male report. We also wondered, given what we know of the values that males and females carry into their jobs in schools, whether a woman is more likely to focus on an instructional issue or a matter concerning a child, whereas a man is more likely to discuss an administrative problem.

Furthermore, we were curious about role discomfort in communicating with a member of the other sex and its effects on a supervisory conference. We knew that male teachers exhibit more hostility in dealing with female administrators than do female teachers, and that women administrators have to work harder to get male teachers to "hear" them (Shakeshaft, 1987), and we asked what this might mean for supervisory interactions.

We also believed that perceptions of competence might influence supervisory styles and effectiveness. Because we knew that women are initially evaluated less favorably than equally competent men (Shakeshaft, 1987), we wanted to know whether these perceptions might unknowingly affect supervisory interactions, both when the woman is being supervised and when she is the supervisor.

The following discussion uses data from five different studies (Garfinkel, 1988; Perry, 1992; Shakeshaft, 1987, 1989; Shakeshaft, Nowell, & Perry, 1991) to try to answer some of these questions. We believe our data document differences in male and female administrative actions and communication styles. Furthermore, we believe that these differences help to explain why women are reported to do as well or better than men on most behavioral measures in school administration and what it is about women school administrators' communication styles that makes them more participative and democratic in their leadership.

Gender Differences in Supervisory Conferences

We examined the supervisory conferences of principals with teachers to determine whether or not there are gender differences in the ways male and female principals interact with teachers. We chose the supervisory conference because we felt that this was a required part of the job description of all principals and that there is some uniformity of expected practice. We believed that if there were differences, we would most likely see them in this context because the format of supervisory conferences tends to be contractually defined in New York. We chose to observe five pairs of elementary principals—one female and one male and each pair from the same school district—in supervisory postobservation conferences with two teachers—one female and one male. Thus, 20 postobservation conferences between a principal and a teacher were observed. We selected male/female pairs by district so that district expectations of supervisory behaviors would be the same for each male/female pair. All 10 elementary principals had been trained in the Hunter technique, so each came to the conference with the same basic supervisory guiding knowledge.

In addition to observing 20 supervisory conferences, interviews with each principal and each teacher were conducted in an effort to understand the meaning that they gave to the event. We found several differences in the ways in which the principals encountered the supervisory task.

Content. We found that the women principals not only gave more instructional feedback to their teachers than did the men, but that the feedback included more detail and specific recommendations for changes. We observed the women principals giving more databased feedback, pointing out more often why and how an action was effective. The teachers we interviewed confirmed our observations, telling us that the women principals with whom they worked gave them substantial and useful feedback. Typical of the women principals is the following feedback by the principal to a teacher:

> Your praise was good. [You said to the children], "Let me hear what you learned from this experiment," [which was] very effective. You really get them to summarize and put it in their own words, "Why did you change? Let's look at the result." I thought the flow of your questioning and your direction throughout was very strong.

The teachers speaking of the female principals told us that even if they did not agree with the feedback from the principal, they understood why it was being given. No teacher criticized a female principal for a lack of critical feedback.

In contrast, those teachers who worked with male principals talked about their frustration with the lack of substantive feedback they received. Supporting the analysis of the teachers, we observed that the male principals tended to give vague, but complimentary feedback. Typical of a male principal was this exchange with a female teacher:

> The lesson was filled with exuberant responses, terrific student/teacher rapport, a tremendous degree of success, and it was a superb lesson. . . . I observed about fifty lessons, and this was one of the most memorable for the whole year, certainly the top two or three. You really did a very fine job.

Thus, we found differences in the communication patterns of women and men principals that might help to understand why women are more effective. They tend to give more detailed and useful feedback, and the teachers tend to report this as not only helpful, but empowering. Many of the teachers coded this feedback as making them feel valued and important, not trivialized or patronized. Both men and women teachers wanted more detailed feedback and gave the principals who gave it high marks and those who did not, low ones:

> It's more like I want more feedback on my teaching. I know what the lesson is about. I know what I did. Is that a good thing? Is there anything else I could have done? [Female teacher talking about lack of feedback from male principal.]

> I don't mind having someone tell me, "Alan, what you did was okay, but maybe this would be a better way to handle that," or "Have you heard about the new technique in doing this?" I'd love that. I want to continue to improve. [Male teacher talking about the lack of feedback from male principal.]

In this study, women principals were also more likely than men to include educational content in their conferences, connecting what they recommended with current research. Women were observed talking about current trends in educational research more often than men principals, and teachers noted this emphasis in their women principals, pointing out that it occurred outside the supervisory conference as well. Typical of the descriptions of the women principals was this comment: "She's always inserting things in our boxes, encouraging us to go to workshops and conferences. She wants to have everyone be on top of things, and be fresh and learn."

Women principals in this study were also more likely than the men to display concern for the students. They asked about individual students during the conferences with the teachers, and they were more likely to stress the importance of maintaining a student's dignity than were the male principals. Finally, women principals knew these students by their first names, whereas the male principals tended not to know the students by name.

Delivery. We found that not only was the content of the feedback different by female principals, but also the way in which the content was delivered showed gender differences. For instance, the women principals were more likely than the men principals to use questions in their interactions with the teacher. They were also more likely to approach the situation as a learner and to use the pronoun *we* rather than *I*. They also allowed the teachers to talk during the conference.

Thus, the approach of the women principals was more collegial, professional-to-professional, asking what the teacher thought of the lesson and discussing various approaches. It was a climate that focused on identifying both what was effective and what was not. The conferences with the women principals had more the flavor of a teaching session, in which two professionals said, "Let's learn together."

Men, on the other hand, were more likely to make their points using statements, rather than questions, and to use the pronoun *I*. Male principals outtalked their teachers and were more likely to lecture and to limit teacher talk.

The women principals spent more time focused on personal issues and relational processes than did the men. Women principals asked the teachers personal questions or made personal comments ("How's your mother feeling?" "What happened with your daughter?") and volunteered their personal stories. Male principals were much less likely to have personal or relational conversations with their teachers.

We also found gender differences in the way women and men structured their interactions. Male principals were more likely to establish a hierarchical relationship with the teacher and to tell the teacher what was wrong and what was right with the lesson, just giving the "facts." Males, more than females, approached the task as expert and judge. Women principals interacted more as facilitator and helper. Male principals also discussed power issues more often than female principals. For instance, one male principal said that he always read everything in a teacher's file before a conference because he "loved to throw things at them from before I got there." He used this technique to maintain status and to remind the teachers who was boss. Women, on the other hand, tried to minimize the status difference.

Focus. We also found some other gender differences in this study that did not relate directly to style, but to whom we value and why. For instance, both male and female principals spent more time with their male teachers in conference. Although there might be several explanations for this difference (and we did not seek to ask principals why), one might be found in the work of Sadker and Sadker (1986), who found that teachers spend more time with male students in the classroom. Across the board, males tend to get more time, and it appears to be true in the supervisory conference as well.

Gender Differences in Written Teacher Evaluations

In an attempt to examine whether or not the supervisory differences we observed also appeared in written evaluations, we used the data from two studies to answer questions about gender differences in written evaluations (Perry, 1992; Shakeshaft et al., 1991).

In the Shakeshaft et al. study (1991), we found that men and women principals respond differently to teachers in their written evaluations. A content analysis of the written evaluations of 108 female teachers by 8 principals (5 males and 3 females) was undertaken to determine whether or not male and female principals highlighted different things. All of the principals worked in the same school district, and all had received the same amount of training in the Hunter technique (Hunter, 1984). The evaluations were coded without knowledge of the sex of the principal; interrater reliability was 77% before conferencing, 100% after conferencing.

We did find some differences in the things that women and men focused on. Women were more likely than men to encourage the empowerment of their teachers, to establish instructional priorities, to be attentive to the social and emotional development of the students, to focus on student relationships, to be attentive to the feelings of teachers, to include more "facts" in the evaluation, to look for the teachers' personal effects on the lives of children, to place emphasis on the technical skills of teaching, to make comments on the content and quality of the educational program, to provide information gathered from other sources, to involve the teacher in decision making, to issue directives for improvement, to provide immediate feedback on performance, and to emphasize curricular programs. Men, on the other hand, were more likely than women to emphasize organizational structure and to avoid conflict.

In the Perry (1992) study, a sample of all the written evaluations of the principals studied was analyzed. We found that male principals produced longer write-ups for their male teachers whereas female principals delivered longer write-ups for their female teachers. Finally, principals wrote longer commendations for teachers who were the same sex as the principal. The female principals averaged 2.1 additional commendations for their female teachers than for their male teachers, and the male principals averaged 2.7 additional commendations for their male teachers than for their female teachers.

Thus, the two studies that looked at written evaluations reinforced all but one of the behaviors that we found in the face-to-face evaluation conferences. The one exception was that in their written evaluations, principals did not uniformly give males more attention. Males gave males more written feedback and females gave females more.

Overall, in the supervisory tasks—conferences and written feedback—we found that the principals empowered the teachers by treating them as professionals and by making connections that encouraged participation. Women principals engaged teachers as professionals and educational colleagues by discussing specific teaching behaviors that were either commendable or needed improvement, or by focusing on educational aspects of behaviors and connecting them with current research. Women principals were able to build a collegial, participative climate through the following behaviors:

- Asking, not telling
- Listening, not lecturing
- Using connecting language, such as "we," "Let's learn about this"
- Making personal and relational comments for connection
- Focusing on students and their needs.

The language and behaviors of women principals, much more than of men principals, was empowering. The women principals were also powerful, using the concept of power with rather than power over. The male principals were more likely to exert power over their teachers, especially in their tendency to let the teachers know who was boss and who was in charge. Thus, we would argue that the power with, rather than the power over, behaviors might account for women principals' greater success in motivating and helping teachers, which has been documented in research in the field.

Gender Differences in Critical Feedback

We were also interested in understanding other ways gender might intersect with supervision. In a series of observations and interviews with school administrators at all levels (superintendents, assistant superintendents, directors, principals, assistant principals) and with subordinates (other school administrators as well as teachers), which focused on the issue of negative or critical feedback (Shakeshaft, 1987), we discovered that male administrators treated females differently than they did males. Female administrators, however, interacted pretty much the same with male and female subordinates.

We found that male administrators are less likely to give direct feedback to females, but more likely to give it to males. For instance, when a male subordinate makes a mistake or does not live up to the expectations of his boss, his supervisor tends to level with him, "telling it like it is." When a female errs, she often is not even informed. Instead, the mistake is corrected by others without her knowledge. The results are twofold. For the male, learning takes place instantly. He gets criticism and the chance to change his behavior. He learns to deal with negative opinions of his work and has the option of improving.

Females often never hear anything negative, being given neutral or slightly positive cues, even if their performance is less than ideal. This may result in a woman's misconception of her abilities or at least the level of her performance. If she is not directly told that her work is not meeting expectations, she has neither the opportunity to improve nor the opportunity to reassess her abilities.

As we mentioned earlier, the women supervisors treated both males and females in much the same way. Thus, the gender differences in feedback patterns occurred both on the giving and on the receiving side. Male administrators tended to give differential feedback, and female subordinates who worked with male administrators tended to get less specific and helpful feedback. These results support what we found in the supervisory conferences, in which male principals tended to give less detailed feedback—whether positive or negative—to all teachers.

Gender Differences in Interpretation

In our work we found that men and women not only have different communication content and delivery, but also that they often mean different things with the same language. An example of gender differences in meaning can be found in a dissertation by Garfinkel (1988) in which he found that men and women mean different things when they talk about trust and loyalty. Garfinkel interviewed male and female superintendents and their administrative teams in an attempt to determine whether or not men and women superintendents conceptualize their administrative teams differently, and whether or not these superintendents and their team members value different traits in team members. Garfinkel found that both men and women value competence and trust, but that they give each a different priority. For women superintendents, competence is the first thing they look for in a team member; trust is lower on the list. Men superintendents, on the other hand, identify trust as their number one criterion for team membership and view competence as less important.

To complicate matters, especially for team members, men and women define trust differently. Men, both superintendents and team members, are more likely to describe *trust* as the "ability and comfort to say what they wished to say, confident that the persons they were sharing their thoughts or opinions with would not ridicule or repeat these thoughts elsewhere" (Garfinkel, 1988, p. 311). Women superintendents defined trust as "an expectancy held by an individual, that the word, promise or written statement of another individual or group can be relied on" (p. 311). These differing conceptions of trust call for different indicators of proof. For men to see a person as trustworthy, that person must not divulge information or discuss actions or conversations with others. Women did not code those actions as untrustworthy. They expected people to discuss conversations, actions, and feelings with others. What women saw as untrustworthy was someone failing to do what they said they would do, when they said they would do it. Men did not identify a person as untrustworthy if he or she did not deliver on time. Rather, they saw that as a time management or competency issue. Garfinkel's study clearly points to differences in how we evaluate the job performance of those with whom we work and how that evaluation may be related to gender.

Explanations of Gender Differences in Communication

We tried to think about why there might be gender differences in administrative communication, and we were brought back to the messages that males and females receive as they grow up. Girls are much more likely than boys to be taught to pay attention to the emotional meaning of interactions. They are also more likely to be taught to listen, not to interrupt, to be polite, to make the other person feel good or important.

When children reach school, they are treated differently and are apt to observe gender differences in communication patterns from their teachers. The work of Sadker and Sadker (1986) describes gender differences in teacher-to-student communication in K-12 schooling, in which boys receive more feedback and a wider range of feedback. These early differences not only help us understand why we behave as we do when we become adult workers, they also help us understand women's reactions to criticism in the rare instances when they get it firsthand (women always get criticism, the issue is whether or not they get to hear it).

In interviews with women administrators (Shakeshaft, 1987), the women were found to take criticism hard. They tend to think it is an assessment of their very essence. The first time they receive criticism or the first time they fail, women administrators code it as a sign that they are inferior and that they never should have tried to become an administrator in the first place. This is hardly surprising for two reasons. First, females in this society are less valued than men. Because of this, women, from birth onward through school and into adult life, receive subtle and not so subtle messages about their worth. These messages are one of the reasons that women have been found to have lower self-images and less self-esteem than men. Second, if, as girls, females received very little direct criticism, women have hardly been given the opportunities to learn not to take critical comments personally. This lack of experience lends itself to an understanding of why supervisors of women tend to shy away from giving them this critical feedback.

It is not only women who learn stereotypes as children. Men learn them as well. They learn that it is masculine to be aggressive, to interrupt, to take command and control. They also learn—whether they act on it or not—that a gentleman is not supposed to hurt a lady, and that girls and women are sensitive and get their feelings hurt more easily.

We found these stereotypes at the base of some of the reasons why male administrators were reluctant to give women harsh feedback. In interviews with male superintendents and principals asking them why they did not confront women with their misgivings and dissatisfactions, one of the major reasons that was given was the fear of women's tears (Shakeshaft, 1987). Most of the men were uncomfortable with the prospect of tears. When questioned about what they expected from men to whom they gave negative feedback, most anticipated anger. Although none of the administrators in this study liked confronting any-one with negative feedback, the prospect of an angry response was easier to face than the prospect of tears. Male superintendents and principals said they did not like to deal with angry subordinates, but that they had the skills to do so. They were much less comfortable with crying, and because of this discomfort most failed to give women important corrective feedback that would have allowed the women to improve their performance as educators.

This fear of tears led us to examine who cries and how often. What we found was that there is not a lot of crying in public schools, and that although women cry in front of supervisors slightly more often than men, the difference in frequency is very small. However, women are reported to cry equally often in front of females and males, whereas males only cried in front of women. Thus, we learn that it is the fear of tears—rather than overwhelming evidence of actu-al crying—that paralyzes male administrators. We also learn that both men and women cry, so it is not solely a "female" problem. Finally, we learn to under-stand that although it is not solely a female problem and although nobody cries very much, the fear of tears or the gender expectations about what women do keep women from getting honest feedback about their performance and impair the effectiveness of the supervisory styles of male administrators.

Thus, it was the stereotype of females as sensitive and easily hurt and the societal message that men internalize that led them to believe that giving women critical feedback would hurt their feelings, and that it would not be a "nice" thing to do. When we asked them about hurting men's feelings, the male administrators looked at us in bewilderment. This idea of hurting a man's feel-ings had not occurred to them. This was a stereotype about females, and the male principal response was the stereotypic gentleman's action.

SUMMARY

Although socialization and stereotypes may not explain all of the reasons why there are gender differences in communication styles, we believe it explains some. We also believe that it is socialization that accounts for women's greater ability to provide an environment that is empowering for teachers. Because women have been taught to pay attention to relationships, to be polite, to give technical and specific feedback, and to use power with rather than power over, they are more likely to use language that helps achieve these ends. Thus, the effectiveness of women as administrators has much to do with their socialization about what it is to be a woman. The language of empowerment is a language that may sometimes be tentative, that asks questions, that encourages participation. Quite simply, teachers are more likely to feel they are being treated as professionals and equals if they are encouraged to speak, to give their opinions, and to problem solve. Women administrators are much more likely than men to use language that promotes participation and problem solving. As a result, it is not the traditional language of hierarchy that turns out to be the most powerful. It is the language of empowerment that is really the language of power. Women administrators are most likely to use this language of power.

3

Power, Discourse, and Styles of Female Leadership in School Committee Meetings

Ruth Wodak
University of Vienna

In this chapter I first offer some general remarks on the relationship of power and interaction in institutions and then examine them in light of the results obtained in a recent study carried out in three Viennese schools. The study registered (its quantitative aspect) the presence and frequency of specific discursive mechanisms in the interaction between participants in committees established by law as part of the Austrian "school partnership." At the same time, selected qualitative analyses of discourse data serve to illustrate in detail how certain power relationships function. Because those in charge of all three schools under investigation were female, moreover, it allows us to take a closer look at styles of female leadership, specifically, the different discursive strategies women in authority in traditional hierarchical institutions (like schools) use to justify, legitimize, and achieve their agenda.

School partnership is a concept contained in a 1985 Austria law adopted to regulate the communication and participation of teachers, parents, and pupils in school affairs. The law also established a School Welfare Committee (SWC), a Parents' Association (PA), and school and class forums (SF and CF, respectively) to embody this partnership. There is, however, a basic tension between the aims the law wishes to achieve and the means it has set up for doing so. For how can a school partnership that prescribes equal opportunity, participation, and democracy for its deliberative bodies be reconciled with the rigidly hierarchical Austrian school system? In my view, it cannot. To demonstrate this theoretically as well as empirically, I consider briefly the notion of power and examine how power may be exerted, expressed, described, covered up, or legitimized in the social and communicative interaction in institutions such as schools. In short, I examine how power "works" and how power structures frustrate possibilities for democratic participation.

POWER, CONTROL, AND INSTITUTION[1]

Power and Hierarchy

> Power arises from the human capacity not only to act or to do something, but to join up with others and to act together with them. The basic instrument of power is the instrumentalization of a foreign will in a communication directed towards agreement. (Habermas, 1982, p. 104)

Van Dijk (1989) summarized the interaction between those with and those without power as follows: The person exerting power (A) is in control of the cognitive conditions such as wishes, plans, and so on, of the other person (B); at the same time, this control is also accepted by B. Social power is thus largely indirect and occurs through mental processes, for example, evaluating the information necessary to plan and carry out (communicative) actions. The cognitive process itself, of course, also provides the means of coming to terms with and resisting this power. In other words, exerting power is not simply a form of action, but a form of social interaction that has to be more or less negotiated each time. In our study of power relations within a school partnership (Wodak, Andraschko, Lalouschek, & Schrodt, 1992), we attempted to take due account of this complexity by using detailed discourse analysis to uncover the dialectics of power and helplessness, of controlling and being controlled, as well as of activity and passivity in institutions (see Habermas, 1982). Those factors typical of an institution—rules and regulations, assigned roles, and a rigid internal organization such as the hierarchy of positions and the ritualization of procedures—collide ineluctably with structures designed to promote democratic control.

The ultimate ratio here is the legitimacy of power. The free and secret election of persons to committees is the principal means for acquiring this legit-

---

[1]Various disciplines such as psychology, sociology, philosophy, psychoanalysis, and so on, have been concerned with the complex phenomenon of power. Berkowitz (1986), Strotzka (1985), van Dijk (1989), and Wodak (1989) provide a good overview of basic approaches and additional literature: These summaries form a basic foundation for the discussion in this section.

imacy. The majority of voters is normally what determines legitimacy in institutions with democratic procedures. But this is only possible if the election is really secret, everyone is entitled to vote, and the political climate allows enough information about the electoral candidates to be secured. Moreover, the possibility of opposition views and candidates also has to be available. These latter conditions, however, are frequently lacking in Austrian schools. Moreover, as Schneider (1977) points out, in addition to power based on reward, force or attraction, power can be based on the knowledge of facts, that is, power based on information and power based on the selection of information; on legitimation through a position in the hierarchy of an institution; or on the control of a given situation, for example, presidency in a legal sense. Persons in an institution or school in higher hierarchical positions, for example, headmistresses or headmasters, automatically have direct access to relevant information and are therefore in a position of control based on the selection of information (see Text 2 and Text 5 later in the chapter); likewise, they have a legal presidential function in committees such as the SWC or SF and therefore have control of these interactive situations as well.

Even when the available means of participation, criticism, and debate in school committees are really used as intended, their efficacy is by no means assured. Beyond this difficulty, however, is the far less tractable problem of the authenticity of this consensus itself; for the shared perception of which structures ought to exist and how and why they ought to work is also analyzable in terms of power relations. Methodologically, our investigation was required continually to relate several sets of related questions to various levels of discourse, trying to examine the efficacy of the procedures, that is, the correspondence (or lack of it) between the stated objectives of the law and the mechanisms devised to institutionalize the supervisory control; the way a consensus about and within the given procedures was obtained; and whether the outcomes of the procedures validated or undermined (in the minds of the participants) either the controlling structures themselves or the democratic premises underlying them.

Power and Interaction

What then is the relationship between discourse and social power? How do power and power relationships interact, and how is power exerted in terms of language? Bourdieu (1984), Foucault (1977), and van Dijk (1989) all interpret social power as ways of discursive control. In other words, who has access to the various types of discourse, who can talk to whom, in which situations, about what, and who cannot? The more powerful the people, the larger their verbal possibilities in discourse. This is apparent particularly in institutional discourse, for example, doctor-patient interaction, interaction in court and in school (Wodak, 1992a, 1992b). In these situations persons entering the institution from outside, such as patients, clients, or parents, do not act on their own initiative, but react by answering questions, listening, and giving the desired information. In the institution, persons who determine the interaction occupy an institutional role (doctor, teacher or headmaster/ headmistress, etc.) and their language behavior is consequently supported or legitimized by the existing institutional power. These factors beget and stabilize language barriers and failed communication in institutions (cf. Wodak, Menz, & Lalouschek, 1989).

Persons with power determine the course of the interaction or the issues discussed. Through the choice of words, they can determine the length of the verbal contributions by allowing, continuing, or interrupting these contributions. Such persons also determine the beginning and end of the interaction. In addition, the interaction can be manipulated by passing on information selectively, for example, withholding information that could undermine those in power. This issue is a central theme in this illustrative qualitative analysis of interaction sequences.

THE DATA

The Origins of the Study and the Collection of Data

The aim of this study is to measure the actual workings of the statutory committees in the various types of schools against the explicit intentions of the school partnership law that established them. It was necessary to collect comprehensive data in order to be able to describe the setting and meaning of the committees in the individual schools and to illustrate issues that were of a more general interest. Thus, the data included not only committees such as the SWC, the SF, and the CF, but also the meetings of the PA. In addition, we decided to include situations from the everyday life of the school (such as classroom interactions, teachers' meetings and parents' evenings) in order to grasp the structures of the institution as a whole. Data were collected at three different types of schools—a grammar school (GS), a secondary modern school (SMS), and a junior school (JS)—to enable us to compare how the committees of the schools dealt with problems specific to these types of schools. Finally, in the study we employed the methods of participant observation, tape recordings, and written reports of every communicative event as well as in-depth interviews (in the concluding phase of the project) with selected people involved. This took much time and was very labor intensive. The frequent presence of those collecting the data over a long period of time in the schools meant that the subjects of the study became used to their presence; it was therefore possible to observe undistorted communication because it is more difficult to control one's own behavior over such long periods of time (cf. Wodak, 1986).

The transcription of the cassette recordings was carried out concurrently with the collection of further data in several phases. This approach proved to be particularly reliable when dealing with interactions involving more than two people (cf. Lalouschek, Menz, & Wodak, 1990). Initially, a rough transcription of all the communicative situations or of selected passages was made by people trained for this task; the observers then corrected or amended the transcription. These intermediary transcripts were suitable for rough analyses. A further, more refined transcription was necessary for microanalyses of discursive data.

Data Overview

School Statistics. The following statistics obtained from the headmistresses give a sense of the respective schools' demographic profile:

Junior School (JS)
  1 Headmistress
  1 Psychologist
  14 Core teaching staff (13 female, 1 male)
  13 Additional teaching staff (religion, foreign languages, etc.)
  14 classes with 179 girls and 171 boys (total 350), including 72 foreign pupils (20.6%)
Secondary Modern School (SMS)
  1 Headmistress
  1 Psychologist
  28 Core teaching staff (22 female, 6 male)
  1 Accompanying teacher
  10 classes: 137 boys, 90 girls (total 227), including 153 foreign pupils (67.4%)
Grammar School (GS)
  1 Headmistress
  56 Core teaching staff (45 female, 11 male)
  40 Additional teaching staff (all on fixed contracts)
  23 classes with 226 boys, 279 girls (total 505, no foreign pupils)

The Data.

Committees:[2]
[Grammar] School Welfare Committee (SWC)

---

[2]School Welfare Committees, School Forums, and Class Forums are bodies established by Austrian law. They contain elected representatives of pupils and teachers as well as the headmaster or headmistress. These are deliberative bodies with authority to make decisions on matters related to the school such as organization, teaching, finances, and so on.

   [Secondary Modern] School Forum (SF)
   [Junior] School Forum (SF)
   Class forum in 2nd form (CF)
   Class forum in 3rd form (CF)
Parents' Associations:[3]
   GS Parents' Association GSPA
   SMS Parents' Association Committee 1 (SMSPA1)
   Parents' Association Committee 2 (SMSPA2)
   JS Parents' Association (JSPA)
Daily School Life Situations:
   GS: Classroom teaching
      Teachers' Meeting
      Parents' Open Day
   SMS: Classroom teaching
      Parents' Evening for 2nd Form
      Parents' Open Day

The Complexity of the Data and Consequences for the Analysis

In contrast to many previous studies on institutional communication (e.g., Lalouschek et al., 1990), these data consist of interactive events that differ from each other in many respects, but that are related to each other on many different levels. On the one hand, the school partnership committees we recorded owe their existence to and observe the guidelines elaborated in the school legislation; on the other hand, the communicative situations such as teachers' meetings, open days for parents, and classroom teaching derive their forms and procedures from the institutional framework of the school.

   Because the collection of data took place in three different types of school, there were influences specific to the type of school and to the individual school itself. Examples of such influences include the different styles of leadership among the headmistresses (see later in chapter; Wodak & Andraschko, 1992) and the variant possibilities of involving the parents and the pupils in classroom and school activities. Another problem was the high proportion of children or parents in the SMS with no or little knowledge of German. Two final factors of some significance were the proportion of girls to boys and the respective subjects being taught.

   The following sections contain an overview of the length of the individual meetings, the issues discussed, the length of the dialogues, and those features influenced by the type and geographical location of the school. The subse-

---

[3]The various Parents' Associations are equivalent to the Parent/ Teacher Associations in schools in the United States and are, according to the law in Austria, to be involved in ongoing school affairs.

quent qualitative text analyses illustrate how one important phase in the meetings (i.e., voting behavior, which we used as an indicator of "democratic attitudes") was "managed" in verbal terms. On the basis of these it is possible to estimate the extent to which these patterns were dependent on the type of school, the meeting, or the people and indicate the consequences that different strategies employed in the course of the meetings had, that is, which aspects of participation and partnership were realized and which were subverted.

THE ANALYSES

A Quantitative Overview

Length of Dialogue. In every setting and type of school, the main portion of time used for dialogue was taken by the president, that is, the headmistresses and the chairwomen of the parents' associations, followed by the co-chairperson. The amount of time used for dialogue by the other officers and by others present was minimal by comparison. As the following description of issues discussed shows, the participation by the nonofficials present, when it did occur, was mostly connected with one issue of general interest. Yet, large sections of many meetings take place without any verbal participation by the nonofficials attending the respective forum.

The Individual Types of School

Secondary Modern School (SMS). The headmistress claimed for herself a large proportion of the time used (e.g., 47% head vs. 11% chairperson), not only in the SF where she was president, but also in the PA committee meetings to which she was invited. This was connected with the fact that the chairwoman's role was mainly a structural one—she reads out the motions and "administers" the vote; the contributions of the headmistress, on the contrary, contain detailed, additional background information relating to the motions on financial support of various activities and projects and the everyday life in school, for the most part, general statements about the difficult position faced by the school, or the problem of the high proportion of foreign pupils and the like. The headmistress was frequently requested to speak by the chairwoman, resulting in an exact mirror image of the clear division of labor between the chairwoman and headmistress.

Junior School (JS). The opposite was true of the JS. Here the chairwoman claimed most of the time used for dialogue for herself in the JSPA and in the SF; she took over the structuring of the meetings and offered additional

information, ranging from the uses to which the parents' association membership fees might be put to the description of a planned experiment in a class.

   Grammar School (GS). The GS offered a more complex picture. In the
settings, in which the president was responsible to the headmistress, the headmistress claimed a large amount of the time used for dialogue for herself,
emphasizing her hierarchical status. In the GSPA, the chairwoman took over the
procedural and substantive parts of the agenda. The long dialogue of the headmistress in this setting resulted from a lecture she gave on the issue of sixth-
form reform, which was a separate part of the meeting. The functions of headmistress and chairwoman were therefore divided up according to the meetings
and were separated much more clearly from each other than in the other
schools.

The Issues[4]

In general, it can be said that the purely organizational issues predominated in
all settings in all schools. Even educational issues such as films for Third World
Day or for the school library were seen from a purely organizational aspect,
such as that of financial support.

   Educational issues were dealt with above all in more "open" settings,
for example, in the CF of the JS, which was entirely preoccupied with the
experimental "oral reports." One exception was the SF of the SMS; there, issues
such as school field trips, theater productions, and stopping the school experiment—"heterogeneous German"—were examined on their educational merits.
This positive result was qualified by the fact that the headmistress and one
female teacher simply reported on these issues without there being any discussion involving the rest of the forum. Eighty-five percent of the time used for
dialogue was taken up by this headmistress and this one teacher; the remaining
15% of the time was spent on eight requests by the participants in the forum for
additional information.

   Those few issues addressed in the committees and in the PA meetings
in addition to the planned agenda were purely organizational and dealt with
school holidays, additional financial support for events, or for the school
library. Issues not concerned simply with information became the subject of
motions.

---

[4]A partial list of the issues discussed may illustrate the nature of such meetings: At the
GSSWC: Smokers' room—organization of corridor duty by the teachers, permission
from parents, and so on; film about Third World Day—motion for financial support;
communication studies—spatial problems and the pedagogical pros and cons; afternoon
class supervision—a new ruling was a great financial burden for the parents; money for
the volleyball team: money transfer issue was cleared up.

The Motions

The motions were a fundamental and therefore particularly important area of participation. Presumably, active participation should be characterized by a discussion of the motions on the agenda and by a voting behavior in which votes against the motion, deferring action, or outright rejection belong as much to a normal voting pattern as unanimous acceptance. In our study, however, the picture was completely different: In the settings examined by us, not one of the 31 motions was rejected, and only 1 motion of the GSPA was deferred.

Votes against the motions were cast on only three occasions. The issues concerned the smokers' room (in the SWC), an increase in the membership fee of the PA (in the GS), as well as the extension of the school experimental "oral reports" (at the parents' evening in the JS). All the other motions (27 in all) were carried unanimously.

Initiatives from the Forum

The forum comprises those attending who, unlike the president, do not have the right to speak first. The category verbal initiatives include such activities as asking questions, interjecting comments, providing descriptions, and so on. These develop the issue being discussed or introduce new topics. At first glance, the GS and SMS seem to have witnessed a considerable number of participant initiatives in each setting, suggesting the possibility of an active participation of those present. On closer examination, however, these initiatives turned out to be connected predominantly to one issue only, whereas the questions and interjections dealt simply with the agenda.

If one were to examine the connection between the individual issues and the initiatives, the picture could be described as follows. Five issues were discussed in the SWC of the GS. Seventy-five percent of the initiatives from the forum referred to the smokers' room. In the GSPA, 8 different issues were discussed and 7 motions put forward. Initiatives put forward by the forum referred almost exclusively to the issue of refurbishing the classrooms. In the PA1 of the SMS, 12 issues were discussed and 9 motions put forward. The initiatives were concerned essentially with the issue of the buffet and Christmas Bazaar.

In some of the settings, the forum hardly gave any verbal response: In the SF of the SMS, 7 different issues were discussed in 33 minutes. In total, only 8 initiatives were put forward by the 28 participants. The situation in the JS was even more extreme: The SF, in which two issues were mentioned and three motions put forward, was conducted without any verbal participation by the 46 people present. In the PA, 8 issues were discussed and 4 motions put forward. Only 5 initiatives came from the 46 participants.

Thus, if a neutral issue of general interest, such as the organization of the buffet or the classrooms, had not been on the agenda, the forum would hardly have participated at all. The greater proportion of the time used for discussion was limited to a few of those present, most of whom have either the role of president or a high position in the hierarchy; the various issues were dealt with predominantly from an organizational point of view; there were practically no debates with educational content; and the voting behavior was stereotypical and inactive.

The Qualitative Analysis: Selective Information as a Means of Power

As studies on communication in institutions, mostly in hospitals, have shown, information issues are an important indicator of power structures because the privileged possession of information bestows power on the person who possesses it. Institutional outsiders can easily be excluded from communication and therefore from participating in an event when information was withheld from them. The PAs are seen as the link between the institution of the school and the "outside world" of the parents. For this reason it seemed advisable to use the PAs to examine the areas in which and the issues about which the schools informed the parents, when they did not inform the parents, and how requests for additional information were handled.

The PA was run according to the law, that is, by reports by the committee, the accountant, approval by the committee, elections, as well as a decision about the membership fee. These different voting and election procedures require information about the activity and financial situation of the PA as well as about the organization of the association, the active representatives, and the relationship between PA and school committees, such as the SWC. In other words, one main function of the PA is to provide the parents of children attending the school with information about the school and its activities.

Power structures can thus be illustrated in this setting by looking at the gap between the minimum information one might consider that the parents required in order to make a reasonable judgment on the issues discussed and that information actually provided them by the school authorities. In the examples I have chosen—those involving election procedures— it is obvious that most of the parents were insufficiently informed about the agenda of the ongoing subcommittee as well as about the candidates and the voting procedure. The democratic procedures provided by the participation law were thus in themselves insufficient, and the chairpersons and headmistresses easily managed to push their preferred candidates and private agendas.

Text 1. The chairwoman and treasurer delivered their detailed reports on activities and projects, such as refurbishing the school building, school events, the purchase of teaching materials, as well as those undertakings that were to be financed by membership fees and donations. This information was presented clearly and comprehensively and corresponded fully to the legal requirements. Indeed, provision was even made for the "new parents" sitting in the hall, that is, those parents of first-form pupils.

CH   = Chairwoman
TR   = Treasurer
TR: about the membership fee—
CH: yes! o.k.
TR: I want to mention—for the new people. I would like to but I
        think there were a couple of new parents here who probably
        don't know yet. Er for example it remains at 160 schillings and
        say you've got children at other schools and one here—then of
        course you only pay half and if you've got several children at
        this school

The situation was different, however, regarding information concerning organizational issues about the association. Exact information about who will be elected in the first place, how the list of electoral candidates was put forward, how a person can put him- or herself up for election, was not forthcoming. Only the names and functions were read:

L = Mr L. from the election committee

L: Madam counselor—members of the parents' association and er parents. It was my task again to put forward one of our election proposals to this hall and then I shall ask you to make your choice as appropriate.—er—I shall perhaps first of all read out the names—

This led to the following situation: the election of the committee takes place after the chairwoman (Mrs. K.) delivers a very detailed report on those projects that have either taken place or were planned by the parents' association:

L = Mr L. from the election committee
H = Headmistress
X = female member of the audience

L: I would like to request the hall, well, I shall read out the chairperson alone, then I shall ask a vote to be taken, as I said, er Mrs—K. has been put forward as she has put in more and more hard work for many years now. That she should continue to do this work. Those in favor please hm
H: There! That's her
L: raise your hand /pause/ Well—that's
X: Who's that? Mrs K.? I don't know her
L: the lady who gave a report—yes. Crosscheck.

Due to this basic lack of information, the person who had been talking for the past 30 minutes was not clearly identified as the chairwoman of the PA. Thus, it is hardly surprising that all the voting procedures for the election of a new committee proceeded without any opposing votes.

A similar situation occurred during the voting on who should represent the PA on the SWC: Despite the question at the beginning of the meeting about the abbreviation SWC, the information deficit was not perceived by those present. Although mention was made of the importance of this decision prior to the vote, those present were offered no basic information about the SWC as a body whose decisions could significantly influence internal school events.

Text 2.

CH = Chairwoman
H = Headmistress
U = Mrs. U/female member of the audience

CH: Oh, Mr L.—er—I would like er—regarding the that's the SWC. We need
H: we certainly need
CH: yes
H: a president or a deputy. Up to now we've gladly had
CH: yes, so it's also
H: Ms. A here with us
CH: necessary to have a parents' representative and it's proved to be
H: yes I er
CH: very practical when the parents on the committee take part in the meetings as well because they know about the issues. er do you agree?
[names were read out and vote takes place]
CH: Thank you for taking part in this very important election. er we now come to the next issue to the /um/ the fixing of the membership fee
U: excuse me, I've got a
CH: yes
U: a question. What's the purpose of the SWC?

It is clear in both passages that there had not been enough information available about the issues that were the subject of the voting, a fact that shows the proforma nature of the elections.

The same approach to a "selective" willingness to give information was also evident in the JSPA: There was a great willingness to provide information on activities related to outside purposes such as school projects and purchases of equipment; information concerning the organization of the association itself was limited to the reading of the names of the candidates who had put themselves forward for various positions. There was no information provided about how and why these decisions had taken place and how one might have been able to participate in them.

Text 3.

> CH: So thank you. With this the association's work of the past year has finished—and would like the new candidates for the parents' association election to be introduced. You've all received a slip of paper. Over the last few days. It was given out in school to your child—that—er—the following people were standing for election for a position in the parents' association committee. That's me. I was chairwoman for the previous year—[name] and I'm standing for election as chairwoman again for the coming year 89/90. The next candidate was Mrs K.
>
> [CH reads the names and explains the voting procedure.]
>
> CH: so—you have the BOTTOM—at the bottom of the agenda. Have you all got a slip of paper? Agenda was at the top—then there's a line in the middle and underneath there's the election proposal, i.e., the voting slip—underlined on the right-hand side. I would like to ask you to tear off the bottom part or fold it together and: —the people on the slip—which/with which you do not agree—whom you don't want—you can cross them out.

The election result that emerges during the meeting is hardly surprising:

> CH = Chairwoman
> K= Ms. K., deputy chairwoman
> H = Headmistress
>
> CH: —right I hear that Ms. K's looked at the slips. How many were there
> K: 35 voting slips and none invalid
> CH: 35 voting slips and none invalid therefore
> H: We'd like to congratulate Ms [name CH]
> CH: thank you [applause] thank you very much
> H: and the parents' association

The actual power of a group or a system in this context was linked to its unity and lack of transparency, and this in turn concerned its inner organization. Important decisions were made, although the parents were not provided precise information and not explicitly requested to participate. Criticism, debate, and the open questioning of issues were preempted and thereby effectively prevented. Selection and manipulation of information thus provide good examples of how the hierarchy and power relations in institutions are reinforced: Democratic rules and means were neglected, often enough without the interactants actually noticing the infractions. Everyone seemed eager to participate in the quasi-democratic game.

DISCURSIVE STYLES OF FEMALE LEADERSHIP: A CASE STUDY

Male versus Female Leaders?

Studies on female leadership figures are rare and deal primarily with women in management positions. Thus, we were curious as to how women use their power and status in institutions such as schools. Helgesen (1990) offers a dichotomous model to describe differences between male and female managers: Men work at a constant speed, without taking breaks; their work days are characterized by discontinuity and interruptions; they do not have any time for activities outside their work; they show a preference for short and directed conversations and meetings; they maintain a complex social network only to people outside of the company; they do not have or do not take time to contemplate; they identify totally with their work; they rarely pass on information (monopoly of knowledge). Women, according to Helgesen, have a different style of leadership: Women plan breaks within their working day; they cope better with interruptions; they make time for other activities and must integrate their familial responsibilities into their everyday routine; they have a complex system of relationships within the institution as well; they think about an "ecological" style of leadership (working atmosphere).

The women described by Helgesen, however, were exceptions: They all worked in small companies that they partly or totally owned, thus they were able to be flexible and use their creativity and imagination to adapt the companies to their own needs. They could not afford to devote themselves purely to their work if they had children and a family. It would seem to follow from this that for this reason women are also able better to cope with interruptions because it could well be that they carry over features and strategies of the mother's role into their work.

It also emerges from Helgesen's observations that these women were less hierarchically orientated, preferring to "weave a net in their companies" rather than to "build a pyramid." However, the freedom to mold the atmosphere at the place of work as in, for example, small companies is normally not present in traditional institutions such as schools. In the three schools that were examined, we dealt with headmistresses—the most powerful individuals in the school hierarchy and the most influential members of the committees. Nevertheless, in this case study, we wanted to see whether or not similar patterns of "female styles of leadership" could be present in an institution such as the school. As a matter of fact, we expected to find a tension between the fantasy of a family atmosphere and the institutional reality, in which power and control were used to achieve one's own aims.

Traditionally, women were assigned a clear role within the institution of the family. This role consisted mainly of looking after the family and its environment. The role of the mother, which neither did nor does allow the woman much opportunity to divide up her roles as she would like, arose out of this old division of labor, that is, the woman's responsibility for reproduction, which forced her to sacrifice many of her own interests and needs. She was also subject to the pressure of the social expectations of the mother figure. The norms that were set as a result of those expectations reached far beyond the private sphere of the family; motherliness came to be seen as a quality in itself, which was also available as a potential strategic approach to the organization of relationships in the public sphere. The exercise of power by women within the parameters of the traditional mother role is considered socially legitimate. The picture of the "public mother" can be seen most clearly in the development of the female teaching profession: The few sources from the Middle Ages link the role of teaching with the responsibility of a mother because female teachers were allowed to teach both girls and boys up to the age of 8. The picture of the spinster teacher, which existed in Austria well into the post-First World War era, corresponded perfectly to the ideal of "spiritual motherhood" (Andraschko & Ecker, 1982).

The school as an institution reflects and to an extent also incorporates this public motherliness, which in Austria is scarcely different from the genuine maternity in the family. Even the law acknowledges a division of labor between family and school regarding the education of children. This no doubt contributes to the fact that norms are created in school that correspond to behavioral patterns in the family. Because part of the responsibility for bringing up children was delegated to the school, the institution and its representatives are expected to exhibit such qualities as responsibility and care, which trigger maternal associations in society at large as well as in the inner world of the institution. These attributes form the basis for the communication within the school: The motherliness of the institution—with its positive and negative connotations—manifests itself in the communicative behavior of those involved in the institution. These discursive patterns can in turn be attributed both to the style of leadership of the headmistress as well as to the discourse between teachers and pupils and to the discourse between the institutional and the genuine mothers.

General maternal strategies exist in society for several reasons, among them the way mother-child relationships establish and maintain the boundaries of intimacy, while combining this with the mothers' own awareness of their wider educational responsibilities for their children. The acquisition of regulation systems and norms is provided by mothers via such management of relationships.

Structuring maternal behavior is presumed to be positive because although it is the respective "mother" who structures the relationship, her counterparts in these relationships have enough autonomy, at least partially, to co-determine the form and the content of that relationship. Controlling maternal behavior, on the contrary, only functions when those involved are prepared to submit to this control.

In school, control as a behavioral form is fostered by the hierarchical structure of the institution and by the patterns of communication that result from this. The constant dialectic between control and subordination represents the most important behavioral ritual on many different levels. The "pyramid" structure of authority is the rule in Austrian schools: At the top is the headmistress (being controlled and controlling), in the middle the teachers (likewise being controlled and controlling), and at the bottom level are the pupils who are subjected to a double control at least within this pyramid. There is no real room for parents within the pyramid, and they are consulted instead, or if individuals really do make a valuable contribution, they are brought into the school life.

All headmistresses have undergone a socialization as teachers. Every teacher is theoretically eligible to apply for the position of headmaster or headmistress of a school after a certain period of professional experience; he or she need not have any additional academic qualifications. Thus, heads of schools know the everyday life of a teacher and identify very strongly with it. This identification, not only with the teacher's everyday routines in general, but also with individual colleagues, their style of teaching and way of dealing with pupils, and so on, erects a kind of structural barrier to their achieving the distance that could be helpful in some situations. As a result, various different relationships between the heads of schools and the teachers develop: On the one hand, there is cooperation as ostensible equals; on the other hand, there is cooperation in which roles and functions are determined by respective power positions. These different relationships engender different strategies, which often serve to disguise the power and authority of the headmistresses; the illusion of parity is reinforced by the fact that many conversations are held on an informal basis.

The headmistresses with whom we dealt in our project were all convinced that a completely open atmosphere existed in their school, in which everyone spoke with everyone else, in which consensus could be reached on every issue, and in which conflicts arose only in exceptional circumstances, as a result of unsolicited interventions by higher bureaucratic authorities or by uncaring parents. The following impressions were obtained from our observations during the recordings in schools and from individual interviews with the three headmistresses.[5]

---

[5]In this chapter I concentrate solely on discursive mechanisms of female leadership and neglect other aspects of power and gender as they arise, for example, in classroom interaction, and so on. See Cameron (1985), Corson (1992b), and Grässel (1991) for extensive reviews on gender-specific communication. Also, it is important here to illustrate

Junior School: The Emotional Head

This woman had been headmistress for 8 years and attributed her success to the fact that none of the teachers who had been at the school before her time as headmistress was there now. In her view, the turnover in personnel favored her efforts to create and maintain the open atmosphere in the school because openness was, as she put it, "not for everybody." Her school was selected by the Vienna school authorities as the site for a number of experimental school classes. This added to the image of flexibility, openness, and the willingness to experiment, which she believed characterized her school. The headmistress gave the impression of being available for everyone and everything, but this also led to her in fact being somewhat beyond everyone's reach as well as appearing noncommittal. She organized the emotional level of the institution as a whole; the technical side of the organization was left to the head of the Parents' Association, who identified very strongly with the school. One could almost call this a distribution of workload between these two women. The one saw her responsibility in the practical everyday things, the other in the world of "beautiful" emotions.

Although there was no obvious authority handing down orders, there were nevertheless norms that had to be fulfilled. "Her" teachers were indeed very aware of the norm and of the emphasis on openness; it was clear from interviews, mostly with female teachers, however, that this demand for harmony was not always seen as being supportive. "If I become aware of [conflicts]," the headmistress insisted, it was due to misperceptions rather than to structural difficulties inherent in the power relations that existed in the school. As headmistress, she initiated a talk ("and that means, let's talk, let's talk. What's your problem—get it out!"); she does not "want any disruptions"; indeed, avoiding disruptions was her top priority.

Secondary Modern School: The Missionary

At the time of the study, the headmistress of the secondary school had been in her position for less than a year. Confronted with difficult problems, she presented a very different picture of herself and of her professional expectations, as compared to the "emotional" headmistress of the junior school. The SMS headmistress was correspondingly concerned with the present and took every opportunity to try to convince the teachers and parents of her views on "how the school should be and what the school should do." Her demands had a strong tendency to create an image that functioned outwardly and that moved away from a reflexive, problem-solving strategy ("I've told my teachers that the

---

the variation and the differences that exist within the same sex and not just to contrast women with men (see Wodak & Andraschko, 1992).

school always has to present itself"). Another reason that may account for this is the fact that this school has a high proportion of foreign children. The conditions with which she was confronted at the very beginning were not particularly promising. She was not able to "look after herself," as she stated in the interview, "if I can allow myself to say this." The crisis (i.e., the number of foreign pupils) was a challenge for her to motivate all the groups involved in the school to the greatest possible activism ("I would like to take over this position in full power of my spiritual maturity and my physical strength, and do something for the school, the children, and the parents").

The "we" in her discourse was characterized by an authoritativeness that her position as headmistress afforded her. However, it does seem questionable whether this strategy, which rules out any deviations, really permits any individual initiative, whether on her part or on the part of the teachers: "An open discussion. Yes. Above all no anonymity in any direction." Open doors were also described by her as desirable; nevertheless, this very openness allowed the headmistress to superintend, even control, everything and everybody.

The atmosphere in the school as well as the minimal presence of the teachers and others involved in the shared discourse can be compared with the "pyramid" mentioned earlier. The headmistress exhibited little if any ambivalence in her interview. She was convinced of her opinions and advocated them in an insistent manner.

The Grammar School: The Fighter

This woman had been headmistress of this grammar school for 14 years. She was formerly very active in the trades union and had carried over the style learned there into her school. In a combative spirit, she doggedly pursued her own school's interests, often fighting against the superior power of the ministerial authorities. She "navigated" skillfully between maternal care and motherly control. She "operated" her school just like a family; if the authorities should ever dare to intervene, she defended it and did not allow anybody to speak badly of the school.

Unlike the other two examples, this headmistress was still active as a teacher; the teaching seemed to offer her access to everyday life and also seemed to renew her identification with what in her view was the essential purpose of the school, namely, the education of the children. As she spoke about how she first started as a headmistress, her use of the metaphor of the "open doors," of which the pupils only need take advantage, was not surprising. Her opinion that the open doors could be used equally by everyone (regardless of rank, gender, or age), that she did not acknowledge differences between pupils and teachers in her maternal style, corresponded to her style of leadership. She treated all the various groups of people in the school as her pupils; she always behaved in the different school situations as a teacher ("I've gotta try to keep everything here up to standard and to be the boss, encouraging one, supporting the other a bit, keeping the other one in check if he always comes too late or whatever. Or the children, who of course need much more attention"). Her strong identification with teaching and, as a consequence, with all "her" teachers, enabled her to conceal her authority as headmistress and created the fantasy that everyone could be completely open with her. Even her provision for "institutionalized conflicts" (the so-called "grumble time"—two hours every week to air disagreements) did not represent any solution to the structural conflicts between the teachers and the headmistress, for these meetings usually ended up in declarations of unity of purpose ("we teachers" against "those authorities"). In a controlling manner, aware of her authority, this act of solidarity of everyone in the school insulated the headmistress from any kind of institutional aggression.

Some Examples

Text 4. JSPA, 24.10.1989: "Withdrawal of affection in a show of cooperation."

PA = chairperson of the PA
HE = the "emotional head"

PA: Oh, yes—and something else—Mrs. H. has asked that SHE be allowed to intr - one or even TWO hours for parent consultations. The
HE: two   [HE smiles, raises two fingers]
PA: for the following reason—she would like—in the future and sadly she hasn't always succeeded in the past as she would have liked to be more in the classroom. To look after the children and teachers. See how things run. And unfortunately the thing was she's overrun with many administrative things—and since we're a very open house and the parents were able to—come any time and want to talk to the head—it's often the case that she doesn't do anything else from 8 in the morning 'til 12 [laughs] apart from talking about this thing and that thing. Talking. Telephoning was an important point— and then various things don't get done and—therefore she would like you: —she would like to ask the parents to—she will be there for you in future on TUESday from 8 to 9 o'clock and on WEDNESday from 12 until 1. Once at lunchtime and once in the morning. Do you still want to [PA to HE] add anything
HE: [laughs] Yes, I would like to add—I am of course here every day—but I would like to have just a little more peace and quiet and a little more time for important talks. It's often the case—those coming to see me often see it—that the door just keeps opening and shutting the whole time. That whenever someone comes in and that you

never actually reach the point of being able to continue and finish a decent conversation. There have been times when I've gone to the café with parents or with teachers if I wanted to talk without being interrupted. And I would like to do this a little differently. But I'm quite willing if you—say if you've tried it—say to me that it's NOT possible or that there's another way—even to try something different. That's the first step now. Let's see if we
PA: Are there any questions
HE: that/if that brings me a bit of relief.

At the decisive point, the head of the PA introduced the wish of the headmistress: She would like to offer institutionalized parents' consultations and limit her accessibility. This "withdrawal of love" (for mothers always have to be available), however, has to be portrayed in a positive manner in order to be acceptable and understood. The reason given by the chair of the PA succeeds both on the factual and on the emotional levels: Unfortunately, the headmistress with all her commitments did not always succeed in being approachable. And if she tried to be, then much did not get done; although, naturally, the school was and should be "an open house." Here, then, is an appeal to reason, for no one profits from a headmistress who cannot fulfill her commitments. She would still be there for everyone, but only at two arranged hours per week, instead of all the time. "Open house" and "being there for you" were phrases that were employed cleverly as packaging. The headmistress would, she said, "always be there for everyone, but . . ." And the arguments she advanced gave even more of an insight. She would like to have more time for everyone, and she would like to finish conversations in a more relaxed atmosphere. Cooperation and the willingness to talk were therefore emphasized. However, the contradiction remains: If so many people want to speak to her, then the two hours allotted for this purpose are clearly insufficient, and, in the end, the individuals would actually receive even less time. No one, however, notices this contradiction. Finally, her offer merely to try this plan, while leaving open the possibility of adopting other alternatives, enabled her to deflect any possible criticism. By emphasizing cooperation, her withdrawal of affection was cleverly disguised.

Text 5. GSPA, 19.10.89: "Information as a limitation on freedom of action."

    CH = Chairwomen
    HE = "The fighter"
    Uf: = Parent
    Xf = Parent

    CH: Yes
    HE: The School

Uf: A question. What does the School Welfare Committee do?

HE: The Welfare Committee consists of three parents, that was parent parties, so to speak, of three teachers, male and female, and of three pupils, both male and female, and they speak about certain issues—for example, the pupils participate in the decision-making process as regards the school regulations. I can't tell you about everything because I can't remember every detail about every rule. We'll certainly be talking about the School Welfare Committee in the next meeting, about whether we'll be having a smokers' room or not.—because this matter has already been brought to my attention. There were also a few other issues

Xf: Oh God [murmurs]

HE: that have also been brought to my attention. It's the things which were important for the pupils, which were important for the teachers, which were important for the parents that they discuss there. And if possible, of course, with all the information they can gather. The representatives of the pupils have to hold a meeting beforehand so that they know more or less what their fellow pupils want. The teachers also hold a meeting where they discuss what they think was important for them and the parents will hopefully also do this and think about what they need

Xf: Yes

HE: or what they want. Of course, very often we're confronted with

CH: Yes

HE: problems and then we sit there and just think and sometimes even adjourn the meeting. Just because sometimes we don't really know what we should do there and go and [we] look for more information.—after all it's a committee, so that all those involved in the school should have a—a certain insight in a certain part in the decision-making as to what everyday school life should be.—I know—believe me—I know we won't revolutionize the world with it.

In this passage the headmistress succeeded in presenting a redefinition of the tasks, possibilities, and functions of the SWC. She could not even explain everything, because she herself could not remember all the committee's functions rules, which conflicted with the level of information about the school headmistresses might be presumed to have. Her appeal for others' trust, her assurances that she only wanted the best for everyone, and that one could always rely on her suggest an implicit adoption of a "mother" role. The elected teacher and student delegates acquiesced in the headmistress' ploy and seemed not to consider it worth trying to come to terms with each individual regulation. In so doing, they voluntarily relinquished a bit of their own autonomy. The headmistress mentioned an example of the needs of the pupils—the smokers' room—and at the same time deferred it until the next meeting, indicating that she really was informed about the individual requests. In the text, the head-mistress repeatedly emphasized that everything that was important (for pupils, teachers, and parents) should be discussed. Such parallelisms have a persuasive and reinforcing function. She then presented the preferred preparation for the SWC—everyone should discuss beforehand in their groups—and made an appeal to the parents that they should make their preparations as well—an implicit and indirect accusation. This interpretation was immediately confirmed because—as she said—one could not discuss something that one does not know about beforehand. In such a situation, she indirectly threatened to adjourn the meeting.

In the headmistress' view, the SWC should provide insights into the school's everyday life. Yet, this definition clearly limited the possibilities for the SWC foreseen in the legislation: The possibilities go far beyond pure report-ing. Finally, the headmistress concluded with the commonplace "we [she means the school here] can't revolutionize the world," to which the chairperson of the PA replied weakly with an equally common platitude, "we can have a bit of influence at any rate." By her apparently objective representation of the com-mittee's function, by giving repeated assurances that there should be a time and a place for everything, while simultaneously defining the (limited) conditions under which the committee should function, the headmistress succeeded not only in circumscribing the committee's authority, scope and potential, but also in disguising the actual power play this entailed.

Text 6. SF/SS, 9.11.89: "We're great!"

HE = "the missionary"

HE: What wonderful teachers we have here! And I was actually very pleased about it and I passed these on as quickly as possible of course—these reports. That means that people were really very impressed by the classes here—the way in which people get on with each other here—and I have to tell you I am familiar with a lot of schools and I am also very impressed. We were all very happy with EVERY class. That there's also something going on—that the chil-dren were involved everywhere—that may well cause an odd prob-lem here and there—we're quite aware of that, of course. We've still got A FEW problems, a few worries with the first-year classes—did I say something wrong? They're still very unruly—and still aren't quite used to the way things run at a secondary modern school—what we expect of them. They've still got a few problems with the discipline, but I think we're hoping that soon enough it'll be all right and we'll soon have them just like in the other classes. And that's also something that I would like to point out as very positive—you notice here that all the teachers chime in together. They're all in the same boat together—of course, everyone's free to use his or her methods—but they're all in the same boat. I think that has a really good effect on the atmosphere here. I think that I can really say that—and I really do support it. We had a really good experience— the school trip of class 4C. It was in a wonderful castle—near Radstadt—we saw a video—which Mr. T made—the class teacher of 4C. He was there with Ms L. and the children really enjoyed it— had a great time. That was a sporting week—the little angels were everywhere—the weather was excellent—and I haven't heard a single complaint, just enthusiasm from everyone. And I must say that a fourth-year class was able to do this right at the beginning—that it was so successful. We'll be doing more school trips this year—with the first-years and

The president (the headmistress) gave her report at the beginning of the School Forum. This report had several functions: On the one hand, it was intended as information; on the other hand, the teachers as well as the pupils were supposed to be praised. Third, the importance of this school in comparison to others was supposed to be evaluated. The fourth and most important function was to challenge all those involved and to produce a strong identification with the institution. Therefore, this text had a strong persuasive function, and the "we" discourse was particularly noticeable. This constitution of solidarity possibly had the additional function of disguising one's own power (placing oneself on the same level as the teachers, rather than acknowledging the fact that she has power over them) and could signify the headmistress' insecurity in the exercise of power.

The headmistress in this example constantly oscillated between distance and identification: "We're all very happy with the classes" was ambiguous in its reference. It could be a kind of pluralis majestatis, or it could refer to the school authorities, but certainly it could not refer to those involved. "We've had a very good experience," on the other hand, clearly meant the school, the one available group. Later on, those involved were addressed as "them," and she talked in the first person singular, thus signaling the hierarchical distance.

The most important issues in her speech were the opinions of the authorities, the comparison to other schools, the good atmosphere in her school and the school trip as an example of a good achievement. Problems were played down ("there were problems everywhere," "children are like that," "a bit in the first years"), the positive side—that is, the solidarity and the consensus among the teachers ("we're all in the same boat")—came immediately. Slogans and catchwords followed each other. And the criticism itself became weaker, strategically, through the use of a rhetorical question: "Am I saying anything wrong?" The text was full of appeals ("but I think we're hoping that soon enough") as well as strong positive norms and attributes ("enthusiasm," "very well," "wonderful," etc.). Thus, the emotional level was addressed and the teachers praised. This headmistress dispatched several issues in a very clever way. Criticism was disguised with praise, solidarity and a feeling of community had been aroused, and at the same time a break with the hierarchy had been achieved. She was informed about everything, she was pleased about the success, and she was impressed with the achievements of the teachers and pupils. If "everyone was in the same boat," then no criticism would be spoken aloud; conflicts indeed would be made impossible. Therefore, there was another function of the meeting—avoiding open conflict by creating a general consensus. Many similarities with the speeches of politicians were suggested. The persuasive function dominated: convincing oneself and everybody else of the superb position and achievements of the school and enlisting everybody in a collective enterprise—a fine example of strategic, institutional thinking.

CLOSING REMARKS

As the examples have shown, dichotomies—be they in regard to language behavior specific to gender or with regard to female styles of leadership (e.g., Helgesen 1989)—cannot be maintained. The embedding in specific social and institutional contexts leads to an essentially more differentiated analysis and interpretation. We were actually confronted with a system of strategies that was molded by the leader's personalities, self-perceptions, and personal goals and by the institutional conditions in the specific settings. In contrast to the generally positive evaluation of the "female style of leadership" as something cooperative and egalitarian, our examples show that these three women applied controlling and authoritarian strategies to achieve their aims, which they might have taken from the mother's repertoire of social rules. Because the pattern of maternity was shared by all those involved in the institution of the school, that is, everyone played along with it, acceptance of these strategies was consensually achieved and was not seen as an uncomfortable exercising of power. Now and again, however, this clever packaging did not even seem necessary, and the direct and powerful norms of the institution explicitly dominated.

4

The Micropolitics of Successful Supervisor-Teacher Interaction in Instructional Conferences

Jo Roberts Blase
Joseph Blase
University of Georgia

In this chapter we report a study in which we explored the micropolitical elements inherent in interactions between either prospective or practicing supervisors (i.e., administrators or instructional supervisors) and teachers in successful instructional conferences. Our results suggest that attaining deep reflection and free exchange in conference situations—recognized goals of the supervisory conference (Garman, 1990)—is, at best, difficult to achieve and is profoundly complicated by political factors. The results of the study are examined in terms of new conceptual ideas about the micropolitics of conference interaction. Practical implications of the study data are also discussed.

RESEARCH ON SUPERVISORY CONFERENCES

The bureaucratic nature of the supervisory conference is invariably reflected in the power, authority, and control conferred on the hierarchically defined position of the supervisor. Most current research on the relationship between supervisors and teachers reinforces this bureaucratic perspective. This perspective assumes that the supervisor's *technical* proficiency (e.g., contrived, mechanical, or intentional use of such factors as empathy, positive prefixes to begin verbal responses, conference analysis, or evaluation systems) rather than the participants' collaboration (authentic or genuine interaction—an alternative to supervisor control) leads to teacher growth and development (Holland, 1989).

Although there are a variety of approaches to supervisory practice, most are grounded in paradigms reflecting the perspectives of positivism, phenomenology, or critical theory (May & Zimpher, 1986). For example, the collaborative approach, first posited by Cogan (1973) in his original conception of clinical supervision and supported by such writers as Eisner (1982), Garman (1982), Glickman (1990), and Sergiovanni (1982), challenged traditional approaches to supervision. More recently, Garman (1982, 1990) has questioned the viability of the "ritualistic" instructional supervisory conference; she has called for a transformation to genuineness and mutual problem solving in the conference. Moreover, studies of conference interaction have reinforced Blumberg and Amidon's (1965) early research, which suggested the importance of open-ended, collaborative, and nondirective behaviors in supervisory conferences (see also Waite, this volume).

Despite such developments, there is little systematic research on the supervisory conference. This fact, in addition to recent commentary in the professional literature (see, for example, Holland, 1989), has generated renewed interest in verbal interaction in conferences. The small body of research produced primarily during the last decade indicated that supervisory conferences are dominated by supervisors and encompass narrow concerns (Zimpher, deVoss, & Nott, 1980); provide short, prescriptive feedback to teachers (Blumberg & Cusick, 1970); threaten teacher self-esteem and self-determination (Roberts, 1992a); reveal gender differences regarding power and behavior control (Kraft, 1991); show unequal power relationships (Retallick, 1990; Roberts, 1992b); and lack teacher reflection or self-evaluation (Gitlin, Ogawa, & Rose, 1984; Zeichner & Liston, 1985). Several writers have recently argued that these and other power-related issues in schooling may best be resolved through "critical" practices of educational administration and instructional supervision (Bates, 1984; Foster, 1984; Smyth, 1985, 1988, 1990).

Current studies focusing on *teacher reflection* and engagement have also contributed to our understanding of the supervisory conference. Retallick (1990), for example, using a critical-inquiry method, analyzed conference discourse by applying depth hermeneutics. He described supervisors' and teachers' talk during postconference discussions of thoughts underlying conference interaction. This constituted a form of "reflection on the reflection," which targeted participants' language and communication structures.

In related work, Zeichner and Liston (1985) expanded van Maanen's (1977) ideas about teacher reflection. Van Maanen's work encompassed Schön's (1983) and Habermas's (1971) related concepts regarding reflection and analytic, hermeneutic, and critical reasoning. The researcher employed philosophical rather than theoretical methods to study practical reasoning during supervisory conferences. These and similar studies have revealed dismally low levels of reflection, reasoning, critical inquiry, and symmetrical communication in supervisory conference interaction.

In summary, studies of supervisory conferences raise serious questions about a conference's contribution to collegiality and teacher growth. This body of research suggests instead that social and political power regimes (St. Maurice, 1987) dramatically undermine conference success. The aforementioned studies explicitly and implicitly point to the problematic, political nature of the supervisory conference.

This chapter presents an analysis of supervisor-teacher interaction in conferences, an analysis generated from a micropolitical perspective. To our knowledge, there exists no theoretical or empirical work on the instructional conference using such a perspective.

A MICROPOLITICAL FRAMEWORK FOR INVESTIGATING THE SUPERVISORY CONFERENCE

Blase (1991a) has demonstrated the theoretical and practical import of research focusing on the principal's micropolitical orientation vis-à-vis teachers. Among other things, he has shown that the political actions and purposes of administrators strongly affect a number of aspects of teacher performance (Blase, 1988c). Ball (1987) has linked school heads' use of control-oriented, didactic, and proactive micropolitical strategies (including, for example, the manipulation of language, roles, structures, agendas, and participation) to such outcomes as teacher frustration and fatalism. Micropolitical research in general has suggested that a multiplicity of organizational factors are critical to understanding micropolitical processes and structures in schools (Ball, 1987; Blase, 1988a, 1988b, 1991a; Hoyle, 1986; Iannaccone, 1975; Marshall & Scribner, 1991). Politics, as the allocation and use of power, is reflected in language, and "communication is inseparable from it" (Lakoff, 1985, p. 13).

Taken together, research on micropolitics in schools and on supervisory instructional conferences implies that the power dynamics between supervisors and teachers may be fundamental to understanding conference interaction. Blase's (1991b) comprehensive definition of micropolitics was used to interpret data drawn from supervisory conferences:

> Micropolitics refers to the use of formal and informal power by individuals and groups to achieve their goals in organizations. In large part, political actions result from perceived differences between individuals and groups, coupled with the motivation to use power to influence and/ or protect. Although such actions are consciously motivated, any action, consciously

or unconsciously motivated, may have political "significance" in a given situation. Both cooperative and conflictive actions and processes are part of the realm of micropolitics. Moreover, macro and micropolitical factors frequently interact. (p.11)

AN ANALYSIS OF CONFERENCE INTERACTION

The primary purpose of the study reported here is to describe the micropolitics of conference interaction in terms of verbal and paraverbal elements (i.e., interruptions, overlaps, incomplete utterances). These features constitute metamessages about the intentions associated with verbal messages and about relationships between participants' behaviors (see, for example, van Dijk, 1985). The following questions were examined by the study:

1. What events in supervisor-teacher interaction reflect political constructs (e.g., purposes, values, roles, influence) (Blase, 1991b)?
2. What strategies and counterstrategies do supervisors and teachers use to influence each other in supervisory conferences, and what are the specific factors (i.e., practices) identified with these strategies?
3. How do micropolitical strategies vary in frequency and type by the demographics of experience and gender of conference participants?
4. What consequences or outcomes are associated with micropolitical interaction in conferences (Blase, 1991a)?

Method

The study reported in this chapter is part of a larger research project conducted with prospective and practicing administrators and supervisors in a variety of public schools in the southwestern and southeastern states. The databank generated by the study consists of over 100 different cases of supervisor-teacher dyads for which written reports documenting case backgrounds, recall interview transcripts, transcriptions of conference video- and audiorecordings, and demographic data were collected.

The findings presented here were drawn from an analysis of the political dynamics (consistent with Blase's definition) of 20 dyads as the participants engaged in postobservation instructional (feedback) conferences. These cases were selected on the basis of a preliminary content analysis of data as well as an attempt to maximize variation among participants with regard to experience and gender (Bogdan & Biklin, 1992; Bogdan & Taylor, 1975). Those conferences perceived by both participants as nonthreatening and conducive to professional growth were considered to be *successful*, or effective, conferences.

Transcriptions of supervisor-teacher postobservation conferences were coded for micropolitical strategies. Critical constructs and concepts (e.g., strategy, influence, purpose/goal, and effects) from the micropolitical perspective (Blase, 1991a) were used to guide analyses of supervisor-teacher interaction in conference. Using Blase's definition of micropolitics and protocols for inductive-grounded research (Bogdan & Biklin, 1992; Bogdan & Taylor, 1975), coding categories were generated from emergent recurrent patterns.

The transcripts are discussed in terms of the micropolitical factors that appear to influence instructional conference interaction. Those strategies that were determined to be interactive (i.e., affecting each other and used in combinations, thereby increasing or decreasing a participant's overall influence) and were used by both conference participants are emphasized in this analysis.

In the sample dyads, male and female supervisors representing a range of supervisory experience from beginner (within the first year of supervisory work; in some cases, true "novices" engaged in their very first supervisory conference) to experienced supervisors met with male and female teachers also representing a range of teaching experience. All supervisors had completed a classroom observation of the teacher, during which they made verbatim transcripts as well as anecdotal records of selected class events. None of the supervisors was responsible for formal evaluations of the teachers with whom they conferenced, although a few of the supervisors were formally appointed administrators (assistant principal or administrative assistant).

Political Elements of Conference Interaction: Strategies and Related Factors

Analysis of instructional conference interaction between supervisors and teachers demonstrates that a range of factors influence the political dynamics of the conference. Specifically, this analysis produced four major micropolitical strategies: personal orientations, conversational congruence, formal authority, and situational variables.

The data suggest that each of these strategies facilitated or constrained supervisory conferences, and that the two latter strategies were enacted primarily (but not exclusively) by the supervisors. Factors associated with each of these four strategies are also described in Table 4.1. Together, these strategies and related factors constitute a working framework of micropolitical conference interaction. It should be mentioned that examination of the study data with regard to gender revealed no differences. This, of course, may be a function of the small sample size.

Reflecting personal orientation to define conference interaction. The complexity and reciprocity (i.e., conference participants' perception of the degree to which views are shared and equal involvement exists) of supervisor-

Table 4.1. Political Elements of Instructional Conference Interaction: Strategies and Related Factors Used by Conference Participants that Facilitate or Constrain Interaction.

	STRATEGY			
	Use of Participants' Personal Orientations	Use of Conversational Congruence	Use of Formal Authority	Use of Situational Variables
RELATED FACTORS	Cognitive Framework opinions & beliefs individual philosophy personal expectations achievement motivation	Shared Meanings instructional approaches, concepts, ideas	Role Expectations fulfilling traditional roles	Place & Physical Arrangement
			Social Proximity or Distance	Time to Confer
	Affective Framework praise success shared values moral commitments purposes	Shared Assumptions how to work with children purpose of conference	familiarity informality	Teaching Resources and Materials
		Semantic Congruence jargon, terms, references	Status equality of participants	Policy Requirements
				Topic Control
		Professional Credibility expertise experience	Rewards reinforcement feedback	
	Interpersonal Histories shared events knowledge experiences			
	Individual Agendas congruence on instructional goals & objectives			

teacher interaction are most evident in the strategy of reflecting personal orientations in conference talk. Both conference participants used cognitive and affective frameworks and, to lesser degrees, interpersonal history and agendas to advance or to limit conversation. To illustrate, *cognitive frameworks*—the academic, social, cultural, and political realities of participants, which are shaped by formal education and experiences—were evident as participants espoused, supported, or contradicted opinions and beliefs about teaching and supervising:

Teacher: That day I chose to use WRAP, which is a language program developed by a linguistic systems company.

* * * * *

Supervisor: One of the things I think as teachers that we do on a daily basis is a lot of diagnosis. This is the purpose of the [observation] process . . . to be able to reflect back on our own teaching and do that same diagnosis.

* * * * *

Teacher: That was just another indicator to me that this lesson was too long.

* * * * *

Supervisor: Another thing that I know you're real interested in is having
               them do "experience stories."

By reflecting personal cognitive frameworks during conference talk, participants were able to impose certain realities and boundaries on interaction; this
strongly influenced improvement plans made during conferences.

The efficacy of individual philosophy—an aspect of cognitive frameworks—was apparent as teachers attempted to defend, explain, and expand on
their teaching practices, particularly when these practices were questioned by
supervisors during conferences. These comments by three different teachers are
illustrative:

Teacher: I'm not an advocate of performance objectives philosophically. I
               do not believe the teacher should have three things, that students
               will do that, and they will do that by the end of the day. My thing
               is a more long-range approach. I have certain goals.

* * * * *

Teacher: I don't want these kids walking out after one day saying, "Wait a
               minute!" I don't want Hitler in here.

* * * * *

Teacher: I want them to learn the skills, but more than that it's more the
               philosophy of what I want them to learn: to be able to sit in the
               classroom, know how to act, be able to feel good about education
               and feel good about learning.

Personal expectations and achievement motivation—further examples
of cognitive frameworks—were noticeably more salient for beginning supervisors than for experienced supervisors. Less frequently, the data emphasized the
importance of teachers' ideals. This is particularly interesting in light of the
motivating effect of professional goals. The comments of three supervisors and
a teacher illustrate this point:

Supervisor: The purpose of this is for me to gain an experience.

* * * * *

Supervisor: I hope I was able in talking with you to have you either learn or
               relearn something.

* * * * *

Supervisor: One of the things about teaching is that we're so isolated, and there aren't other adults that can come in and say, "Good job!" and/or, "I learned a lot."

* * * * *

Teacher: That's one of the areas I'd really like to work on—[students] having more of the experiences that will relate directly to them.

Appeals to participants' *affective frameworks*—feelings shaped by one's values, moral commitments, and purposes—were often reflected as praise about excellent performance and specific teaching behaviors; achievements related to deeply held beliefs or values were profoundly meaningful to teachers. However, in the case of an unsuccessful conference, a volley of escalating disagreements and interruptions, accompanied by intensely negative emotionality, was evident as in the following teacher-supervisor interactions:

Supervisor: One of the things I really liked about the lesson was the way you explained the vocabulary. I liked the way you did the analogy of the witch's vat.

* * * * *

Supervisor: Do you really feel that they came away learning what you wanted them to learn that day?

* * * * *

Teacher: I don't agree.
Supervisor: You don't have to agree.
Teacher: I *don't* agree, No. But I'm just telling you . . .
Supervisor: —OK, but from my notes . . .
Teacher: —Alright!
Supervisor: —OK! But from where I was . . .

The introduction of negative affective elements in conference talk invariably led to adverse emotional effects; feelings of failure and conflict were linked to hostility and resentment. In contrast, feelings of success were linked to motivation, and expressions indicating shared values, commitments, and purposes seemed to enhance rapport between participants.

In successful conferences, supervisors and teachers tended to agree on the use of instructional methods, the value of methods, and the reasons for practicing particular methods. In these conferences, participants often appealed to interpersonal histories and alluded to their shared knowledge of events or shared experiences to support an argument or facilitate a discussion. Congruence between individual agendas (participants' long- and short-term goals and objectives regarding instructional improvement) was also observed in successful collaborative conferences.

The following counterexample to successful conferences is illustrative.

In this case an overloaded teacher repeatedly lobbied the supervisor for either smaller classes or the assistance of an aide or volunteer. To explain his weak teaching, he declared to the supervisor, "The weaknesses [you mention] would evaporate if I had one class, one class [fewer students] at a time." These words were wasted because his and the supervisor's agendas were far too different for him to broach the subject of overcrowded classes and have a successful discussion of the issue.

In summary, the study data demonstrated that the personal orientations of conference participants—manifest and latent, conscious and unconscious—can significantly constrain or facilitate conference interaction. Conference participants indicated their awareness and sensitivity to the impact of declaring personal orientations, whether this occurred by drawing on a cognitive framework or an affective framework. Participants' interpersonal histories and agendas also affected conference interaction, although to a lesser degree.

Reflecting conversational congruence to define conference interaction. Supervisors and teachers used the strategy of reflecting conversational congruence in conference talk. The goal was to define talk in terms of meanings, assumptions, semantics, and credibility. When *meanings* (of approaches, concepts, ideas) and *assumptions* about instruction were made explicit and were shared by participants, conferences were seen as successful, and teachers were more inclined to follow through on action plans. One teacher, for example, was enthusiastic about the supervisor's proposal to use a special observation strategy to isolate data about the relative level of attention she gave to various students. It was clear to her that the supervisor understood her situation and her needs.

By comparison, silence or resistance ("I *don't* understand what you're referring to") often resulted when participants erroneously assumed that meanings were shared. Shared assumptions about the purpose of the conference itself or how best to work with children were often made explicit:

Teacher: I can't tell you *how much* help it's been to me. It made me aware how little time I spend with that child . . .

* * * * *

Supervisor: The purpose of the appraisal process is to do that same thing, to reflect on our teaching and do that same diagnosis.

Participants in successful conferences also demonstrated semantic congruence, that is, educational jargon, professional terminology, research references, and general talk about teaching and learning tended to be defined similarly. Although it was difficult to determine whether semantic congruence derived from prior familiarity or established trust between the conference participants or whether it emerged from direct attempts to establish semantic congruence, deliberate attempts at semantic manipulation were common in unsuccessful conferences:

Supervisor:	We'll see if you are improving.
Teacher:	. . . if I am improving?
Supervisor:	If you are . . . You know . . . We talked about how to make your situation better.
Teacher:	. . . to see if the *situation* is improving. I prefer that way of putting it.
Supervisor:	OK. If the situation is improving.

Furthermore, more devious reasons for seeking semantic congruence may exist (e.g., to curry favor, to feign deference, to resist oppressive ideologies). This contrasting negative side of semantic congruence raised a haunting specter of supervisory power and control over professional teachers, subtly achieved through the use of language.

Lastly, it was evident that supervisors and teachers referred to their own or each other's professional credibility (expertise or lack of expertise) to facilitate or obstruct conference conversation. Beginning supervisors, in particular, searched for and often directly requested confirmation of their credibility:

| Supervisor: | I really like your approach. Us coaches were never ashamed to go find out who's doing it well. |

* * * * *

| Supervisor: | How do you feel about me, with limited teaching experience, giving you feedback? |

* * * * *

| Teacher: | I think that you're very qualified to do that, and to look at those two things I gave you. |

As the following examples demonstrate, less effective beginning supervisors tended to make excuses for their lack of experience. They also emphasized their own expertise and frequently asserted how they would have done things differently:

| Supervisor: | These codes are to help me, cause . . . I'm not an expert at using them. |

* * * * *

| Supervisor: | I've been a teacher for 20 years. |

* * * * *

| Supervisor: | I would do . . . |

Such behaviors represent a sharp contrast to conferences in which experienced supervisors comfortably interact with unthreatened teachers who desire frequent assistance and peer observation.

Use of formal authority to define conference interaction. Enacted primarily by the supervisor, the third strategy found in conference talk was the use of formal authority; related factors included participants' role expectations, social proximity or distance, status, and rewards.

Although all supervisors used formal authority to influence the conference roles and norms, it was less prominent in successful versus unsuccessful conferences and for experienced versus beginning supervisors. In addition, beginning supervisors appeared to be especially cautious about exceeding the role expectations teachers hold for them:

Supervisor: I'm not supposed to be looking at that right now [since it wasn't part of our observation plan].

Teacher: But I'd appreciate some suggestions from you.

* * * * *

Supervisor: The conference tries to take a good teacher like yourself to a place where eventually that teacher is growing toward a point of making self-appraisals.

However, the same beginning supervisors frequently mishandled social proximity and distance issues (e.g., using titles and last names to formalize talk or using familiarity to lessen formality) as well as status (e.g., emphasizing their superior position) and thus threatened and alienated teachers. The words of several supervisors illustrate this point:

Supervisor: OK, OK [uses teacher's formal title and last name]. The data are here. It shows they were confused. They were not on task.

* * * * *

Supervisor: So you've accounted for their not perhaps doing exactly what you wanted them to do, but in my mind what I need to know specifically is what you wanted the students to accomplish that day.

* * * * *

Supervisor: If you had done this prior to [now], they should have known that. They shouldn't have had to wait to get this. And it seemed a lot of them really didn't know the words.

* * * * *

Supervisor: What do you think you could have done, knowing they have a short attention span?

Teacher: I don't agree with that at all.

Supervisor: But they *don't* listen . . .

Teacher: I *don't* agree.

Infrequently, supervisors rewarded teachers with personal reinforcement or growth-oriented feedback. Positive remarks from a supervisor, technical success, and improvement in areas of interest appeared to motivate teachers:

Supervisor: I think you're very consistent.
Teacher: I'm strict.
Supervisor: But the kids respect you.

                        * * * * *

Supervisor: Can you see how this [data-collection instrument] would help
               you?
Teacher: Uh, huh, I sure can. Yes, it's very interesting to see how they
               stay on-task, looking at the chart.

Use of situational variables to define conference interaction. The use of situational variables constitutes the fourth strategy for influencing conference interaction. Although it is beyond the scope of this chapter to discuss fully the factors associated with this strategy (particularly in regard to contextual elements), several primary factors are noted. Again, this was a strategy enacted primarily—but not exclusively—by supervisors.

Supervisors determined the conference place and its physical arrangement. This, according to the data, influenced the value of the conference to participants. References to the lack of available conference time, the lack of needed teaching resources and materials, and the press of fulfilling district policy requirements regarding teacher evaluation and student behavior were more evident in less successful conferences. The importance of using situational variables to influence conference interaction was most apparent in comments made by various supervisors:

Supervisor: I know your time is very valuable so we're going to move on to
               our real reason for being here. My objective is . . .

                        * * * * *

Supervisor: I hope you don't mind me coming in. I know it's the last minute
               and the last week of school, and we're real busy, but if you don't
               mind, could we go ahead and have our postconference from my
               observation?

                        * * * * *

Supervisor: I know you're moving from campus to campus. I'm here to help
               you. Feel free to use me any time.

A final factor related to this strategy is controlling or shifting the conference topic. Topic control was typically achieved subtly by experienced supervisors and more explicitly by beginning supervisors. Beginning supervisors often disregarded teachers' agendas and teachers' ability to reflect on teaching. For example, two beginning supervisors stated: "I want you to look at the results of the observation instrument and tell me what you see," and "As you will see, a lot of them weren't at their desks."

Experienced supervisors, in contrast, usually requested information from teachers and followed their reflective talk with reinforcement and additional questions ("Tell me a little bit about this class. . . . That's really different. . . . You like working with these kids. . . . That's got to feel mighty good. . . . How do you get them to do that? . . . You listed a lot of problems; what do you see as their strengths?"). Such follow-up comments appeared to be critical to reflective talk; in fact, without these comments, conference participants seemed to wander aimlessly through subsequent talk.

Inexperienced versus experienced supervisors. This study indicates that both teachers and supervisors extensively use personal orientations and conversational congruence to facilitate or constrain conference interaction. The strategies of formal authority and situational variables, however, were used far more by supervisors than teachers; this is to be expected, given the supervisor's positional authority. Nevertheless, it created problems and constrained dialogue. To achieve a closer look at this phenomenon, the data were disaggregated according to supervisor experience.

Other research has indicated that beginning supervisors are at a disadvantage in comparison with experienced supervisors when conducting instructional conferences (Roberts, 1991, 1992a, 1992b). Similarly, our data point out that beginning supervisors (especially the novices who had virtually no supervisory experience) employed fewer political strategies than their experienced counterparts; they also tended to rely on a limited number of potentially offensive strategies without success.

As suggested earlier, beginning supervisors' use of micropolitical strategies differed from that of experienced supervisors in every area. The factors of personal orientations they emphasized included their personal expectations (of self) and their achievement motivation ("I'm learning how to do this. . . . The purpose is for me to learn how to assist you. . . . I was trying to script without a bias. . . . I'm trying to take teachers to a place where they are growing . . . . I'm not an expert, but I'm working hard on my skills."). In reflecting conversational congruence, beginning supervisors sought confirmation of their credibility, and they emphasized their knowledge and experience ("You know I've been a teacher for 20 years . . . I can help you improve; that's what we're all about. . . . Do you see how my data prove that? and I understand these students and what it takes to teach them."). Such supervisors used formal authority often. They also mishandled social distance/ proximity and status and yet were wary of exceeding their perceived role expectations ("I don't mean to tell you how to do your job. . . ."). Beginning supervisors also tended to strictly control the situational variable of discussion topic, moving from topic to topic at will and seemingly without hearing the current conversation.

In addition, beginning supervisors frequently imposed their agendas on the conference. For instance, one teacher initially justified and rationalized his actions, then attempted to avoid traps and "loaded" questions posed by the supervisor, and finally retreated into silence. In this case, the supervisor invoked random use of multiple political strategies to recover from the conflictive episode. However, each of the supervisor's strategies were challenged by the use of a parallel counterstrategy by the angry teacher. Overall, the study data suggest that beginning supervisors have difficulty in tolerating high levels of dissonance in conference interaction; consequently, they escalate their attempts to guide or control ensuing conference interactions.

It was also apparent that beginning supervisors frequently used inappropriate strategies (i.e., conversationally unmatched, and incongruent) during conferences. For example, they emphasized policy expectations rather than teacher instructional expertise. Failure of conferences involving beginning supervisors and inexperienced and experienced teachers was related to technical and political aspects of their orientation; they neither adequately guided nor appropriately controlled the conference. Clearly, beginning supervisors failed more frequently because they seemed to lack a repertoire of strategies, used strategies unmatched to a given conversation, and were dominated by experienced teachers. In contrast, these supervisors succeeded when they worked with (a) inexperienced teachers with sufficient intellectual and practical abilities to change their own behaviors, and (b) experienced teachers who helped them through the morass of conference political interaction.

SUCCESSFUL CONFERENCES: SUMMARY OF FINDINGS

In general, the study data suggest that successful conferences—conferences that both participants reported as nonthreatening and growth-oriented—differ from less effective conferences in terms of the strategies participants employ. Effective conferences are characterized by supervisors' (as well as teachers') reliance on the strategies of using personal orientations and conversational congruence more than on using formal authority or situational variables; congruence between the personal orientations of participants' affective and cognitive frameworks and personal expectations of self and others; similar agendas and mutual credibility; and shared meanings, assumptions, role, and personal expectations for one another. Use of formal authority as a political strategy is limited to elevating the status of participants to equalize and balance the conference, to build trust, and to foster openness.

Finally, in successful conferences, supervisors tend to provide nonthreatening opportunities for teachers to talk and explore their work. In this "safe haven," risk is tolerated, suggestions are offered in a positive manner, and mutual goals are emphasized. This results in interactions that more closely approximate the ideal of a collaborative, nonevaluative, and reflective conference (Smyth, 1988). Teachers who participate in such conferences reported increased self-esteem and respect for their supervisors.

In relatively less successful conferences, verbal agreements between participants appear to be forced and contrived. For example, participants often lapsed into perfunctory expressions of agreement or silence (e.g., "uh huh," "mmm," "oh yeah"). These conferences are characterized by a lack of agreement on roles and personal expectations and a lack of shared meaning or assumptions about teaching or learning. Moreover, although teachers tend to respond positively to supervisors' initial attempts to engage them in reflection about their work, subsequent strategies used by supervisors, including authority and situational control, seem to limit the potential of developing viable conference interactions. Generally, in less successful conferences, supervisors encounter teachers' counterstrategies of resistance (see, for example, Waite, this volume); this reduces the probability of addressing the conference goal of reflection. In some conferences, supervisors restore viable interaction by changing from the strategy of formal authority to the strategy of emphasizing personal orientation (i.e., shared assumptions, knowledge, and philosophy).

DEFINING THE MICROPOLITICS OF CONFERENCE INTERACTION

The four strategies discussed in this chapter provide a beginning perspective on the micropolitics of supervisor-teacher conferences. In addition, the study data suggest that all four strategies discussed are interactive (affecting each other and used in combinations). Only two of these strategies—reflecting personal orientation and reflecting conversational congruence—prevail in conferences defined positively by participants. These two strategies are useful not only in creating and maintaining effective instructional conferences, but also in salvaging a conference that has deteriorated because of use of the strategies of formal authority or situational variables.

The bureaucracy, policies, traditions, and evaluative orientation of the instructional conference promotes the use of two micropolitical strategies—formal authority and situational variables—by supervisors. These strategies are frequently considered inappropriate by teachers, and dissonance occurs. This, of course, severely diminishes the quality of the supervisor-teacher interaction during instructional conferences.

IMPLICATIONS

As noted earlier, the number of studies of micropolitical processes and structures in education has increased rapidly during the last several years. Although a wide range of topics has been explored (Blase, 1991b), the study of such processes and structures in supervisor-teacher interaction has been virtually ignored in the supervision literature. The descriptive and conceptual results of the present study represent an initial effort to redress this problem and to advance work in an area that appears to be critically important to understanding instructional conferences.

More studies of the strategies, goals, purposes, and consequences of political interaction in the instructional conference are needed. Research on the relationship between school organization factors and micropolitical interaction in conferences would be valuable. Studies focusing on changes in micropolitical interaction over time in conferences would also be useful. Additional work might compare and contrast the micropolitical aspects of conferences varying by participant experience, ethnicity, gender, class, and language. More broadly, the phenomenon of instructional conferring should be studied within the social, cultural, and academic—as well as political—context of the school. Finally, investigations into additional elements of successful conferences (e.g., the supervisor's preparation and skills vis-à-vis factors and, more important, the participants' interpretation of the use of micropolitical strategies) should be initiated.

On a practical level, students would benefit from university programs that provide academic preparation in micropolitical knowledge and skills. Such preparation could focus on building awareness in participants of the range of strategic interactions that tend to occur in conferences and the consequences of such actions. For example, prospective or practicing supervisors should become cognizant of their everyday political orientations; understanding the elements of trust, respect, and support as well as the nature of professional collaboration and reflection would be helpful to constructing effective supervisory practice. Further micropolitical understandings could be derived from observing conferences in an interactive mode and developing awareness of the interplay of strategies, purposes, and consequences.

Perhaps most important is that supervisors should be made aware of the differences between control-oriented strategies and empowerment strategies. Most supervisors are prepared to use only standard evaluation systems and procedures (as opposed to growth-oriented, collaborative interactions based on nonthreatening classroom observation and data gathering) that encourage them to assume a control orientation. To reduce the salience of such an orientation, it would be useful to focus on the effects of supervisory behavior on teacher performance and student achievement. With current school restructuring efforts emphasizing collegiality and power sharing, understanding both control and empowerment will be especially critical. Without such awareness and knowledge, supervisors may inadvertently undermine attempts to build new and dynamic forms of collegial, professional interaction in public schools.

5

Teacher Resistance in a Supervision Conference

Duncan Waite
University of Georgia

Every word is ideological and each and every application of language involves ideological change.—V. N. Volosinov (1973/1986)

This chapter is premised on the belief that studies of teachers and their lived experiences should enhance our understanding of supervision, especially teachers' roles in the process. Presented here is an examination of a particularly problematic teacher-supervisor conference. The data for this chapter, taken from a larger study (Waite, 1990, 1992a), inform an analysis of one teacher-supervisor conference, which I chose because it illustrates beautifully what I have come to understand as teacher resistance.[1] This discussion is meant as a contribution to the dialogue of supervision, hegemony, and resistance.

---

[1]Use of a single case or example may trouble some readers. However, in that regard, Wolcott's (1988) pithy retort to the what-can-we-learn-from-just-one-of-anything-question is appropriate: "All we can!" (p. 16). More academically, Friedrich (1989) made the argument for studying the individual, at whatever level of analysis:

> Individuals at these and yet other levels of analysis should be included because they give critical margins of understanding, insight and intuition into "how political economy works" and how it is lived out in real life . . . —margins that elude the rigidly sociocentric or socioeconomic modes of research. When the biographical and autobi-

THE CONTEXT(S)

The mainstream supervision literature reflexively defines itself as being growth-inducing for teachers, as "the improvement of instruction" (see, for example, Weller, 1971). Seldom is this notion problematized.[2] Indeed, within the mainstream literature teachers are subject to objectification, rationalization, and commodification.[3] This lamentable state of affairs is reflected in the questions of even the most well-meaning educators who ask, "But what are we to do about the 'dead wood'?", as it is voiced in public and political spheres in calls for reform, in which teachers, who are primarily women, are perceived to be the only culpable party (Goodman, 1988).

Of course, supervision as a field of study cannot be separated from the larger historical-political milieu in which it operates (Bolin & Panaritis, 1992). Through the years, supervisory research and theory have reflected, both methodologically and ideologically, the times that gave them birth. Recently, theorists of a critical persuasion have begun to examine supervision (Smyth, 1985, 1991; St. Maurice, 1987); whereas, concurrently, critical theory itself is being refined (see Burbules, 1992; Burbules & Rice, 1991; Ellsworth, 1989). The application of critical theory to the study and development of supervision is felicitous given that a prime motivation of critical theory is its educative agenda (Fay, 1987). However, as Fay asserts, critical theorists have not dealt adequately with the problem of resistance.

The School University Program

The program that frames this study was modeled after the Harvard master of arts in teaching summer school program (see Garman, 1990; Goldhammer, 1969). It was a collaborative university school program designed to offer beginning teachers field support and graduate courses culminating in a masters

ographical dimensions are not dealt with, the study of language . . . and of political economy . . . tends to remain somehow unreal, and hence vulnerable to the charge of objectification and even of structuralist fetishization and alienation. . . . [T]o exclude the unique individual as matter of methodological principal is disturbingly analogous to the suppression of dissent in a totalitarian society. Also, ideologies, like poems, are always originally generated and contributed to by individuals. (p. 299)

[2]Elsewhere (Waite, 1994), I discuss the problematic character of this taken-for-granted notion in more depth. The mainstream literature of supervision pays scant attention to the notion that a technico-rational perspective puts out of focus the larger contexts and issues framing teachers, teaching, students, and their learning.
[3]These three processes—objectification, rationalization, and commodification—are what West (1990, p. 35) refers to as "major impediments of the radical libertarian and democratic projects of the new cultural politics." *Objectification* transforms living beings into manipulable objects. *Rationalization* fosters and supports "bureaucratic hierarchies that

degree. After meeting university requirements for admission to graduate study, candidates were interviewed by the principals of the buildings in which they were to work. Those selected attended summer courses on the university campus before leaving for their assigned districts, where they had probationary contracts for that year. At the end of the year, each principal decided whether to offer a more permanent contract to the teacher placed in his or her school.

The program's teachers were under the tutelage of a school district supervisor—a "Clinical Professor," in the program's terminology. These supervisors were the liaisons between their local district and the university. The districts involved usually accepted five or six beginning teachers each year. Supervisors were responsible for the weekly graduate seminars offered on site to the local group of beginning teachers and visited their classrooms each week to observe and confer. The supervisors in this program were restricted by teachers' union contracts and by the program's goals and philosophy from offering summative personnel recommendations of the teachers whom they supervised. These school district supervisors did, however, determine their teachers' grades for their graduate school course work.

The Actors

The supervisor protagonist of this chapter, "Faye," was to retire in another year. She had been with her district, "Milltown," population 15,930, for more than 20 years. Faye was a primary school teacher when she first accepted a quasiformal role as a mentor to new teachers. Later, this role was formalized through her appointment as the Clinical Professor from Milltown. As she gained more education and experience she took on more responsibility in her district, eventually moving out of the classroom and into the central office. Faye had been a Clinical Professor for 16 years and was referred to as the resident historian of the group, having outlasted several university professors who served as program directors.

"Bea," one of Faye's charges and the teacher protagonist of this chapter, was a nontraditional student—pursuing a career as an educator after having raised her family. She had done her student teaching in this mill town and came to the attention of a local principal. But Bea's matriculation into the program had been problematic from the outset: She had difficulty passing the state minimal competency teacher's exam required for certification. However, that local principal lobbied heavily for her inclusion in the program, and so it came about.

---

impose impersonal rules and regulations in order to increase efficiency, be they defined in terms of better service or better surveillance." *Commodification* makes teachers susceptible to "market forces . . . that centralize resources and powers and promote cultures of consumption that view people (/teachers) as mere spectorial consumers and passive citizens." Commodification of the original forms and intent of clinical supervision is discussed at length by Garman (1990, pp. 202-203).

Faye had uneasy feelings about Bea and her abilities early in the year, feelings she had vaguely expressed to me concerning Bea's language. Later, she recounted her estimation of Bea's idea of what it meant to be a teacher: "Bea's notion of teaching is pretty heavy handed, offensive and domineering. Her motivation system is extrinsic. It's a role conflict—she needs to compensate for her life experience by getting the kids to like her while still being heavy handed" (fieldnotes, 06-06-89).

The observation and conference I witnessed occurred in the late spring/early summer, a week before the end of public school classes. Bea was carrying an "incomplete" in her graduate courses because she had yet to complete all her assignments from the previous term. Faye structured her seminars around certain teaching and observation techniques. Her students, the beginning teachers in this district, were then to complete the observations and practice the teaching methods as assignments. The most recent teaching technique Faye had taught the group was that of role play, and that was what we were to observe. Earlier on the day of the scheduled observation, Bea called Faye's office to change the time of observation to one more suitable to Bea and her schedule. Faye obliged.

The Lesson

Faye brought a videocamera to record the lesson. Addressing Bea's class, Faye mentioned the camera, reminded them that they had all seen cameras before, and asked that they not act any differently than usual. Bea began the lesson, posing the problem that they were going to deal with in the role play. Well into the lesson some students suggested "punching out" the miscreant. Faye interrupted to share that she thought some of the resolutions she had heard students voice were inappropriate. (An interruption of this sort is a particularly strong violation of the supervisory norms respecting teacher autonomy [Waite, 1992c].) The lesson ended soon thereafter. When the students left for recess, we sat at a table in the back of the room, me off to one side, and began the conference.

A WORD ABOUT METHODOLOGY AND THE RESEARCHER'S PERSPECTIVE

The conference reported here is taken from a larger study (Waite, 1990, 1992a) in which epistemological concerns led me to combine two distinct research methods: conversation analysis and ethnography. Moerman (1988) was the first, to my knowledge, to combine these two approaches, resulting in what he terms "culturally contexted conversation analysis" (p. 5). Moerman's resolution allayed my reservations surrounding strict conversation analysis—a method whose adherents claimed to be both "context free" and "context sensitive" (Sacks, Schegloff, & Jefferson, 1978).

The problems remain those of context and the relation of text to context.[4] McDermott, Gospodinoff, and Aron (1978, p. 245) flatly claim that "the object of any ethnography is to describe some people's activities and to locate these activities within the various contexts of their occurrence." What are the contexts for the interaction one wishes to analyze?

Elsewhere (Waite, 1992a), I have referred to the contexts of supervision conferences as "unbounded." By that, I wish to portray conferences as reflexively embedded within numerous contexts, any of which are available as a resource to conference participants in their interactional construction of the conference. Similarly, Cicourel (1992) reports on the interpenetration of communicative contexts in medical encounters. He believes that "all social interaction and/or speech events presuppose and are informed by analogous prior forms of socially organized experiences" (p. 308) and encourages researchers to "justify what has been included and what has been excluded according to stated theoretical goals, methodological strategies employed, and the consistency and convincingness of an argument or analysis" (p. 309). For, as he states, "meaning and understanding in everyday life are contingent on cognitive and linguistic activities" and, therefore, "some specification of the environmental conditions in which these language practices emerge, are embedded, and evolve should guide the researcher's depiction of context" (p. 309). Cicourel strongly advises the use of ethnographic material in cases where conversation is the primary focus.

Interested as I was in supervision from the participants' perspectives, I undertook an ethnographic study of the teachers and supervisors in the university-school collaborative program described earlier during the 1988-89 school year. When my observations of these particular teacher-supervisor, face-to-face interactions began I had been in the field for nine months.[5] It was now near the end of the school year. I had completed what Agar (1986, p. 64) terms "career history interviews" of three supervisors, had interacted with both teachers and supervisors at numerous university seminars and in the field, had visited on-site, supervisor-led seminars, had met with the supervisors at their district offices, had accompa-

---

[4]I am grateful to Phillip Payne for clarifying this point. Others phrase the problem in terms of the "micro/macro" distinction. See Hargreaves (1985) for a discussion of the relation of "micro" to "macro" and the relation of theory to evidence. I do not mean, by relegating this discussion to a footnote, to minimize the importance of the question. Indeed, the relation between local, face-to-face processes and larger, societal structures is of paramount importance. For researchers, the question hinges on the nature of the evidence necessary to substantiate one's claims. Conversation analysts insist that one cannot assume beforehand what has relevance for interaction—propositions must be shown to have relevance for the participants, in the talk, and as it transpires. The interested reader is directed to Wilson (1991) for a discussion of the structural implications of talk. Another promising line of inquiry is Giddens's structuration theory (Giddens, 1984; Shilling, 1992).

[5]During the fieldwork phase, I also served as Assistant Director for the program, although I had been a program supervisor myself for three years and had come to know the other supervisors during that time.

nied all the supervisors on their rounds, and had interviewed some of the teachers extensively. I took fieldnotes, recorded and transcribed interviews with the supervisors and teachers, and recorded six supervision conferences. I transcribed the conferences using the conversation analysis protocol (see Figure 5.1).

TEACHER RESISTANCE TO COMMUNICATIVE HEGEMONY

During the observation, Faye worked from a checklist; something she felt she needed to do because Bea was prone to "arguing" (fieldnotes, 06-06-89).[6] Faye asked Bea questions from the checklist and Bea responded. Aside from topic initiation, Faye exerted control of the conference in other ways. One such technique manifested itself in competition for the floor, or turns-at-talk. When simultaneous talk occurs (i.e., overlap), generally it is up to the participants to

-	a dash signals a slight pause, generally of less than .2 seconds
(0.0)	parentheses show longer pauses, timed in tenths of seconds
^	a caret shows rising intonation
^	a subscripted caret shows falling intonation
o o	superscripted ⁰s enclose passages which are quieter than the surrounding talk
[ ]	brackets enclose simultaneous talk, marking onset and resolution
___	words underlined are given stress by the speaker
( )	parentheses show transcriber's doubt, or inaudible passages
(( ))	double parentheses are used to note occurrences in the setting, not necessarily part of the talk
> <	arrows show passages spoken at a much quicker rate than surrounding talk
=	latches show where one speaker begins immediately after the preceding speaker with no pause
:	colons show elongated sounds; generally, each colon represents a beat
CAPS	show talk which is louder than surrounding talk
.h	shows an audible in-breath
h	shows an audible out-breath

Figure 5.1. Transcript notation

---

[6]The complete text of the conference transcript is available in Waite (1990, pp. 159-170). I only excerpt portions of the original text here to illustrate the points I wish to make. I do, however, retain the original line numbers to give the reader a relative sense of the flow of the conference.

With regard to the checklist Faye employed: It was entitled "Guide for Evaluating Your Performance: Role Playing and Interactive Teaching" and consisted of 11 questions. Only "yes" answers were scored, the highest possible score being 11. Faye had scored Bea's lesson as a 5 1/2. In response to the last question, "What suggestions would you make for improvements?", Faye wrote, "Clarify the purpose of the lesson at the resolve it locally. In nearly all such overlap, especially that occurring early in the conference, it was Faye who managed to retain the floor. Bea dropped out (see Waite, 1992b, p. 359).

However, even if supervisory conferences can be characterized by their "communicative hegemony" (Briggs, 1986, p. 90), within the most hegemonic of systems there remains room for resistance (Foucault, 1981; Lindstrom, 1992). I have chosen the following transcript segments as representative of sites of contestation to demonstrate the resistance tactics Bea employed even though the entire conference, indeed Bea's whole experience with supervision, may well have been such a contest (as Faye's might have been).[7]

Breaking the Frame of the Conference

Briggs's (1986) sociolinguistic reappraisal of the interview as a communicative event led him to the conclusion that "the respondent's principal means of sub-

beginning and focus the discussion by responding to the reality of the whole scene when they debrief following each enactment." She had also attached a page-and-a-quarter summary of the lesson, including further suggestions that went into Bea's file. She also made the videotape available to her.

[7]I have no qualms characterizing Bea's tactics as resistance, although others might take exception with my use of this (ideologically loaded) term: Walker (1985), for instance, prefers the term *recusant* for that oppositional behavior that is not "actually or potentially, consciously or unconsciously, contributing to progressive social change by undermining the reproduction of oppressive social structures and social relations" and reserves "resistance" for those behaviors that are (p. 65). Other pedagogues, espousing a critical perspective, privilege the conscious, that is, the rational (the Frankfurt school, for example) and/or the collective and progressive aspects of oppositional behavior in their definitions of resistance (Giroux, 1981, 1983b; McLaren, 1985). However, such appropriations of the term are not without their disadvantages and critics. Recently, the multifaceted nature of oppression and resistance has been adumbrated by such authors as Apple (1992), Davis (1992), Ellsworth (1989), hooks (1990c), Lather (1991a), Minh-ha (1986/87), and Shilling (1991).

As an example of the increasingly complex conceptualization of hegemony, resistance, and the Other, Ellsworth (1989) came to see herself and her students as "inhabiting intersections of multiple, contradictory, overlapping social positions not reducible either to race, or class, or gender, and so on. Depending upon the moment and the context, the degree to which any one of us 'differs' from the mythical norm . . . varies along multiple axes, and so do the consequences" (p. 302).

Ellsworth saw that "'there are no social positions exempt from becoming oppressive to others . . . any group—any position—can move into the oppressor role' depending upon specific historical context and situations" (p. 322). This more complex view of hegemony, resistance, and the subjectification of the Other is actually more liberatory than simpler definitions: It permits a constructed subjectivity in place of normalizing categories, and it encourages an historical and relational examination of those structures and processes in which one is embedded and to which one contributes.

Bea resisted her supervisor—whether or not she was conscious of what she was doing, and whether or not she was part of a larger collective with a progressive agenda. Her resistance in itself is ripe with implications for supervisors and supervision.

verting [the interviewer's] power lies in breaking the frame of the interview" (p. 56). When supervisors control the topics, ask the questions, and even determine the relevancy and adequacy of the teacher's responses, little more is left to the teacher if he or she chooses to resist than to refuse to play by the rules.

As Faye was addressing the questions from her checklist, she and Bea were discussing what for the students would be the result of the scene enacted in the role play. Faye brought up her own interruption of the lesson and apologized (Transcript Fragment #1, lines 106-108, 110-111, and 113-116):

Transcript Fragment #1.

102	Faye:	FIRST PREDICT WHAt's gonna <u>happen</u> as a <u>result</u> of this
103		scene. Now when Dorothy did <u>hers</u>, she predicted (0.2)
104		another way, like you did. And so <u>that</u> was the next
105		scene. Well that kinda gotchu into trouble when they
106		predicted that they were gonna punch out - and - I -
107		could not (0.6) °listen° - I tried to stay out of <u>it</u>, but I
108		₍could NOT leave ʌ<u>it</u> [I could <u>n</u> ot lea₍ve - <u>that</u>
109	Bea:	<u>OH</u> I'M <u>GLAD</u> you d₍id tha t's fine] °that's fine°]
110	Faye:	because <u>it</u> - evolved so - naturally - that - >it got
111		<u>worse</u><
112	Bea:	um hum um ₍hum um ₍hum
113	Faye:	>th]<u>at</u> it <u>escalated</u>< once] you use an
114		escalation - whether it involves t - I mean <u>they</u> were
115		just <u>thrilled</u> - because here's a scene they hadn't seen
116		before=
117	Bea:	((Bea goes to window))
118	Bea:	=I'm just concerned that <u>my</u> <u>kids</u> are out <u>there</u> ((at
119		recess)) with no supervi₍sion
120	Faye:	<u>OH</u>::] <u>well</u> you'd <u>better</u> get out
121		^the₍re, ʌthen.
122	Bea :	ʌno] <u>he's</u> <u>still</u> out there - that's good (1.2)
123		>just let me <u>check</u> and make <u>sure</u>< - okay=
124	Faye:	=the - <u>intent</u> of <u>this</u> <u>question</u> - is (0.8) if - you were=
125	Bea:	=oh, I - to take ₍my ( )
126	Faye:	<u>IF</u> - YOU WERE TAKING] °a pencil -
127		at the <u>end</u>° see what you're after here - IS: - THEM to
128		think
129	Bea:	UM HU:M=

Bea's protestations (line 109) may be seen as an attempt to close discussion of this topic. Recall that such an interruption by a supervisor is a strong violation of the norms of supervisory conduct and can be read as such by both parties. (During our debrief, Faye said, "I try not to ever interrupt a lesson, but that one [of Bea's]!") It may even be construed as a negative evaluation of the teacher's performance, her ability to conduct this type of lesson and to manage the class. Even after Bea's protestations, Faye continued on this topic—possibly wishing to present her warrant for the earlier interruption.

This discussion made Bea uncomfortable (notice the repeated overlaps, line 109, in raised voice). She then broke the frame of the conference, getting up and physically distancing herself from the face-to-face interaction to go to the window. When she returned, talk of the interruption was not resumed. However, Faye had retrieved the discussion of the scene and the intent of the teacher's question during the role play (line 124). Bea attempted to radically shift the topic, to break the frame again (line 125), but Faye held her to the task by not allowing her to finish. Faye retained the floor through the escalation technique of raised voice (note how Faye paused briefly to ascertain whether she had indeed been successful in her bid for the floor, whether or not she was "in the clear," before resuming, line 126).

Another radical topical shift, a break in the frame of the conference, instituted by Bea, came much later in the conference (Transcript Fragment #2, line 268):

Transcript Fragment #2.

251	Faye:	Uh - did they generalize >whatda you think?< do *you*
252		think your kids left here with - a (1.0) °way - of dealing
253		with that problem?°
254	Bea:	°no - I don't think they did° - because I th - I don't
255		think they were in tune with what was goi-I don-th-I
256		didn't feel comfortable.
257		(0.4)
258	Faye:	I think it's °right,° and I think you're right - I think it
259		was right here=
260	Bea:	=yeah=
261	Faye:	=I think we °got off right there°
262	Bea:	um hum
263	Faye:	and they needed - uh - EIther - explanation °at the
264		beginning,°
265	Bea:	um 'kay
266	Faye:	it's - realistic to tell 'em (0.4) that you're gonna play
267		something you've seen (0.6) you've seen ₍kids
268	Bea:	>SEE₎ I didn't
269		know whether - a - because see - the boy that was in the very
270		back:< (0.9) Cody? - um - he - he is. I mean I have a huge
271		ba:g - he's - he has done that. a₍lot
272	Faye:	um h]um

Here (lines 268-271) Bea begins talking about Cody and the number of times he has taken things from a bag she keeps. Note how Bea has taken the floor in overlap, using raised voice and increased speed—two escalation tactics which, when used together here, gain her the floor. This constitutes an interruption (as compared with other occurrences of overlap that do not so constitute an interruption). Faye's "acknowledgment token," the "um hum" of line 272, projects Faye's orientation to Bea's continuing—in essence, Faye concedes to Bea.[8] And so, Bea continued (Transcript Fragment #3).

Activation of a Counterdiscourse

Terdiman (1985) stated that:

> Dominant forms of discourse have achieved unprecedented degrees of penetration and an astonishingly sophisticated capacity to enforce their control of the forms of social communication and social practice. . . . But at the same time, in intimate connection with the power of such an apparatus, discourses of resistance ceaselessly interrupt what would otherwise be the seamless serenity of the dominant, its obliviousness to any contestation. For every level at which the discourse of power determines dominant forms of speech and thinking, counter-dominant strains challenge and subvert the appearance of inevitability which is ideology's primary mechanism for sustaining its own self-reproduction. (pp. 39-40)

Although supervisory discourse may have a decided advantage, no discourse is so totalizing, so unified, as to be immune to some form of counterdiscourse. The readily available distinction in teacher culture between "us" and "them" is one such counterdiscourse.

One point of contestation in this conference was Faye's questioning of why the student, Cody, was not included in the role play. She argued that his inclusion may have mitigated against his disruptive behavior. In response, Bea invoked the teacher collective as part of her rationale (Transcript Fragment #3, lines 278-281 and, especially, the "we" of line 286):[9]

Transcript Fragment #3.

273 Bea: and the reason - I didn't call on him today, is just because
274   he's been totally off the ∧wall: and so (0.6) having him up
275   there - participating >would've been a very bad< choice.
276   Because - he would have - just been (0.4) more obnoxious

---

[8]Goodwin and Heritage (1990, p. 288) define an acknowledgment token as use of "uh huh," "okay," "u hum," and so on which "projects (but does not require) the continuation of another speaker's talk. Simultaneously it usually displays an analysis of the other speaker's prior talk as being incomplete so far."

[9]This particular segment also highlights the collective group estimation of Faye's role and hints at a normative response to it: that subterfuge is permissible in protecting oneself from the supervisor's gaze.

```
277              - than he was by sitting back there - stacking: - books
278              around and doing the things that he's - IN FACT - he's been
279              so bad throughout the whole school - that - somebody said -
280              if Faye's coming to watch - today you don't wanna be
281              sabotaged by Cody - >send him outta the room - and I didn't
282              - do that
283   Faye:     do - uh - yet - but - someti:mes - his - thorough -
284              involvement in it
285              (0.9)
286   Bea:      well we tr₍ied ₍al ready
287   Faye:                   cut] ou ts]      the behavior.—but you're
288              saying that wouldn't work f₍or ₍(    )
289   Bea:                                   it] di dn't w—] it hasn't
290              worked so far: - today - >an I'd< - 'cause I was really
291              going to use him.
```

Invoking the collective and activating its counterdiscourse puts Bea and her rationale beyond Faye's reach. In essence, this counterdiscourse recognizes the teacher as the authority on classroom occurrences (Waite, 1992b).[10] The tension and negotiation between discourses is evident, even within Bea herself, in her "and I didn't do that" (lines 281-282). This may be Bea's way of indicating to Faye that she took the middle ground (it may be conciliatory): Bea is stating that other teachers suggested a more radical solution than that which Bea chose. Also of interest is Faye's acknowledgment of Bea's estimation of the boy's status as a potentially worthy participant (lines 287-288), a legitimization of the power of the counterdiscourse.

Once activated, Bea defends herself, her choices, and her actions, using this counterdiscourse. To counter Faye's insistence on Cody's inclusion, Bea uses phrases (not reported here in their entirety) such as: "I'd already given him many chances, he hit a kid in the head" (lines 306-307); "(he's just) totally off the wall" (line 310); and "not today, because he would have made a circus, a three-ring circus out of it up there today" (lines 316-318). These are all opinions based on the boy's actions "throughout the whole school" and before Faye's arrival. This effectively places the teacher's decisions beyond Faye's power to judge.

Stepping Over the Line: From Resistance to Hegemony

As Ellsworth (1989) reminds us, "any group any position can move into the

---

[10]Kanpol (1988) described the tensions between teacher and administrator "cultures." Teachers' perceptions, he found, are of teachers as adept and administrators as inept. Kanpol (1991, pp. 140-141) wrote that this group norm reinforces what teacher solidarity was evident in the group of teachers he studied. Such taken-for-granted beliefs may, however, serve hegemonic ends when they stereotype and, thereby constrain, others' (for example, supervisors') self-determination (see Burbules, 1986, p. 97).

oppressor role." (p. 322). Likewise, Burbules (1986) wrote of a "relational conception of power," whereby, "in the power relation itself each party might gain a particular gratification from the negotiated balance between compliance and resistance" (p. 103). Seeing power relations as a web, Burbules believes, reveals that "relations of power are to some extent reciprocal . . . [in that] a person in power over another in one respect may be relatively powerless in other respects" (p. 104). Burbules' web analogy also provides that "power can be transitive in its nature and effects (the father beats the boy, and the boy kicks the dog)" (p. 104). Similarly, Terdiman (1985) spoke of the counterdiscourse that "situates its struggle somehow and somewhere within the conflicted cultural field . . . [and] functions by a kind of violence" (pp. 65-66).

These complex notions of power, compliance, and resistance further our understanding of this particular teacher's resistance. Bea can be seen as at once resisting the supervisor's discursive intent, while in turn acting to suppress the supervisor, even while she may, at times, be an oppressive agent in her students' lives (as Faye has stated she believes). There is no inconsistency here. Just how might Bea oppress her supervisor, Faye?

Power imbalances often arise where there are conflicts of interest, especially in zero-sum games (Burbules, 1986). Such conflicts between teacher (culture) and administrator/supervisor (culture) have been well documented (Hargreaves, 1990; Kanpol, 1988; and others).

Faye and Bea collude in the interactive construction of this conference.[11] One important aspect of that construction is the production and interpretation of what Gumperz (1992) refers to as "contextualization cues"—such cues signal participants' orientations to "what is happening now" and "who we are" in the process. Through her activation of the counterdiscourses of teacher culture, Bea has signaled her orientation toward who Faye is, how Bea expects her to behave, and what Bea thinks her own role is. Such firmly held role expectations "constrain the alternatives the agents see as possible" and "constitute a template or pattern which the relationship will tend to follow" (Burbules, 1986, p. 97). When role expectations are not mutually shared or negotiable they are hegemonic, that is, when compliance to role expectations is enforced against the wishes of one of the parties.

In an important essay on the social construction of the stranger, Bauman (1988/89) noted how: "The presence of the stranger always carries the potential for an end. The stranger has the freedom to go. He [sic] may be forced to go or, at least, forcing him to go may be contemplated without violating the order of things" (p. 9). In addition to the tactics cited earlier, Bea presses her attack on Faye's position through manipulation of her rights as a supervisory conference participant, especially those that accrue to the teacher during the last phase of the conference.[12] The last phase of the conference—the programmatic phase—commences after Faye has

---

[11]See McDermott and Tylbor (1983) for a discussion of collusion as a necessary condition of conversation.

[12]Elsewhere (Waite, 1992a) I have identified the three phases in the supervisory conferences

completed her supervisor's report phase. Faye has just offered Bea an alternative action by which she might remedy the shortcomings Faye has articulated. Bea agrees to pursue the suggestion (Transcript Fragment #4, lines 516-517). The boundary between phases comes with Faye's "ALRIGHT," said at line 518. This may be seen as Faye's first attempt to close the conference. However, Bea hurriedly begins another turn (shown by the fact that she "latches" her turn immediately to Faye's prior turn, with no pause and with rapid voicing). Refusing to accept the closure, she begins the programmatic phase. Bea begins discussion on the topic of her class assignments in anticipation of resolving her incomplete grade.

Transcript Fragment #4.

```
515   Faye:   if    [IF she's willing to exchange.
516   Bea:          I'D LI KE - to do ʌthatJ          °yeah° okay - we
517           can talk about iit -
518   Faye                AlJRIGHT=
519   Bea:    =>I ME - another thing< - is I have my u:m (1.4) I have -
520           everything ready to turn in to you - today - except for my
521           unit.   °can I turn it in on thursday? - 'kay there's°=
```

In the discussion that follows, Faye mentions that she thinks Bea has one more assignment due. If Faye wanted to leave, this was a tactical error. Bea is incredulous and queries Faye on this (Transcript Fragment #5, line 540). Faye attempts to disengage from that contest (that is, of whether or not there is actually another due) at that time (lines 541-542). Bea persists.

Transcript Fragment #5.

```
535   Faye:   YE:s but I have to °get back to you. I have to look back
536           through - your file and t - t - con - I ma:rked it ʌdown and
537           penciled ʌin but I have to >make sure - what time.<°
538   Bea:    ok[ay:
539   Faye:    the]re's one - more: (0.3) [that you
540   Bea:                        >I have an]other one to do?<
541   Faye:   well - let me talk to you about it - tonight, when you
542           come, so I - you can look - through your folder.
543   Bea:    ʌoh ^oʌkay
```

Both stand and Faye moves toward the door.

I studied: (a) the supervisor's report phase, (b) the teachers' response phase, and (c) the programmatic phase. The "ownership" of this last phase I have assigned to the teacher—due to consideration of local conversational issues such as resolution of overlap (who drops out and who "wins" in competition for the floor), who employs acknowledgment tokens most often during any particular phase, and who initiates topics. It could be said that during this phase the teacher is more privileged or more dominant than the supervisor.

Bea continues to call Faye to account until the end of their face-to-face encounter. She enumerates those assignments she has completed and turned in and those she has yet to complete. Faye's only defense (and, at the same time, her defenselessness) is that her records are at her office. The degree of contestation is evidenced in the following example (for example, in the amount of overlap and competition for the floor):

Transcript Fragment #6.

```
577  Faye:    . . . - so: I'll talk to you tonight,
578           [WHEN I HAVE IT in fr[ont of - me
579  Bea:     alright—good]         ʌye:ah] okay k - because I - I wasn't
580           awa[re that there was any thing
581  Faye:          without being - more]
582  Bea:     ʌelse
583  Faye:    explicit about it.
584  Bea:     oka[y
585  Faye:          th]ough Bea, don't get nervous about it - until I: -
586           check it out more.
```

Faye instigates a radical topic shift (recall that Bea used this tactic earlier). It is accomplished through interruption, by asking a question in a raised voice (Transcript Fragment #7, lines 597-598):

Transcript Fragment #7.

```
595  Faye:    and then we'll do the - uh - folder (2.5) thursday °okay°
596           Your - curriculum=
597  Bea:     =I HA[VE
598  Faye:          ARE] YOU DOING - poetry?
599  Bea:     >yeah<=
```

This topic shift, while deflecting Bea's onslaught, does not get Faye out of the room. To do this, she first enlists my aid (Transcript Fragment #8, lines 612-614) and then refers to the group outside (lines 616-617, 619). Referring to the group outside reactivates Bea's role vis-à-vis her students. Bea responds affirmatively.

Transcript Fragment #8.

```
612  Faye:    ((to observer)) well Duncan - do you wanna go: - or are
613           you gonna stay. Here I am - walkin' outta here and he's
614           stayin' here. ((laughs)) And he's - watching me -
615  Bea:     ((to observer)) yeah, thank you ((laughs))
```

```
616  Faye:   leave. it's because - I'm thinking you need to be out on
617          that playground.
618  Bea:    I'm going out - I'm gonna take=
619  Faye:   =I SEE YOU looking out there - so - [frequent      ly
620  Bea:                                         I'm gonna t - ]
```

We quickly say our goodbyes and leave.

Faye was aware of how Bea had manipulated her. Afterwards, she commented, "I'm not going to win . . . because when I try to deal with problems, it becomes a personal assault" with Bea. "So I just literally kind of backed away. . . . She wins either way." Faye was planning to return to her office to check Bea's course grades, because, as she said, "There'll be a war if I don't. She really holds me to it" (fieldnotes, 06-06-89).

Bea finished the year in Milltown and was subsequently rehired. She continued there until her husband was transferred and she sought employment in another district. Bea also finished her masters degree, although not until two years later. Faye retired the year after the fieldwork for this study was complete.

DISCUSSION

In order to make sense of Bea's resistance tactics and the fact that she was able to retain her job in Milltown in spite of Faye's negative evaluation of her teaching ability, I employ Hall's (1959) notion of levels of culture. Hall wrote that there are three levels of culture: the formal, the informal, and the technical. Adeptly, Bea realized where her support laid and aligned herself with the formal and informal levels of teaching culture. The technical level, with which Faye was charged, proved relatively inconsequential in the scheme of things. Faye holds that this is because the program's grades are not performance based, although the issue is much deeper than that. Elsewhere (Waite, 1992c, p. 438) I suggest that teachers are highly regarded by their colleagues (and administrators, it seems) if they are well versed in the formal and informal cultures of teaching.[13]

Although the supervision discourse may well be the dominant form in schools, Bea was able to invoke the counterdiscourses of teacher culture successfully in this case. These counterdiscourses were of two types: alignment with the teacher collectivity; and invocation of the tenets of teacher culture—specifically, the firmly held belief that teachers know more about their students than any stranger can. Such counterdiscourses may put immediate conference

[13]I am indebted to Harry Wolcott (personal communication, May 16, 1989) for this insight.

issues beyond the supervisor's control. Bea also used local conversational processes and the rights accruing to teachers in conferences to parry the imposition of the supervisor's agenda: In effect, she ran Faye off. A tactic Bea employed was that of breaking the frame of the conference, a tactic that may be seen as a tactic of last resort when the discussion became too sensitive, too embarrassing for her, or when the supervisor's control became too burdensome.

CONCLUSION

Throughout much of their history, teachers have been marginalized by the mainstream literature in supervision.[14] However, the agency of teachers now has been revealed and will need to be dealt with by theorists and practitioners alike. Groundbreaking work in this area already has been initiated by authors such as Gitlin and Smyth (1989). But such work itself is done on the margins of supervision. It will need to be incorporated, not coopted, by the field as a whole if the field of supervision is to remain a viable one.

Teacher resistance ought to clue supervisors that something is seriously wrong with either the total process of supervision or with particular supervisor-teacher relationships. Other bases on which to establish teacher-supervisor relationships are needed. Indeed, the interested supervisor may need to do a lot of work in overcoming historically hierarchical relations and the connotations engendered by the term *supervision*.[15] As has been suggested, concretized roles and their relations prove oppressive to all parties involved. Revolutionary actions, however, serve to break down artificial bureaucratic barriers, just as resistance problematizes them (Bullough & Gitlin, 1985). Supervisory energies would be well spent if this were to become supervision's educative agenda.

---

[14]Welcome exceptions may be found in the work of Blumberg and Amidon (1965), Blumberg and Jonas (1987), Munro (1991), and Smyth (1991).

[15]Perhaps we might now write of "superVision" in an attempt to denote the visionary potential of collegial relations between an insider and an outsider in which both may benefit if both take an educative/inquisitive stance.

6

Ideology and Distortion in the Administration of Outgroup Interests

David Corson
Ontario Institute for Studies in Education

In this chapter, I examine how power is exercised through language in a meeting of school administrators and community representatives. I ask to what extent the distorting influence of ideology affects proceedings in a school meeting, even one conducted along formal lines, and how that distorting power is manifested in the discourse itself. Building on earlier studies (see Chapter 1), I try to give more attention to three particular areas: analyses of prosody, second-order interpretations by the interactants themselves, and ideology.

PROSODIC ANALYSIS AND SYMBOLS*

Prosodic analysis of discourse provides transcribed detail using symbols to show intonation, speed of delivery, stress, timing, or interruption patterns. The absence of this detail limits the quality of the message that readers can take from the transcripts and makes them imperfect replicas of their originals. This abstracting of language from its context has often been advanced as a weakness of discourse and conversation analysis. As a result, the information content of

---

*See appendix

prosodic features, including laughter and other interjections, now figures much more prominently in the analysis of texts than was once the case. Like the interpretation of all features of language, the "reading" of prosodic information depends on context. There are no fixed rules for determining the meaning of a word or expression; similarly there are no firm rules for interpreting prosodic features. The meaning of any given prosodic feature is at least as culture and context bound as the meaning of a lexical item in a language. As Wittgenstein argued: The meaning of a word is its "use" (cited in Corson, 1995). So, too, the meaning of a prosodic feature is its use in language. In interpreting prosody, we combine vague conventions of use with patterns of meaning in the text and argue from that evidence toward a more certain grasp of the semantic intentions underlying that use of language. The use of prosody adds to the semantic evidence available to us.

INTERVIEWS

Interviews after the event help the researcher to interpret what has taken place. This view is supported by discourse analysts (Potter & Wetherell, 1987) and by recent developments in the philosophy of the social sciences (Bhaskar, 1989; Hughes, 1990). The human capacity for second-order monitoring enables people to reflect on their discourse and to render an interpretation. This new account has priority as evidence over other accounts of the discourse, such as those offered by a researcher who is unable to perform that retrospective monitoring. Interaction with participants also readdresses the original context of situation, and this also softens the criticism that discourse analysis as a method "decontextualizes" the language. In every study of language in context, there will be some spillage of context because no single discursive setting can be isolated from others.[1] In this study I try to minimize that problem by isolating a physical and linguistic context in which the discursive practices of interactants are controlled by the subject of the study and in which episodes of interaction are artificially structured through the formal agenda regularly set for a meeting of policymakers.

---

[1]Social scientists seem increasingly reluctant to view their domains of study as closed contexts that are walled off from the overflow of other contexts. This is an overdue development because it seems clear that the domain of the social is unconstrainedly open. Even laboratory experiments that were once interpreted as closed studies and judged to be free from the residual influence of outside variables, now are seen as "leaking" contexts, not least because the presence of the researchers themselves always brings with it the overflow of many other contexts into the experimental situation. This present study uses discrete discourse episodes so that spillage of context is at least minimized for the reader. This is also consistent with current analytical practice: Contemporary discourse analysis tries to avoid isolating specific language forms or focusing on one structure or selecting one process or indeed lifting any feature of a discourse out of its context because to do so risks distorting the meaning of that feature.

IDEOLOGY

A common criticism of "conversation analysis" in sociological research is that it does not grapple with matters of ideology and power. In this chapter I am giving ideology a higher profile because its role in the exercise of power clearly makes it an important point of entry to the analysis of administrative texts. In this study I am using *ideology* to refer to any system of ideas, expressed in discursive practices, that distorts reality in order to serve the interests of a privileged individual or group. This use of ideology can operate at a macro level and affect a large political community, or it can operate at a micro level and affect a smaller group such as the single school board in this chapter. Often people are quick to spot ideology at work in macro contexts, but overlook its influence at the micro level, especially when dealing with the interests of people who are not members of the in-group of the moment.

Ideology and Discourse

Modern ideology studies examine language from two vantage points (Corson, 1991b; Thompson, 1984). In the one approach to the study of language and ideology, questions are asked about the development of "political narratives" and their effects. These narratives seem to take on a power of their own so that structural relations of domination become represented as "legitimate" through the stories that are told to justify the exercise of power by agents who hold it. The other approach questions not so much the discourse of the ideologues themselves as the language of everyday life and the taken-for-granted semantic structures that mundane discourse distributes among men and women. Above all, ideology operates to distort human communication and thereby the use of human reasoning in power relationships. There are three principal distorting functions that ideology is said to serve (Giddens, 1979):

- type 1—the representation of sectional interests as universal, for example, by defining interests specific to a group so that those interests are perceived as universally valid
- type 2—the denial or transmutation of contradictions, for example, by reformulating fundamental system contradictions as more superficial issues of social conduct
- type 3—the naturalization of the present through reification, for example, by defining present or past organizational realities as "the way things are" and objective, so that alternatives seem unworkable or unrealistic. In the discourse examined in this chapter, examples of the type 3 function of ideology are uncovered and discussed.

Distorted or ideological communication in social institutions is an interest of Habermas (1970, 1985), whose solution to the problem is his "ideal speech situation." He abstracts from the nature of human language itself certain principles that people usually take for granted in any communicative situation. When a person says something to another, he suggests that the second person is able to make the following claims:

- that what is said is meant to be intelligible, offering a "meaning" that can be understood
- that the propositions or factual assertions offered by the speaker are true
- that the speaker is justified in saying what is said, not going outside social rights or norms for that context of speech
- that the speaker is sincere in what is said, not intending to deceive the listener.

In ideal and undistorted communication, speakers can defend by word or deed all four claims: What is said is meaningful, true, justified, and sincere. These claims are ethical codes in themselves, embodied in the structure of human language. When all participants in a speech context are able to defend these claims, when all related evidence can be brought into play, and when nothing apart from logically reasoned argument is used in reaching consensus, then the circumstances provide an ideal speech situation. This is a setting in which people can sort out their real interests from their illusory ones and agree on the things that they have in common and on other things that may divide them.

Such a setting is rarely available in human affairs, but we do try to create it in certain formal settings. For instance, in the context of official meetings, weight and respect is given to certain "conventions of meeting procedure" that have developed over time. Rules of debate and decision making are applied under the guidance of an impartial chairperson, usually with the help of a minutes secretary. In this study, I examine this very approximate example of the ideal speech situation at work. I ask to what extent the distorting influence of ideology is excluded from a meeting conducted along these formal lines.

A Board of Trustees in Process

The context for this study is a monthly meeting of a Board of Trustees in a secondary school. In New Zealand, a radical devolution of power away from national level has given school decision-making responsibility to Boards of Trustees elected for every school in the country. These comprise staff and community representatives. The basis for each Board's operation is a charter or contractual agreement with the Ministry of Education. These spell out the obligations of each institution to its community, and they are the basis on which schools are guaranteed state funding. For this study the Board responded to a letter by giving permission to tape-record its next meeting for research purposes.[2] I selected the school, from the eight secondary schools in its region,

---

[2]Government legislation requires Boards of Trustees to allow members of the public to attend their meetings, except for those parts of the meetings that deal with "in commit-

because its student body is socioculturally representative of the community and because the membership and concerns of the elected Board at this randomly selected meeting would probably tend toward similar representativeness. My letter to the Board set out the aim of the research: to analyze the formal discourse of the meeting with regard to linguistic and paralinguistic features. The letter guaranteed anonymity in the later use of discourse transcripts. I recorded the meeting while present in the boardroom, using a pressure-zone microphone feeding into a cassette recorder. A stenographer made transcriptions shortly afterward, helped by copies of the Board's minutes and other documents circulated for the meeting. I checked the transcripts back to the original sound tapes and added prosodic notations that were also checked against the original by a third party. Later I gave four of the Board's members the final transcripts and interviewed them in order to cross-check "what was going on" and other matters of background relevant to the three episodes.

The Board meeting was held late in the afternoon of a school day in a room regularly used for the purpose. The room was furnished with armchairs, comfortably spaced around a rectangular table that allowed eye contact; the pressure microphone was in the center of this table. The agenda had been in progress for 20 minutes before discussion in the first episode. The meeting followed an agenda, beginning with "Apologies," "Confirmation of Minutes," "Correspondence," and "Principal's Report." The people present and their roles are as follows:

1. Doug = Board *Chair*
2. Mary = Board *Secretary*
3. Aileen = *Principal*
4. Dulcie = *Associate Principal*
5. Andy = *Vice Principal*
6. Pam = Parent Representative Coopted by the Board
7. Fred = Community Education Representative
8. Shastra = Elected Teacher Representative
9. Rangi = Elected Parent Representative
10. Jason = Elected Student Representative
11. Moana = Minority Parent Representative (does not speak)

The italicized names or roles appear in the transcripts (see Appendix). The asterisks indicate the four members whom I interviewed later. Member 11 did not speak in the meeting, and members interviewed indicated that she rarely speaks. Because Moana is a Maori New Zealander and filled a special role on the Board, this raises a question that is not addressed in this chapter, but which

---

tee" matters deemed confidential. In this research, the "in committee" proceedings of the Board were not recorded; the researcher left the room while the Board dealt with these matters of student discipline, suspensions and the like.

clearly invites research: What discursive processes, in such a setting of relative empowerment for individuals, exclude the interests and constrain the contributions even of a few of those who are present and empowered by that presence?

Episode 1: "Attain" (see Appendix: lines 1-93). The topic of this episode is an item in the Principal's Report. She is describing the responses of the public to a major innovation that the school has introduced. The ATTAIN program is in its first year of operation. Other schools have become interested in borrowing ideas from the program. So far the school has provided several open days for visiting parents and teachers, but interest in more formal teacher workshops is growing. In this episode the Principal introduces a problem associated with the cost of freeing the school's teachers to provide these workshops. Although the Ministry brings visitors to see ATTAIN in operation, now that it is successful, the school received no additional funding from the Ministry for ATTAIN. The school is now faced with the expense of helping other schools, who may be taking up the innovation, in spite of the fact that under educational policies that are now in place in New Zealand the school is actually "in competition" with its neighbors to attract both students and other sources of income. Although encouraging the school in its plans, the Ministry declines to provide any funding support for workshops. The Principal is seeking comments from the Board on the school's interest in helping other schools while charging them for that help. The debate is complicated by the fact that the Chair of the Board, an academic, is a colleague of a team of researchers who have been contracted by the Ministry of Education to evaluate the ATTAIN program in its early years of operation.

Analysis. This episode highlights a professional dilemma that can arise for educational administrators when they must operate within systemwide policies that promote competition between schools for students and resources. There is evidence at many points in the transcript that administrative tension is growing because of a clearly perceived dilemma: The commitment of the educationists to wider educational aims is affected by the need to meet what they perceive as unreasonable financial objectives because their failure to meet those narrow objectives may affect the overall educational effectiveness of their program. Line 22 reveals the personal tension that this dilemma causes: The Principal interrupts the Chair with a spirited challenge on the matter of royalties. Down to line 75, the dynamic exchange between the Principal and the Chair is a powerful statement of conflicting interests expressed by people who are unwilling agents of systemwide policies. There is mention of the "bitterness" (25), the innocence of the victims (30), the "irony" (31 & 64) and the embarrassment (49) that the dilemma causes. Lines 35-39 reveal the extent to which marketplace ideas such as "ownership" and "selling services" have intruded; they prevent teachers in "rival" schools from behaving as colleagues in sharing ideas to improve the quality of education for all. In the follow-up interviews, the Board members remarked on the pressures that these demands were placing on their activities and on the social distance that they were creating between their school and other schools in its neighbourhood.

Although this issue might easily create grounds for distorted communication, there is none in the discourse of this episode. Instead, the exchanges, especially between the Chair and the Principal, are powerful statements of personal or group interests, sincerely and freely expressed in a context that resembles an ideal speech situation. The Principal's defense of her interests is a fearless and challenging series of statements. She begins with a loud question (22), but follows with more subtle prosodic strategies that are at least as effective in getting her points across. Her use of word stress and of rises in intonation adds power to her argument: stressing words and phrases related to values choices and affective concerns ("fault" and "feeling" in 30, "disquiet" in 34, "unpleasant" in 38, "injustice" in 73), emphasizing the problem of ownership ("own" and "ownership" in 35, "as ownership" in 36, "share" in 39), and highlighting the distance developing between schools and between teachers ("other schools" in 63-64, "our school" in 64, "other schools" in 68, "our kids" and "their teachers" in 84). She leaves little room for doubting her sincerity and adds emphasis to key points in her case. The mildly embarrassing situation in which the Chair is placed, "trying to wear two hats" (49), leads to no distortion or dissembling on his part. He wears his two hats with aplomb and manages to argue cogently that the injustice of funds going into an evaluation, rather than into the program itself, may have good results for the school (57-60), although the Principal is skeptical of this (68-70). The Chair's response is less impassioned and more conciliatory. Its power comes from his gentle use of self-mocking humor (49-51), from his frank admission of a conflict of interests, and from his portrayal of himself as the powerless object of external forces (51-53). In achieving this effect, he stresses only one word in his opening passage ("anything" in 53), but his choice of this word is the nub of his argument. It provokes an accepting murmur from the Principal (54) that allows him to be even more conciliatory later in the passage (57-60).

There is no distortion in any of this, nor is there any introduction of personal ideologies that might give advantage in the debate to one or another party. Discursive power is exercised, received, and exchanged with good will and sincerity. In the context of this episode, there may be several reasons for this. First, the power expressed through the discourse is supportive of the Principal and the school (80-82, 91-92). She has looked for guidance from the Board and has found expression of support for her plans, which is positive and comforting: a group desire to support one another by making the best of the situation and by preserving the ideals that are most important to the members (76-78, 83-85). Because they are all headed in the same direction, there is little reason for distorted communication to arise. A second reason for the absence of distortion surfaced in later interviews. Clearly the Board members see one another as having a similar philosophy of education, and this is liberating for their discussions because the presuppositions for many debates are shared. This gives them respect for one another's views, even if strongly expressed as in the range of prosodic reinforcers that are used throughout this episode.

The power exercised through the functioning of the various discourses in this episode is of a relational kind, belonging to no single individual. This power is invested in the real and effective exchange of views that takes place between respected equals. The undistorted quality of the communication does not seem to depend on formal meeting procedures. Although the conventions for running meetings provide an understood framework, the things that are said are meaningful, true, justified, and sincere because the participants are alike in their commitment to representing the needs of their school and the community served by it. The discourse may resemble an ideal speech situation because all of those with a stake in the topic of debate (parents, teachers, administrators, students) are present or represented by people who can communicate without distortion on their behalf on this topic.

Episode 2: "School Trips" (see Appendix: lines 94-223). This episode occurs early in the second hour of the meeting, shortly after a break for a light evening meal. The Board has a written policy for dealing with requests to undertake major student excursions. Here the request has come from a teacher [George] in a letter. Other members are aware of the planned trip, and George has lobbied the teacher-elected representative in advance (169-173). The key topic of the debate appears in 104-105: whether the Board will approve leave with pay during term for the teachers, although the trip is still three years away. There are complicating factors: There will be Board elections in the interim, and another Board will be responsible for any commitment made; also the Board's financial responsibilities may be extended to include "bulk-funding" (132-134).

Analysis. The discursive power here is much less one-directional than in Episode 1. The Board is no longer dealing with the interests of one of its own members, so there is more need for members to act as advocates supporting the teacher or the school community. The three administrators unite to oppose George's request (124-125, 130, 208-211). Their solidarity, expressed in overlapping (//), speedy (> <), or contiguous discourse (=) (see symbols in 129-136, 157-163), seems to win out over the strong but isolated support for George that is offered by other members (107, 126-128, 138-140, 154-156, 169-173). The supporters are neither as well organized as a group nor cogent enough in their choice of language. They use polite expressions of tentativeness, such as "but I think" (126), "sort of" (128), "could we say" (137 & 154), and "p'haps ahh expenses" (173). One also introduces a type 3 function of ideology that allows him to change sides (107, see also later). To develop their points the administrators use different prosodic means: The Principal again uses word stress and word lengthening (106, 119 & 120) or emphasizes phrases of number or quantity (141-150, 191-200), the Vice Principal's strategy is to come in quickly with supportive remarks (130 & 159), and the Associate Principal makes discrete remarks marked by clear pauses (109-115) or recapitulates her previous points at speed (208-211). Like word choice, use of prosody varies from person to person. It offers many means to reach an end, and these can complement one another in the service of a single discursive purpose.

In spite of the apparent solidarity of the administrators on the issue, later interviews suggested that there was no prior discussion of the matter. The Principal knew only that a request was coming to the Board. There are good reasons for the administrators to be concerned with the long-term consequences of this decision because their roles on the Board would continue beyond the present Board membership, as would their responsibility for the school. So their solidarity on the matter is not surprising, and it is sufficient to overwhelm the arguments of George's supporters, who have less direct stake in the outcome of the debate. Although the arguments of the latter may be as good or better, their status in the organization and their uncertain role in the Board's future seems to affect the power of their presentation so that they may not represent George's case as well as it could be. His supporters do present his case in a context of openness, but there is some room for doubting that the best set of arguments has won out on the day. This is especially so because the administrators manage to introduce an argument predicated on an uncertain future scenario becoming a highly likely one. This allows them to define interests specific to themselves as universally valid, which is a type 1 function of ideology at work (130-161). However, the Chair acknowledges that his earlier position on the matter (137-140) is changed by the arguments he has heard (164-165), and his response to a strong point sympathetic to George's case (171-173) indicates that he has been persuaded by force of argument (176-179). He even repeats his own words (in 177-179 from 164-165) as though they were someone else's. The Principal too makes a concession to the need for leave with pay (152-153), apparently influenced by the force of the debate. Although this concession does not show up in the motion that she later moves (218-219), her words are lodged in the discursive structures of the school and may return to influence the institution and its policies.

The only other hint of an intruding ideology in the episode comes from Fred in lines 204-207. This (type 3) function of ideology occurs when a person or persons define present organizational realities as naturalistically necessary. In this case Fred generalizes from his own "experience" in such matters to argue that taking children on school trips "is the kind of thing that you do for love." Now if accepted uncritically by the Board, this argument from Fred would have been sufficient on its own to rule out George's request for leave with pay. It is curious that no one challenged George on this assertion of his. Did everyone agree with his generalization? The answer from later interviews was ambiguous. Although one member "agreed in practice" with Fred's assessment and disagreed "in theory," two other members strongly disagreed with Fred. They both believed that teachers should be paid for any time given to the school and to its students that is approved by the Board. In spite of this contrary view, Fred's view went unchallenged, partly because he "tends to go on a bit and people don't always listen to what he says," and partly because there was already a strong consensus in the prior discourse that the issue of leave with pay would become a Board matter in the future (180-183). So Fred's ideological point seemed redundant.

Leaving aside this and the earlier distorting incident, the episode seems to be free of insincerities, unjustified claims, untruths, and meaningless statements, although the discursive solidarity of the administrators does tilt the debate unequally in their favor so that not all of the speaking members may be swayed by the power of the best arguments presented. But because the members in this episode are still dealing by proxy with "one of their own," there is scrupulous fairness and attention to detail. In the final episode the Board is dealing with a matter raised by the members of an outgroup.

Episode 3: "Community Use of Facilities" (see Appendix: lines 224-334). This episode occurs about 10 minutes after Episode 2. The hiring of the school's premises to community groups is a well-established practice at this school. In this episode a request has come from a fundamentalist Christian sect, in a letter to the Secretary, following discussions with the Secretary and the Caretaker (Janitor). This sect wants to lease some of the school's facilities for Sunday worship over one or two years.

Analysis. The discourse in this episode shows a remarkable transformation: a sharp deterioration in the even-handedness of arguments and comments. The sect's request is countered through an ideological challenge supported by an array of unjust verbal and prosodic practices. Again, this (type 3) function of ideology occurs when a person or persons define present organizational realities or practices as naturalistically necessary so that alternatives seem unworkable. Several Board members generalize, from their unhappy experience of an earlier arrangement involving another fundamentalist sect, to argue against approving this request (256-262, 298-300). They do so on grounds that are not challenged by others because of the distorting power of the maneuver outlined later, although the grounds are spurious: That is, their argument by implication is that the same factors that caused difficulties for the school in the earlier instance would reoccur if this unrelated request were approved because in all relevant respects one religious sect is the same as another. This claim is neither demonstrated discursively nor is it likely to be because its demonstration would depend on an impossible act of induction in order to predict that factors, behaviors, and outcomes in the future would be the same as in a dissimilar past.

Although none of the members speak up on behalf of the fundamentalist sect against the ideological argument, several reinforce it with negative points that create a bandwagon effect of opposition to the request. Some points hint at valid objections, but their effective power is only to reinforce an ideology-based argument sustained without opposition. In the resulting debate, no one raises any points in favor of the request or suggests any compromise measure that might appeal to the sect as a partly positive response to their request. Well before the ideology begins to do its work, there is clear evidence in the discourse to show that this request faces severe prejudices that smooth the way for the ideology to work: A number of key verbal and prosodic contributions scaffold the discourse in such a way as to make the possibility of opposition seem unwise or risky and to encourage collusion in a conspiracy of distorted communication into which those around the table are drawn. The discourse itself seems to structure subsequent discourse, and an ideological distortion goes unchallenged. How does this happen?

The Scaffold

1. The Secretary of the Board steps out of her official role of objectivity to use an ambiguity in the text of the sect's letter to play for a laugh at their expense (232-234). She signals that she is not disinterested in this matter. She solicits comments on the ambiguity by putting a raised intonation on her words *kitchen* and *hall* (232 & 234) and by deliberately pausing in her reading (234).
2. On cue, several participants deliver laughter and ironic comments (235).
3. The Principal reinforces these with an audible aside (236).
4. The Chair adds a frivolous interjection (242).
5. Several participants reinforce the Chair's expression of mild contempt (243).
6. Pam adds an ironic exclamation (246) perhaps renderable as "I am impressed."
7. The Secretary inserts an extremely hostile aside into her reading of the letter, adding the absent caretaker's view to her own in a new layer of opposition (249-251).
8. With the groundwork for the ideology laid, the Principal introduces it and solicits corroboration with a raised intonation (256).
9. The Secretary responds, providing the first in a chain of enthusiastic statements creating and supporting the ideology (257).
10. Overlapping or contiguous contributions reinforce the distortion until it becomes a forecast of school chaos, complete with alarm bells ringing (258-264).
11. With her chuckle, Shastra signals that she for one is aware of the cynical game that the Board is playing, but contributes to it nonetheless (265).
12. The Secretary interrupts Shastra, highlighting the number of alarms (267) and getting the response from the Board that she expects (268-269).
13. The Principal brings the discussion back to the point, but gives the Secretary grounds for another interruption (272-273).
14. The Secretary interrupts with a very hostile choice of words (274-275).[3]

---

[3]Some verbs actually entail acceptance of the speakers' view of the truth or falsity of

15. The three administrators suggest some genuinely undesirable consequences of agreeing to the request (277-300). Again, they back one
another up in overlapping contributions (290 & 291).

16. The Secretary makes an ironic characterization of her own actions,
"fobbing off" the sect when they had asked to plead their case in person (304-305). (Note that this act is very prejudicial to discursive
fairness because it occurs soon after the only moment in the debate
in which some form of compromise action is foreshadowed [287-
289], and it preempts other members from suggesting that the sect be
allowed to vary their request or to state their point of view more
fully.)

17. By now the request is tacitly defeated and the Chair offers a humorous
allusion to a problem that has affected other Boards of Trustees in the
country, when they have been "captured" by sectional interests (306).

18. A motion to decline the request becomes a formality. Rangi moves it
sotto voce, and Fred hurriedly seconds it (318-319).

19. The Chair gives a mild display of intolerant impatience in hurrying
through the motion (321-322).

This discursive scaffold distorts the communication; it moves it away
from a debate in which the best argument advanced has the best chance of suc-
ceeding because only one spurious argument has had the floor. Most crucially,
the distortions of communication seem to structure the power arrangements in
the debate. Up to a point, they solicit both the verbal and the prosodic contributions that participants seem willing to make (233-236, 242-246, 257-264). By
the time several members realize that the Board might have been less than fair
in its treatment of the request (325 & 330-331), the motion has already been
passed and the opportunity to act more fairly has been lost.

Clearly many events, feelings, and attitudes, which do not show up in
the transcript itself, provide a backdrop to this episode and contributed to the
distortion of the debate. Later interviews allowed this to be pieced together. The
influential thing seems to have been the way that the representatives of the sect
presented themselves to the school's staff in their preliminary meetings (230-
231, 247-251): Although they were seen as respectable people, they were also
seen as demanding, blunt, rude, and hasty. This created a strong feeling of
antipathy that worked against them in at least two ways. It went directly into the
discursive structures of the school, coloring official attitudes to the request; and
it showed up in the presentation made to the Board by the Secretary and indirectly by the Principal. Prior to the meeting, the Principal saw the request as a
matter of slight importance that would quickly be dismissed; the Secretary was
also opposed to the request in advance, hoping it would not succeed because of

what they are saying. These are called "implicative verbs" by Bolinger (1980). The
Secretary's claim that "they even had the cheek to ask for it at half the normal rates"
does this sort of work.

her antipathy and because of the hidden expenses that such hirings create. Clearly, memories of the earlier sect's use of the facilities created prejudice against this request. Also the Chair confirmed that he was not just intolerant of fringe sects, he was somewhat intolerant of religious groups of all kinds and acknowledged that this sometimes affected his objectivity in dealing with them. Even the Vice Principal responsible for room bookings, who showed some readiness to compromise (287-289) and then to correspond on the matter (330-331), was less than impartial as it turns out. He was influenced by his memories of a recent experience, hiring the school hall to a society for caged birds and entering the room the next day to find it "full of shit and feathers." Other Board members were genuinely opposed to the request because of the long-term commitment; this was helpful in allowing the ideology and the antipathy it expressed to do its work without any voiced opposition, especially when the sect provided so easy a target as a fringe minority outgroup. A most telling contextual factor, which summarizes the episode, was suggested by the Chair in his words: "They had no patronage on the Board."

CONCLUSION

This study suggests how easily distorted communication can arise in formal administrative discourse when the interests of those with some stake in the matter under discussion are not represented among the participants in the discourse. The Board members were highly successful in debating and reaching suitable conclusions when the agenda item concerned their own close interests; they were only a little less successful when the agenda item concerned the interests of an absent member of their school in-group. In both episodes they were able to create a discursive context that was relatively free of highly distorting ideologies and that allowed participants to make the four validity claims that Habermas recommends. However, when the agenda broached the affairs of an out-group, who had no known patronage on the Board and who seem to have been less than sensitive in handling their preliminary dealings with the school, distortions in communication and small injustices became common and the out-group's interests were compromised. In this instance, the out-group was a fundamentalist sect, but it could have been the members of some other culturally different minority whose views were not well represented among the Board members. It is likely that if the sect had had the opportunity to state their case and engage the Board in discussion, their request might have received fairer treatment. But, as Board members confirmed, no other public group had ever been invited to plead their case in this way, and constraints of time made it unlikely any ever would. So how could discursive power have been exercised more fairly, both in this case and in the generality?

Habermas (1971) believes that social institutions have a pathological quality about them. They operate with the same damaging consequences that human neurotic behavior causes; they are a collective manifestation of the "repetition compulsion" of individuals; and they act to defend a rigid uniformity of behavior and to disguise that behavior in such a way as to remove it from criticism. To modify this pathology, his "ideal speech situation" provides for all those with an interest in an affair to have an equal and open chance of entering into discussion and weighing evidence and argument. Reinterpreting his ideas into the everyday practice of managing schools as social institutions, the key seems to lie in the way the concept of "impartiality" is put into practice. Habermas shares this concept with Rawls (1972), who may offer a little more guidance about its application in real-world institutions. Using Rawls's account, Barry (1989) suggests fleshing out the idea of "impartiality" in two different ways. The first approach is to ask interested parties what outcome they would favor if they did not know which position they were to occupy under a new policy. Doing this prevents powerful participants from abusing their superior bargaining power because it denies them various kinds of knowledge, especially knowledge of their own identities in the hypothetical arrangements. Barry's second approach is more like a debate than a game. Its method is to ask those involved to propose and defend principles for the distribution of benefits and burdens that they sincerely believe ought to be acceptable to everyone affected and that no one could reasonably reject. This approach could enable participants to think of themselves as representatives of groups in the wider society, although not if this meant excluding the real representatives of minorities or other social groups. Clearly the cultural knowledge that different groups possess is not something that actors in a debate can take on or put off at will, and this makes Rawls's and Barry's recommendations seem less than practical in the pluralist contexts of modern schools. When out-groups have very different cultural values, their participation in the debate cannot be "fobbed off" with justice.

   In the contemporary world this conclusion now receives widespread support among emancipatory theorists and practitioners of all kinds. In their relations with minority peoples and with other out-groups, policymakers do need to develop methods for finding out about very different sets of human needs and interests that will allow them to know when the exercise of power through language in any setting is useful and benevolent and when it is harmful. Bhaskar is one contemporary theorist who offers an approach for doing this, which is already influential. Elsewhere I introduce his conception of discovery, which has its base in his scientific realism (Corson, 1991a).[4] The organizing theme of Bhaskar's enquiry is a straightforward one: the nature of, and the prospects for, human emancipation. Emancipation for him occurs when we substitute a wanted policy for an unwanted one. The task of policy research is to establish what is really wanted. In approaching any form of social policymaking or inquiry, Bhaskar's conception includes, as real entities, any emergent proper-

---

[4]Elsewhere too I link Bhaskar's views with Habermas and Bourdieu in discussing social justice and minority language policy; and language and gender (Corson, 1992a, 1992b, 1993b).

ties of the social world, such as the reasons and other accounts in language that people use to direct and affect social or individual behavior and change. If human reasons or accounts are to be awarded this deserved status, then the twin tasks of any inquiry are first to confirm the existence and then to detail the operation of these real entities—to show that the reasons or accounts are real and important influences in the lives of actors affected by policy. Once confirmed, this evidence not only guides policy inquiries, but it also morally compels policymakers to act on their findings by inserting into the social world the emancipatory policy actions that their inquiries uncover. To do otherwise is to act as if those reasons or accounts do not exist or as if they have no status.

As this chapter argues, even when conditions of debate come close to an ideal speech situation and when participants are skilled in taking a balanced point of view, an in-group of policymakers will find it difficult to engage dispassionately with the special interests and rights of socially or culturally different people. Not long ago, any form of accommodation to minority group views, expressing cultural or spiritual values, was discouraged in most societies. Although policy accommodations to majority group cultural or spiritual values were regularly made, as they still are today, because one function of dominant ideology is to represent dominant group interests as universal in this way. But in the culturally pluralist societies that are becoming more common in today's world, people often accept and give weight in their social policies to the reasons and accounts offered by minority peoples. Decision makers increasingly accept this state of affairs on moral or political grounds.

In the account offered here, recognizing the interests and rights of outgroups means beginning with the evidence of out-group values and intentions that is expressed in the group's reasons and accounts because these aspects of discourse in turn produce, shape, and are shaped by the sociocultural structures that the groups value. It seems impossible to avoid the conclusion that any policymaking that does not engage with those cultural structures, and with the reasons and accounts that produce and are productive of them, will consistently act against the emancipation, through education in this case, of people drawn from those groups. In place of policymaking that disempowers in this way, we need a form of decision making that sincerely responds to the reasons and accounts that minority people offer as expressions of their intentions and as evidence of the cultural structures that they value. In some places, this may mean that minority cultures and groups need to be in control of the educational decision making that mainly affects their interests. In other places, a thoroughly pluralist organizational arrangement may be needed, incorporating minority representatives at every level (Corson, 1990, 1993b), if just decisions are going to be reached.[5]

---

[5]This chapter is extracted from "Discursive bias and ideology in the administration of minority group interests." *Language in Society, 22,* 165-191. © 1993 Cambridge University Press. Reprinted with permission.

APPENDIX: TRANSCRIPTS AND TRANSCRIPT SYMBOLS

The symbols are a modification of those developed by conversation analysis, which uses transcripts of naturally occurring talk as a practical strategy for understanding social life. They are thought to capture the minimum number and degree of features of talk that persons seem to apprehend and respond to in some way in conversations. They have the virtue of leaving the transcripts reasonably intelligible to nonspecialists. They also replace normal punctuation:

//	(e.g,. see line 20)	When one speaker begins while another is still speaking, two oblique lines mark the place at which the overlap begins. The next utterance in the transcript begins at that place in the relevant passage.
//. . . //	(see 81)	If there is a second set of oblique lines in a passage, then the next utterance but one in the transcript begins at the second marked place in the passage.
=	(see 82 & 35)	When one utterance runs on from a prior utterance without a break, an equal sign links the two utterances. When a speaker runs together parts of a single utterance without a break, the same sign is also used.
(1.1)	(see 1)	Timed intervals within or between utterances are shown by bracketed numbers marking seconds and tenths of seconds of the interval.
(.)	(see 2)	For discernible intervals of less than one-tenth of a second a dot is placed in brackets.
?	(see 22)	A question mark indicates a rising intonation that may not necessarily accompany a question.
^	(see 22)	A circumflex indicates rising shifts in intonation.
:::	(see 88)	When a sound is extended or prolonged, colons mark relative length; the more colons the longer the extension.
o o	(see 224-225)	Degree signs indicate that the part of the utterance they enclose is spoken more quietly than the rest.
CAPS	(see 22)	Talk that is louder than the surrounding talk is marked by capital letters.
> <	(see 1)	Sections of an utterance that are delivered more quickly are enclosed between less-than and greater-than signs.
heh arh	(see 28 & 30)	Laughter, chuckling, fill-ins and so on, are represented by using sound particles that are close to the sounds made.
_	(see 7)	Parts of an utterance that are stressed are underlined.

( )	(see 239)	Brackets enclosing a blank space show talk that was inaudible or left out for some other reason.
[ ]	(see 17)	Square brackets surround a change made in a name for the sake of anonymity.
(( ))	(see 268)	Double brackets surround a description of a sound or an activity supplied by the transcriptionist.

Episode 1: "Attain."

1. PRINC.:   The problem is >you see< if if it gets to the stage where (0.5) there is
2.   there was were a number of schools there (.) we feel we have to charge
3.   'em because (.) so that our resources don't get (.) depleted (.) but if it got
4.   to be ahh more schools than one and if they're wanting you to help
5.   them set in place something that we had to work hard to do last year
6.   (.) it's going to be a very big time commitment and therefore that time
7.   won't be spent with the people who are there (.) the other implications
8.   that it has is that I believe from indications (.) I may be wrong (.) but I
9.   believe that ATTAIN itself will grow within the school (.) so
10.   therefore we have to spend time training our own teachers as well (.) ·
11.   And ahh it it's ahh quite umm >a dilemma< my I'm clear that our
12.   priorities are first (.) other schools we'll help if we can (.) but they
13.   have second priority to us (.)
14. CHAIR: One of our objectives (.) in the evalu- when the evaluation (.) part of it is
15.   finished one of the things that we hope to do is to put the projects::s (0.2)
16.   an outline of the project plus the evaluation on the network (.) >on the
17.   electronic network< (.) we've got one and which [this school] is about
18.   to join (.) °I understand° um and at that point we will be preparing
19.   (.) resource materials for sale (.) which will have the names on them of
20.   the people who developed // them=
21. PRINC.:   ehm (.)
22.   BUT WHO'S GOING TO GET THE FUNDING FOR TH^AT? (.)
23. CHAIR: and the school will get the royalties (.)
24. PRINC.:   Yeah (.) as long as it is the school (.) because >y'know< there was a bit
25.   of umm I suppose bitterness about the fact that umm the school who set up
26.   the program is being given (0.2) virtually nothing yet the evaluators
27.   have been given 60,000 dollars plus and if we hadn't set the
28.   pro^gram up (0.2) you heh could've had 60,000 that you weren't
29.   evaluating anything for (.) >y'know< the group that's doing it (.) and
30.   that's no one's fault (.) but (0.3) ahh there is a lot of feeling ahh among
31.   um ^people in the school that um (0.4) that the irony of getting large
32.   (0.4) well a large amount of money (.) if it was split halfway think what
33.   we could have done (.) um to in fact evaluate a program that gets (0.2)
34.   no fun^ding (.) um and I think that arh there is some disquiet about that
35.   and and then you see all the things of ownership come about=who owns

36.	the program? is there such a thing ^as ownership? and if you're talking
37.	about selling services (.) >you know< it's a whole new world and it's
38.	sort of an unpleasant (0.2) feeling because mostly teachers have said
39.	we'll share this with you (.) arrh and in fact there were people
40.	photocopying off resources right left and c^entre (.) they were doing
41.	that=that day (.) other teachers from other schools (0.1) so I think
42.	there's an ethical issue as well as (0.4) a marketing issue as well as a
43.	time issue that we hadn't really heh heh heh thought about until the
44.	open days led to >quite a lot of interest< the good thing is that there was
45.	very very positive feedback from the people who were there (.) why
46.	this happened years ago (.) those sorts of comments people were
47.	making (0.1)
48. VOICES:	((coughs))
49. CHAIR:	It it's a bit embarrassing (.) I guess I'm (0.2) trying to wear two hats here
50.	and it doesn't really (0.1) they don't fit either of them (.) well (.) >they
51.	do< but not both together (0.4) but one of the points that (.) we've been
52.	had >it made clear to us< is that the Ministry is not going to fund
53.	anything that hasn't been evaluated (.)
54. PRINC.:	mmm
55. CHAIR:	and the point about them being willing to put money into the evaluation
56.	(.) they wouldn't have put that much money if they thought it wasn't
57.	going to (0.2) if it didn't have a good chance of succeeding (0.2) and the
58.	point about it=if the evaluation is of a (.) is favorable in that sense then
59.	that evaluation itself can be used as a claim for further resources (0.1) to
60.	develop it further
61. V/PRIN.:	Nevertheless it becomes a chicken // and egg situation<
62. VOICES:	(embarrassed coughs and laughter))
63. PRINC.:	But (0.2) But the thing is it won't be ((cough)) for us (.) it'll be for ^other
64.	schools that is that is the irony of it all (.) that the staff at ^our school
65.	have done all the hard work (0.1) and the funding wasn't ^given to us to
66.	float it which it ^has been in other places=you look at [Freetown High]
67.	with their computers they got ^lots and lots of money and lots and lots of
68.	equipment to do that umm it'll be ^other ^schools that will benefit from
69.	your evaluation >we will too< but we won't be funded because we've
70.	already got it up and running (.) and umm this is where (.) I I talked with
71.	[a Ministry official] about it and he's going to talk with the [Secretary
72.	for Education] about it umm because it seems to me a little bit of an un-
73.	injustice basically (.) that >there isn't much< incentive for curriculum
74.	initiatives really is there if you look at it and that's one of the things
75.	they're talking about (0.1) but // ummm
76. PAM:	I think if we keep in mind that the program's for the children and the
77.	children's needs are priority (.) then I think you've got every right to (.)
78.	sort of argue that // >you know<
79. PRINC.:	mmm

80.	PAM:	in order to meet those <u>needs</u> we do need th'extra money (.) so (.) ch^arge
81.		people that want to come and learn // from your experience // I think
82.		that is quite=
83.	PRINC.:	That's why (.) that is actually why because umm it's going to have err
84.		why should <u>our</u> kids in fact be deprived of <u>their</u> teachers and n::not have
85.		<u>any</u>thing back for it (0.2)
86.	PAM:	yeah=
87.	PRINC.:	and umm that is basically why >you know< it's been a bit hard >no it's
88.		quite hard< ah but th'th' other schools in fact i::if they want it they
89.		will (.) pay for it (.) >if they don't< well::ll it it's not our ^worry
90.		basically
91.	PAM:	No (0.2) I would support you I think I would
92.	CHAIR:	°Yes I think it's a good idea°
93.	PRINC.	:>OK well that's< ATTAIN

Episode 2 : "School Trips"

94.	CHAIR:	umm school trips (1.0) are those (0.2)
95.	SECR.:	I have a letter to read out ((reads letter to the Board from George, a
96.		teacher planning to take a party of pupils on a trip overseas in three
97.		years time)) (2.0)
98.	CHAIR:	Any (.) any comments (.) any (0.5)
99.	PAM:	Are they asking just to <u>fund</u> it or just to give them // approval for
100.		fundraising
101.	SECR.:	No no [a] approval in (.) in principle and [b] approval for them to
102.		fundraise (.)
103.	PAM:	mm=
104.	SECR.:	and [c] approval for leave with pay for two teachers (0.2) for at least two
105.		teachers (1.0)
106.	PRINC.:	At <u>least</u> two teachers (1.0)
107.	FRED:	>Mr Chairman this is just a wonderful idea< ((Fred speaks at length in
108.		support of George's proposal))
109.	A/PRIN.:	There is one (.) point I when I took a trip to Australia a couple of years
110.		ago with some students (.) if we'd <u>taken</u> them during <u>term</u>-time (.) the
111.		teachers' salaries would <u>not</u> have been <u>paid</u> (.) you were only <u>paid</u> if you
112.		were traveling with students with<u>in</u> New <u>Zea</u>land (.)
113.		now I don't know whether that
114.		anomaly still exists (.) but in fact the two weeks that he's asking for paid
115.		leave for with the Board would have to fund if that is still existing (.)
116.	PRINC.:	mm I I was going to suggest that we approve a. and b. and reserve our
117.		<u>judge</u>ment on::n ^<u>c</u>. // until we get(.)
118.	CHAIR:	It's 1993
119.	PRINC.:	It's 199<u>4</u> asking for leave of two weeks for (.) at <u>least</u> two teachers at the
120.		beginning of 199^4 (.) And I and I believe that it's <u>long</u>::gg way to look

121.		into the future and if we had 50 kids going are we going to having be
122.		looking for leave for six teachers or whatever=so I believe that we
123.		y'know I would like to move that we approve the (.) trip in <u>prin</u>ciple
(.) 124.		that we approve for them to <u>fund</u>raise (.) but that we reserve our
125.		<u>judg</u>ment on the <u>leave</u> with <u>pay</u> until <u>clo</u>ser to the <u>trip</u> (0.2)
126.	CHAIR:	Well (.) they need but I think they would need some <u>pos</u>itive indication
127.		though otherwise it's not worth doing the <u>first</u> two things if you if the
128.		<u>last</u> one which what is the really <u>cru</u>cial one (.) if that's sort of // ahhh=
129.	PRINC.:	Mm well::ll=
130.	V/PRIN.:	trying to crystal ball gaze though=we don't know//
131.	CHAIR:	No I understand that=
132.	V/PRIN.:	ahrr::rr what decisions the Ministry or th'the is likely to make in terms
133.		of funding in the future (.) >by then we could be on bulk-funding and it
134.		could be a ^Board decision<
135.	PRINC.:	I mean if they fundraise // the money could go back to them if it fell
136.		through but (0.2)
137.	CHAIR:	Could we say=if we if we approve the
138.		first <u>two</u> and then said with
139.		regard to the third one (.) as far as we can <u>see</u> (.) <u>now</u> there appear to
be 140.		no problems but no <u>final</u> decision can be (.) entered into until 199^3=
141.	PRINC.:	Well I don't know about the no problems bit=I mean if it's <u>one</u> teacher you
142.		can ^<u>cov</u>er them at the beginning
143.		(.) If it's <u>two</u> teachers you can probably cover
144.		them t^oo but it's saying at <u>least</u> two teachers what say it's <u>six</u> teachers
145.		um y'know I'm not saying it is (.) what I'm what <u>I</u> feel uneasy about is is is
146.		umm ((reads)) "for leave with pay for at least two staff for a period of
147.		two w^eeks at the beginning of the year"(.) now I think these trips are (.)
148.		really good ^things but then you have to look at the <u>over</u>all functioning of
149.		the school as well (.) <u>and</u> I would be very loath to give (.) to approve
at 150.		<u>least</u> two teachers going (.) umm at this stage ahh with <u>leave</u> with <u>pay</u>
151.		umm I think that once we know how many st^udents are going we can
152.		make a decision on it then and I think <u>yes</u> there needs to be some
leave 153.		with pay but (.) maybe we need to put a <u>lid</u> on how many=
154.	PAM:	Could we say in principle <u>up to</u> two teachers (.) and then if they get the
155.		required number of students surely there'd be ^parents available who
156.		might end up being able to take // a
157.	A/PRIN.:	Yes (.) you're still probably committing yourself to about 4,000
158.		dollars (.) // for two teachers for two weeks=
159.	V/PRIN.:	I don't (.) I don't think you can do that on on pay at this stage on that=
160.	PRINC.:	If we've got bulk-funding we might have bulk-funding salaries by then=
161.	A/PRIN.:	Yeah=
162.	PRINC.:	an' an' >y'know< I think to <u>me</u> <u>yes</u> we might think >yes it's a good idea<
163.		but what we're doing is a <u>pol</u>icy=it's a <u>pol</u>icy thing (.) that umm
164.	CHAIR:	Well can we say we can approve the idea in principle (.) but that we this

165.		Board cannot ((slowly)) commit a future Board to ahh //
166.	PRINC.:	Leave with or without=
167.	CHAIR:	>a financial commitment<
168.		in terms of teachers' pay (1.5)
169.	SHASTRA:	umm I agree with what you say [Doug] umm (.) [George] actually passed
170.		on some other material to me I'd like I wonder if I can read that here
171.		((reads a letter from George)) so I think [George] is saying that um he has
172.		had a background of (.) umm going away with students without claiming
173.		for p'haps ahh expenses he could be entitled // to=
174.	CHAIR:	He makes a tremendous contribution to the school in this way (.)
175.	SHASTRA:	mmm
176.	CHAIR:	My own children have benefited from it enormously ah I understand that
177.		>but we still< (.) we can't commit (.) I think you're correct (.) we can't
178.		commit a future Board to those >sorts of things< so far away (.) with so
179.		many things in the // being changed on us all the time=
180.	PRINC.:	Umm (.) that's not to say that a future Board wouldn't do that >I mean<
181.		the fact that we can't commit it now doesn't mean that it might never
182.		happen (.) // it just means that they can go ahead= it's approved in
183.		principle and they can go ahead and fundraise=
184.	RANGI:	If we (2.0) if we approve those first two parts it really leaves it in their
185.		court to decide whether or not it's worthwhile proceeding with (3.0)
186.	CHAIR:	Well I think (.) no I don't think we ought to drop a lid on them that way
187.		(.) it's something that the school ought to support in principle (1.0) or the
188.		future Board (.) we ought to be able to convince them that the future
189.		Board will do everything that it can (.) to make sure that it happens
but 190.		at least we can't make the undertaking // definitely now=
191.	PRINC.:	Yeah (.) but I think the Board would make that decision in the light of
192.		(.) the needs of the wider school an::nd umm being fair to the staff who
193.		take °such a trip° (.) those two things have to be weighed up and that
194.		would depend on how many students were going and how many teachers
195.		were ^seeking leave=there might be four teachers seeking leave and we
196.		might only grant leave to ^two of them >with pay< =they they they're
197.		the sorts of issues that I think would need to be (.) discussed (.) when we
198.		knew more information (.) but to say >y'know< th'way that's worded is if
199.		we approve that we're saying we're=leave with pay for at least two
200.		teachers (1.5)
201.	FRED:	Um Mr Chairman I wonder if anyone knows what the um::m what
202.		precedents there are (.) for example, [Maple] High with it's trips to
203.		France and um::m (.) yes [Dulcie] the one you mentioned to Australia
204.		ah::h my (.) experience has rather been that um this is the kind of thing
205.		that you >do for love< and while [George] is very strong on ah ahh
206.		costing everything to very fine detail ahh the sting in the tail about I'll
207.		do it as as long as I get paid (.) grates a little bit (2.4) ((coughs))
208.	A/PRINC.	As I say wh't we found was that if the teachers went in the holidays

209.		they received their holiday pay if they went during term-time they
210.		receive <u>noth</u> ^ing< and um::m it's the term-time bit that's difficult with
211.		this (.)
212.	VOICES:	Yes (1.5)
213.	CHAIR:	Well is:s someone like to word a m' // a motion?
214.	A/PRIN:	I think I'd like to move one=
215.	PRINC.:	I move that we approve the ahh trip in <u>princ</u>iple (.) and give approval
216.		for them to <u>fund</u>raise for this purpose (0.4)
217.	CHAIR:	And avoid th'=
218.	PRINC.:	And then that we reserve any decision on <u>leave</u> with <u>pay</u> for <u>staff</u> until
219.		we know <u>more</u> >information< (1.5)
220.	CHAIR:	Have we got a second // a seconder for that=[Jason]
221.	PRINC.:	Two motions really
222.	JASON:	Yes=
223.	CHAIR	Thank you

Episode 3: "Community Use of Facilities"

224.	CHAIR:	An' now there was an<u>other</u> (.) request >I think< as well (0.5) // °I'll
225.		keep quiet this time°=
226.	SECR.:	Yes there is (0.2) it's from the [Praise the Lord Congregation] ((reads)) ( )
227.		"we ( ) are part of an international church movement with over
228.		200 centers ( ) at present we are meeting at [Freetown]
229.		School and have outgrown our facility and are looking to move to larger
230.		premises (.) after prior discussion with [the principal] of your college and
231.		on the inspection of your hall and other buildings (.) we would like to
232.		apply for the use of your facilities (.) i.e. hall and adjoining ^kitchen the
233.		drama room and two classrooms (.) although these two rooms do not
234.		necessarily need to be attached to the h^all" ((stops reading))
235.	VOICES:	((laughter)) ((ironic interjections))
236.	PRINC.:	That's good because // they're not=
237.	SECR.:	We offered them room 35 but we didn't offer any <u>other</u> room
238.		((continues reading)) "we will require these facilities every Sunday with
239.		a view to commence on or near the 22nd of July ( ) we
240.		understand that we are liable for any damage and have both public
241.		liability and <u>cont</u>ents insurance to cover any such occurrence"=
242.	CHAIR:	Or act of God
243.	VOICES:	((loud laughter)) ((ironic interjections))
244.	SECR.:	((still reading)) "we do not see this as a problem as the children have
245.		trained supervision at all times" (.)
246.	PAM:	<u>o</u>hhh=
247.	SECR.:	((still reading)) "we ( ) thank you for the positive response ( ) so far
248.		from both the caretaker and the secretary and look forward to working
249.		closely with them in the future" ((stops reading)) ((aside)) they <u>don</u>'t

250.   know what the caretaker and the secretary were saying to each <u>other</u>
251.   about it ((continues reading)) "we look forward to your reply (.) yours
252.   faithfully ( ) Pastor" (.)
253. PRINC.:   And they want it for one to two years // every Sunday=
254. SECR.:   Yes (.) and they're prepared to lease it=
255. SHASTRA: What time >I mean< is it the whole day going into the <u>evening</u> 'n=
256. PRINC.:   We used to have the [Revival Center] here did'n they^
257. SECR.:   Yes n' that was for the whole day (.)
258. PRINC.:   And the=were got=the <u>rooms</u> got more and more rooms that they had and
259.   things went missing 'nd=
260. SECR.:   And kids went ^all over the school // and the <u>staff</u>room and //
261.   everywhere
262. VOICES: All over the school=kids running=yess ( )
263. SHASTRA: We've got places that are already al<u>arme</u>d haven't we ? in the school=
264. SECR.:   Exactly=
265. SHASTRA: and I think that w'd jeop- that would jeopardise heheh our security
266.   system for one thing let alone any other (.) // problems that might crop up
267. SECR.:   <u>Twenty</u> <u>three</u> calls at the weekend (.) the alarm systems
268. VOICES: ((gasps of surprise))
269. PRINC.:   How m::=yeah that was a fairly lucrativ::e operation last <u>time</u> but::t if
270.   ^you let out your hall <u>every</u> Sunday for two years (.) >I mean< you really
271.   are uh I can think of a clash the first Sun th'second Sunday that they're
272.   th^ere=it's Science (.) at least they're <u>paying</u> I s'pose // it's the Science
273.   // Technology Roadshow=
274. SECR.:   Yeah (0.4) this is where I have to say something=they even had the
275.   <u>cheek</u> to <u>ask</u> for it at <u>half</u> the normal rates (.) because it was a
276.   community thing (.) ((murmurs from several voices))
277. V/PRIN.:   They're go-going to be some problems in that we already have a
278.   commitment to one or two organizations who have made prior bookings for
279.   the hall for a long period of time umm that would not be available for
280.   the exam period because once the exams um::m desks and so on are set out
281.   there 's a major operation to get those out back in and so on um and that
282.   will apply (.) or coming up anyway we've got the school exams at the
283.   start of Term Three and they will go over a weekend=we will have um::m
284.   two to three weeks for um public examinations and remember that this
285.   year we are also having the bursary and schol- exams and so on within
286.   the school and not up at a::hh [the university] so that would take out at
287.   least two or three weekends a::hh for that (.) if we were going to hire it it
288.   would have to be on the understanding that on <u>certain</u> times for <u>certain</u>
289.   things it would <u>not</u> be available on the Sunday (.) um::m // yes
290. A/PRINC.:   You mean things like the School Ball // and
291. PRINC.:   Well that's r^ight an' and also there'll be the intersecondary
292.   athletics=I just think it restricts us ^<u>too</u> much in the use of the
293.   hall=because (.) you have to think about (.) >I mean< sometimes that

294.		place is cleaned on a Sunday as w^ell umm it just I just think that two
295.		years to know that y'r hall and y'r classrooms every day are actually (.)
296.		used I just don't honestly (.) think that=well my view is that umm that is
297.		too much of a commitment of our facilities to some some other
298.		organization (.) and I can remember back to the [Revival Center] days
299.		when there were enormous problems there um with and we were very
300.		pleased when they said // they were going // I can remember
301.	SHASTRA:	Mmm (.) mm it could be added that we don't want to commit a future
302.		Board heh ahhh
303.	VOICES	((laughter))
304.	SECR.:	They ahh also wanted to come along to the meeting tonight to plead
305.		their case but I fobbed them off (0.5)
306.	CHAIR:	Well they might stack the next Board elections y'know
307.	VOICES:	(inaudible comments and interjections)
308.	FRED:	I've struck criticism ahh (0.5) along the lines of um::m we don't hire our
309.		facilities enough >you know<=organizations want t' use classrooms on a
310.		regular basis=that kind of thing=for meeting rooms (.) and when you
311.		point out what they w' would have to be responsible for and that really
312.		the the use of the facility for the community at large tends to pre-
313.		preclude um::m (.) such block bookings for a particular ahh section so that
314.		you have the utmost mobility for the community at large (.) then um I
315.		think::k they have to be declined (3.0)
316.	CHAIR:	Further com^ment=discussion? (1.5) would someone like to::o (.) put
317.		motion (0.5)
318.	RANGI:	°I'll move that the application be declined=°
319.	FRED:	Second=
320.	CHAIR:	Seconded by [Fred]=any further discussion? (1.0) motion is that the
321.		application from the (.) [Praise the Lord] (1.5) Church or whatever they
322.		are=be declined (.) >All those in favor please say Aye<=
323.	VOICES:	Aye=
324.	CHAIR:	All those against say No=Carried=
325.	PAM:	Are we going to give them reasons // why //
326.	CHAIR:	Yes=
327.	PRINC.:	Yes (.) I think so like the the the longg commit the long-term //
328.		commitment
329.	SECR.:	already done that=((background murmurs))=
330.	V/PRIN.:	>I think we should put it I think we should put it in writing< ((murmurs
331.		of agreement)) >so that they know where we stand with it<
332.	CHAIR:	Think it cuts across other activities of the °school°=
333.	FRED:	The work^ of the ^school must come first=
334.	VOICES:	((murmurs of agreement))

7

The Identification and Evaluation of Power in Discourse*

Viviane M.J. Robinson
University of Auckland

When I see a title such as "Discourse and Power in Educational Organizations," I anticipate a concern to identify how power is exercised in educational programs and practices and how such exercise might be connected to a wider social context of inequalities between various social groups. In addition, I anticipate an attempt to trace the implications of such exercise for the conduct of educative practices and the attainment of educational goals and some discussion of how the negative impact of power-related phenomena can be challenged and changed.

THE NEED FOR A NORMATIVE THEORY OF POWER

Among the intellectual resources needed for the pursuit of such a broad agenda is a theory of power that is sufficiently detailed to enable researchers to identify

*I thank the Research and Statistics Division of the New Zealand Ministry of Education (then Department of Education) for funding the empirical research, a portion of which is reported in the case study. The principal and staff of Northern Grammar welcomed me and my co-researcher Michael Absolum into their school and were generous in granting time and access.

how it is instantiated in particular examples of discourse. In addition, a normative theory is required that enables discourse patterns to be critically evaluated in terms of the qualities that are selected by the particular normative theory. Given the title of this book, one would assume that these qualities would be closely linked to a theory of educative practices. Answering the normative questions incorporated in this book's agenda, therefore, requires judgments to be made about the desirability or undesirability of particular patterns of discourse and the defense of the normative theory that underpins those judgments.

As a relative newcomer to discourse analysis, I must admit to some confusion about the contribution of discourse analysis to these normative questions. That discourse analysts are prepared to make normative judgments about the texts they analyze is apparent from the negative, even condemnatory tone that accompanies some of their illustrative analyses (Fairclough, 1989; Nairn & McCreanor, 1991; Potter & Wetherell, 1987). What is less apparent is the normative theory that justifies these evaluations. What is the theory of power, or of education, that leads to the condemnation of, for example, interruptions, unequal participation, and the bureaucratic processing of individuals? My uncertainty about how discourse analysts justify these evaluations can be illustrated by examining Fairclough's (1989) analysis of two discourse extracts that appear in his Language and Power.

Early in the text (pp. 18-19 and p. 41) he presents a 12-line extract from an interview between a police officer and a female witness to a violent crime. The subsequent analysis includes 12 critical comments about the policeman's treatment of the female witness, ranging from his interruptions, to his failure "to mitigate the demands he makes of her," to his control of her contributions, which he neither fully acknowledges nor thanks her for (p. 18). The need for an explicit justification of these evaluations can be assessed by imagining the policeman's reaction to Fairclough's critique. Although agreeing that he interrupted and controlled the sequence in which the witness told her story, he might justify his approach by claiming the importance of being efficient so that the offender could be apprehended as soon as possible. Although part of the contribution of critical discourse analysis has been to show that people in roles such as that of a police officer typically appeal to such values, additional arguments are needed about why those values are any less desirable than those that are presupposed by the analysts themselves.

In the second example, Fairclough presents a 21-line dialogue between a doctor and one of a group of medical students accompanying him on a clinical round (pp. 44-46). Once again, Fairclough is highly critical of the more powerful speaker, criticizing the doctor for his abruptness, for being curt, and for making the student look silly. Fairclough concludes that the extract illustrates "how power in discourse is to do with powerful participants controlling and constraining the contributions of non-powerful participants" (p. 46). Once again, one can imagine the doctor defending himself by appealing to, for the sake of argument, a theory of learning that connects the fear of public embarrassment with conscientious preparation for clinical rounds. If discourse analysts are to contribute to the elimination of counterproductive discourse patterns, then they must show why their evaluative judgments are more soundly based than those of the people they seek to criticize.

Although Fairclough (1989) does not explicitly defend his criticism of these two extracts, one can extrapolate from his earlier chapters on the relationship between discourse, social structures, power, and capitalism to construct two possible justificatory arguments. The first is embedded in this comment on the police interview:

> But mundane and conventional practice such as we have in the extract also indirectly contributes to the reproduction of the unequal social relations of our society, through naturalizing hierarchy, the routine insensitive manipulation of people in the interests of bureaucratic goals of efficiency, and the image of the police as helpers and protectors of us all (rather than an arm of the state apparatus). (p. 41)

Phrases such as "reproduction of the unequal social relations" and "naturalizing hierarchy" suggest that it is the inequality of power, as reflected in the respective positions of the participants, that justifies the negative evaluation of the police officer's speech. But surely his conduct of the interview cannot be condemned simply because it reflects or reproduces inequality? There is nothing inherently undesirable in inequalities that result from differences in expertise, information, and responsibility for the completion of particular tasks. The police officer's greater power reflects his greater knowledge of the information required to apprehend the offender and his greater responsibility for obtaining it. The doctor's unequal power reflects his greater knowledge of the content to be learned and of the instructional processes by which it can best be communicated. Because inequality of position and of associated power is not necessarily undesirable, we must ask whether Fairclough offers an additional basis for his evaluations.

A second possible justification can be found in Fairclough's subsequent discussion of power: "Power in discourse is to do with powerful participants *controlling and constraining the contributions of non-powerful participants*" (p. 46; emphasis in original). Here Fairclough has shifted from appeal to inequalities in power associated with position to a more interactional concept of power as the exercise of control. But once again it cannot be the mere exercise of control that justifies the criticism of the doctor and the police officer, because control is essential to achieving the goals appropriate to the tasks they are engaged in. What Fairclough fails to provide is a normative theory of the precise features of control that render it reprehensible in these cases and that enables one to distinguish justified from unjustified instances of control. Given the interest of discourse theorists in precise features of interaction, this gap in Fairclough's work is puzzling. Perhaps the answer lies in Fairclough's (1989, chapter 2) emphasis on wider social structures, in particular those associated with capitalism, which he sees as both undesirable and as determining the patterns of discourse associated with particular social roles. The undesirability of the behavior of the police officer, in this view, lies in its connection to a pattern of discourse (an order of discourse), which is itself determined by the power relations associated with the institution of policing in our society. This type of argument will not do, however, because even if Fairclough could establish the validity of his claim that the social relations of capitalism were, in general, normatively undesirable, it does not follow that every interaction relevant to the maintenance of capitalism is, ipso facto, undesirable. Such a claim would require an implausible degree of structural determinism because it would rule out the possibility that people can create microcontexts under capitalism that avoid the alleged abuses associated with it (Swanton, Robinson, & Crosthwaite, 1989). In addition, as Huspek (1991) has pointed out, Fairclough cannot subscribe to a strongly determinist position without contradicting his claim that discourse can be both structured by power relations and the means for transforming them.

Given that normative judgments of macrocontexts cannot be directly applied to the evaluation of interactions that occur within those contexts, discourse analysts need to justify their criticisms of the exercise of power in terms of the particular features of interactions that violate their normative theory of power. It is to the development of such a normative theory that I now turn.

THE EXERCISE OF POWER IN DISCOURSE

What concept of power might be appropriate to the task of making normative judgments about how power is exercised in particular interactions? Given the variety of relevant literature, some distinctions are necessary in order to select or construct a concept that is appropriate to the task. The first distinction to be made is between concepts of power that locate it in particular positions sanctioned by formal authority and concepts that locate power in the way it is exercised in interactions, whether or not those interactions are associated with formally sanctioned authority (Dunlap & Goldman, 1991, pp. 7-11). Research on power in discourse requires an interactional concept of power that focuses on the precise features of how it is exercised in particular discourse examples.

The second distinction to be made is between those concepts of power that build their normative judgment into the very definition of the concept and those more descriptive concepts that require additional normative criteria to distinguish between what I call the legitimate (normatively desirable) and the illegitimate (normatively undesirable) exercise of power. The work of Burbules (1986) and Lukes (1974) illustrate the former type of concept, whereas that of Fay (1987) and Dunlap and Goldman (1991) illustrate the latter. For Lukes and Burbules, power is by definition undesirable because it involves acting against the interests of another. Under their concept, the identification of power requires prior determination of another's interests and the relationship of the actions in question to those interests. For Fay and Dunlap and Goldman, power is a more neutral term that describes an influence process whose desirability must be judged separately from its identification as power. Dunlap and Goldman (1991), for example, argue that power in schools can be either facilitative or coercive. Similarly, Fay (1987) offers a normatively neutral definition of power: "A exercises power with respect to B when A does x a causal outcome of which is that B does y which B would not have done without the occurrence of x. (Does is meant to include both positive actions and forbearances; A and B refer to collective entities as well as individuals.)" (p. 120). Under this general rubric, Fay then goes on to demarcate a number of related power phenomena, namely, force, coercion, manipulation, and leadership. The inclusion of a concept of leadership (p. 121), in which power is fundamentally consensual, demonstrates how Fay's concept of power embraces both desirable and undesirable influence processes. I prefer this latter approach because it reflects the way common usage incorporates both the desirable and undesirable aspects of power relations.

We speak of both the "power of an argument," and of being "power hungry," and to restrict the concept to its undesirable referents would require an awkward change in our common usage. More telling is the confusion that results when we juxtapose Burbules' definition of power with the idea of being powerless. If to exercise power is by definition undesirable, then to be powerless, must, contrary to common sense and common usage, be desirable! The second related reason concerns the difficulty and controversy that frequently surrounds normative decisions about power. If we cannot speak of power until difficult questions about interests and consent have been determined, then we have to find some other term to describe the interaction prior to the making of this decision. This awkwardness and conceptual overload would be avoided if we could separate out the identification of power from normative, context-based decisions about its desirability. In short, there are subtleties in our usage of power and power-related concepts that are lost if we build normative judgments into the definition of power, and this loss would make it more difficult to engage in dialogue with those who had a more neutral definition of power or who wished to bring a different normative theory to its analysis.

THE EVALUATION OF POWER IN DISCOURSE

Having argued for a concept of power that is interactional and normatively neutral, there remains the task of proposing and defending a normative framework for distinguishing between legitimate and illegitimate uses of power. In the following I propose that the distinction can be made in terms of the extent to which the influence process matches the qualities of a critical dialogue (Robinson, 1989, 1993). The name signifies a process of mutual critique of validity claims and bilateral or multilateral (in contrast to unilateral) control of the processes and outcomes of the dialogue. The following model of critical dialogue is based on the work of Chris Argyris, a social psychologist who has written extensively on normative theories of interpersonal and organizational reasoning and action (Argyris, 1982, 1985; Argyris & Schön, 1974). The model describes the values and skills associated with the exercise of legitimate power and contrasts them with those that are more likely to be associated with illegitimate power. (For ease of expression the model is described as involving two male interlocutors.) Three values are relevant to the judgment of legitimacy:

1. **Respect.** A must view B as someone who has needs, intentions, and interests of his own and as having an equal right to their fulfillment, even though they may be in conflict with those of A. This value can be contrasted with one in which A treats B as the means to the fulfillment of his aims and intentions. The value of respect ensures what Habermas (1990) calls the general symmetry requirement: fair opportunity to speak, to challenge, to continue or to open up any line of inquiry, to express one's feelings, and to be, in general, unconstrained in one's dealings with other parties to the discourse. This value also alerts one to the way the exercise of legitimate power may be thwarted by structural or interpersonal barriers to participation in relevant discourse or by inequalities that arise within discourse itself.

2. **Commitment to Valid Information.** Argyris's value of valid information speaks to the cognitive requirements of the exercise of legitimate power. To be committed to valid information is to be committed to the conduct of discourse in a way that increases the chances of detection and correction of error in one's own and others' claims about the world and about what is right. This implies that A is open to the possibility that his grounds for influencing B are not as strong as he believed, and conversely that B is prepared to examine his own views about what is in his interests. A commitment to valid information is an essential addition to the value of respect. To embrace respect without valid information is to risk unexamined consensus or compromise; to embrace valid information without respect will undermine the trust and openness needed for a free and full debate of differing points of view.

3. **Freedom of Choice.** The exercise of legitimate power by A requires the freedom of B to accept or reject the influence attempt on the basis of valid information. This value is violated in the case of violence or coercion because in the first case the choice to act otherwise is removed and, in the second, deprivation is threatened if a particular choice is made (Fay, 1987, pp. 120-121).

Normative judgments about A's exercise of power are based on the degree to which these three values of critical dialogue are evident in actual discourse, not on the strength of their espousal by A, no matter how sincere. It is possible, therefore, for actors who are philosophically committed to the practices implied by these values to themselves be guilty of the exercise of illegitimate power because they lack the skills required to make their behavior consistent with their convictions. These skills fall into three broad types:

1. **Openness.** The exercise of legitimate power requires a degree of openness about one's intentions and beliefs that enables the other party to respond in the context of fact rather than supposition and second-guessing. To be open is to disclose one's views and to do so in a way that increases the probability that others can do so in return. The skills of openness can be contrasted with the strategic withholding of information that, if disclosed, may weaken A's chances of prevailing over B.

2. **Public Testing.** The point of openness is not just to hear a range of views, but to express them in ways that increase the chance that errors can be detected and corrected. The cognitive skills involved in testing the various claims that are made during an influence attempt are complex. First, there is a need to identify those claims that are problematic, that is, those whose validity is open to challenge. Habermas's (1984) typology describes the four different types of validity claim that may be problematized in discourse: claims about comprehensibility (claims to understand or to be understandable), claims to truth (about what is the case), normative claims (about what is right) and, finally, claims to sincerity (about the accurate representation of self). Having identified a problematic claim, the skills involved in its testing include identifying and evaluating the evidence or argument that was, or could be, given in its support. The evaluation process could include a number of informal testing processes, such as raising and replying to counterclaims, searching for disconfirming evidence, and constructing and examining alternative hypotheses. Although some of these tests could be conducted privately, the importance of public testing lies in the fact that the same reasoning processes that lead us to believe as we do tend to inform our testing processes (Argyris, 1982). We are more likely to escape from such circular reasoning processes if we expose our reasoning to the critical scrutiny of others.

3. **Facilitation.** Facilitative skills include frequent invitations to others to express their reactions, sensitive listening, and associated nonverbal behaviors. These facilitation skills are particularly important in situations in which there is an imbalance of formal authority or status between participants because lower status participants may be reluctant to question or refuse the influence attempts of those they perceive as having higher status and authority.

Several points need to be made about the way the exercise of power is judged under this model. First, legitimacy depends on the extent to which the interaction between A and B was informed by the values outlined earlier, and this judgment is made from analysis of the actual interaction and not from self-reports of that interaction. This methodological distinction is required by the abundant evidence that when a lot is at stake, people are frequently unaware of the way they have violated their espousals and hence are unaware of the inaccuracy of their self-reports (Argyris, 1982, p. 43; Bifano, 1989).

Second, how the values of the model are manifested in particular skills cannot be precisely specified because context will determine just how they should be employed in particular cases. The contexts in which more complete disclosure, testing, and facilitation are needed are likely to be those in which the views and interests of each party are unknown, or it is unclear how their differing interests can be reconciled. Some social institutions and practices are inherently biased toward the maintenance of existing rules, regulations, and inequalities, and in these cases more complete use of the skills may be required in order to create a microcontext in which legitimate power can be exercised in an institution in which its illegitimate use is the norm (Swanton et al., 1989).

Third, the judgment of legitimacy is made holistically by using the skills as guides rather than as infallible indicators of the value base of the interaction. For example, A's behavior may exhibit frequent disclosure and public testing, but still exemplify illegitimate power because later sections of the dialogue reveal that information crucial to B's interests was withheld. This one failure would be a sufficiently serious breach of the values of the model to warrant the judgment of illegitimacy, despite the frequent use of some of the skills otherwise associated with legitimate power.

I now return to the work of Fairclough and ask how the normative model proposed here would apply to the previously discussed discourse example concerning the police officer and witness. To what extent did this interaction involve the exercise of power, and to what extent was any such power legitimate or not? According to Fay's definition, power is exercised by A over B when the latter engages in an act (or refrains from engaging in one), which he or she would not have done without A's influence. Although the definition appears straightforward enough, complexity emerges as soon as it is applied to concrete examples. Deciding whether Fairclough's example constitutes a case of the exercise of power, let alone whether any such exercise is legitimate, requires a prior decision about which actions of the witness we seek to explain: Is it her involvement in the interview, or is it the manner of that involvement? If the witness went to the interview independently of any request or coercion of the officer, then that action is not the result of the exercise of power over the witness. Given that we have no knowledge of how the witness made this decision, assume for the sake of argument that it is the witness's manner of speaking in the interview that Fairclough attributes to the power of the police officer. Judging the legitimacy of such power requires us to evaluate the extent to which the officer's behavior reflects the values enshrined in the model. This requires us to answer the following questions:

1. Did the officer disclose his reasons for conducting the interview in the manner he did and check that the witness had understood what was involved and that she agreed to the procedures?
2. Did the officer treat the witness as a person who may have needs and interests of her own which should be taken into account in determining how the interview was to proceed?
3. Did the officer give the witness a choice about whether or not to be involved?

The evidence that is provided by the discourse extract (Fairclough, 1989, p. 18) enables us to answer some but not all of these questions. The extract begins with the questioning process, and the reader does not know whether or not consent to act as a witness had been obtained, nor whether the procedures used had been explained and agreed to. This is a critical gap in the evidence required to make a judgment about the legitimacy of the officer's exercise of power, because the officer's control of the sequencing of the witness's story would be judged quite differently if this procedure had been explained and agreed to in advance. We do have evidence, however, that suggests that the officer did not give equal regard to the needs of the witness, because he did not explore her concern about time, nor check that his assurance to her was acceptable. On the whole, although we must reserve final judgment through a lack of relevant evidence, the evidence suggests that the officer's behavior violated the norms outlined, and therefore that his behavior was likely to constitute an illegitimate exercise of power.

In summary, I have argued that making evaluative claims about power related discourse requires a concept of power and an explicit theory of the normative basis of those evaluations, which is applicable at the level of discourse. It remains to show how the model proposed here can be applied to a concrete educational case and how the distinctions it draws are significant in terms of their implications for educative practices.

POWER AND PARTICIPATION: A CASE STUDY

Organizations cannot function without the exercise of controls over their members, so that individual actions are at least loosely coordinated in the pursuit of shared goals and tasks. The development and maintenance of such controls raises major questions about the exercise of power within organizations, for they are designed to rule out options that organizational members might otherwise have chosen. There are questions to be asked, therefore, about how these controls arise and about the legitimacy of the power that they represent. How does the model of legitimate power help us evaluate the way organizations make decisions about the nature of such controls?

So far, the model of legitimate power has been discussed in the relatively simple context of a dyadic exchange. In the following case I examine its utility for the evaluation of a staff debate about the controls that are to be set on students about their wearing uniforms, and on staff about their duty to enforce this.

The Administrative Context of the Uniform Debate

The meeting that is the focus of this case was part of a series of discussions about school uniforms that took place in Northern Grammar, an Auckland co-educational secondary school. The parties to the discussion were the school staff, the students, and the parents as represented by the elected members of the school Board. It is important to understand that most state high schools in New Zealand have a school uniform, and that all decisions about uniforms, including whether or not there will be one, are made by the parent elected Board, with varying degrees of consultation with school staff. Although many staff believe that debates about uniforms are a trivial distraction from more important educational matters, the amount of energy and controversy that such debates attract suggest otherwise. The question of school uniforms raises fundamental issues about a school's stance on adolescent socialization, on individual freedom versus institutional control, and on the nature of its hidden curriculum. In addition, the recent relaxation of zoning requirements in New Zealand and the consequent competition for students has made many staff acutely aware of how parents use uniforms as a standard by which to judge many other aspects of a school's functioning.

Northern Grammar was a uniform school, and the principal and most staff were under no illusions that the relatively affluent European community in which it was set would agree to it being otherwise. There was widespread agreement, however, that there was a problem with the current uniform because over 80% of staff had nominated it as an area of concern during a school development day held some months earlier. Despite the agreement about the existence of a "uniform" problem, staff disagreed about whether the cause lay, for example, with poor uniform design, poor staff enforcement, or negligent parents. The staff of 70 included the whole spectrum of opinion from those who saw uniforms as an authoritarian attempt to control adolescents, to those who saw their colleagues, through their nonenforcement of the policy, as jeopardizing the high standards embodied in the English grammar school traditions of the school. Many staff were skeptical of ever reaching a consensus position on the issue.

The immediate trigger to the uniform debate was a paper written for staff by Terry, Head of English. His two concerns about uniforms were that "attitudes to the enforcing of what constitutes uniform are inconsistent within the teaching staff," and that "uniform has become a visible area of discontent particularly amongst senior students." He proposed that the staff discuss eight recommendations for change to the uniform, and that if change was desired by a majority, that this view be conveyed to the Board. He also recommended that student opinion be canvassed.

The very fact that the uniform issue had been placed on the meeting agenda was indicative of the changes that had been made in the school administration since the arrival of the new principal, Tony, one year earlier. Tony was determined that the school be managed in a far more inclusive way than under the previous more traditional, hierarchical arrangements. Meeting agendas were no longer controlled by the management team, and all those who would be affected by a decision, including parents, junior staff, and students, were now to be consulted. Tony's hope was that the problem of uniform enforcement could be reduced, if not resolved, by the intellectual commitment of staff, students, and parents to an educationally sound uniform policy. The means to such commitment was to be a sustained debate in which all parties could express their own views and, through listening to those of others, become aware of the diversity and complexity of the issue.

The Research Approach

The data for this case were obtained as part of a much larger study of the relationship between school leadership and the quality of administrative problem solving (Robinson, 1993). Only those methodological details that are directly relevant to this chapter are described here. Access to the uniform debate was gained via the permission that had been granted by the Board, principal and staff to attend meetings, analyze relevant documents, and approach individual staff for interviews. Two full staff meetings and one Board meeting were devoted entirely to the uniform issue. The appended transcription extracts are drawn from the second of these staff meetings because this meeting provided the best quality recording of proceedings. Data on how staff experienced and evaluated the uniform debate were gathered as part of a series of 10 individual interviews with staff chosen to represent a range of reactions to the leadership style of the principal. Because the focus of these interviews was on the much wider question of school leadership, no direct questions on uniforms were asked, although, as it turned out, much of the interview material was germane to the analysis. The final source of information was a school development day held three weeks after the second uniform meeting. A transcription was made of the report-back phase of the day, during which time a representative summarized each group's discussion of aspects of the school's administration.

The meeting from which the appended extracts are drawn took place after school in a cramped square room that served as the staff common room. It was attended as usual by about 40 of the 70 or so staff of the school and lasted one hour. I recorded the meeting while present in the room via a radio microphone worn by the principal. The transcription was checked by the author against the original recording, but detailed prosodic notations were not made because the size of the room and of the group precluded quality recording of such details with the equipment that was available.

In the remainder of the chapter these data are used to evaluate the extent to which the staff debate met the conditions required for the exercise of legitimate power and to discuss the consequences of any deviation from the model.

The Meeting Process

By the end of the first meeting on uniforms, staff had passed two motions to accept the first of the eight recommended changes to the uniform and the recommended decision procedures. The principal began the second meeting by reporting that the Board had accepted these decision procedures and agreed to meet with staff. He then invited Terry to reintroduce his discussion paper.

Extract 1. This extract (Appendix A) illustrates the meeting process that was employed throughout this and all other full staff meetings I attended during the course of the wider study of school leadership. Once the topic was introduced, Tony controlled the speaking turns of staff by calling on those who had put up their hands. By keeping a list of speakers, he was able to give priority to those who had not yet had a turn and to achieve a rough balance of gender and seniority.

The first speaker (Sethka) challenged the appropriateness of the agenda itself, claiming that staff should be debating the very existence of uniforms rather than its modification (15-17). By sticking to his role as a facilitator of turns (18) rather than as a participant in the debate, the principal placed the responsibility for deciding whether or not the challenge would be taken up back onto his staff. Because the subsequent four speakers were more concerned to express their opinions on the changes rather than on the question of the uniforms itself, Sethka's challenge, for the moment at least, was publicly ignored.

The recommendations on uniforms included in Terry's paper contained numerous claims about the current and desired state of the Northern Grammar uniform. The right hand side of Table 7.1 lists seven challenges made to these claims within Extract 1. Six of the seven challenges are to the desirability of the claims embodied in the recommendations, whereas the seventh questions the truth of the claim that students cannot wear blue longs under current regulations. The model of legitimate power requires that when a claim is problematized by another speaker, that it be identified as such, and that a systematic process of evaluating the basis of the claim be made. Those claims that survive such discourse are then integrated with other such claims; those that do not are publicly dropped so that the group can focus on integrating those claims that have withstood their scrutiny.

Resolution of the claims and counterclaims listed in Table 7.1 requires direct engagement of the protagonists because it is they who must clarify their

Table 7.1. Challenges to Validity Claims in Uniform Recommendations (Extract One)

Recommendation	Challenges
1. That the regulations on earrings be changed so that any student may wear simple keepers in either gold or silver. [Passed at previous meeting]	
2. That long trousers in blue or grey be available to any student	•Only blue trousers should be allowed (19-21) •Current regulations permit any student to wear blue trousers (45-50)
3. That mufti, restricted only by decency, sense, and safety, be permissible in forms 6 and 7.	•A uniform school should apply it from 3rd to 7th form (50-56)
4. That a regulation winter sports jacket (bomber type) be available to any student.	
5. That a limited range of standard sweat shirts be available with school identification.	
6. That the only restrictions on the type of jacket be denim or offensive labeling.	•Restriction on denim jackets is unreasonable (29-36)
7. That a more practical range of tights be available.	Problem with tights is school furniture not the range available (24-26)
8. That sensitivity be shown to cultural differences with respect to jewelry.	•Recommendation is open to too wide an interpretation (26-27) •Too hard to enforce and can be easily abused (37-43)

understandings, give their reasons, and signal acceptance or rejection of each other's arguments. Such direct engagement was precluded by the meeting process that Tony enforced. Although speakers could have their say, they could not obtain feedback nor clarify misunderstandings and reply to objections, because all such interventions required that both they and their potential discussants wait for their next speaking turn. With 40 staff present and priority given to first-time speakers (57), it was practically impossible to pursue a line of inquiry through to a resolution. The result was a nonadditive, highly fragmented expression of individual views that increased rather than rationally reduced the complexity of the decision process.

Extract 2. After one and a half hours of debate over the two meetings, during which time the principal had remained silent on the substance of the debate, an unidentified staff member asked whether it was possible to hear the principal's views (58). Tony's reply reveals a lot about his theory of power in a situation like this. First, he attributed to staff that they were attempting to second guess his views by reading his body language (60-61). Second, he believed that by reducing such cues he would help "to get the stuff in the air" (62), so he indicated that he would like to stay silent until the end of the first round at least. His "neutral" role was predicated, therefore, on the untested assumption that staff were inappropriately sensitive to his views, and that their expression would distort their own contributions to the debate. Procedurally, his wish for staff to listen to each other with respect did seem to be working. Geoff's confession to being impressed by the possibly contradictory views of his colleagues (70-73) elicited sympathetic laughter.

Extract 3. This extract illustrates part of the process Tony used to bring the meeting to a close. The turn taking procedure had finished with Tony's speech, after which he turned to Terry and asked him whether he wanted the vote to be taken or not. Terry replied that he did not want to vote on whether or not there would be a uniform, but he wanted to continue the discussion on his recommendations. The extract begins with Tony expressing confidence that progress would be made, and asserting that this would not be achieved by taking a vote on the recommendations. Given the diversity of views he had heard, Tony probably believed that a vote at this stage was not going to achieve the commitment that he sought. He then searched for a way forward and suggested that staff who wish to meet with the Board nominate themselves (83). Everyone seemed to have forgotten that they voted at the previous meeting to adopt procedures that stated that an elected staff committee would perform this function. The meeting ended with various staff suggesting that the consultation process should be broadened to include parents and junior and senior students.

Analysis of the Process

The model of legitimate power requires that discourse be conducted in a way that the views of all parties are heard and that those parties have equal opportunity to influence the decisions reached. This principle of respect must be combined with a commitment to valid information such that points of view are not only expressed, but challenged, tested, and, if necessary, revised. The meeting procedure was exemplary in fulfilling the first requirement, but it failed on the second. Twenty-four different speakers, of whom 11 were women, were heard in the course of the hour-long discussion, and the chairman's control eliminated interruptions and created a nonthreatening opportunity for everybody to speak. In addition, the staff were mindful of the interests of those who were not present, and by the end of the meeting a commitment was made to solicit the views of parents and of junior and senior students.

Inclusiveness, however, is a necessary but not sufficient condition for the exercise of legitimate power. Not all problems of power arise because voices are suppressed or excluded. As I have written elsewhere (Robinson, 1993), legitimate power "also requires rational and mutually acceptable ways of silencing voices, so that dissent and plurality, while recognized, does not preclude consensually co-ordinated action" (pp. 259-260). Although the principal repeatedly stated the importance of reaching a rational consensus (64-67), and several staff stated how failure to coordinate their effort had "got them into this mess," the meeting procedure was inappropriate for the attainment of this goal. Staff were encouraged to express their points of view, but not to defend them, even when they were challenged by subsequent speakers. Although resolution of some of the claims and counterclaims would no doubt have been difficult, others could have been easily resolved by, for example, clarifying the current regulations on long trousers, by asking girls whether snagged tights were a problem, and by making an early decision on whether or not the debate was about the modification or the retention of the uniform.

It could be argued that even though dialogue was precluded, speakers could test their claims privately by listening to the relevant counterclaims of other speakers. Private testing would not advance the debate, however, for the process and results of such testing could not be made available to the group unless another turn was gained. Each speaker remained ignorant of the impact of their contribution on others; the absence of feedback and reaction precluded the type of mutual adjustment essential to the development of a group perspective. It is ironic that a staff who so genuinely wanted a public commitment to a uniform policy adopted procedures that empowered them as individuals, but prevented them from learning how to act as a group.

Tony could defend the meeting procedure by appealing to his previous experience of meetings in which dialogue was distorted by such irrational considerations as status, formal authority, and various defensive maneuvers. In a sense, he was caught in a dilemma; either he adopted a procedure that prevented such abuse of power at the price of the evaluation and integration of competing views, or he allowed such evaluation at the risk of allowing the most articulate and forceful speakers to swamp the interests of those who were less forthcoming. The model of legitimate power suggests that there is a third alternative, one that combines the interpersonal and cognitive skills needed to facilitate the expression and the reduction of difference (Robinson, 1992).

The practical consequences of the discourse mode employed are also relevant to its evaluation. The interviews revealed that staff were very appreciative of their greatly increased opportunities to participate in school decision making:

> **VR**: How do you see that (decision-making) process?
> **Staff**: Well, I see that process as being certainly more open than it used to be—there is this discussion process we go through now.

The invitation to staff to contribute to meeting agendas was also seen as a sign of greater openness.

> **Staff**: It's something that is just starting to change its nature, in that issues are being discussed, people are being asked, "Is there anything you want to add to the agenda?"

Along with this appreciation was a parallel frustration with the time taken to reach decisions and uncertainty about the process by which the final decision was reached and communicated to staff. This was a major theme of the feedback that staff gave the management team after their third-term review day held two weeks after the uniform meeting. The following two extracts, taken from a recording of the small group report phase of the day, convey the concern and frustration of staff:

> **Group Reporter**: We have a lot of staff meetings on important topics—we felt we should finish and get a decision on one topic before we start discussing something else. . . . In some areas we seem to follow a consensus method with a lot of exhaustive staff discussion on the topic. All points of view represented, and sometimes a decision coming late or not at all, and on other occasions, a sort of executive decision seems to have been made on an ad hoc basis without anybody even knowing what the decision was officially.
> **Staff Member**: My opinion is that we have been incredibly democratic this year and we've had lots of staff meetings and things like that where ideas have been put forward, on various topics, but my opinion is that at some point or other there's got to be somebody who's appointed to make decisions.

The concerns of the staff quoted here could have been met by taking rather than postponing the vote on the uniform recommendations. But given that the various objections raised in the discussion had not been resolved, staff were right to sense as Tony did that a vote would not have produced the intellectual commitment they all desired. What they did not realize, however, was that even with considerably more time, they would not reach a rational conclusion under their current meeting procedure, for it did not allow for the progressive and public development of a position that integrated those views that had survived the critical scrutiny of the group. The uniform debate was continued at a tense meeting between staff and the Board, at which the Board chairperson expressed dismay that the staff were unable to present a coordinated position. The principal indicated that the debate would have to be delayed until the following year because the staff "had no more energy for a uniform at present."

CONCLUSION

Discourse analysts have undoubtedly raised the awareness of both researchers and practitioners about the ways in which power imbues talk in both classrooms and meetings. If this awareness is to become a force for change, it needs to be informed by a normative theory of power in discourse that allows researchers and practitioners to make the subtle, yet crucially important distinctions between what I have called the legitimate and the illegitimate exercise of power. I have suggested in this chapter that power be understood as the exercise of a particular kind of influence, and that the distinction between the two forms of power be drawn on the basis of the nature of the values and skills that inform the influence attempt. These values and skills refer to both the interpersonal and cognitive qualities of the influence attempt, and it is only through the integration of both that legitimate power is exercised.

The importance of this integration was illustrated through the case of a highly participative yet ineffective administrative decision process. The school leader at the center of the case was highly sensitive to the fact that his own position and the hierarchical structures of the school were open to abuses of power. He attempted to avoid such abuse by consultative procedures that encouraged the expression of differences and respect for the complexity of an issue. His strategy was ultimately ineffective because it was one-sided; his achievement of more inclusive debate only increased the complexity and uncertainty of the decision process, because it was not matched by the skills required to rationally reduce the options and alternatives generated through such participation.

There is something of a parallel one-sidedness in the academic debate on the use and abuse of power. Given a diversity of views and a requirement for coordinated action, the exercise of legitimate power requires discourse patterns that both recognize and reduce diversity. Although there has been much written about the former (Corson, 1993a; Ellsworth, 1989; Gitlin, 1990), there has been less attention paid to the way such diversity of interests and voices can be legitimately coordinated in those contexts in which a unified rather than diversified response is required (Burbules & Rice, 1991; Robinson, 1993). The model of legitimate power described and illustrated in this chapter is designed to address these twin requirements through inclusion of both the interpersonal and cognitive skills needed to publicly reduce, revise, and coordinate the claims made about how organizational life should be regulated. Illegitimate power not only arises through the exclusion of relevant voices, but it also arises through the adoption of processes that, although highly participative, fail to raise and publicly resolve the genuine doubts and criticisms that participants hold about the validity of each others' claims.

APPENDIX

Extract 1.

1.	Terry:	Now I know that some of those recommendations are open to all
2.		sorts of interpretation and I know that teachers are notoriously good
3.		at saying that pupils say practical range of tights better be defined
4.		absolutely or else we will be in trouble. I would suggest that we look
5.		at those recommendations in a wide-ranging sense, and look at the
6.		absolute fine details at some later stage. I would therefore like to
7.		move recommendations two to eight, and I would like to suggest that
8.		after that, we then work out some system of forming a group that can
9.		meet the Board as soon as possible to offer them our suggestions.
10.	Tony:	Okay, how many people haven't got their paper from last week?
11.		Right, quite a lot. Well, it comes down to, long trousers, multi, jackets
12.		and sweatshirts, tights and cultural sensitivity. So I'll open it up
13.		to people who want to contribute to that part of the debate. Right,
14.	Sethka.	
15.	Sethka:	Really it seems to me that you're putting the cart before the horse,
16.		because what we need to discuss first of all is how many are in favor of
17.		not having school uniform at all, before we start modifying it, surely.
18.	Tony:	Further speakers?
19.	John:	As far as long trouser go, if they're to come in I think they should
20.		be blue, to be consistent. There are so many shades of grey for a
21.		start. One of the problems of wearing uniform of course, is that it is
22.		not worn consistently and there is a great range of interpretations.
23.	Tony:	Jean.
24.	Jean:	In reference to the subject of tights, I would suggest that perhaps it's
25.		the school furniture that needs to be looked at, rather than quality
26.		of the school tights that are offered. And the item of cultural sensi-
27.		tivity to jewelry opens itself to very wide interpretations indeed.
28.	Tony:	Alan.
29.	Alan:	I'd be concerned about two things. One, I think there's a social stratifi-
30.		cation hanging out very largely over the denim jackets. I think that
31.		there is a—don't know whether it's middle-upper class New Zealand
32.		snobbery or something about wearing denim. It's quite obvious that
33.		there are members of staff who wear denim to school and to define that
34.		as being something which, I think [ ] is working class is pretty inap-
35.		propriate in a school this day and age anyway. That's the inference that
36.		I get from it. The other thing is I think, the cultural thing about the jew-
37.		elry, I would agree with Jean. So what if your religious symbol says
38.		you do this or that or the other? I think it's just another excuse for peo-
39.		ple to be able to express their individuality when, for some, to express

40.		their individuality when others are unable to, and that if we're going to
41.		base that on cultural differences, I think we're opening up a great big
42.		trap, I will certainly say that my culture says that I wear earrings in my
43.		car, and I definitely get my ears pierced specially to do it.
44.	Tony:	Right, further speakers? Ian.
45.	Ian:	I'd like to just comment that at present blue trousers are allowed to
46.		be worn by any pupil. It's on the regulations at the moment. I
47.		haven't got the actual things here, but if a pupil in the third form up
48.		into the sixth form wishes to wear blue trousers, they may do so, if
49.		they are asked to bring a note from home. That's just a point of
50.		information it's not an opinion. If this is a uniform school, or going
51.		to remain a uniform school, I would just like to speak in favor of a
52.		uniform being applied in some way to third and right through to sev-
53.		enth. It it's not going to be a uniform school that's another issue. I
54.		agree with Sethka. I would not support a type of multi being avail
55.		able in the sixth and seventh and the rest of the school having to be
56.		in uniform. I would sooner have the school a school or not.

Extract 2.

57.	Tony:	Other first timers first.
58.	?:	Can we hear what you think about it?
59.	Tony:	Yes, yes, certainly. The question was can you hear what I think? Um.
60.		I'm trying not to, I'm conscious of everybody looking at me, and say-
61.		ing is he nodding, is he smiling, is he frowning, and I'm trying to do
62.		none of those things because I really want this stuff in the air, and I
63.		want it, perhaps more importantly, I want the feelings out and on the
64.		table, so that when we resolve what we are going to do, because we
65.		are going to do something, we kind of all know where we started from
66.		and we can pull together on whatever the final outcome is. So can I
67.		reserve until it looks as though there is nobody else going, or I might
68.		perhaps go in at the beginning of the second round. Is there anybody
69.		else who hasn't had a first speech who would like to speak? Geoff.
70.	Geoff:	I've listened to all these opinions, I agree with everybody's (laugh-
71.		ter). I find it difficult to take a stance, without taking cognizance of
72.		the other people's points. I just find it very difficult to take a position
73.		on it
74.	?:	That's nice to know.

Extract 3.

75.	Tony:	It's fair to say the next step in the process is going to be closer
76.		towards a decision than we are right now. And a decision, when it is
77.		made, we will want to be able to live with. But I take Terry's point, I
78.		don't think that there is any point in going into a series of votes on

79.		these things because we won't be any wiser than we actually are
80.		right now, at the end of it. Therefore, unless there is a screaming
81.		objection I think the thing to do would be to, well, here's another
82.		suggestion, I looked on the board when the Melbourne Cup has been
83.		run, if it hasn't already, and then that people self-nominate on there
84.		if they would like to meet with the Board. I feel that everybody
85.		should feel free to put their name up there. And that when the Board
86.		does meet with the staff that it's, if necessary, a big meeting.
87.		Because there is a lot of views to be expressed, and the Board needs
88.		to know that, just as we need to know theirs. Peter
89.	Peter:	I think that in some ways we haven't really consulted the students over
90.		how much the students want to ( ). I think in the senior school we
91.		probably should try to get some kind of identifiable feeling from the
92.		students. We might be making a rod for our backs, I don't know, but I
93.		think they are also they're entitled, they're directly affected. . .
94.	Tony:	Absolutely. Well if we could simply indicate that consultation with
95.		the student body is like another matter to be resolved.
96.	Tony:	Ron.
97.	Ron:	How much input do you expect from the parents on the subject?
98.	Tony:	How much are we expecting from parents? Alright, so we should
99.		expect something from them.
100.	Ron:	They've got to buy it after all.
101.	Tony:	Well, yes, well technically the Board represents the parents, and they
102.		are elected to represent them. One look at the Board and you can see
103.		that that is not quite true. That is the problem with representational
104.		democracy, of course. There is also the PTA. There is also your
105.		knowledge of what parents think, because they send the kids along
106.		day by day.
107.	Ron:	So it really boils down to, between us and the Board.
108.	Tony:	The power to decide certainly does. Yeah.
109.	Mary:	If the senior school is going to be asked for their opinion, I really
110.		think that it is really fair to ask the junior school as well. Because
111.		they have to wear the uniform and they do have opinions.
112.	Tony:	Right, well then the degrees of consultation are fair grounds for the
113.		next step in the process to resolve. Well people it's 28 minutes to 5
114.		now, so we ought to be stopping. I'd like to pick up all those threads,
115.		I'd like to get in touch with the Board. I'm not entirely delighted
116.		with the prospect of turning up late at night to discuss the issue.
117.	?:	We could have it after this meeting on next Wednesday. If they
118.		could come at 4:30pm, we could just continue it.
119.	Tony:	We'll have to hunt around in our planner. We'll try and find some
120.		gaps. Righto people, there's a way point along the road. Thanks.

PART TWO

THE DISCOURSES OF
POLICY AND CURRICULUM

8

Power and the Discourses of Policy and Curriculum: An Introduction

David Corson
Ontario Institute for Studies in Education

EDUCATIONAL POLICIES AND THE "DISCOURSE ETHIC"

Policies adopted across an educational system ideally begin with principles as norms for use at the system level; they elaborate on the ways in which these principles can be related to one another, and they lay out what makes different principles appropriate to different situation types. Having done all this, good system-level policies devolve as much policy decision making and power as possible to schools themselves so that fair compromises can be reached that are appropriate to local contexts and consistent with the original normative principles. These recommendations are very like the "discourse ethic" of the German social theorist, Jürgen Habermas (see Chapters 1 and 6 in this volume). While introducing the second part of this book, this chapter discusses the use of the discourse ethic at three levels of education: at the whole system level, at the school or local level, and in the classroom itself.

The Discourse Ethic at the Whole System Level

Following the discourse ethic, then, the first task in an act of social policymaking is to achieve consensus at system level by establishing any universal norms that could operate as principles across the system and that could increase the scope for meeting social justice goals. I use the example of language policy-making. In this form of policymaking, the clarification of principles means finding a realistic set of shared values that overarch all the various social and cultural groups that the political system contains (Smolicz, 1984). Although most of these values may come from dominant groups in society, they cease to be merely dominant values once they are found to be consistent with the just treatment of the interests of other groups. They then become the property of the political system as a whole. At the whole system level—whether national, provincial, or state—two principles guaranteeing key language rights seem essential (after Spolsky, 1986). The first principle guarantees the right of children to be educated wherever possible in the same variety of language that is learned at home, or, failing that, at least in a school that shows full respect for that variety's existence and for its role in preserving important ethnic, traditional, social, gender, or religious values and interests. The second principle guarantees the right of children to learn to the highest level of competence possible the standard or official language(s) or the languages of wider communication adopted by the society as a whole.

Action in devolved local settings provides the second stage in the discourse ethic. There are three clear reasons why the devolution of decision making down to local levels is essential in specific areas of policymaking. First, devolution is needed to establish subnorms for determining local compatibility between interest groups, whose views may not be well represented at the whole system level because of the degree of pluralism that most political systems contain.

Second, devolution is needed to agree on any necessary compromises should genuine incompatibility exist. For example, incompatibility will arise when the values of cultural or religious minorities support pluralist versions of "the good life" that are very different from the norm. A just form of policy action does not need a conception of what *the* just society would be. Rather, it requires as many conceptions of justice as there are distinct possible conditions of society or subsets of society or culture.

Thirdly, devolution to local levels is usually the only practical way to focus attention on the outcomes of any implemented process of change. Only rarely do the utopian intentions that lie behind complex centralized policies combine with the final outcomes of their implementation (Corson, 1986b). In recommending that more attention be given to the likely results of reforms, Cleo Cherryholmes in Chapter 9 links pragmatism with the limits of modernity and its impact on educational change. After critiquing a review of hundreds of studies of planned educational change, he finds that the methodology of many of the change efforts displays key weaknesses reflecting these limits of modernity. He advances pragmatism, in its classical form, as a remedy for the modernist assumptions and social practices of conventional reform processes in education. A pragmatic approach to change focuses attention holistically on likely outcomes. The chapter draws links between critical realist, critical hermeneutic, and pragmatic approaches to policymaking.

So after any overarching policy principles have been agreed on and elaborated on at the whole system level, which is a difficult enough task, the most important and even more difficult work will occur at the local level. This may be no larger than a single town, board, district, or school.

The Discourse Ethic at the Local School Level

Local schools, collaboratively managed through critical policies that are continually revised using the best available evidence about changing circumstances (Corson, 1990), are more likely to be places of staff and community commitment. This is because community and staff participation has to be deliberately sought in order to get at that evidence. But participation is both an end in itself and a device for producing other ends. When people come together to plan something, there is obvious value to them in the feedback, skill development, social interaction, and knowledge growth that they receive. More than this, participation usually fosters a commitment in people to the results or product of their participation, provided those results seem reasonable to them. In this way, a form of critical policymaking can become a development activity that has rewards for a school at several levels. For example, by using democratic and relational management practices, schools tend to escape the trap of having their procedures and styles of operation modeled only on dominant and often outdated points of view.

Clearly by implementing genuine collaborative management involving their own staff and community, schools limit the degree to which the wider system of education can constrain social action within them. In other words, collaborative management lessens the extent to which wider social formations, such as the relationships that exist between schools, the economy, and the state, create the ideological framework that constrains discourses of reform and initiative within them. Those same external and constraining relationships can be challenged by school policymakers to advance the interests of the school and its community. When challenged in this way, unjust social formations themselves can often be transformed, and their undesirable impact elsewhere may also be lessened. At the same time, by lending approval and support, schools can reinforce the values in the wider social formations that are worthwhile and desirable.

There is evidence to support claims of this kind. For example, it has been found that active parent involvement in decision making can bring children from minority social or class groups closer to their teachers, who often come from the dominant class and culture. It has also been found that the parents themselves grow in confidence and develop a sense of their own efficacy, which impacts positively on student learning, and that the harmful stereotypes about pupils that teachers often develop fall away as teachers begin to collaborate with parents (Comer, 1984; Cummins, 1986; Garcia & Otheguy, 1987; Greenberg 1989; Haynes, Comer, & Hamilton-Lee, 1989; May, 1994; Rasinski & Fredericks, 1989). In the eyes of the public, autonomous schools are also more "legitimate" places. This is a concern addressed by Habermas who wants to lessen the discursive randomness that typifies the management styles of organizations. In its place, he wants to instill a discourse arrangement for resolving conflicts of interpretation as they develop, using a situation in which asymmetrical relations of power do not prevail or even operate. For him, a "new" form of "institutionalized discourse" is needed in public institutions if they are to recapture their legitimacy for people in general, their sense of direction, and the motivation of participants and adherents. In this section I look selectively at this complex set of ideas from Habermas, which seems to have important applied value for policy action at the level of the school.

In ideal and undistorted communication, Habermas suggests, speakers can defend by word or deed all four of the validity claims: what is said is meaningful, true, justified, and sincere (see Chapter 6). When all of the participants in a given speech context are able to do this, when all related evidence can be brought into play, and when nothing apart from logically reasoned argument is used in reaching consensus, then the circumstances provide an "ideal speech situation." A starting point in appreciating what Habermas is up to here is to note that when he talks of an "ideal" situation, he is not suggesting that any possible speech context has the characteristics of this "ideal speech situation." He admits that the conditions of actual speech are rarely if ever those of the "ideal speech situation." What he wants to show is that all exchanges of speech tacitly presume that near-ideal conditions apply. Indeed, if communication is going to take place in speech situations, and if rational consensus is an aim of the interaction, then these things on their own require the presumption that ideal conditions are met.

Habermas sets out the conditions that people expect when they enter into purposeful discourse. First, most people expect that a speech situation that they enter will be one from which the true interests of the participants in the discussion can emerge:

- all participants must receive an equal distribution of opportunities to select and use speech acts
- all participants must have an equal chance to initiate and maintain discourse
- all participants must have an equal chance to advance their points of view, to question ideas, and to give reasons for and against claims made in language.

Second, people expect that argument and debate will proceed without undue external pressures:

- all participants must accept that accidental or systematic constraints on discussion will play no part in it
- all participants must be assured of an equal chance to express feelings, attitudes, and intentions
- all participants must be assured of an equal chance to oppose, permit, command, instruct, forbid, and any of the other things that any other participants are entitled to do.

Third, people expect that the "force of argument" will prevail, that the outcome of discussion will depend on the force of the better argument.

What remains after meeting all these conditions is a democratic form of public discussion that provides a forum for an unforced flow of ideas and arguments: Domination, manipulation, and control are banished. Again Habermas is recognizing an ideal that does not really exist, an ideal that is merely promised and expected in almost every activity of language. The existence of this ideal situation is inherent in the nature of communication itself. Humans expect that it operates every time they begin to speak; in making an utterance, people are holding out the possibility that a form of social life exists in which individuals can have free, open, and equal communication with one another.

From these ideas Habermas extracts a "critical measure" of the "quality of interaction" that takes place in social settings and in social institutions. Clearly certain things are often lacking in ordinary speech situations and their absence distorts communication. Usually other things also will be present, such as ideologies that distort communication in favor of the powerful (see Chapter 6). Bureaucratic communication as often used in schools, especially larger ones, regularly falls short of the ideal because its purpose is usually to command and to control; it always has some strategic purpose. This strategic use of discourse assumes the existence of roles, based on legal authority of some kind; it assumes that it is the role of some to receive impersonal messages and to act on them with little debate or question; and it assumes that the weight of tradition, of power, or of domination is more important in decision making than the need for rational consensus. In all these respects, the normal bureaucratic communication of schools runs counter to the kind of collaborative and participative decision making that an ideal speech situation might allow. I want to reinterpret these ideas into the everyday practice of managing schools. The key to implementing this approach to management seems to lie in the way the concept of "impartiality" is put into practice. Habermas shares this concept with Rawls (1972), and the latter may offer a little more guidance about its application in real world institutions.

Following Rawls's account, Barry (1989) suggests fleshing out the idea of "impartiality" in two different ways. The first approach is to ask the interested parties in any problem-centered discussion what outcome they would favor if they did not know which position they were to occupy under a new policy. Doing this prevents powerful participants from abusing their superior bargaining power because it denies them various kinds of knowledge, especially knowledge of their own identities in the hypothetical arrangements. This device creates a kind of game in which participants ask what result rational self-interested players would end up with if they did their best in presenting to each other the greatest possible challenge in support of their case. But Barry's second approach is more like a debate than a game. Its method is to ask those involved to propose and defend principles for the distribution of benefits and burdens that they sincerely believe ought to be acceptable to everyone affected, and that no one could reasonably reject. The criterion for choosing these principles is that they should lead to an outcome in the situation that is both preferable to what would result if there were no agreement and productive of as satisfactory an outcome as would be obtained under conditions in which bargaining pressure is removed. In other words, this approach asks participants to argue not for what they *would do* if given a free hand in the matter, but for what they *should do*. In this second approach the objective is to convince opponents by making them see things as you see them, but in a two-way process. The debate is in good faith in that participants must be prepared to be convinced as well as to convince others. For some purposes this approach could enable participants to think of themselves as representatives of groups in the wider society, although not if this meant excluding the real representatives of minorities or other social groups. Very often these groups will have views and interests that are systematically different: In other words, they will not only have interests that others do not understand, but often, too, they will have interests that others cannot understand.

As an example of this point and as an instance of policies and practices in education that remain discriminatory, Chapter 10 discusses sign language and the discursive construction of power over the deaf through education. Jan Branson and Don Miller argue that the discourse on sign language in education is vital to the assertion of symbolic power by the hearing establishment over the Deaf community. Using case studies of policies for the Deaf from Western countries, their chapter exemplifies the educational and political processes at work as individual Deaf communities, with their own distinct native sign languages, confront the ideology that education can only proceed through the dominant language and the accredited modes of the hearing. In line with the discourse ethic, Deaf communities are increasingly seizing the emancipatory opportunities of managing schools for themselves so that those schools have as their priority the development of organizational forms and practices that are organic to the culture of local Deaf communities.

This development suggests how the discourse ethic can be put to work to secure emancipatory ends. But there is a common objection to putting the ideal speech situation to work: If we are to achieve genuine balance in discourse, all participants need to have similar knowledge about the subject matter of the policy discussion. As well as having particular details relevant to the policy issue itself, Young (1981) concludes that all participants approaching social policy issues need to have broad and specific knowledge of the particular society that they are considering. They need to know the basic, natural constraints of their location, the climate, topography, the character and general amount of land and material resources to which they have access, and so on. They need to have basic demographic knowledge, such as how much space they have per person or what resources can be produced relative to the population. They need to know the sort of problems their technology can solve and the level of productive capacity at their disposal. They need therefore to have a good grounding in the culture and traditions of their society. They need to appreciate the tastes of their artistic and decorative tradition. They need to have a set of shared symbols and stories, and they need to know their language, the games that they play, their educational practices, and so on. In short, for participants to engage in free, open, and equal communication with one another, on matters of policy complexity and managing an institution collaboratively, to begin with they need to be well educated.

If participants are in possession of this knowledge, and if there is genuine goodwill in the administrative setting, the ideologies of special interest groups should have fewer distorting effects. Indeed, given continual practice and the incentive that comes from having genuine policy purposes and decision making power, the influence of the three principal distorting functions that ideology itself is said to serve (Giddens, 1979; see Chapter 6) may lessen or disappear. Public policymaking regularly incorporates these functions of ideology into its decision-making practices. In doing so, it marginalizes the interests of less powerful stakeholders and blocks genuine reform. In some places, though, the interests of minority and other disempowered groups are being deliberately consulted, and school policymakers are responding to the results of that consultation. This change in policy in some countries is producing a few schools that are beginning to break away from the ideologies of control that have dominated modern education since its inception (Corson, 1993b; May, 1994).

A look at the history of modern schooling helps explain some of the limitations of conventional schools and classrooms. The concentration on control and passive student activities in classrooms reflects the ethos of control that is still an outstanding feature of conventional school organizations. In this respect, modern schools have not changed very much in their general aim since their inception in the middle of the 19th century. The political architects of modern universal schooling were contemporaries of the political architects of prisons, asylums for the insane, and hospitals for the diseased poor. It is no accident that all four types of institution use the term *superintendent* to describe their executive officers, and operate through hierarchical and controlling structures. In education, beginning in English-speaking countries in the decades around the Taunton Report in Britain (1864-1868), these policy architects were acting in direct response to fears about what many children would otherwise become if an attempt were not made to change them by controlling their socialization through compulsory schooling. These architects had before them the recent memories of the democratic revolutions across Europe and North America in 1848 and earlier, and they were mindful of the bitter and costly contemporary uprisings of culturally and linguistically different peoples acting in defense of their cultural and language rights. They were anxious to avoid any extension of similar experiences, and they saw schooling for the masses as a way of initiating their own lower orders into the technologies and values of the mainstream culture and as a way of assimilating and taming the culturally and linguistically different. These architects saw schooling as a way of making children "better," as a way of "civilizing" them in line with the canons for civilized man that the architects themselves or people very like them had established.

Structurally schools remain very much in this mold. Often in spite of teachers' best efforts, classrooms tend to reflect the structures of the wider institution. These structures in their turn often reflect wider discourses of repression that persevere in modern states, as Chapters 11 and 12 contend. Jim Cummins in Chapter 11 discusses the role of wider social formations in shaping bilingual policies for minority language users. After reviewing the present policy norms for speakers of minority languages in English-speaking countries, he locates those norms within wider discourses of economic and political oppression in capitalist nation states, especially the competing and conflicting discourses blown in by the winds of changing political fashion in the United States. While indicating how those policies work to constrain socially just reforms at national, regional, school, and classroom levels, he makes clear recommendations for reform that range across matters of cultural/linguistic incorporation, community participation, critical pedagogy, and sensitive assessment policies.

The Discourse Ethic in the Classroom

In Chapter 12, Alan Luke, Joan Kale, and Michael Garbutcheon Singh show how these wider structures of power impact on culturally different children in classrooms, right from their earliest years of schooling. The authors use critical discourse analysis to examine a key element of early schooling for many culturally different children: how literacy instruction makes available particular discourses for talking and thinking about cultural identity. The chapter describes an array of spoken and written texts generated by students, teachers, and textbooks that position and construct children and their culture in ways that mark cultural differences at the same time as they silence them.

If the discourse ethic is a true reflection of the ideal context of interaction for human beings, then classrooms everywhere are also much in need of this kind of reform. The discourse ethic is said to obtain when all contributions to human interaction in a setting are meaningful, true, justified, and sincere. Most of the time, teachers assume that they are communicating meaningful content, in a context in which that communication is a legitimate or justified activity. But truth and sincerity themselves are often missing from contemporary classrooms; this may occur because of the pressures of externally imposed curricula, with their emphasis on "outcomes," or because of the strategic professional purposes of teachers and administrators themselves, which can receive priority ahead of the interests of students as Chapter 12 illustrates. When class-room events do take place in an environment in which trust and sincerity are missing, those same events tend to lose their meaning and their legitimacy for pupils; all four validity conditions required by the discourse ethic disappear from classrooms. But it is not just fairness that suffers under these conditions. There is clear evidence to confirm that if there is no trusting context of interac-tion in classrooms, student learning itself is severely affected.

Extensive studies of classrooms in a variety of school systems report that when trusting relations exist, students spend most of their time and energy on learning. But when they do not exist, teachers spend excessive amounts of their time on marginal activities: organizing and negotiating relationships, establishing rewards and punishments to make reluctant children perform tasks, and disciplining and censuring children who are not working or who are dis-rupting the teacher's activities. Trusting relations develop when teachers and students perceive one another as involved and at work on the project of learning (McDermott, 1977). In a study of many American secondary classrooms, this kind of trust-developing environment seemed to be missing from classes at all ability levels. Instead, children were seen as passive receivers of humdrum tasks: listening to the teacher, writing answers to the teacher's questions, and taking tests. They had only limited opportunities to answer open-ended ques-tions, to work in cooperative learning groups, or otherwise to control the class-room's discursive activity. Moreover, when the study focused on students in lower ability classes, there were even greater restrictions on students because the content of the learning seemed to be watered down for the weaker ones: "High-track students got Shakespeare; low-track students got reading kits. High-track students got mathematical concepts; low-track students got compu-tational exercises. Why?" (Oakes, 1985, p. 192).

Moving more in the direction of the discourse ethic would help to change all this by structuring classroom activities to promote cooperative, active, interactive, and purposeful learning, in which the control function of the setting, of the teacher, and of wider social forces becomes an instrument of last resort, not first. The simple act of the teacher withdrawing from center stage and abdicating the "absolute rights" suggested later, removes the key cause of com-municative distortion in classrooms and allows cooperative discourse practices some room to develop. Informal approaches for doing just this are widely avail-able for teachers (Corson, 1987). But using more formal cooperative learning approaches is also known to result in increased academic achievement, more positive attitudes, and better relationships (Slavin, 1983). Oakes (1985) sees three advantages in the cooperative strategy: First, it offers an incentive for stu-dents to interact with each other, as learning resources; second, it offers a way of accommodating learner differences; and third, it offers a way of softening the effects that initial differences in student ability have on assigning rewards for learning. Cooperative group work expresses the cultural values of a greater number of girls and boys in classrooms than do pedagogies based on the individualization of instruction and on direct teaching. Cummins (1988, p. 144) contrasts the major characteristics of this kind of interactional model with the transmission model of teaching. For him the interactional model offers:

- genuine dialogue between student and teacher in both oral and written modalities
- guidance and facilitation, rather than control of student learning by the teacher
- encouragement of student-student talk in a collaborative learning context
- encouragement of meaningful language use by students, rather than correctness of surface forms
- conscious integration of language use and development with all curricular content, rather than teaching language and other content as isolated subjects
- a focus on developing higher level cognitive skills, rather than on factual recall
- task presentation that generates intrinsic rather than extrinsic motivation.

Many teacher interaction styles, suited to culturally different children, also apply to interactions with girls and young women in general. Female discursive norms are often different from male norms. Because females tend to place high value on strengthening affiliative links between people, their discursive norms seem to be different in broadly the same collectivist directions as are the discursive interests of many minority peoples. Indeed, it would seem that dominant male norms of interaction are really the "marked" variety in spite of their dominance; they constitute a norm that most people would not prefer if allowed the choice. Perhaps the real interests of boys and men would also be served by changes in teacher-pupil interaction practices to eliminate imbalances in the use of power such as the following: the unrestrained use of the imperative, the use of the (absolute) right to speak last, the use of the (absolute) right to contradict, the use of the (absolute) right to define the world for others, the use of the (absolute) right to interrupt or to censure, and the use of the (absolute) right to praise or blame in public. These negative things are deeply ingrained habits that many teachers consider to be part of the very stuff of teaching. I believe that this is a teacher ideology that would not withstand critical inspection and challenge. In Chapter 13, Jill Blackmore and Jane Kenway offer a poststructuralist account of gender regimes and organizational culture in schools. The authors begin by pointing to the ways in which dominant models of policy have been informed by theories of change that are not helpful in explaining the gap between policy and practice, especially as played out in schools among girls. They offer an interpretation of feminist poststructuralism that is helpful both in the process of gender reform in schools and in the professional development of teachers.

There are other positive steps that can be taken. Stanworth (1983) recommends that teachers give higher priority to reshaping the sexual distribution of interaction in classrooms: by singling girls out for more recognition, by remembering their names and using them, or by creating a comfortable and non-threatening environment for interaction (by sitting down in a child's desk to address the class, for example, or relaxing the posture). Other changes can express an ethic of care; they involve making the discourse practices of classrooms courteous, respectful, and caring. Above all, classrooms need to offer an environment in which children can develop forms of "critical language awareness" that will enable them to take charge of their own discursive practices.

CRITICAL LANGUAGE AWARENESS

Power and the Language Norms of Education

Education's legitimate influence on language use is clear: It seeks to capitalize on the central role of language in learning, in understanding, and in knowing. Although language development is a major aim of schooling, language is also the most accessible pedagogy and form of evaluation available to schools. But a more subtle and greater influence that education has on language is its power to promote and disseminate certain ideas about the appropriacy of language, whether relating to standard or nonstandard codes, majority or minority languages, gender speech styles and functions, high-status forms and structures, and so on. This pervasive influence is institutionalized in education; it comes from the power that social institutions such as education have to do things that individual human beings could never do. For instance, education has the power to enforce its linguistic demands by excluding dissenters, by rewarding conformity, by pillorying deviation, and by sanctioning the "legitimate." These sanctions go far beyond the benign, direct, and deliberate influences that education properly exercises in the course of providing "an education."

In other words, education can routinely repress, dominate, and disempower language users whose practices differ from the norms that it establishes. Furthermore, it can do this while concealing the structural relations that underlie its power and while conveying a reality that can be highly partisan. For example, the syntax of a language offers a ready vehicle for converting power relations and for distorting perceptions of the world. Because of the role of syntax in drawing causal relationships between participants and processes, it is always available to designate the relative status of social actors by putting them in different roles in sentences—as agent, experiencer, or object—or by deleting them entirely through using the passive or a transformation or a substitution. This kind of deception is always possible; and it is not uncommon when problems

arise that involve demarcations, such as those that exist in schools between people of very different statuses and social power. Whoever has the power to define
the context and the language code that describes it is empowered; all others who
accept that definition without question accept to a degree their own disempowerment in that setting. In this way the powerful position other social actors
through their discourse so that the disempowered perceive and respond to the
world in particular ways. But subtle distortions in language frequently arise
when humans use language to describe reality and to create personal realities
because everyone's reality can be very different from the realities of others.

Edelman (1984) observes that when it is in our interests to do so,
human beings often rationalize and call this reasoning; they distort through language and call this creative and original description; and they repress others
through language and call this "being helpful." The counseling profession
seems especially adept at these practices. Fairclough (1985) provided some
apposite examples. He presented four expressions that belong to a particular
lexicalization of young people who are perceived as misfits by their families,
their schools, and their communities: They are seen as "incorrigible," "defiant,"
"lacking in responsibility," and "delinquent." He showed how these four
expressions could be placed within an alternative lexicalization creating an
"anti-language" of matching descriptors for the same young people viewed
from a different ideological position: "irrepressible" (incorrigible), "debunking"
(defiant), "refusing to be sucked in by society" (lacking in responsibility), and
"spirited" (delinquent). Here neither code can really capture reality because
each depends on the viewpoint of the speaker; both are ideologically loaded.

However, when one ideological rationalization or another becomes
dominant, the distortions and "helpful repressions" that they contain become
naturalized and win acceptance as neutral codes. Professional groups do this all
the time when establishing the limits of their interests. Edelman (1984) noted
that professionals in schools commonly engage in rationalization, distortion,
and repression in their language activities; they even see these practices as part
of their professional duties. Indeed, an important part of those duties is to define
the status of their clients in education: the underachievers, the gifted and talent-
ed, the disabled, the retarded, the discipline problems, or the delinquent. By
doing this, policymakers, administrators, and teachers also define their own status in relation to those of others and thereby justify the work that they do. They
use and apply many special terms as labels in an exercise of power that would
be rather meaningless or misplaced if the terms were used by nonprofessionals.
But in the hands of the empowered professionals, the terms and the categories
that they create become tools of power that shape and repress other people's
destinies and legitimize professional value systems: The language becomes
powerful in ways that the study of education itself still leaves untheorized.

As part of a growing movement of critical linguists, Norman
Fairclough sees the capacity for critique of language as a prerequisite for effective democratic citizenship. In Chapter 14, he describes two elements of an

approach to the general societal problematic of language and power: the first involves the overdue development of a critical tradition within language studies; the second is the application of this critical theory and method in developing critical language awareness work in schools and in other educational settings. He offers examples of critical language awareness at work in schools.

Critical language awareness denies the possibility that humans can be fully objective in making judgments about complex language matters. In this and other respects it is very different from the rather descriptive approach to knowledge about language known as language awareness. Most language awareness activities accept the descriptive account of language as a given; they assume that the norms for language behavior established in conventions of use over time are rather unproblematic and uncontested. But critical language awareness goes beyond these assumptions. As it has developed to date (Clark, Fairclough, Ivanic, & Martin-Jones, 1990; Clark, Fairclough, Ivanic, & Martin-Jones, 1991; Fairclough, 1992c), critical language awareness works from the 10 claims summarized as follows:

1. Critical language study tries to explain and not just describe the discourse of a society.
2. Socially dominant forces have the power to shape the conventions that underlie discourse, just as much as any other social practices.
3. Conventions of language and discourse tend to be "naturalized"; they are accepted as unproblematic givens.
4. Conventions of language, such as rules of use, receive their value according to the positions of their users in systems of power relations.
5. Different conventions embody different ideologies.
6. Critical language study needs an historical orientation to link it with the past events that structure language and that determine its forms and the future effects that its present structures might have.
7. Discourse is determined by its conventions, but it is also a voluntary and creative activity that allows its users to critique the same conventions.
8. Discourse is both socially determined and creative.
9. Discourse itself is a site and practice of struggle.
10. Critical language study is a resource for developing the consciousness and self-consciousness of dominated people.

By reducing these ten theoretical claims to manageable curriculum themes, the approach to critical language awareness identifies three major categories of issues (Clark et al., 1990). These provide some direction for a curriculum (Corson, 1993b).

Promoting Social Awareness of Discourse

The intention in this theme area is to encourage students to approach meanings more critically, rather than take them for granted. A sophisticated understanding of discourse as a site of human struggle is not a prerequisite because acquiring that understanding seems to be one of the goals of study in this theme. Working within the theme, students examine why access to certain types of discourse is restricted and how imbalances in access affect individuals and groups. For example, students might examine the routine imbalances in communication that occur between teacher and student, doctor and patient, or judge and witness. If handled skillfully, skepticism about legitimate power relationships need not result. On the contrary, students may come to see how power that derives from justified authority, greater knowledge, or legitimate expertise often results inevitably in an unequal distribution of access to discourse. At the same time, because of the critical component in such a study, students would become more alert to those occasions when an unequal use of discourse in special contexts is used unjustly.

Promoting Critical Awareness of Variety

Working within this theme, students can examine why some languages and varieties are different in status from others, why they are valued differently in different settings, what historical events have produced different valuations of language varieties, and what are the effects that devaluing a language variety has upon its users. There are as many possibilities for pursuing this theme as the school's social context allows because every local community contains examples of variety. They may be the relatively subtle markers of status that distinguish groups in monolingual societies, or they may be significant boundaries that keep cultural and subcultural groups isolated or alienated from one another, even while sharing the same social space.

Promoting Consciousness of and Practice for Change

Mere critique of the status quo is not enough for critical language awareness. The critical study of language tries to encourage students to contribute to improving wider practices. Any language awareness activity will be useful here if it stresses the dynamic nature of language and the reciprocal role that every individual's discourse has in creating and being created by social structures. For example, adolescents will take some pleasure in discovering new and reasonable ways in which the conventions of standard language appropriateness can be subverted, perhaps following tactics not unlike those followed by the reformers of sexist language forms and functions in recent decades. Working within this theme, students can examine how social struggles and changes in power relations can change language, what potential for language change and what constraints on change exist in contemporary societies, and how improvements can be brought about.

Critical language awareness also extends to classroom discourse practices. When teachers encourage their students to reflect critically on the language practices used within the school itself, this is an important step toward implementing the discourse ethic in the school. It is also a statement by teachers that this is the way they would like the world of discourse outside the school to be. By looking at real acts of discourse in the school's own context rather than at abstract examples, students are empowered by the activities rather than just informed and perhaps demoralized by them. If mundane discourse practices in schools are not connected in children's minds to a critical awareness of that discourse set in its wider context, then the discourse conceals the structures of domination within which it is located. In doing so, it creates a deceitful illusion of freedom that is clearly miseducative.

Gender imbalances in communication offer a guide here. The unequal power relations in many male-female conversations often force females into conceding to the world view of males in their conversations, which are then conducted so as to favor the male's style of operating, often with unwelcome consequences for the females. For example, young women as a routine part of their educational experience in many institutions have to develop discursive tactics for dealing with unwelcome forms of harassment from male students and teachers. This continues in spite of the best phrased antiharassment policies, because even to engage with harassment at a verbal level often means that females have to recognize and accept the discourse used by males as natural and normal, thus accepting at the same time complicity in the harassment itself and thereby reinforcing sexual harassment as a legitimate attribute of masculinity. Those of lesser power are often drawn into supporting the practices of the powerful, thereby reinforcing the structures of power that allowed those practices to develop in the first place. This point can be reapplied with equal force to the situation that confronts all children in schools.

Young children engaging in dialogue with powerful adults such as teachers almost always accept that discourse on the adult's terms. Habermas talks about the "strategic" communication that adults engage in with children. Usually there is some further purpose behind an adult's discourse with children, and the talk is only instrumental to that end. When teachers are bent on reaching some curriculum or personal goal through their interactions with children, the imbalance in the power relationship gives many children a distorted view of the purposes of language. They often develop perceptions of their own powerlessness in school that reinforce their sense of powerlessness outside the school. Many girls are routinely disempowered in this way. School experiences finish off a long process of discursively distorted socialization for many young women who go on to accept roles that they perceive to be their lot in life because most of the structural narratives that they have encountered leave them with no alternative. Nor are girls the sole victims of this process of disempowerment. Many girls and boys from minority social groups and from cultural minorities are in great need of empowering classroom practices.

If critical language awareness is to find a place in classrooms, teachers may have to reduce their heavy reliance on several favored approaches to teaching. One major "pedagogy of disempowerment" spans and affects the entire process of education. The conventional classroom questioning technique of the "initiation-feedback-response" cycle (IRF) is the basis of most teaching acts (Young, 1992). In Chapter 15, Robert Young begins with a critique of the relevance of poststructuralist/postmodernist theorizing to practice and reform. He examines the ideology-producing processes of classrooms, especially that universal cornerstone of traditional pedagogy: the IRF cycle. A structural and functional study of the IRF cycle shows that the possibility of rational responses by students to the validity claims of teachers is excluded in principle. Typical patterns support a form of strategic action by teachers, appropriately labeled *instructional action* rather than the *educational action* necessary for learning aimed at the learners' eventual autonomy. Students are seduced or indoctrinated, not educated. The chapter offers some possibilities for reform. In Chapter 16, Stanton Wortham discusses another widespread and taken-for-granted pedagogy: experience-near examples. These objects or events from a students own experience are introduced into lessons to illuminate curriculum content. From his data, Wortham argues that the superficiality of many experience-near examples reflects larger historical ways of thinking and speaking to do with the peculiar character of products and social relations in capitalist society. Rather than creating pedagogical moments that are productive, this commodification of classroom discourse may be leading schools to produce passive not critically reflective students.

9

Pragmatism, Modernity, and Educational Change*

Cleo H. Cherryholmes
Michigan State University

The Soviet Union launched Sputnik 1 on October 4, 1957. From that time to the present the schools and educational system of the United States have episodically been targeted for change and reform.[1] There was little reason to believe that reforming an educational system consisting of some 110,000 public and private schools would come quickly or easily. It has not. Movements to produce changes and reforms have been organized repeatedly; they seem to come in waves in which each wave has been driven by events far removed from individual schools and classrooms, not unlike the way unseen storms at sea generate huge and noisy breakers at the shore. It is possible that the overall failure of educational reform has been due in part to the remoteness of the precipitating events from the immediacy of targeted schools and classrooms. The character of

*I thank David Corson, David Labaree, and Thomas Popkewitz for comments on earlier versions of this chapter.

[1]For present purposes I use the terms change and reform interchangeably. Obviously, all change does not generate reform, although one cannot have reform without change. My argument, simply put, is that planned changes attempt to bring about reforms, and in a very limited context they can be substituted for each other. Also, I refer occasionally to educational change in the United States, although I do not claim this argument is nation specific, even though most of the studies on which it is based were conducted in the United States.

these external events has ranged widely, although for the most part they have been linked to issues of national security. In the early 1960s, educational changes were driven by a perceived military threat from the Soviet Union. By the early 1990s, that military threat had disappeared along with the Soviet Union itself. Demands for educational reform were then driven by an increasingly competitive international economy. In a changing and uncertain world it is likely that schools will continue to be targets for change and reform.

This chapter discusses a major review and assessment of educational change—Michael Fullan's *The New Meaning of Educational Change* (1991). This is how he described his task:

> This book is concerned with educational change affecting elementary and secondary schools. Those involved with schools are constantly embroiled in small- and large-scale change. In Canada this means some 5 million elementary and secondary school students and their parents, 300,000 teachers, and 30,000 school and district administrators. . . . In the United States there are close to 45 million students . . . over 2 million teachers, 200,000 school and district administrators, and tens of thousands of regional, state, federal, and university based personnel; the 88,000 (public) schools are organized into over 15,000 school districts. (pp. 3-4)

Here is Fullan's reason for focusing on the meaning of educational change:

> Implicit in discussions of educational reform, but rarely recognized, is the confusion between the terms *change* and *progress*. Resisting certain changes may be more progressive than adopting them, but how do we know? The key to understanding the worth of particular changes, or to achieving desired changes, concerns what I call "the problem of meaning." One of the most fundamental problems in education today is that people do not have a clear, coherent sense of *meaning* about what educational change is for, what it is, and how it proceeds. Thus, there is much faddism, superficiality, confusion, failure of change programs, unwarranted and misdirected resistance, and misunderstood reform. (p. 4)

Progress, educational or otherwise, is difficult to assess, and it is worth noting that Fullan's book is entitled *The New Meaning of Educational Change* and not *The New Meaning of Educational Progress*. Clear, unambiguous, and agreed upon (because progress is a social idea) standards and criteria are required in order to strike a progressive/nonprogressive distinction. Additionally, methodologies must be available to compare such standards with enacted changes. For present purposes, however, I am little concerned that Fullan pays a great deal of attention to change and, for the most part, ignores questions of progress.

Fullan thoughtfully reviews in rich detail hundreds of studies of educational change. His book should be read closely by anyone interested in planned educational change because it reports the experiences of many reform efforts and is a source of numerous insights. My present concern, however, is with the methodology, or perhaps the metamethodology, of many of the change efforts that he describes. My reading of Fullan's book is built around two themes. First, I suggest that he documents in great detail the limits of modernity concerning educational change. This should not be confused with the limits of technical instruction that may have less to do with institutional reform than with amassing technical expertise and resources in the production of specific learning outcomes. Many of the educational change efforts that he describes were planned and implemented as thoroughly modern undertakings, more about this shortly. Second, if it is the case that Fullan describes how modern attempts at change have failed, it is plausible to interpret his commentary as advocating a thoroughgoing pragmatism. The various pragmatisms of Charles Sanders Peirce, William James, John Dewey, Richard Rorty, Cornel West, and others reject modernist assumptions and many of the social practices that are built on them. I first give brief introductions to modernity and pragmatism and then review two parts of Fullan's analysis and conclusion (Chapters 3 and 16) to illustrate my argument.

MODERNITY AND MODERNIZATION

The term *modernity* is often used, as I will use it here, to refer to the rationalization of Western societies that began with the Enlightenment and the rise of modern science in the 17th and 18th centuries. Writing of Enlightenment intellectuals that included John Locke, Jean Jacques Rousseau, David Hume, and the Marquis de Condorcet, among many others, Berlin (1990) gave the following description of some of the beliefs Enlightenment thinkers shared:

They [Enlightenment thinkers] believed in varying measure that men were, by nature, rational and sociable; or at least understood their own and other's best interests when they were not being bamboozled by knaves or misled by fools; that, if only they were taught to see them, they would follow the rules of conduct discoverable by the use of ordinary human understanding; that there existed laws which govern nature, both animate and inanimate, and that these laws, whether empirically discoverable or not, were equally evident whether one looked within oneself or at the world outside. They believed that the discovery of such laws, and knowledge of them, if it were spread widely enough, would of itself tend to promote a stable harmony both between individuals and associations, and within the individual himself. . . . They believed that all good and desirable things were necessarily compatible, and some maintained more than this—that all true values were interconnected by a network of indestructible, logically interlocking relationships. The more empirically minded among them were sure that a science of human nature could be developed no less than a science of inanimate things, and that ethical and political questions, provided that they were genuine, could in principle be answered with no less certainty than those of mathematics and astronomy. A life founded upon these answers would be free, secure, happy, virtuous, and wise. (p. 60)

Much of the contemporary discourse about educational change, I submit, continues in this tradition that began some 300 to 400 years ago.

Toulmin (1990) has argued that modernity distinguished between "*rational freedom* of moral and intellectual decision in the human world of thought and action, and the *causal necessity* of mechanical processes in the natural world of physical phenomena" (p. 107), separating what is human from what is nonhuman. This is related, Toulmin asserts, to the mind/body as well as many other distinctions: "mental vs. material, actions vs. phenomena, performances vs. happenings, thoughts vs. objects, voluntary vs. mechanical, active vs. passive, creative vs. repetitive" (p. 108). These are not "assumptions" as much as "presuppositions" about how best to study and understand the world (p. 116). One such presupposition, for example, is that "the 'human' thing about humanity is its capacity for rational thought and action" (p. 109).

Havel (1992) summarized many characteristics of the modern world that developed from the Enlightenment in the following extract.

The modern era has been dominated by the culminating belief that the world . . . is a wholly knowable system governed by a finite number of universal laws that man can grasp and rationally direct for his own benefit. This era, beginning in the Renaissance and developing from the Enlightenment to socialism, from positivism to scientism, from the Industrial Revolution to the information revolution, was characterized by rapid advances in rational, cognitive thinking. This, in turn, gave rise to the proud belief that man, as the pinnacle of everything that exists, was capable of objectively describing, explaining and controlling everything that exists, and of possessing the one and only truth about the world. It was an era in which there was a cult of depersonalized objectivity, an era in which objective knowledge was amassed and technologically exploited, an era of belief in automatic progress brokered by the scientific method. It was an era of systems, institutions, mechanisms, and statistical averages. It was an era of ideologies, doctrines, interpretations of reality, an era in which the goal was to find a universal theory of the world, and thus a universal key to unlock its prosperity. . . . [However] we all know civilization is in danger. . . . We are looking for an objective way out of the crisis of objectivity. . . . [But] we cannot discover a law or theory whose technical application will eliminate all the disastrous consequences of the technical application of earlier laws and technologies. (p. 15)

Modern ways of looking at the world, this argument goes, have led us to objectify it in the search for knowledge and control. The story that Fullan tells about educational change, I suggest, is one small part of the failed search for an "objective way out of the crisis of objectivity."

There are several ways in which modernist inquiries in search of "an objective way out of the crisis of objectivity" play themselves out in education and the social sciences. Sometimes the desire for a rational technology of educational change and innovation has exhibited itself in attempts to be ultraorganized and systematic: stating goals, describing tasks designed to bring them about, breaking tasks into component parts, evaluating outcomes following task implementation, and introducing modifications based on evaluations. We live in an era of "systems," to use Havel's term, of change and innovation that seek to counteract the failed "systems" of the past. The educational change proposals and activities since October 4, 1957 are a series of thoroughly modern adventures.

These adventures have not met with overwhelming success—a series of failed modern quests perhaps. Several explanations, to invoke a modern usage of this term (along the lines of Hempel, 1965), can be offered for this lack of success. Some failures can be attributed, no doubt, to the fact that many of these change efforts were not sufficiently modern. Some, quite likely, failed because various goals and objectives were not specified with sufficient clarity or precision to permit an adequate description and implementation of instrumental tasks. Or, they were due to the fact that insufficient resources were available for adequate planning and implementation. Or, perhaps, goals and objectives were never adhered to with sufficient consistency, thereby blocking their systematic implementation and proper evaluation. Or, it could be that many change proposals were not supported by teachers, principals, neighborhood groups, and others necessary for their success. Or, perhaps the necessary expertise in terms of research findings and expert personnel was simply not forthcoming.

In addition to modernist accounts of failure such as those listed in the preceding paragraph, I believe that Fullan's account of the educational change literature can profitably be read in terms of the limits of modernity itself. Instead of adopting the view that our educational change failures can be reversed if only we become more rational and systematic, more modern if you will, I argue something quite different. Many of these failures resulted not from failed attempts to be rational, systematic, and instrumental, but followed from the fact that many of these change efforts were quite modern indeed. Rationalization, systematization, task fragmentation, and specialization that are marks of the modern are themselves limited in what they can bring about. Instead of crediting the failures of educational change to the fact that the changers and how they went about their tasks were insufficiently modern, I argue that many educational change failures were induced by limitations inherent in modernization and rationalization. In broad outline this argument shares many themes with those emphasized by Labaree (1992a, 1992b). Although Labaree does not refer to modernity or pragmatism in his analysis of the rhetoric of *The*

Holmes Group Reports (1992a) or in his account of the genealogy of the movement to professionalize teaching (1992b), his analyses complement much of what follows.

PRAGMATISM

There are as many versions of pragmatism, perhaps, as there are pragmatists. Whereas many pragmatic arguments made at the turn of the century have explicit as well as implicit modernist and instrumental nuances, contemporary versions of pragmatism or neopragmatism, as you wish, include postmodern as well as modern themes. If to be modern means to be scientific, rational, systematic, and controlled, to be postmodern is to acknowledge the confines, ambiguities, and contradictions intrinsic to science, rationality, system, and control. Modernity, it is arguable, always already contained elements of postmodernity, including indications of its own incompleteness and flaws. Pragmatists openly embrace both what is modern and postmodern. What might this mean?

Because pragmatism has many variants a few comments are in order about the pragmatic assumptions upon which I draw. I begin with Charles Sanders Peirce and his version of the pragmatic maxim circa 1905:

> The word *pragmatism* was invented to express a certain maxim of logic . . . [that] is intended to furnish a method for the analysis of concepts. . . . The method prescribed in the maxim is to trace out in the imagination the conceivable practical consequences—that is, the consequences for deliberate, self-controlled conduct,—of the affirmation or denial of the concept. (Peirce, 1905, reprinted in Thayer, 1984, p. 494)

Pragmatism was originally concerned with meaning and so, it should be noted, is Fullan in his account of educational change. Not only is meaning the operative word in the title of both editions of Fullan's book, but chapter 3 (1991) is devoted explicitly to "the meaning of educational change."

Whereas Peirce sought to clarify meanings of intellectual concepts by tracing out their "conceivable practical consequences," William James and John Dewey shifted attention to the importance of the consequences of actions based on particular conceptions. Here is something Dewey (1925/1989) wrote along these lines:

> Pragmatism . . . does not insist upon antecedent phenomena but upon consequent phenomena; not upon the precedents but upon the possibilities of action. And this change in point of view is almost revolutionary in its consequences. . . . [W]hen we take the point of view of pragmatism we see that general ideas have a very different role to play than that of reporting and registering past experiences. They are the bases for organizing future observations and experiences. (pp. 32-33)

Menand (1992) provided the following summary of pragmatism in his review essay of Westbrook's (1991) *John Dewey and American Democracy*:

> Put most simply, pragmatism is what follows from the view that there is nothing external to experience—no World of Forms, City of God, independent cogito, a priori category, transcendental Mind, or far-off divine event to which the whole creation moves, but only the mundane business of making our way as best we can in a universe shot through with contingency. . . . Distinctions are valid, therefore, only when they make a practical difference, since there is no other authority for them to appeal to. Separate a distinction from its use, or change the context in which it is made, and it becomes an idle abstraction. (p. 52)

Pragmatism is neither programmatic nor is it a systematic logic or methodology each of which, it should be noted, is characteristically modern. Pragmatism, it can be argued, is a modern-postmodern collection of methods of analysis and thought that are antiessentialist, antirepresentationalist, and antifoundationalist. Antiessentialism for a pragmatist is the belief that events and objects have no essence, no ultimate or final nature. Any event or object is subject to multiple descriptions and interpretations. Accordingly, there are multiple "conceivable practical consequences . . . of the affirmation or denial of a concept" (Peirce, 1905, p. 494) when one traces them out in one's imagination because different purposes produce different assessments of the same concept, action, or outcome. Once antiessentialism has been accepted, antirepresentationalism follows right along. If there is no essence of, say, intelligence or classroom climate, then it is a mistake to believe that one can truly represent or measure intelligence or classroom climate.

Any descriptions tracing "conceivable practical consequences" are purposive because unless one has a purpose there is no motivation to describe anything. Rorty (1990) framed this point with the vocabularies we use in different areas of our lives:

> [I]t is useless to ask whether one vocabulary rather than another is closer to reality. For different vocabularies serve different purposes, and there is no such thing as a purpose that is closer to reality than another purpose. In particular, there is no purpose that is simply "finding out how things are" as opposed to finding out how to predict their motion, explain their behavior, and so on. (p. 3)

For the sake of argument assume, contrary to the pragmatists, the opposite of each of these two assumptions: Things have essences, and it is possible, in principle, to represent them. An additional problem arises even if these points are granted. How would we know that our representations, say of either the success or failure of educational change, are true and correct? To have true and correct answers one must have foundational criteria, standards, and rules that enable one to recognize them as true and correct. But pragmatists do not claim to know how words hook onto the world, therefore, they do not pretend to have an answer to this question, nor do they believe that anyone else has one either. Pragmatists appreciate the successes and victories of modern science and technology, yet reject foundational interpretations of them. This is called *antifoundationalism.* If we had foundational criteria, standards, rules, and procedures, so the argument goes, then we would be able to build a positive body of scientific knowledge and account for the successes of modern science. Such foundational rules have yet to be formulated. A thoroughgoing pragmatist is basically agnostic rather than militantly atheistic on these issues because sometime in the future, say 200 or 300 years from now, if not next week, someone may discover and conclusively demonstrate that events and things have essences and in the process specify the foundational rules to follow in representing them truly and correctly. Do not block the road to inquiry has been a pragmatist tenet since Peirce.

Because antiessentialism, antirepresentationalism, and antifoundationalism are central to whatever passes for a pragmatist's web-of-belief, it is relatively straightforward to understand why pragmatists seek the meaning either of concepts or actions in their "conceivable practical consequences." Pragmatists can observe and learn about the consequences of an idea being affirmed or denied because they are not distracted by questions about whether they have "got things right." Pragmatists are also fallibilists (Rorty, 1980), look to the consequences (James, 1907/1981), are pluralists (Dewey, 1925/1989), are democrats (Dewey, 1925/1989), are cultural critics (West, 1989), draw no hard distinction between text and context (Rorty, 1991), and value community (Dewey, 1925/1989).

THE NEW MEANING OF EDUCATIONAL CHANGE

Fullan's complex story flirts with open criticism of modernist approaches to educational change and comes close to endorsing pragmatism. Yet he declines to acknowledge or to come to grips with either. His account of much of the educational change rhetoric is that it is thoroughly modern in advocating standards, accountability, control, productivity, and specialization. He shows in detail, however, that many actions taken under the guise of this rhetoric have not been sufficiently powerful to bring about desired changes. He takes four tacks in addressing the meaning of change:

1. "the meaning of individual change in the society at large,"
2. "the *subjective* meaning of change for individuals,"
3. "description[s] of the *objective* meaning of change," and

4. "the implications of subjective and objective realities for understanding educational change" (p. 30).

As in point 1, he quoted Marris (1975), "*all* real change involves loss, anxiety, and struggle" (Fullan, 1991, p. 31):

> Real change, then, whether desired or not, represents a serious personal and collective experience characterized by ambivalence and uncertainty. . . . The anxieties of uncertainty and the joys of mastery are central to the subjective meaning of educational change, and to success or failure—facts that have not been recognized or appreciated in most attempts at change. (p. 32)

The subjective meaning of change (point 2) has been described differently by different writers. Huberman's (1984) summary of "classroom press" in shaping subjective meanings, for example, includes press for immediacy and concreteness, multidimensionality and simultaneity, adaptation to everchanging conditions or unpredictability, and personal involvement with students (p. 33). The effects of "classroom press" push for short-term perspectives, isolation from other adults, exhaustion, and limited opportunities for sustained reflection (p. 33). When these characteristics of teaching are combined with "the hyperrationalization of change" (Wise, 1977) in the form of "rational assumptions, abstraction, and descriptions of a proposed new curriculum . . . there is no reason for the teacher to believe in the change, and few incentives (and large costs) to find out whether a given change will turn out to be worthwhile" (Fullan, 1991, p. 34). What results is often either false clarity without change or painful unclarity without change. Here is a concluding sentence to this section that anticipates Fullan's later (Peircean) pragmatic arguments: "Ultimately the transformation of subjective realities is the essence of change" (p. 36).

The objective reality of educational change (point 3) is elusive. Fullan quoted Berger and Luckmann (1967) on the difficulty of defining objective "reality." There are two questions: (a) "What is the existing conception of reality on a given issue?" (b) "Says who?" (Fullan, 1991, p. 37). Fullan quickly deconstructs the objective reality/subjective reality distinction by pointing out that objective realities are always subject to (subjective) individual interpretation. He makes a pragmatic move at this point by implicitly acknowledging that different individuals can trace differently the "conceivable practical consequences" of the same practices and actions (Peircean pragmatism). In addition, innovations and changes are multilayered because some occur on the "surface" of things whereas others involve basic beliefs and identities. The question of objective reality, therefore, becomes more complex because each classroom innovation is multidimensional and multilayered in which each dimension and each layer of every innovation is open to multiple interpretations. Fullan explains:

> The real crunch comes in the relationships between these new programs or
> policies and the thousands of subjective realities embedded in people's
> individual and organizational contexts and their personal histories. How
> these subjective realities are addressed or ignored is crucial for whether
> potential changes become meaningful at the level of individual use and
> effectiveness. (p. 43)

Fullan ultimately contests one subtext of many proposed educational
changes that can be thought of as a series of causal, although ambiguous,
hypotheses. Educational failures follow from the fact that our schools and educational systems are not sufficiently modern. It is not that what educators have
been doing is wrong-headed or inappropriate, the problem is that educators and
educational reformers have not done well enough what they set out to do in the
first place—produce a modern educational system. Fullan problematizes this
subtext. Is it possible for teachers and other school personnel to bring about the
desired changes by becoming sufficiently modern? Is it possible to train, induce,
cajole, reward, educate, or coerce teachers and others so that they will be rational, systematic, controlled, linear, and specialized enough to take the risks necessary to change fundamentally existing schools? Fullan answers in the negative.

In the section, "Why Planning Fails," Fullan (1991) identifies several
constraints on attempts to institute rationalized change:

> [I]t might be . . . useful to accept the nonrational quality of social systems
> and move on from there. Patterson, Purkey, and Parker (1986) suggest that
> organizations in today's society do not follow an orderly logic, but a com-
> plex one that is often paradoxical and contradictory, but still understandable
> and amenable to influence. They contrast the assumptions of the rational
> conception with those of nonrational conception on five dimensions. *First*,
> goals: School systems are necessarily guided by multiple and sometimes
> competing goals. . . . *Second*, power: In school systems, power is distributed
> throughout the organization. *Third*, decision making: This is inevitably a
> bargaining process to arrive at solutions that satisfy a number of constituen-
> cies. *Fourth*, external environment: The public influences school systems in
> major ways that are unpredictable. *Fifth*, teaching process: There are a vari-
> ety of situationally appropriate ways to teach that are effective. (p. 97)

Rationally conceived plans and actions are always subject to such contingencies. Nonrational factors, then, are always already present whenever one
attempts to think and act rationally. Fullan continues:

> Proponents of the rational model believe that a change in "procedures" will
> lead to improvement. When their "if-then" procedures don't work, they
> become only "if-only" procedures, tightening up rules to influence what is
> seen as a deficiency in response. Proponents of nonrational models recognize
> that organizations do not behave in a logical, predictable manner and try to

work this to their advantage. Wishing for, waiting for, and urging the system to become more rational is in itself irrational—it won't happen. (p. 97)

With occasional variations he tells this story repeatedly. Rational procedures have a long history of failing to meet the aspirations and promises of educational change agents and reformers.

In his last chapter Fullan advocates moving to new "paradigms" for educational change. His use of the term *paradigm* may not be well advised, however, because paradigms imply modern solutions along with the normal, if not routinized, science that comes with them (Kuhn, 1972). Be that as it may, the following are Fullan's six themes for the future of educational change. The six involve moving from an old, unsuccessful way of managing change to a new mindset:

1. from negative to positive politics
2. from monolithic to alternative solutions
3. from innovations to institutional developments
4. from going it alone to alliances
5. from neglect to deeper appreciation of the change process, and
6. from "if only" to "if I" or "if we." (p. 347)

This is a thoroughly pragmatic approach to educational change. The move from a negative to a positive politics (point 1) includes moving *from* a politics of resisting change from below and imposing it from above *to* a politics that focuses on the implementation of a few principles. The move from monolithic to alternative solutions (point 2) rejects universal rationalistic solutions that, to some, are a mark of what is quintessentially modern. Monolithic solutions marginalize specific contexts of change and thereby limit one's flexibility in responding to the contingencies of the change process. In moving away from what is monolithic Fullan emphasizes the importance of planned variations when it comes to changing educational practices. This is one instance, if you will, of what pragmatists believe about plurality. Bernstein (1989) wrote that, "there can be no escape from plurality—a plurality of traditions, perspectives, philosophic orientations" (p. 10). A pragmatic belief in plurality parallels Fullan's alternative approaches and "capacity building."

A major theme that runs throughout his conclusions is that we would be well advised to take our eyes off the text of innovation and focus, instead, on the context of the institution (point 3) and the situation within which we find ourselves. This shift from innovation to institution is, perhaps, Fullan's most overtly pragmatic recommendation. When he directs our attention away from innovation to institution building, he invites us to look at the social and physical context of change as well as the plurality of interests and visions of those involved.

Even though Fullan documents the limitations of modernity in *The New Meaning of Educational Change*, his is *not* an antimodern argument (see Burbules & Rice, 1991, for a discussion of modernity, postmodernity, and antimodernity). Fullan is not opposed to thoughtfully and systematically surveying one's problems and acting on the resulting insights. Instead, his argument is to the point that shortsighted concern with innovation may lead one to overlook the fact that successful change often requires inclusive institutional changes:

> Instead of tracing specific policies and innovations, we turn the problem on its head, and ask what does the array of innovative possibilities look like, if we are on the receiving or shopping end. Thus institutional development . . . is the generic solution needed. Taking on one innovation at a time is fire fighting and faddism. Institutional development of schools and districts increases coherence and capacity for sorting out and integrating the myriad of choices, acting on them, assessing progress, and (re)directing energies. . . . We cannot develop institutions without developing the people in them. (Fullan, 1991, p. 349)

This shift from innovation to institution parallels the way pragmatists deconstruct the proposed distinction between text and context.

Sarason (1990) made a similar argument in *The Predictable Failure of Educational Reform* when he asked, "For Whom Do Schools Exist?" Educational reformers who highlight innovations often, rhetorically at least, place the needs of students first. Sarason put a counterposition like this, "If you, as I have, ask teachers . . . how they justify the existence of their school, the answer you get is that schools exist to further the intellectual and social development of students" (p. 137). If most educational reformers believe that schools exist for students, then it follows that their change efforts will be designed to enhance the "intellectual and social development of students." This belief underlies an approach to school reform whereby the "text" of an innovation is emphasized and the "context" of the institution is deemphasized. But Sarason rejects the idea that schools exist solely for students. Sarason wrote: "If, as I have asserted, it is virtually impossible to create and sustain over time conditions for productive learning for students when they do not exist for teachers, the benefits sought by educational reform stand little chance of being realized" (p. 145).

Interpreted in simple benefit-cost terms, Sarason is making the not so obscure observation that whatever change is desired must be perceived if it is to be sustained to be to everyone's advantage. Everyone—students, teachers, administrators, staff, parents—must believe that change provides them either with a net benefit or at least not a net loss. Otherwise, those who see themselves losing out because of proposed changes will either have no incentive to support it or believe that it is in their interest to subvert it. Continuing with this line of argument, it is not likely that everyone—students, teachers, administrators, or others—involved in schools will share the same interests and desires. Furthermore, if these different people were "to trace out in the imagination the conceivable practical consequences" (Peirce, 1905, p. 494) of a proposed change, it is likely that different individuals—educators and students for example—will many times value the same outcomes differently.

At this point Sarason anticipates requests for a plan for educational reform:

> It is easy to say that schools should exist coequally for students and educators. But what does it mean in practice? What are starting points? (p. 146)

> [I]t makes no sense to offer a prescription for what it would mean in practice for schools to exist coequally for students and teachers. . . . I trust that the reader will comprehend my reluctance to offer a prescription in regard to a problem that is not regarded as a problem! And that is the point . . . the complete inability of educational reformers to examine the possibility that to create and sustain for children the conditions for productive growth without those conditions existing for educators is virtually impossible. (p. 147)

In more pragmatic terms, educational reformers are often so caught up in modernist conceptions of progress and education that they simply are unaware that they tend to highlight the "text" of educational innovation at the expense of the educational "context." Modernist proposals are thereby transformed into conceptual and incapacitating straightjackets.

This theme from Fullan and Sarason overlaps Fullan's next point "from going it alone to alliances" (point 4). But here the argument takes an unexpected detour—unexpected in terms of his previous observations. Instead of citing, say, Dewey on democracy, Fullan introduces the idea of interactive professionalism. An interactive professionalism suggests an underlying tension, if not outright contradiction, in his position. Professionalism is a most modern conception and development. It appeals to expertise, control, hierarchy, accountability, and rationality, and Fullan's discussion of professionalism ignores the operation of power through professional structures and subjectivities (see Cherryholmes, 1988). More professionalism may not be the cure for the failures of professionalism (from Havel quoted earlier and Labaree, 1992a, 1992b). Fullan's interactive professionalism requires nuanced and sophisticated elaboration.

Successful change often requires a willingness to embrace contradiction and inconsistency (point 5):

> Change is difficult because it is riddled with dilemmas, ambivalences, and paradoxes. It combines steps that seemingly do not go together: to have a clear vision and be open-minded; to take initiative and empower others; to provide support and pressure; to start small and think big; to expect results and be patient and persistent; to have a plan and be flexible; to use top-down and bottom-up strategies; to experience uncertainty and satisfaction. (p. 350)

Paradoxes, dilemmas, contradictions, and ambiguity subvert modern impulses to linearity, control, and clarity. These complexities highlight, again, limits to modernity.

His last suggestion (point 6) breaks with modernist conceptions of change in yet another way. He argues against relying on causal hypotheses because the contradictions and paradoxes of practice and the context within which it is situated often undermine attempts at isolated interventions that are suggested by if-then thinking. The best chances for successful change are found when change efforts have personal meaning for the individuals involved, "Acting on change is an exercise in pursuing meaning" (p. 351). This brings us once again to Peirce's pragmatic maxim. For Peirce the meaning of an intellectual concept was found in the "conceivable practical consequences—that is, the consequences for deliberate, self-controlled conduct—of the affirmation or denial of the concept" (Peirce, 1905, p. 494). For Fullan successful change requires "pursuing meaning" as the "conceivable practical consequences" of affirming or denying an idea and acting or failing to act on it.

Some three decades after Peirce formulated the preceding definition of pragmatism John Dewey (1934/1980) extended the pragmatic conception of consequences to what is aesthetic in experience, "the aesthetic . . . is the clarified and intensified development of traits that belong to every normally complete experience" (p. 46). Dewey also outlined a number of ways in which modern organizations and planning restrict and limit the aesthetic:

> Experience is limited by all the causes which interfere with perception of the relations between undergoing and doing. . . . Zeal for doing, lust for action, leaves many a person, especially in this hurried and impatient human environment in which we live, with experience of an almost incredible paucity, all on the surface. No one experience has a chance to complete itself because something else is entered upon so speedily. . . . Resistance is treated as an obstruction to be beaten down, not as an invitation to reflection. An individual comes to seek, unconsciously even more than by deliberate choice, situations in which he can do the most things in the shortest time. (pp. 44-45)

Productivity that is thought of primarily in terms of efficiently implementing innovations, according to Dewey, undercuts broader conceptions and interpretations of experience. Living on the surface and doing things in the shortest time denies the aesthetic component of what we do. If modernist ideas are allowed to develop in this direction, as Dewey argues and Fullan documents, then alienation and an overall lack of success will often follow. Modernist efforts at reform that emphasize rationality and control threaten to dehumanize the very institutions they are designed to change.

The modern and postmodern meet and part in pragmatic attempts to bring about change. Fullan's argument ends, rightfully so, in an assortment of paradoxes that he fails to state or investigate. Here are a few:

1. Rational attempts to bring about change are likely to be enhanced when they incorporate irrational commitments.
2. Hierarchies that promote change are likely to improve their chances of success when the hierarchy itself is subverted.
3. Coordinated efforts to bring about change often depend for their success on uncoordinated responses to the complexities and inconsistencies of specific situations.
4. Impersonal goals are more likely to be achieved when they are personalized.
5. In order to understand the meaning of the "text" of an innovation one must carefully and thoughtfully attend to its "context."

It is not clear where he stands on these matters. Is he nostalgic for modernist aspirations? Does he call for more modernization that will cure the ills of modernity? Or, does he wish to break with the modernist ambitions of contemporary educational reformers and establish a "new" and pragmatic professionalism that embraces what is postmodern as well as what is modern? His argument is clear; the conclusions he draws from it are less so.

As this review of Fullan's text nears its end, a reader of empiricist leanings might remain unconvinced by this pragmatic/postmodern reading. I propose, therefore, an empiricist reading of these change efforts. Empiricist research is often designed to test hypotheses. Specifically, as a result of Popper's (1976) argument about falsification, any empirical study designed to test a hypothesis should satisfy the following criterion. The study must be designed so that it is possible, in principle, to collect negative evidence, that is, evidence that could falsify the hypothesis under test. The change studies that Fullan investigates, in fact, falsify many specific hypotheses concerning educational interventions. But perhaps the most important hypothesis that is falsified by his narrative is neither explicitly mentioned nor discussed. This central and overarching hypothesis is not made explicit perhaps because it seems so intuitively obvious it needs no testing. The hypothesis is that modernist approaches to change that emphasize rationality, hierarchy, accountability, and linearity of thought (independent variables) will produce successful educational change (dependent variables). Fullan's metaanalysis, if you will, serves to falsify this hypothesis. The repeated results of empirical investigations into educational change provide a great deal of negative evidence for our modernist hypothesis. Empiricism, a product of modernity, in this case documents the limits of modernity. If being modern enables us to learn systematically from our mistakes, then we would be well advised to view with caution admonitions to be modern. This is one example in which what is modern points toward what is postmodern. In light of Fullan's story to be thoroughly modern entails acknowledging the limits of modernity while embracing its possibilities. Pragmatism, I submit, is where the wholistic and subtle embrace and rejection of empiricism leads.

POSTSCRIPT

Three final thoughts. First, the implications of pragmatism for education are currently being explored after decades of neglect. I have (1988) provided a variety of poststructural interpretations of contemporary educational theories and practices and have argued for critically pragmatic responses to the contingencies of teaching and learning. Skrtic (1991) has shown how the crisis in modern knowledge is working itself out in the field of special education. Maxcy (1991) has illustrated how pragmatism provides insight into the theory and practice of educational administration. And, Stanley (1992) has provided a thoughtful and penetrating analysis of pragmatism in the area of curriculum.

Each of these writers explored and elaborated, among other things, Dewey's (1934/1980) insistence on the wholeness of experience:

> It is not possible to divide in a vital experience the practical, emotional, and intellectual from one another and to set the properties of one over against the characteristics of the other. The emotional phase binds parts together into a single whole; "intellectual" simply names the fact that the experience has meaning; "practical" indicates that the organism is interacting with events and objects which surround it. (p. 55)

In affirming the wholeness of experience by looking to the consequences of belief and action pragmatism qualifies claims made in the name of modernity and progress.

Second, if for purposes of argument it can be assumed that pragmatist assumptions are correct that there is (a) *no* essential nature to education or educational change, (b) *no* foundational knowledge about education or how to change our schools, *and* (c) it is *not possible* to truly represent either of these, then it is fair to ask what does it mean to "trace out in the imagination the conceivable practical consequences . . . of the affirmation or denial of the concept [of change]" (Peirce, 1905, p. 494). This turns my argument against itself; what are the pragmatic consequences of Peirce's pragmatic maxim when it is applied to educational change? A pragmatic approach to change keeps attention holistically focused on the likely outcomes. Criticism is essential to the endeavor. The following is Gunn's (1992) observation about pragmatic criticism:

> [I]t should be clear that while pragmatic criticism advocates no particular policies, it does possess a specifiable politics. It is a politics distinguished by the democratic preference for rendering differences conversable so that the conflicts they produce, instead of being destructive of human community, can become potentially creative of it; can broaden and thicken public culture rather than depleting it. (p. 37)

Hierarchies that avoid pragmatic criticism act to "render differences [non]conversable" and thereby truncate and desiccate discourses that otherwise might contribute to change. One-way flows of communication, for example, whatever their rationalized intent, will if pursued long enough eventually subvert pragmatic criticism even though pragmatists may choose, from time to time, to so communicate.

Gunn continued:

> Pragmatism does not pretend to be without prejudice: it merely holds that all prejudices are subject to revision if we can learn how to replace the foundationalist "quest for certainty" . . . with a more provisional relation to our convictions and a more quizzical attitude toward where they may carry us and what sorts of criticism they can sustain. (p. 38)

One of Fullan's more important points is that those who would change educational practices have not always resisted "the foundationalist 'quest for certainty.'" To the contrary, educational reformers have often successfully resisted the notion that their prejudices were provisional. Pragmatism, however, pushes in a different direction: "Such a (pragmatic) perspective is located beyond ideology and transcendence alike not because it can escape their superventions but only because it can resist their simplifications" (Gunn, 1992, p. 36).

Third, even though pragmatism is only now being given explicit attention in North America, it has influenced continental thinkers in recent decades. I cite three aspects of Habermas's (1979) thought that have a distinctly Peircean flavor:

1. Habermas's consensus theory of truth bears a striking resemblance to Peirce's view that what is true is that which is fated to be agreed upon at the end of inquiry.
2. Habermas's conception of the ideal speech situation that allows only the pursuit of the best argument is remarkably similar to Peirce's pragmatic admonition not to block the road to inquiry.
3. Habermas's extension of neo-Marxist thought into symbolic and discursive realms was foreshadowed by Peirce's investigations in semiotics.

10

Sign Language and the Discursive Construction of Power Over the Deaf Through Education

Jan Branson
La Trobe University
Don Miller
Monash University

The real political task . . . is to criticize the working of institutions that appear to be both neutral and independent; to criticize them in such a manner that the political violence which has always exercised itself obscurely through them will be unmasked so that one can fight them. (Foucault, quoted in Lane, 1992, p. viii)

It is precisely the unmasking of the unrecognized violence that is central to the exercising of power, "symbolic violence," and associated "symbolic power," to use Bourdieu's terms, that is the purpose of this chapter. Power is a dynamic relationship, a relationship that involves the control of one person's access to resources by another, a control that is usually not simply individuated and temporary, but is the embodiment of a wider structured relationship between categories of people—between employers and employees, teachers and pupils, parents and children, the able-bodied and the disabled, white and black, male and female, the hearing and the deaf, and so on. The formation and transformation of power is an ongoing process, *a discursive process* in the sense that control must be justified, legitimized, through a discourse, through an essentially implicit dialogue that establishes certain physical conditions, behaviors, and ideas as superior to others. Like the concept of *ideology* that it compliments and to a degree has displaced, the concept of *discourse* refers to the ongoing construction of discriminatory processes, through the formation and transformation of discriminatory categories that structure attitudes and behavior—the discursive construction of gender, of race, of disabilities, and so on.

But we must insert a vital cautionary note at this stage. As we turn to consider the role of education in the discursive construction of power over the Deaf[1] by the hearing establishment, it is vital that we correct a tendency to regard discourse as essentially intellectual, that is, of the mind. Although such discourses might indeed be articulated in word or print, such articulations are but expressions of wider discourses, expressed most importantly in practice. The discursive construction of power by men over women, whites over blacks, the able-bodied over the so-called "disabled," involves a series of discourses in the sense that historically and culturally specific approaches to gender, race, and behavior are articulated. But they are articulated most importantly through experience, rather than in an abstract intellectual sense. That experience also involves not only the experience of discriminatory behavior, but of particular material conditions of existence. These material conditions of existence embody privilege or lack of privilege, the degree and nature of access to society's resources.

Considerations of the discursive construction of power over the Deaf necessitates a clear understanding of the material and indeed physical nature of the discursive processes. To lay the ground for the effective analysis of the situation of the Deaf, we turn to recent feminist theory that has challenged much of the literature on the discursive construction and consolidation of power. In particular, we turn to literature that, in seeking to move beyond an intellectualist view of discursive processes, lays bare the epistemological assumptions that remain untheorized in much of the literature on discriminatory behavior. So, for example, in much of the literature the "resources" or "means of production" to which the disadvantaged must gain access are assumed "neutral." Break down the barriers—economic, political, or ideological—and "equal access" will pre-

---

[1]The use of a capital letter for the word *Deaf* in this context signifies the way the shared experience of deafness is associated with the development of a subculture, a sense of community linked very closely to the use of sign language. Written with a capital d, the word therefore refers to a social network linked by a particular perception of the world and by resultant dispositions toward that world, dispositions sensed and expressed in a way not experienced or understood by the vast majority of hearing people, a marginalized "way of seeing" ignored and thus devalued by the dominant culture that labels those who are deaf as "lacking hearing" and thus as "disabled." For many of the Deaf, deafness does not render them disabled, although they acknowledge that they suffer an enormous social handicap due to discrimination against them by the hearing world, but rather simply renders them different. And so they see their deafness as a mark of identity, something to revel in and be proud of rather than as something to be embarrassed about, to be partially hidden beneath a mimicry of hearing people. They are thus not simply "deaf people" but the "the Deaf."

vail, it is assumed. So too is the accumulation of knowledge about such "minority" groups on which such theorizing is based and assumed unproblematic.

Recent feminist scholarship has challenged the conventional wisdom that something such as equality can be achieved by providing for equal access to society's resources, including education and culture. It has demonstrated that our economic, political, juridical, and cultural conditions of existence are framed in such a way as to marginalize women, irrespective of the enactment of legislation guaranteeing women "equal access" to jobs, political office, the law, and the full range of educational and cultural resources that are assumed to be neutrally "available." It has pointed out that this is not simply due to the fact that people are mentally conditioned to regard certain conditions of existence and certain practices as appropriate for men or women. Such conditioning does of course exist and is a vital component in the discursive construction of the gender-based differences that are basic to the exercise of male power, but deeper than this mental conditioning is the construction of a world that is materially, not simply mentally, oriented toward the physicality of maleness, that demands male bodies—culturally conditioned male bodies—a world in which female bodies are not only inappropriate but out of tune. "One could argue," wrote Gatens (1992), "that gender is a material effect of the way in which power takes hold of the body rather than an ideological effect of the way power 'conditions' the mind" (p. 127). Women who enter this male world must recondition their bodies, not just their minds, in order to fit. They must control menstruation so that it is invisible and does not interfere with work routines—routines assumed to be gender neutral. They must control menopause for the same reasons. And when they are pregnant they must leave the environment once their "inappropriate" condition begins to interfere with work routines. The routines are designed for male bodies. Gatens summed up the situation:

> Female embodiment as it is currently lived is itself a barrier to women's "equal" participation in socio-political life. Suppose our body politic were one which was created for the enhancement and intensification of women's historical and present capacities. The primary aim of such a body politic might be to foster conditions for the healthy reproduction of its members. If this were the case, then presumably some men would now be demanding that medical science provide ways for them to overcome their "natural" or biological disadvantages, by inventing, for example, means by which they could lactate. (p. 132)

As we explore the failure of mainstreaming in the context of the education of the Deaf, it must therefore be understood that the power that controls and marginalizes the Deaf is not only exercised through the discursive construction of an educational environment in which certain linguistic and cultural skills that the Deaf cannot achieve are required, but through the construction of an educational environment that demands hearing bodies, in both a physical and cultural sense. Within the "normal" educational environment deafness remains an *embodied pathology*, irrespective of the access provided.

The embodiment of their pathological status occurs within an environment not only designed in hearing terms, but an environment that *defines* the Deaf, that constructs an understanding of deafness via an epistemology that is framed in terms of and informed by hearing sensibilities. The Deaf are understood in terms that come not from their own experience of deafness, but from the "expertise" of hearing professionals. In more than a simply metaphorical sense, the Deaf have been colonized, studied, and described by outsiders. Related theorizing again provides the conceptual apparatus required to understand the social impact of such phonocentric views of the Deaf and to move beyond them. Within the fields of Anthropology, History, and Literary Criticism, in particular, there has been an attempt by more progressive scholars to move beyond Eurocentric views of society and history in general, and in particular to move beyond such Eurocentric views of the culture and history of non-Western, former colonial territories and their peoples. This postcolonial criticism has also been informed by and has itself served to inform feminist critiques of male-dominated scholarship. In Spivak's terms, the male incorporation of women in its scheme of things is as imperialist as the Western definitions of non-Western societies, cultures, and histories or the white-middle class definitions of non-white, and/or working-class behaviors within Western societies. An essentially white, male, middle-class, intellectual tradition has defined itself and the rest of humanity in essentialist, unitary, logocentric, and phallocentric terms, a mode of understanding that has served white, male, middle-class interests at home and abroad.

Here, therefore, within the context of Bourdieu's analyses of language and symbolic power, we explore the imperialist domination of the Deaf, epistemologically via the encapsulation of their subjectivities within a hearing cosmology and materially through the demand that they fit into and succeed within an environment that is designed for culturally constituted hearing bodies. The symbolic violence that contains and oppresses the Deaf will be shown to be exercised via the agency of an apparently "neutral and independent" institution—the school—a vital site for the discursive construction of discriminatory ideas, practices and material conditions of existence.

THE DEAF AND MAINSTREAMING

The total subjection of a deaf child to a means of communication which he cannot understand in a school setting is not only unprofessional and usually ineffective, but it could well be viewed as a violation of the rights of another human being. (Merrill, 1975)

Like the sociology of culture, the sociology of language is logically inseparable from a sociology of education. (Bourdieu, 1991, p. 62)

This challenge to the mainstreaming of the Deaf claims, at the most general level, that such a policy is oriented not toward the educational needs of the Deaf, but toward the reinforcement of the dominant ideology of equality of access to educational resources, an ideology that is in fact the foundation for the reproduction of structured inequalities. Bourdieu (1977b) encapsulated the process:

> Indeed, among all the solutions put forward throughout history to the problem of the transmission of power and privileges, there surely does not exist one that is better concealed, and therefore better adapted to societies which tend to refuse the most patent forms of the transmission of power and privileges, than that solution which the educational system provides by contributing to the reproduction of the structure of class relations and by concealing, by an apparently neutral attitude, the fact that it fills this function. (p. 488)

> By doing away with giving explicitly to everyone what it implicitly demands of everyone, the educational system demands of everyone alike that they have what it does not give. This consists mainly of linguistic and cultural competence and that relationship of familiarity with culture which can only be produced by family upbringing when it transmits the dominant culture. (p. 494)

Mainstreaming thus becomes a form of symbolic violence, reinforcing the cultural, linguistic, and physical incompetence of the Deaf in the eyes of the hearing establishment, marginalizing them as effectively as ever, reinforcing rather than destroying their status as "disabled" and thus in need of "care" or control.

In documenting the failure of education through oralism and manually coded forms of dominant sound-based languages for the Deaf, we are not ignoring the fact that there have been exceptions to the general and overwhelming trend toward failure. Individual Deaf have succeeded through oralist systems, showing exceptional abilities to cope with voicing and lip reading, and have achieved high standards of literacy in the dominant language. But they are exceptions to the rule. The Deaf as a whole should not be judged by these exceptions, nor should policy be based on the abilities and achievements of a very small minority. Ideological assertions of the existence of equality frequently claim legitimacy on the basis of the exceptional. Denials of the existence of class-based, gender-based, racially or ethnically based barriers to success within the middle-class labor market are often supported by publicity being given to the working-class boy who made it, the woman in a high position of responsibility, or the "black" lawyer or "migrant" businessman. These denials, which revel in the cult of the individual, ignore the copious sociological research that time and again demonstrates that these cases of upward mobility are exceptional and that for the vast majority of the population, the cultural, economic, and political forces that restrict access to society's resources, operate to reproduce structured inequalities. Ladd (1991) poignantly paced his own experience and "success" in this very context:

He was paraded in front of parents at the clinic: "Now Nigel, show the parents how well you speak. Thank you. Now, if you work hard, your children will be able to speak like Nigel." (Implied, if your child doesn't, then you are to blame for not working hard enough.) This was grossly deceitful for two reasons. One, that many of the parents had profoundly deaf children, who had little hope of being able to speak like Nigel. And it was also calculated to make Nigel feel better than those other deaf children, so that he would make the springboard into the hearing world, and leave those nasty traces of deafness behind. Thus Nigel began life with a carefully instilled pattern of self-deceit. The parallels between this approach and the capitalist Great Lie are remarkable—both say "You can make it to the top if you work hard. Anyone can." In reality, of course, only those with the resources can do it, apart from a determined few who trample everybody before them. For the majority of people who have neither resources nor killer instinct, there is nothing but the branding mark of failure. The fact that this is not the only approach to life or to deafness is kept well hidden. (p. 89)

The links to the capitalist Great Lie are direct; the treatment of exceptions as justifications for the rule are integral to the ideological conditions of existence for capitalism. The resources required to succeed are as much linguistic and cultural as economic.

The sociolinguistic characteristics of the Deaf generate unique problems in relation to the achievement of effective educational outcomes. Deprived of access to and the right to use the only language to which no sensory barriers exist—sign language—the only language through which they can acquire complete understanding, all but the very few who have grown up in signing households (approximately 10% of the deaf) have been deprived not only of access to information, including literacy in English, but of the very ability to conceptualize and communicate an understanding of the world around them. (There are exceptions to this general statement that will be discussed later.)

In addressing the problems of why and how the majority of existing educational practices fail to address the particular linguistic, cultural, and educational needs of Deaf communities throughout the world, but rather operate to reproduce their marginality through the promotion of what the establishment interprets as linguistic and cultural incompetence, we open a can of worms that reveals much about the fundamental nature of Western society and its politics. We look below what Dumont called the "threshold of consciousness" (Dumont, 1980; Miller, 1991) to the processes that serve to reproduce inequality and marginality in a society that asserts equality of opportunity through equal access to society's economic, political, educational, and cultural resources. It will be this task that requires an appropriation of Bourdieu's theory of practice (Bourdieu, 1977a) and in particular of his discussions of "language and symbolic violence" (Bourdieu, 1991). At the heart of all that is discussed here is the awareness that: "one must not forget that the relations of communication *par excellence*—linguistic exchanges—are also relations of symbolic power in which the power relations between speakers or their respective groups are actualized" (Bourdieu, 1991, p. 37).

Through this distinctly imperial orientation, teachers, linguists, and policymakers become the unwitting agents of an "epistemic violence" that "effaces the subject," to quote Spivak's recent and devastating deconstructive critiques of Western scholarship (Spivak, 1987), "insidiously objectifying" the "colonized" through a conceptual apparatus that robs them of their individual and cultural integrity, devaluing and distorting their differences. (For further discussion see Branson & Miller, 1989.)

SIGN LANGUAGES—THE STRUGGLE FOR RECOGNITION

When we deal with native sign languages we are faced with issues and problems that do not arise in relation to other languages. Here we turn briefly to consider the history of the linguistic deprivation that has been part and parcel of the history of the Deaf. Although linguists have now established that sign languages are distinct, *bona fide* languages, with each Deaf community having developed its own distinct language, such recognition is recent and often still not accepted by those who control access by the Deaf to society's resources.

Formal histories of the education of the deaf begin conventionally with Ponce de Leon in 16th-century Spain, Pascha in Brandenburg in Germany at the same time, and then Juan Martin Pablo Bonet and Ramirez de Carrion in Madrid in the early 17th century. All were involved in teaching deaf children of the nobility above all to read and write, with some mention of the teaching of speech and lip reading. During the intellectual turmoil of the 16th century, we see a redefinition of deafness as a medical condition and an interest in the deaf as medical "specimens." Also evident is philosophical speculation about the relationship between deafness and language acquisition. These treatises herald a debate that emerges and reemerges in the literature on deaf education, on the nature and merits of sign language versus speech and lip reading. But the stress was firmly on the development of medical and educational techniques to generate speech, especially evident in the work of the Spanish-born Frenchman Periera in the 18th century, highly praised in his day for his success in teaching the Deaf to speak via the sensitization of his pupils to touch and vibrations, receiving honors for his "scientific" work in France and England.

But it was the Abbé de l'Épée, first Director of the National Institute for the Deaf and Dumb in Paris, who moved to educate not only those who could pay, as with Periera, but to educate the poor as a matter of public duty. His importance lies in his championing of education through sign language.[2] He

---

[2]It should be noted here that a great innovator inspired by de l'Épée but usually missing from the histories of the education of the deaf is the founder of the first school for the Deaf in Denmark—P.A. Castberg—who in 1807 established a school based on sign language. But "whereas de l'Épée believed in construction of a sign system to support French words and syntax, Castberg mainly based his teaching on the Sign Language he found was already existing among his pupils" (Hansen, 1991, p. 3).

established an educational method and tradition that was to be developed by his successor Sicard throughout Europe and carried by one of Sicard's Deaf pupils, Laurent Clerc, to the United States with Gallaudet in the early 19th century, there to survive against the onslaught of oralism throughout the world.

THE ORALIST OFFENSIVE

> There stands opposed to the true history of my people, whose modern era began when the abbé de l'Épée discovered how to educate us through sign language, quite another history. It is a record of the efforts of hearing people to supplant the language of the deaf with their language, to replace signs with speech. It calls itself the history of the deaf—yet it is an account not of my people but of our hearing benefactors, who affirm that the only proper route for elevating the deaf is oral instruction. (Lane, 1988, p. 67)

In Paris, under Sicard's successors, in England where oralism was the accepted method in the tradition of Braidwood, and particularly in Germany where oralism had been championed and developed since Heinicke opened his school in Leipzig in 1778, oralism developed as the hearing world's treatment of deafness. The oralist attack culminated in an international assertion of oralism as the only acceptable method of education for the Deaf via the overt suppression of sign language at the second International Congress of Teachers of the Deaf in Milan in 1880. After 1880, the United States was the only country where the so-called "silent method" remained in use, and there too oralism proceeded apace. Oralism became a crusade. The transformation of the Deaf to appear as much as possible like hearing people via oralist educational methods, now aided by "science" and its amplification of sound and the associated development of audiology, became the site for the development of specialist professions in the therapeutic treatment of deafness as an illness and a deficit, despite the opposition of the deaf themselves.[3] The potential future role of the Deaf teachers in the tradition of Le Clerc and Massieu was certainly destroyed for the time being, and the profession of "teachers of the deaf" asserted itself as a hearing profession. The teachers were hearing people, the experts were hearing people, and the aim was to make the Deaf as much like hearing people as possible. In denying sign language a place in the lives of the Deaf and in refusing to use it as a medium for access to the resource central to effective strategic participation in the society, the teachers of the Deaf were above all controlling the Deaf. So the Italian teacher, Abbé Tarra, who led the crusade for oralism at the Milan Congress, stated:

---

[3]This was expressed particularly at the International Congresses of the Deaf following the Milan Congress of Teachers of the Deaf (see Lane, 1988).

The habit of full dependence, which the deaf-mute contracts in catching what is said from the lips and communicating ideas by the orderly, rational, and tranquil means of oral conversation, takes from them that indocile and wild spirit peculiar to those who express themselves by the fantastic and passionate methods of gestures, and always renders them more obedient, respectful, affectionate, sincere, and good. (cited in Lane, 1988, p. 401)

Interest lay not in the achievements of the Deaf, but of the professionals living off them. The achievement of even a mild reflection of oral competence was seen as a grand scientific achievement. So fervent a crusade had oralism become that they even ignored the criticism of other scientific experts. The very people who were to lay the basis for wholesale IQ testing with its disastrous results—Binet and Simon—were completely ignored when they concluded, following a "scientific" evaluation of the achievements of Paris graduates from oralist institutions:

People are mistaken about the practical result of the oral method. It seems to us a sort of luxury education, which boosts morale rather than yielding useful and tangible results. It does not enable deaf-mutes to get jobs; it does not permit them to exchange ideas with strangers; it does not allow them even a consecutive conversation with intimates; and deaf-mutes who have not learned to speak earn their living just as easily as those who have acquired this semblance of speech. (cited in Lane, 1988, p. 400)

Such an approach, still dominant, is based on the assumption that a little hearing is better than none at all, itself based on the assumption that hearing and speech are the only natural form of communication, and therefore that oralism is the only viable mode of communication for society as a whole, the mode to which all members of society should and must adjust. With regard to the first assumption, it should be noted that the transition from education in sign to oral education of the Deaf was accompanied by dramatic deterioration in the performance of Deaf students (BBC, 1988; Lane, 1988). The handicap of oralism created an educational lack to accompany the assumed physical lack. The possibility that a little hearing, extremely distorted via amplification equipment, can be extremely disorienting and indeed a *barrier* to communication, a barrier created by the technologies, is rarely considered. The faith of the hearing world in technology leads to the assumption that once some hearing has been stimulated, the Deaf person can be expected to participate effectively in the hearing world.

THE DENIGRATION OF SIGN LANGUAGE AND DEAF CULTURE

But the hearing professionals remain on the whole unaware of the consequences of their pursuit of the education of their pupils through the varieties of the dominant sound-based language. They exercise a "symbolic violence": "The gentle invisible form of violence which is never recognized as such . . . the violence of credit, confidence, obligation, personal loyalty, hospitality, gifts, gratitude, piety" (Bourdieu, 1977a, p. 192), and we might add the violence of charity, the violence of sympathy, and above all the symbolic violence of therapy. They exercise a *symbolic control* that is often, maybe usually, subconscious as they evaluate the world in terms of their class-specific, gender-specific "*habitus*, those systems of durable, transposable *dispositions*, structured structures predisposed to act as structuring structures, that is, as principles of the generation and structuring of practices and representations" (Bourdieu, 1977a, p. 72). They exercise symbolic violence or symbolic control by virtue of their enculturation to dispose themselves toward language and others in culturally specific ways that become for them "common sense."[4] This has involved a complete insensitivity on the part of the hearing culture to the sensibilities of the Deaf. Oralism is a clear and explicit statement about the unacceptability of a linguistic and thus cultural difference when that difference is not only grammatical and lexical but via a different mode.

Why the antagonism to signing? First, we have to confront the fact that in our society deafness is defined as a "disability," compounded by the essentially subconscious equation of muteness with dumbness, and dumbness with stupidity. Coupled with this, at least within middle class Anglo-American culture, is a definition of politeness and good behavior that explicitly excludes as rude and even grotesque those manual and facial expressions that are an essential part of communication through sign language. In those societies dominated by middle-class English cultural dispositions—in which gesticulating is minimal, pointing is rude, and mouth movements and facial expressions are minimal and subtle, the tongue well out of sight—the mouth movements and gestures integral to signing positively disable the Deaf culturally within the hearing community.[5] The signing Deaf are evaluated as gross and uncultured. They are culturally conditioned as not only physically lacking, but as physically inappropriate.

Added to this is the impact of the Cartesian mind/body dualism on the development of a particular kind of intellectual arrogance associated with the assertion of the infinite creativity of the mind over the limitations of the body. As Derrida has shown, the Western intellectual tradition stresses the phonetic basis of writing as lying at the heart of its meaning. Speech itself is accorded this essentially mind-based status in its representation as disembodied sound— the essential component at the heart of all language—giving even the written word an authorial legitimacy as a representation of sound. So even one of the more perceptive sociolinguists can write, "The basic orality of language is permanent" (Ong, 1982, p. 7), having dismissed the potential problem of sign languages as follows:

---

[4]For further discussion of Bourdieu's sociology of culture, see Miller and Branson (1987, 1991).

[5]Bourdieu's (1991, p. 86) analysis of the "bodily hexis" is particularly revealing in this respect.

> Wherever human beings exist they have a language, and in every instance a
> language that exists basically as spoken and heard, in the world of sound. . . .
> Despite the richness of gesture, elaborated sign languages are substitutes for
> speech and dependent on oral speech systems, even when used by the con-
> genitally deaf. (p. 7)

The statement is made without any care being given as to why sign languages
should be "substitutes" rather than alternative languages or why and in what
way they are supposed to be "dependent."

Communication through sign is thus perceived of or evaluated as, limited and nonintellectual in the same way as manual labor and indeed the language of the working class is regarded.[6] Of course, the contradictions are as
apparent as ever, for just as painting or sculpture are evaluated as art and creative despite their being manual because they are middle-class pursuits, manual
labor is devalued not simply because it is manual, but because it is of the working class. So too was or is the devaluation of sign language due not primarily to
its being manual, but to its being of the Deaf. Its manual nature reinforces its
inferior status.

THE RELATIONSHIP BETWEEN DOMINANT SOUND
LANGUAGES AND MINORITY SIGN LANGUAGES

The principles governing the relationship between dominant hearing languages
and native sign languages are essentially the same throughout the world. As
minority languages, as the languages of subcultural groups of a kind quite distinct from other minority groups, each native sign language has a complex relationship with the sound-based language of the dominant culture, a relationship
that has led to much misunderstanding among linguists, teachers and signers
themselves.

Although linguists have indeed been vital for the Deaf in giving "scientific" support of the linguistic status of sign languages, some have also, usually unwittingly, lent legitimacy to the claims of those who support and promote
the use, particularly in educational settings, of the manually coded forms of
dominant languages. These confusions are associated with an hypothesized
diglossia continuum between a native sign language and its dominant sound-
based language. This assertion that, for example, Auslan or BSL or ASL relate
to English on a continuum with pure native sign language at one end and the

---

[6]Although there is not enough space here to pursue further the complex relationship
between language and social class, it is worth noting that the spoken language of manual
workers has been devalued and dismissed as a viable medium of education, the assumption being that when they do enter formal education the workers must learn and learn in
the language of the middle classes, the language of learning, formal grammatical, written
English.

dominant language—English—at the other, although no more than an hypothesis for it has not been tested at all conclusively, implies a number of unstated premises: that the two languages are compatible; that the dominant language—English—can effectively be represented in a signing mode—otherwise a diglossia continuum cannot occur; that the users of sign language are dependent on the dominant language in some way implying support for the position quoted from Ong earlier; and that the sign language is in some way inadequate on its own. The relationship between native sign languages and the languages of those whose are dominant is indeed an unequal one but this need not imply a lack of coherent and separate identity for the native sign language.

Languages are dynamic aspects of culture that are constantly undergoing transformation, transformations influenced by the unequal dynamics of social relationships. Few languages are truly autonomous in a long-term historical sense from those around them. When English lexical and grammatical elements are used as part and parcel of fluid communication by signers in conversation with each other, they are no more problematic than the linguistic behaviors of the vast majority of language speakers as they manipulate vocabularies and structures creatively and do not detract from the integrity of the language. With this historical and linguistic background in mind, we turn to the problems of sign language and education as they relate to wider cultural issues.

SIGNED ENGLISH AS SYMBOLIC VIOLENCE—THE VIOLENCE OF SILENCE

So far we have stressed the importance of sign language and hinted at the inadequacy of signed forms of dominant sound-based languages. In this section we concentrate on the example of Signed English. Two factors have guided the development of signed forms of English, and both reinforce the control of the Deaf via linguistic and cultural deprivation, through forms of "symbolic violence": first, the assumed superiority of English as a language for the transmission of knowledge; and second, the assumption that the Deaf need to be assimilated as much as possible into the hearing world via the use of the majority language. The development of signed forms of English has not only devalued native sign languages, but it has sought to assimilate the Deaf into the majority language and majority culture as overtly deficient participants. The process is precisely that described by Bourdieu as the educational system "conceals" "by an apparently neutral attitude, the fact that it fills this function" (Bourdieu, 1977b, p. 488), namely, the transmission of power and privilege. The development of signed English has served to reinforce the linguistic deprivation of the Deaf, to represent their sensory differences as linguistic lack.

In the early 1960s, an American teacher, David Anthony, developed a manual system to represent English so that his deaf students could learn English more easily (Seeing Exact English [SEE1]). This encouraged other teachers to develop codes for the manual representations of English, resulting in different variations of manually coded English developing out of SEE1. In Australia, a committee set up in Victoria developed its own version in the 1970s, accumulating a vocabulary from a range of sources, including Auslan, SEE2, other native sign languages from different countries, and those developed by the committee—a "camel" indeed. The Deaf who had been asked to participate in the construction of the Australian version of Signed English in fact walked out of the committee. But the process continued regardless of the boycott by the Deaf, indicative of the conviction on the part of the teachers of the deaf of their authority not only over education, but over signing as a mode.

Certainly their action indicated clearly that Signed English belonged to the teachers of the deaf, not to the Deaf themselves. Each of these diverse forms of Signed English claims to be a manual attempt on the part of the majority, dominant group—the hearing—to understand the alternative, minority mode or sensibility. Both oralism and Signed English give only partial access to language. Their use denies access to the richness and complexities of language that are essential for effective cultural expression and participation and of course for even moderate educational success.

Although Signed English can never become an effective first language, this is not to deny its possible educational role as an aid in accessing English as a second language. In its ideal form, Signed English uses manual shapes to represent English words and thus allows for a signed representation of grammatical English. For the Deaf these signs are devoid of the phonemic level of meaning that is fundamental to the hearing person's reading of the written word or perception of the signed English word. They are shapes devoid of expression.[7] Sign languages, in contrast, exploit space and facial expression to develop a range of grammatical techniques peculiar to sign languages that create an expressive language with as much creative potential as any spoken language, the sort of medium required by children in the early years of their intellectual development. For many of the Deaf, language development is thus completely restricted, and when they do get to school they are provided at best with Signed English, but usually with a combination of oralism and pidgin sign. Available studies of academic performance by the profoundly deaf and severely hearing impaired from international sources show that those students who have access to sign language as a fully fledged first language have higher literacy skills than those who have had no access to sign language, but for whom the language of the hearing community is being promoted as a first language—that is, those using Signed English or oralism.

Thus, although Signed English may give some understanding of the English language, it will always be limited and partial. Signed English, too, is

---

[7]It is worth noting here that the development of Signed English in the 1970s coincided with a stage of linguistic theory that laid emphasis on the role of syntax in language.

not a language of communication, but it is confined to contrived situations such as the classroom. It is not used within the Deaf community and thus has none of the natural dynamics of a natural language being designed and imposed from outside. Its use serves to reinforce the identification of the Deaf as "disabled" by ensuring their linguistic dependence on their teachers who become not only the experts in spoken and written language, but in the legitimate form of signed language as well. The disabling nature of the educational environment is of course reinforced by the fact that Signed English is not a language at all, but an artificially derived code, a visual system superimposed on a language that is dependent on sound. Often individual teachers of the Deaf follow their own mixture of systems and speak at the same time as they sign, a system quite erroneously labeled by the hearing world as *total communication*. In fact, research from America and Denmark has shown that in some cases the signed portion of the so-called "total communication" process is unintelligible (Hansen, 1989; Johnson & Erting, 1990; Strong & Chaarlson, 1987). It should also be noted that Signed English is based on the grammar of written English not spoken English, creating particular confusion when combined with lip reading.

PROFESSIONALISM AS SYMBOLIC VIOLENCE

The Deaf in and through their diagnosis as "disabled" become inevitably involved with a range of professionals, concentrated particularly in the educational sphere, who control their every move. The professionals are hearing, English speaking, and status conscious, protective of their professionalism and scornful of any suggestion that their expertise might be ill founded. Convinced that their charges must be reoriented toward "normality," they concentrate on promoting hearing of and speech in the dominant language. Coclear implants, hearing aids, speech therapy, and the educational promotion of oralism and occasionally Signed English are all oriented to such ends and place the professionals in a position of control. The teachers of the Deaf unconsciously accumulate symbolic capital as they assert their symbolic power over the Deaf via their control of language, both as oralism and as Signed English. Convinced themselves that native sign languages are not a viable alternative, they imbue their pupils with a need, indeed a desire, to satisfy the linguistic goals they as teachers set, disciplining their pupils to accept and reproduce their marginal linguistic and cultural status.

Particularly destructive is the way their therapy constructs their pupils as culturally incompetent in the eyes of the hearing community. Those mouth movements and sounds promoted through speech therapy are oriented primarily toward the production of speech sounds that are above all recognizable rather than culturally acceptable. The orientation is acultural, for the Deaf are not deemed to be normal members of the society. But this very treatment of them as marginal reinforces their marginality in cultural terms through the bodily hexis they project, positively orienting them not only toward a kind of language competence that constructs them as a cultural underclass, but toward the production of sounds and mouth movements that reinforce that cultural evaluation by others.

The recognition of native sign languages threatens these modes of symbolic control. To acknowledge the *bona fides* of such languages is to acknowledge that the lack of speech is not synonymous with communicative breakdown. To go a step further and acknowledge their educational potential is to undermine the expertise of the hearing teacher of the Deaf and to imply that Deaf teachers have at least as equal a place in the education of the Deaf as current professionals.

THE AUSTRALIAN VERSION: SIGN LANGUAGE AND EDUCATION IN AUSTRALIA

Sign language came to Australia with the first migrant settlers. The varieties of British and Irish sign language brought by these early English and Irish settlers developed into a distinct language with its own distinctive lexical and grammatical features—the language that today we call Auslan. In this sense it is as much an Australian language (albeit a minority one) as is English and are the Aboriginal languages, a language unique to Australia. Like "ethnic languages," it is also a community language playing a vital role in the transmission of both Deaf and hearing cultures and in providing members of that community with a social and emotional identity.

The Deaf in Australia are a fluid population. Because only a small minority are from Deaf families, the Deaf as a whole have little sense of inherited tradition, unlike Aboriginal Australians or other minority ethnic groups. They have no territorial focus, their traditions growing from shared experiences in schools, clubs, from much treasured interaction with Deaf families, and most importantly from the discovery of sign language with its immediate and total accessibility. For many, this access comes in early adulthood, their early years spent in a struggle to be oral, to please the parents, teachers, and therapists to produce the sounds they could not hear; to decipher the noises or often faint vibrations that for some came through their hearing aids; to communicate through a language to which they had inadequate access and to which they used in ways that reinforced their disabled status in the hearing world, their voices strange, their misunderstandings rife.

The history of the education of the Deaf in Australia mirrors in many ways the processes at work in Britain, although with idiosyncratic twists and turns along the way. Formal education of the Deaf began in two schools in 1860, the first in Sydney and the second in Melbourne, both established by Deaf men who had migrated from Britain and who had been educated in British schools for the deaf (Crickmore, 1990). Although a fairly strong oral tradition was established from the start, there was, in these secular schools, no antagonism to the use of sign or, more correctly, finger spelling. The more intense and exclusive oralism was first expressed in the schools established by the Catholic church. Later, in the post-Second World War era, the establishment of more oral schools was stimulated by parental demand following the rubella epidemic of the 1940s and legitimized by the visit of the archoralists from Manchester—the Ewings—in the 1950s. In 1953 at the Fifth Triennial Conference of the Australian Association of Teachers of the Deaf at Darlington in Sydney, it was formally resolved that henceforth all education of the Deaf in Australia would be oral and that sign language was not to be used as a medium of instruction, that "finger spelling and gestures" were "outmoded." By the mid-1950s, the pressure for pure oralism was as strong as anywhere in the world and those who were judged incapable of benefiting from oralism were essentially treated as outcasts and as capable of only basic education. They were segregated so as not to pollute those working in the oral tradition, and they were eventually taught together with students with "multiple handicaps." At the Victorian School for Deaf Children in Melbourne, the children were until fairly recently segregated at the kindergarten level on the basis of their family background, with the children of Deaf parents who came from signing households kept apart from the children of hearing and deaf parents who came from nonsigning households. It was feared that the signers would teach the other children to sign and retard their educational potential, with all such potential assumed to be entirely oral:

> Oh Ewing, Oh Van Uden,[8] what a marvellous choice you gave us deaf children! To see ourselves as stupid rather than to be able to see ourselves as deaf and accept it, and to work from there. I hope it gave you a sense of real achievement! (Ladd, 1991, p. 93)

THE PURSUIT OF SOCIAL JUSTICE IN, THROUGH, AND BEYOND EDUCATION

If native sign languages are the only viable first languages for the Deaf, what implications does this have for educational policy, particularly in relation to the integration of the Deaf into mainstream schooling? To understand the symbolic violence that permeated the apparently egalitarian process of "mainstreaming," to what in Britain and Australia is referred to as "integration," we turn briefly to the discourse on integration.[9]

---

[8]Dutch educationalist who promoted oralism.
[9]We have dealt with the theory and practice of integration in detail elsewhere (Branson & Miller, 1989, 1991a; Branson, Miller, & Branson, 1988; Branson, Miller, & McLeod, 1989).

MAINSTREAMING AS A DISCRIMINATORY PRACTICE

Published in 1984, the Ministerial Review of Educational Services for the Disabled, titled Integration in Victorian Education (Ministerial Review, 1984), laid the foundations for the enactment of policy and thereby of a program to enable all children to realize their right (but not an obligation) to be educated in a regular school. The Victorian Government stated its "commitment to provide necessary resources and . . . [its] concern with enrolling and supporting in regular schools children who were formerly segregated, or at risk of being segregated from them" (Ministerial Review, 1984, p. 7) with a democratic model (Fulcher, 1986) that aimed at the equalization of the relationship between parents and service providers and that focused on the educational system or structure rather than on the child's named impairment.

In its move away from the professional assessment of disabilities as qualities of the individual to be understood in terms of established syndromes and treated individually, the Review recognized that schools were often "disabling structures" generating and/or exacerbating disabilities and thus producing handicaps. It proposed the establishment of procedures and structures aimed at "changing the nature of the educational environment (especially that of the regular school) in order to reduce the educationally handicapping consequences which may otherwise follow from certain impairments or disabilities" (Ministerial Review, 1984, p. 8). It asked that explanations for failure be sought not in the child but in "aspects of the education system" (Ministerial Review, 1984, p. 9), and that these be rectified not via an orientation toward the "special educational needs" of the child, because "this belongs to a deficit model," but rather via the provision of "additional educational requirements." The onus was thus placed on the education system to "reduc[e] the handicap which may follow from an impairment or disability" (Ministerial Review, 1984, p. 11). Committees were established and Ministerial Memoranda circulated to regions, principals, and school councils.

Our research into the practice of mainstreaming showed that what resulted was a discriminatory practice far removed from the ideals outlined earlier (Branson et al., 1989). Given that the schooling system already discriminates against a wide range of groups in cultural terms, expecting existing students in all their diversity to mold to the narrow culturally biased demands of schooling, it is hardly surprising that there is no inclination to adapt the school and the curriculum to the diverse and formerly hidden potentialities of these new integration students. Just as Aboriginal Australians and non-Anglo-Saxon migrants were expected to "assimilate," to change to fit existing Anglo-Saxon cultural expectations, so too are the formerly segregated "disabled" to be transformed as much as possible to fit into the school. Few teachers regard total assimilation as possible, but they assume that specialist services will be required on a continuous basis to compensate for assumed "deficiencies." The "disabled," like Aboriginal Australians, remain marginalized by and beyond the dominant culture, effectively segregated within the regular classroom as "other" or as "integration students."

Integration, or *mainstreaming*, is therefore on the whole a discriminatory practice. Its orientation toward the normalization of the formerly segregated demands their assimilation into the educational and cultural environment, demanding of them as much as of the other students "that they have what it does not give . . . linguistic and cultural competence" (Bourdieu, 1977b, p. 494), and to this must be added the even more hidden assumption that they adapt physically to an environment that empowers only hearing bodies. In the case of the Deaf, the demand is that they have a linguistic competence in the dominant language that is unachievable, a demand that is an implicit assertion of their physical "abnormality."

The failure of mainstreaming for the Deaf derives from the fact that they are mainstreamed in terms of a medical model of deafness. Despite the overt opposition to the use of clinically based assessments and thus to the use of medical models of "disability," even the most radical integrationists continue to define deafness as a pathology, as a deficit, rather than as a cultural difference based on a linguistic difference. Given the overriding ideals of the mainstreaming movement, the mainstreaming of the Deaf is a blatant contradiction:

> My experience of mainstreaming in England . . . leads me to believe that it is the most dangerous move yet against the early development of a deaf person's character, self-confidence and basic sense of identity. Forceful clumsy attempts to mainstream not only deny facts about being deaf but destroy much that deaf people and their friends have worked so hard to create, and may in the last resort be seen as genocidal. (Ladd, 1991, p. 88)

Research into the impact of different linguistic environments on the education of the Deaf conclusively shows that the acquisition of sign language as a first language by deaf children, whether they be from Deaf or hearing families, is basic to the effective acquisition of a second language and to educational success (Branson & Miller, 1991b). What cannot and must not be avoided given these research findings is that at least partial segregation of the Deaf in educational settings is essential if they are to begin to achieve their educational potential. The bilingual mode of education requires or demands such segregation, irrespective of whether it offends the latest ideological sensibilities of those dependent on ideological rather than actual orthodoxy—the politicians. The segregation required is of course radically different from the "remedial" and "special educational" practice still associated with the segregation of the Deaf. The denial of segregation is in fact a denial of social justice.

The use of native sign language as a medium of instruction for Deaf people around the world is slowly developing, based on a substantial amount of theoretical and empirical evidence. It is on the basis of this research and theory that bilingual programs are being established unlike the move into oralism that could never claim such support (Ewoldt, 1979), but rested instead on an ideological commitment to speech and hearing as "normal" and deafness as pathological. This research is also supported by many of the Deaf themselves as they reflect on their own linguistic progress (Ladd, 1991; Mason, 1991; Taylor & Bishop, 1991). Many a hearing parent too has discovered the relief of complete communication with deaf children through sign language after struggles with oralism (Fletcher, 1991; Robinson, 1991).

AGAINST MAINSTREAMING: A BILINGUAL/BICULTURAL SEGREGATED SYSTEM OF EDUCATION[10]

What then of the shape of Deaf education? Many Deaf (see, for example, Ladd, 1991) argue for a segregated education through sign language, combining forms of segregation and bilingualism, a bilingual segregated system very different from the sort of segregation that currently exists in many countries around the world, for example, Australia and Britain. For what the Deaf seek is not only the provision of native sign language as a language of instruction, but a meaningful cultural environment, an environment that empowers them through their abilities. The provision of interpreters into either manually coded forms of the dominant language or native sign language therefore does not serve to counteract the discriminatory processes at work in an integrated setting, for the student remains marginal to the linguistic and cultural environment of the classroom and school. The signing Deaf school envisaged harks back not only to a place where the Deaf were educated, but to a place where Deaf children from hearing families have learned their language, accessed Deaf culture, met the full range of Deaf people, and oriented themselves toward the society at large, forging their links within the complex networks that are the Deaf community.

In the environment of fervent mainstreaming in Australia, the Victorian School for Deaf Children has, for example, become a repository for those judged "profoundly deaf," who cannot cope with integration, and "multiply disabled," who are constantly devalued educationally, reinforcing the cultural constitution of the Deaf as physically pathological. Segregation is currently a negative concept, associated with not coping, with not being "normal." Within this context, the segregation of the profoundly deaf is thus indicative of the devaluation of their abilities, their language, and their potential. The educational potential of the segregated school for the Deaf lies in its *transformation* through the provision of a comprehensive primary and secondary curriculum to provide the sort of education for the Deaf that all-girls schools provide for girls.[11] Just

---

[10]For more complete coverage of the issues and literature summarized in this section, see Bouvet, 1990; Branson, 1991a, 1991b; Cummins, 1984; Israelite, Ewoldt, et al., 1989; Lucas, 1989; Rodda & Grove, 1987.

[11]Research here and elsewhere has shown clearly that girls educated in single sex environments perform better on the whole than those in co-educational settings (see Branson, 1988; Branson & Miller, 1979; Yates, 1987a, 1987b).

as the all-girls school, transformed from a discriminatory curriculum based on preconceived notions of the "normal" girl to providing a comprehensive curriculum, is an environment in which girls can achieve without being put down by the male society, without being constantly confronted by a male competitive presence—handicapped, "disabled" by male values—so too do the Deaf need an environment in which they are not subjected to the symbolic violence of a hearing culture. They need an environment in which they are not "disabled"; in which they are not driven to struggle to be like hearing people; in which they can relax into their deafness, communicate effectively via a medium through which they understand everything, not just snippets plucked from a distorted electronic stream of sound, and in which they can feel whole, free to explore additional communicative strategies on their terms.

Because access to and competence in a first language is vital for effective access to and competence in a second language and to education in general, and because access to the appropriate native sign language as a first language is only available to a minority of the deaf through the family, that is, through Deaf parents, first language acquisition must be provided through the education system. A coherent and effective educational system for the Deaf, whether from Deaf or hearing families, must employ a language inclusive curriculum policy involving the provision of a bilingual/bicultural system of education. A bilingual education is one that involves the use of two languages as the media of instruction and provides both subject matter and language-learning experience in both languages (Rado, 1989). Until recently it was erroneously thought that children who learned to speak two languages when they were young would never learn to speak or use either of them properly, what Cummins and Swain (1986) called the "linguistic mismatch hypothesis."

No matter where it occurs, a bilingual/bicultural education for the Deaf requires that the native sign language be made available as a first language for all deaf children from birth, given that partial access to the dominant language through oralism results in severe educational disadvantage and that signed forms of the dominant language cannot function effectively as a first language because they are not true languages. Native sign language gained as a first language enables Deaf children to start school with the same linguistic skills as hearing children, whose first language is not the dominant language. This is the case in Sweden and Denmark in which professional instruction in Swedish and Danish sign language respectively is provided for all parents of deaf children as soon as deafness has been diagnosed, so that a coherent linguistic environment is available to the child from the start of her or his linguistic development.

SUMMARY AND CONCLUSIONS

The issues of mainstreaming on the one hand and the language of instruction on the other are therefore intertwined. Mainstreaming involves the attempted assimilation of minority groups into the linguistic and cultural environment of the mainstream educational system. Mainstreaming seeks to establish homogeneity through assimilation. Such a process of assimilation via mainstreaming therefore involves a monolingual schooling system that assumes, implicitly or explicitly, that language immersion in the dominant language will generate linguistic competence. Such assumptions fly in the face of research findings that consistently demonstrate, as indicated earlier, that the development of linguistic competence in the dominant language by those whose first language is a minority language demands a bilingual environment (see Cummins, 1984; Luetke-Stahlman, 1983). In the case of the Deaf, for whom access to the dominant language can never be as complete as for other minority language students, the inappropriateness of the discourse on mainstreaming is particularly marked.

Many countries aspire to the sort of social justice and educational innovation found in countries such as Sweden, challenged only by its neighbour Denmark in terms of legislation and practice, in which regulations were passed by parliament in 1981 guaranteeing the right of all Deaf to be educated with native sign language as their first language and as the medium for acquisition of the national spoken and written language, Swedish. So Ahlgren wrote in 1990:

> In Swedish schools for the deaf, Swedish Sign Language is officially the language of instruction in all subjects *including Swedish*. According to the official curriculum Swedish Sign Language is regarded the first language for the deaf pupils and written Swedish is their secondary language. . . . The real picture of teaching in the deaf-schools is, however, not as bright as in the curriculum. We are in fact in the middle of a process where *the majority* of the teachers has come to accept Swedish Sign Language as a true language and therefore beneficial to the students but where this same majority still has a long way to go before they know sign language well enough to be sufficiently good teachers. (p. 9; emphasis added)

The gap between policy and practice remains, and even if it is narrowing after nearly a decade under progressive legislation, the struggle for the recognition of a native sign language, even among teachers of the Deaf, is still far from won. An air of threatening symbolic violence still permeates the relationships between the hearing and the Deaf.

What we have been concerned with showing here is that the barriers—cultural, educational, and political—placed in the way of the Deaf are often subtle, placed there subconsciously as people operate in terms that are assumed governed by rationality or common sense, not by prejudice. This, above all, is the awareness that Bourdieu's theory of cultural practice promotes. As people operate as strategic and creative agents of society's myriad processes, structured by and structuring their orientations toward themselves and others, they do so in terms inherited from the past and transformed in the present, classifying the world around them in terms taken for granted, assumed to be "common sense."

They do not see the symbolic violence that their evaluations of language, behavior, and appearance perpetrates on those judged marginal. They do not realize that it is they, those who conform to the desired behavioral, physical, and cultural standards of society, who are served by their dispositions towards others to marginalize and disable.

To condemn the use of Signed English, or its equivalent, in non-English speaking countries, as symbolic violence, as the exercising of symbolic power to maintain symbolic control, is therefore not to judge those who promote these signed forms of dominant sound languages as overt enemies of the Deaf, consciously restricting their access to society's economic, political, and cultural resources. They seek, within the framework of their own rationalities and dispositions toward others, to frame policies and promote practices that they assume are in the best interests of the Deaf. It is the lack of understanding of the way inequalities are formed and transformed in our societies and of the vital part that processes that generate linguistic and cultural deprivation play in the reproduction of inequalities that blinds them to the disabling nature of the environments in which they operate. So too it is with those who promote the integration of the so-called "disabled" into mainstream education, including the Deaf, who see the segregated environment as restricting access to educational resources. Their arguments appeal to a common sense governed by ideological commitment to egalitarianism, individualism, liberty, and social justice and to dispositions toward "normality." Thus, hearing parents seize on integration and oralism as the way through to acceptability for their deaf child, and for themselves. The assumption of their own "normality" and respectability by the hearing establishment has been shown to be interpreted by the hearing as bestowing on them a right, even a duty, not only to make the Deaf "as normal as possible," but the right to control the Deaf, a control that must be exercised through normal means, that is, via oral communication where even marginally possible and via signed forms of the dominant sound language where necessary.

To acknowledge native sign languages as not only "normal communication," but as equivalent languages involves not only challenging the established assumption that linguistic competence is sound based, but potentially handing over control of the Deaf to the experts in Sign Language, the native signers, the Deaf. This would not only challenge the professionalism or the status of "experts," of myriad doctors, scientists, technicians, and specialist teachers, but it would destroy the very basis upon which education through oralism and signed forms of dominant sound languages rest. For the education of the deaf remains in many countries as the last bastion of the medical model in education. They are segregated and integrated, and, of course, educated on the basis of medically diagnosed or constructed pathology. Their education remains therapeutic in orientation. Their difference is treated as a medically diagnosed deficit, not as a linguistic and cultural difference associated with heightened visual sensory development. The symbolic violence of mainstreaming is thus particularly acute for the Deaf, their mainstreaming a measure of society's ignorance of the processes at work beneath its surface, of the subtleties of the political processes through which inequalities and associated injustices are reproduced.

If Bourdieu and Passeron's analysis of Western educational systems revealed the hollowness of the rhetoric of equality of opportunity, revealing a hidden agenda, the reproduction of structured inequalities in terms of class, the power of the establishment in its most effective form a symbolic power exercised through symbolic violence, such an analysis becomes even more devastating when applied to the hidden agenda shaping the education of the Deaf. The ideological denial of the structural importance of cultural difference serves to reproduce those differences as inequalities based on cultural and linguistic deprivation.

And so we return to the beginning. This linguistic and cultural deprivation must be recognized as essentially physical. Assimilation involves assimilation not into a neutral world of objectively achievable ends, but assimilation into a world thoroughly biased, in material and not simply conceptual terms, toward the physicality of a hearing world. This is a world of sound, a world that is linguistically, culturally, politically, economically, spiritually, and educationally framed in hearing terms. Assimilation thus makes not only unreasonable demands of the Deaf in "knowledge" terms but impossible physical demands. Language is physical. Cultural conditions of existence are fundamentally material conditions of existence-sensed worlds. What the material on the education of the Deaf reveals even more starkly than that on sexism is that the transformation of conditions of existence, including educational conditions of existence, in the direction of something like equality of opportunity demands much more than mental reconditioning. What is required is the recognition of different physical realities, differently sensed worlds, different rhythms, linked to but not subsumed by, different mental imagery, different views of the world. What is required is the celebration of difference (see Branson & Miller, 1993). And the celebration of difference must above all be part of the educational experience, not only be an idea conveyed in the abstract—something to understand, believe in, or agree with—but part of the material conditions of existence of education, via the transformation of the very shape and rhythm of the school.

11

Discursive Power in Educational Policy and Practice for Culturally Diverse Students

Jim Cummins
Ontario Institute for Studies in Education

Cross-cultural contact has escalated during the past 30 years both within and between nation states as a result of greater international mobility, the increasing interdependence of the global economy, and refugee resettlement necessitated by conflicts in many parts of the globe. The concrete manifestation of this process of population mobility is evident in the schools of many Western societies. For example, so-called "minority" students (primarily those from African-American, Asian, and Latino/ Latina backgrounds) have become the "majority" in California schools since the early 1990s; students from language backgrounds other than English are projected to reach 70% of the school population in the Toronto Board of Education by the year 2000, and similar patterns of diversity are evident in other Canadian urban school systems (Cummins & Danesi, 1990); on the other side of the Atlantic, about 10% of the European Community school-age population currently comes from families that have a language and/or cultural background different than that of the majority of the country in which they live (Reid & Reich, 1992, p. 231).

Immigration policies are obviously designed to serve the interests of the receiving country and in most cases have been motivated by the twin phenomena of falling birthrates and increasing longevity in Western countries. Increases in immigration have resulted from the fear of economic difficulties

191

arising from the combination of fewer young people entering the workforce and an older population making greater demands on social services. Despite the assumed economic benefits of immigration, however, the increasing cultural and linguistic diversity has not been welcomed by many in the receiving countries. Economic recession has contributed to a rise in intercultural tension on both sides of the Atlantic.

This intercultural tension is evident in schools as well as other societal institutions. In most countries educational professionals are representative of the dominant societal group and yet their clients, the students, and communities increasingly are drawn from culturally diverse backgrounds. The adaptations required to adjust to this new situation are resented and resisted by many educators. At the same time, education systems have come under increasing scrutiny in many countries as a result of concerns that students are not being prepared adequately for the economic realities of the 21st century workplace, in which knowledge and intellectual resources will be key to survival and growth. Educational restructuring to realign policies and programs with changing economic and technological realities is clearly rendered more challenging by the rapid increase in cultural and linguistic diversity in schools.

In their efforts to redefine the goals and methods of education, educators have been buffeted by competing and conflicting discourses blown in by the winds of changing political fashion. United States educators, for example, prioritized "equity" in policies and programs initiated during the late 1960s and 1970s, but by 1983, the prevailing discourse had shifted from "equity" to "excellence." The push to educational reform in the Reagan/Bush era was fuelled by the presumed relationship between educational standards and economic competitiveness. As expressed by the report of the National Commission on Excellence in Education (1983), A Nation at Risk: "Our once unchallenged preeminence in commerce, industry, science and technological innovations is being overtaken by competitors throughout the world" (p. 1). There currently appears to be an emerging pragmatic recognition at a federal level that equity and excellence cannot be isolated from each other because, in most of the large urban school districts, students from culturally diverse backgrounds constitute the mainstream, and thus in an important sense equity is a prerequisite for excellence.

The discourse of equity was effective during the 1960s and 1970s in generating considerable funds for programs and research aimed at improving the academic performance of culturally diverse students. However, this financial commitment did not alter in any significant way the educational structures within which culturally diverse students were schooled nor the ways in which educators defined their roles in relation to students and communities. These structures and role definitions still predominantly reflect the relations of power within the society as a whole.

I argue in this chapter that the lack of progress toward equity-of-achievement outcomes for culturally diverse students in the United States (and other Western societies) is a consequence of the maintenance of coercive relations of power in the society and schools. I analyze the discursive means by which this power structure is maintained in the context of a framework for analyzing causes of minority students' academic difficulties and for planning interventions to reverse these difficulties. A fundamental assumption of the framework is that, to be effective, these interventions must challenge manifestations of coercive relations of power in the school system, and by extension, the society. My concern is particularly the debate in regard to bilingual education for language minority students in the United States, but related patterns of discursive power can be discerned in other contexts.

A distinction between coercive and collaborative relations of power is introduced in the following section, after which a framework for analyzing power relations in educational interactions is presented.

COERCIVE AND COLLABORATIVE RELATIONS OF POWER

The distinction between coercive and collaborative relations of power (Cummins, 1994) is similar to that introduced by Shakeshaft and Perry in Chapter 2 between "power over" and "power with" others. Coercive relations of power refer to the exercise of power by a dominant group (or individual or country) to the detriment of a subordinated group (or individual or country). The assumption is that there is a fixed quantity of power that operates according to a balance effect; in other words, the more power one group has the less is left for other groups. Coercive relations of power are reflected in and shaped by discursive practices (Corson, 1993b) and usually involve a definitional process that legitimates the inferior or deviant status accorded to the subordinated group (or individual or country). In other words, the dominant group defines the subordinated group as inferior (or evil), thereby automatically defining itself as superior (or virtuous).

The experiences of First Nations students in Canadian residential schools clearly illustrates how coercive relations of power have operated historically in educational settings. For more than 100 years, educators in these schools defined their roles as bearers of salvation, civilization, and education to students who necessarily had to be defined as lacking all of these qualities. In other words, the self-definition of educators required that students and their communities be defined as heathen, savage, and without any valid form of cultural transmission (education). This devaluation of identity was communicated to students in all of the interactions they experienced in schools, ranging from brutal punishment if they were caught speaking their languages to widespread sexual abuse of both boys and girls. The process of defining groups or individuals as inferior almost inevitably results in a pattern of interactions that confines them, either psychologically or physically (e.g., in special education classes as children or jails as adults).

The experience of First Nations students in residential schools is not entirely surprising because the interactions between individual educators and students (henceforth, termed *microinteractions*) were merely reflecting the pattern of interactions between dominant and subordinated groups in the wider society (henceforth, *macrointeractions*), in which First Nations communities were widely disparaged. In both micro- and macrointeractions, the process of identity negotiation reflected the relations of power in the society.

This process of identity negotiation is interwoven into all educator-student interactions and is usually nonproblematic when there is a cultural and class match between educator and student, but is often highly problematic when there is a cultural and class mismatch (see, for example, Fordham, 1990). In these cases, coercive relations of power will operate to define the subordinated group in ways that purport to explain its poor academic performance (e.g., attributing the school failure of bilingual children to cognitive confusion caused by two languages).

This perspective clearly implies that in situations in which coercive relations of power between dominant and subordinated groups predominate, the creation of interpersonal spaces in which students' identities are validated will entail a direct challenge by educators to the societal power structure. For example, to acknowledge that students' religion, culture, and language are valid forms of self-expression and to encourage the development of these cultural forms is to challenge the prevailing attitudes in the wider society and the coercive structures that reflect these attitudes.

Collaborative relations of power, on the other hand, operate on the assumption that power is not a fixed, predetermined quantity, but rather can be *generated* in interpersonal and intergroup relations. In other words, participants in the relationship are *empowered* through their collaboration such that each is more affirmed in her or his identity and has a greater sense of efficacy to create change in his or her life or social situation. Thus, power is created in the relationship and shared among participants.

In educational contexts, the empowerment that results from collaborative relations of power has been documented in the outcomes of cooperative learning activities (Kagan, 1986) and in the global sister-class networks described by Sayers (1991). Reciprocal empowerment is also evident in the family literacy projects documented by Ada (1988), McCaleb (1994), and Tizard, Schofield, and Hewison (1982). A central characteristic of these projects is that they challenge assumptions and definitions of culturally diverse students and communities that have operated to reinforce coercive relations of power (e.g., assumptions that certain groups of minority parents do not care about their children's education).

The framework outlined later argues that students whose schooling experiences reflect collaborative relations of power develop the ability, confidence, and motivation to succeed academically. They participate competently in instruction as a result of having developed a confident cultural identity as well as appropriate school-based knowledge and interactional structures. Students who are disempowered or "disabled" by their school experiences do not develop this type of cognitive/academic and social/emotional foundation.

A FRAMEWORK FOR ANALYZING SCHOOL FAILURE

The framework presented in Figure 11.1 proposes that the causes of under-achievement are rooted in the continuation of historical patterns of coercive relations of power between dominant and subordinated groups. These relations of power find expression in educational structures that limit students' possibili-

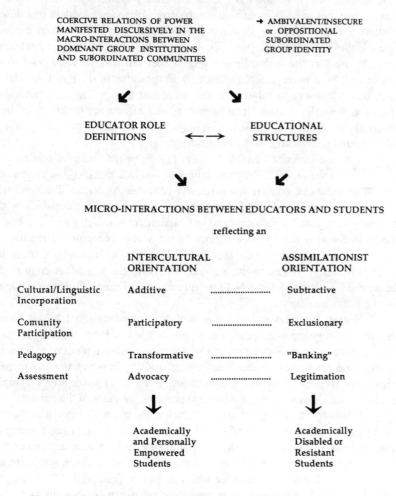

Figure 11.1. Intervention for collaborative empowerment

ties for learning and for developing a strong sense of cultural identity. They also find expression in the ways educators define their roles in relation to culturally diverse students and communities. Both the educational structures and educator role definitions affect the interactions that minority students experience in the school system. Reversal of educational failure requires that the interactions that occur in school between educators and students be empowering for both; in other words, power must be generated in these interactions for both educators and students.

Societal Macrointeractions

When patterns of school success and failure among culturally diverse students are examined within an international perspective, it becomes evident that power and status relations between dominant and subordinated groups exert a major influence. Several theorists (e.g., Cummins, 1989; Ogbu, 1978, 1992) have pointed to the fact that subordinated groups that fail academically tend to be characterized by a sense of ambivalence about the value of their cultural identity and powerlessness in relation to the dominant group. This is what Ogbu refers to as "castelike" status, and its educational effects are strikingly evident in many situations in which formerly subjugated or colonized groups are still in a subordinated relationship to the dominant group.

The phenomenon of what Blauner (1969) called "internal colonies" is exemplified by the fact that the three groups in the U.S. context that experience the most pronounced educational difficulty (African-American, Latino/Latina and Native American students) have each been subordinated for centuries by the dominant group. Similar patterns exist in Scandinavia in which Finnish minority students in Sweden are reported to experience severe academic difficulties, a phenomenon not unrelated to the fact that Finland was colonized by Sweden for several hundred years (Skutnabb-Kangas, 1984). In the Canadian context the academic difficulties of First Nations students and Franco-Ontarian students illustrate a similar pattern.

Within the rules of the social mobility (or educational achievement) game, dominant group institutions and representatives of those institutions (e.g., teachers) require that subordinated groups deny their cultural identity as a necessary condition for success in the "mainstream" society, in which the gatekeepers are invariably representatives of the dominant group or, at lower levels, compliant subordinated group members who have accepted the rules of the game.

Currently in Western democratic states, the overt violence that characterized patterns of societal macrointeractions until quite recently has given way to predominantly discursive means of establishing and maintaining power and status relations. I am using the term *discourse* to refer to the ways in which meaning is mobilized to exercise or maintain power (Foucault, 1980; Knight, Smith, & Sachs, 1990). Discourses constitute what can be thought and what counts as truth or knowledge. Internalized discourses constitute cognitive schemata that allow for certain propositions to be processed in a highly automatized way and accepted as valid, whereas propositions that are inconsistent with the internalized discourse are automatically rejected.

In discussing the historical and current organization of education for culturally diverse students in the present framework, I attempt to highlight the discursive processes that have been used in the attempt to "manufacture consent" (Chomsky, 1987) on both sides of the issues.

Educational Structures

As sketched in Figure 11.1, societal macrointeractions give rise to particular forms of educational structures that are designed to reproduce the relations of power in the broader society. Educational structures refer to the organization of schooling in a broad sense that includes policies, programs, curriculum, and assessment. This organization is established to achieve the goals of education as defined by the dominant group in the society. For example, the historical patterns of educational apartheid in the United States, Canada, South Africa, and many other countries were designed to limit the opportunities that subordinated groups might have for educational and social advancement. As documented by Kozol (1991) for African-American students and by Berman, Chambers, Gadaura, et al. (1992) for recent immigrants in California, similar patterns of segregation still characterize the education of many subordinated groups (see Reid & Reich, 1992, and Skutnabb-Kangas, 1984, for a discussion of similar phenomena in the European context).

Examples of educational structures that reflect coercive relations of power are:

- English-only submersion programs for bilingual students that actively suppress students' first language (L1) and cultural identity
- Exclusion of culturally diverse parents from participation in their children's schooling
- Tracking practices that place subordinated group students disproportionately in lower level tracks
- Use of culturally and linguistically biased standardized tests for both achievement monitoring and special education placement
- Curriculum content reflecting dominant group notions of "cultural literacy" (Hirsch, 1987).

These educational structures constitute a frame that sets limits on the kinds of interactions that are likely to occur between educators and students. As one illustration of the impact of these structures, Oakes (1985) has shown that tracking results in major differences in the quality of instruction that students receive; those in lower tracks receive instruction that is less challenging and motivating than those in higher tracks. She concludes that when schools are structured according to tracks, the academic progress of those in average and low groups is retarded. Tracking also lowers educational aspirations, fosters low self-esteem, and promotes dropping out.

Educator Role Definitions

Societal macrointeractions will also influence the ways in which educators define their roles in relation to culturally diverse students and communities; in other words, they influence the mindset of assumptions, expectations, and goals that educators bring to the task of educating students.

The notion of *educator role definitions* is proposed as a central explanatory construct mediating macro- and microinteractions in the present framework. An earlier version of the framework argued that culturally diverse students:

> are "empowered" or "disabled" as a direct result of their interactions with educators in the schools. These interactions are mediated by the implicit or explicit role definitions that educators assume in relation to four institutional characteristics of schools. These characteristics reflect the extent to which:
>
> 1. minority students' language and culture are incorporated into the school program;
>
> 2. minority community participation is encouraged as an integral component of children's education;
>
> 3. the pedagogy promotes intrinsic motivation on the part of students to use language actively in order to generate their own knowledge; and
>
> 4. professionals involved in assessment become advocates for minority students by focusing primarily on the ways in which students' academic difficulty is a function of interactions within the school context rather than legitimizing the location of the 'problem' within students. (Cummins, 1989, p. 58)

These four dimensions, namely, language/culture incorporation, community participation, pedagogy, and assessment, represent sets of educational structures that will affect, but can also be influenced by, educators' role definitions.

An assumption of the framework is that a major reason why most attempts at promoting equity of outcomes for culturally diverse students have been unsuccessful is that the relationships between teachers and students and between schools and communities have remained essentially unchanged. The required changes involve personal redefinitions of the way classroom teachers interact with the children and communities they serve. In other words, legislative and policy reforms may be necessary conditions for effective change, but they are not sufficient. Implementation of change is dependent on the extent to which educators, both collectively and individually, redefine their roles with respect to culturally diverse students and communities.

MICROINTERACTIONS AS REFLECTIONS OF COERCIVE OR COLLABORATIVE RELATIONS OF POWER

A central tenet of the framework is that the negotiation of identity in the microinteractions between educators and students is central to students' academic success or failure. These microinteractions form an interpersonal or an interactional space within which the acquisition of knowledge and formation of identity is negotiated.

In the past, dominant group institutions (e.g., schools) have required that subordinated groups deny their cultural identity as a necessary condition for success in the "mainstream" society. The historical pattern of dominant-subordinate group interactions has been one in which educators have constricted the interactional space in an attempt to sanitize deviant cultural identities. For educators to become partners in the transmission of knowledge, culturally diverse students were required to acquiesce in the subordination of their identities and to celebrate as "truth" the "cultural literacy" of the dominant group (e.g., the "truth" that Columbus "discovered" America). The constriction of the interactional space by educators reflected a process whereby they defined their role as "civilizing," "saving," "assimilating," or "educating" students whose culture and values they viewed as inherently deficient. Through these microinteractions they reproduced the pattern of societal macrointeractions and limited students' possibilities to define and interpret their own realities and identities. In short, the coercive power of the dominant group historically has been used to define the "other" as inferior, thereby justifying their confinement, either physically (e.g., slavery) or psychologically (e.g., through internalization of dominant group attributions resulting in ambivalence in regard to their identities).

It is important to note that students (and communities) do not passively accept dominant group attributions of their inferiority. Frequently, they actively resist this process of subordination through disruptive or oppositional behavior. Although for some students resistance may contribute to academic development (Skutnabb-Kangas, 1988; Zanger, 1994), in many situations resistance has severe costs with respect to academic success and upward mobility, often culminating in students prematurely dropping out of school (Ogbu, 1992; Willis, 1977). Other students may modify their cultural identity by "acting white" (Fordham, 1990) and by buying educational success at the expense of rejection by their peers and ambivalence about their identity. Still others are never given the opportunity in school to gain either academic confidence or pride in identity and, over time, internalize the negative attributions of the dominant group and live down to their teachers' expectations (Fordham, 1990; Willis, 1977).

What this implies is that the microinteractions between educators and students script an image of the envisaged relations of culture and power in the society. These microinteractions either reinforce or challenge particular educational structures within the school or school system and, by implication, the power structure in the wider society. Educational equity requires that educators define their roles and attempt to orchestrate the pattern of microinteractions in such a way that these interactions actively challenge manifestations of coercive relations of power in the school and by implication in the wider society. Empowerment of both students and educators is postulated as an outcome of this process.

For each of the four dimensions of school organization outlined in Figure 11.1, the role definitions of educators can be described in terms of a continuum with one end of the continuum promoting the empowerment of students and the other contributing to the disabling of students. In the sections that follow the dimensions are described and examples of the discourses that have been mobilized to support both assimilationist and intercultural orientations are outlined.

CULTURAL/LINGUISTIC INCORPORATION

Considerable research data suggest that for subordinated group students, the extent to which students' language and culture is incorporated into the school program constitutes a significant predictor of academic success (see, for example, Campos & Keatinge, 1988; Cummins, 1989; Ramirez, 1992). Students' school success appears to reflect both the more solid cognitive/academic foundation developed through intensive L1 instruction as well as the reinforcement of their cultural identity.

Educators' role definitions with respect to students' language and culture can be characterized along an "additive-subtractive" dimension. Educators who see their role as adding a second language and cultural affiliation to students' repertoire are more likely to create interactional conditions of empowerment than those who see their role as replacing or subtracting students' primary language and culture in the process of assimilating them to the dominant culture.

It should be noted that an additive orientation is not always dependent on actual teaching of the minority language. In many cases this may not be possible for a variety of reasons (e.g., low concentration of particular groups of minority students). However, educators communicate to students and parents in a variety of ways the extent to which students' language and culture is valued within the context of the school. Even within a monolingual school context, powerful messages can be communicated to students regarding the validity and advantages of first language development.

However, the extent to which educators are likely to communicate validating messages to students regarding their language and culture will be strongly affected by the patterns of discourse in the wider society. In this regard, in the U.S. context, the predominant message has been that cultural diversity represents a threat to national unity, and bilingualism constitutes an impediment to academic success. A recent example of the neoconservative discourse on bilingualism and bilingual education comes from Schlesinger (1991) in his book *The Disuniting of America*:

> In recent years the combination of the ethnicity cult with a flood of immigration from Spanish-speaking countries has given bilingualism new impetus. . . . Alas, bilingualism has not worked out as planned: rather the contrary. Testimony is mixed, but indications are that bilingual education retards rather than expedites the movement of Hispanic children into the English-speaking world and that it promotes segregation rather than it does integration. Bilingualism shuts doors. It nourishes self-ghettoization, and ghettoization nourishes racial antagonism. . . . Using some language other than English dooms people to second-class citizenship in American society. . . . Monolingual education opens doors to the larger world. Institutionalized bilingualism remains another source of the fragmentation of America, another threat to the dream of one "people." (pp. 108-109)

A variation on the theme of "bilingualism shuts doors" comes from Dunn (1987), who claims that Latino/Latina children and adults "speak inferior Spanish" and that "Latin pupils on the U.S. mainland, as a group, are inadequate bilinguals. They simply don't understand either English or Spanish well enough to function adequately in school" (p. 49).

It is interesting that in neither of these examples is reference made to any supportive research. By contrast, the discourse that affirms the value of bilingualism and bilingual education relies heavily on published research suggesting that bilingualism enhances aspects of cognitive functioning and that well-implemented bilingual education programs with sustained L1 instruction throughout elementary school result in better academic progress in English than programs with minimal or no L1 instruction (e.g., Cummins, 1993; Ramirez, 1992).

Despite the absence of research support, the negative rhetoric with regard to bilingualism broadcast by the media into every classroom in the nation creates a discursive context that legitimates the eradication of bilingual students' language and culture in school.

Claims that "bilingualism shuts doors" and "monolingual education opens doors to the wider world" are laughable if viewed in isolation, particularly in the context of current global interdependence. They become interpretable only in the context of a societal discourse that is profoundly disquieted by the fact that the sounds of the "other" have now become audible, and the hues of the American social landscape have darkened noticibly. There is anger that schools have apparently reneged on their traditional duty to render the "other" invisible and inaudible. Demographic projections of the growth of diversity, particularly the rapid increase in the Spanish-speaking population, generate tremors presaging dramatic shifts in the structure of power within the nation. The mobilization of discourse is intended to prevent this potential shift in the power structure.

COMMUNITY PARTICIPATION

Students from subordinated communities will be empowered in the school context to the extent that the communities themselves are empowered through their interactions with the school. When educators and parents develop partnerships to promote their children's education, parents appear to develop a sense of efficacy that communicates itself to children with positive academic consequences (e.g., Ada, 1988; McCaleb, 1994; Tizard et al., 1982).

The teacher role definitions associated with community participation can be characterized along a *collaborative-exclusionary* dimension. Teachers operating at the collaborative end of the continuum actively encourage parents to participate in promoting their children's academic progress, both in the home and through involvement in classroom activities. A collaborative orientation may require a willingness on the part of the teacher to work closely with classroom assistants or community volunteers in order to communicate effectively and in a noncondescending way with parents. Teachers with an exclusionary orientation, on the other hand, tend to regard teaching as *their* job and are likely to view collaboration with culturally diverse parents as either irrelevant or actually detrimental to children's progress. Clearly, initiatives for collaboration or for a shared decision-making process can come from the community as well as from the school. Under these conditions, maintenance of an exclusionary orientation by the school can lead communities to directly challenge the institutional power structure. This was the case with the school strike organized by Finnish parents and their children at the Bredby school in Rinkeby, Sweden. In response to a plan by the headmistress to reduce the amount of Finnish instruction, the Finnish community withdrew their children from the school. Eventually (after eight weeks) most of their demands were met. According to Skutnabb-Kangas (1988), the strike had the effect of generating a new sense of efficacy among the community and making them more aware of the role of dominant group-controlled (i.e., exclusionary) education in reproducing the powerless status of minority groups. A hypothesis that the present framework generates is that this renewed sense of efficacy will lead to higher levels of academic achievement among minority students in this type of situation.

The discourse on minority parent involvement represents a subset of the broader discourse on cultural diversity. Despite the fact that the term *parental involvement* lines the pages of the many manuals of school effectiveness that have been produced during the past 20 years, one can search in vain in most of this literature to find examples of genuine partnership between schools and parents from culturally diverse backgrounds. Because parents fail to show up to meetings designed to teach them "parenting skills" or other strategies for overcoming their children's "deficits," educators assume that they are just not interested in their children's education, and this clearly contributes to children's massive rates of educational failure. Dunn (1987), the author of the widely used Peabody Picture Vocabulary Test, explicitly blames Latino/Latina parents for their children's academic difficulties when he argues that "teachers are not miracle workers" (p. 65), and "Hispanic pupils and their parents have also failed the schools and society, because they have not been motivated and dedicated enough to make the system work for them" (p. 78). In short, Dunn shows no interest in factors within the school context that might act to silence Latino/Latina parents, opting instead for a discursive pattern that suggests that educators are powerless to reverse the debilitating effects of apathetic and incompetent parents.

A very different picture emerges from case studies in which genuine collaboration between educators and culturally diverse parents took place. Ada (1988) describes the outcomes of one such program in which she participated that involved a Mexican-American community in a rural area of California. The program focused on promoting family literacy in Spanish through the use of children's books. With Ada as the facilitator, parents and teachers met in the school library once a month throughout the school year to discuss children's books (loaned by the school) that they had read together and discussed as a family during the previous month. The sense of collaborative empowerment that was generated in these meetings is evident in the following quotations:

> Another mother said: "Ever since I know I have no need to feel ashamed of speaking Spanish I have become strong. Now I feel I can speak with the teachers about my children's education and I can tell them I want my children to know Spanish. I have gained courage . . ."
>
> One of the fathers said: "I have discovered that my children can write. And I bring another story [written by his child]. But I have also discovered something personal. I have discovered that by reading books one can find out many things. Since my children want me to read them the stories over and over again, I took them to the public library to look for more books. There I discovered books about our own culture. I borrowed them and I am reading, and now I am finding out things I never knew about our roots and what has happened to them and I have discovered that I can read in Spanish about the history of this country [the U.S.A.] and of other countries." (pp. 235-236)

In summary, a discourse of mutual respect between schools and culturally diverse communities is likely to promote forms of collaborative empowerment, whereas the neoconservative disparagement of culturally diverse communities is a manifestation of coercive relations of power.

PEDAGOGY

Several investigators have suggested that the learning difficulties of culturally diverse students are often pedagogically induced in that children designated "at risk" frequently receive intensive instruction that confines them to a passive role and induces a form of "learned helplessness" (see Cummins, 1984, for a review). Instruction that creates conditions of empowerment, on the other hand, will aim to liberate students from dependence on instruction in the sense of encouraging them to become active generators of their own knowledge.

Two major orientations can be distinguished with respect to pedagogy. These differ in the extent to which the teacher retains exclusive control over classroom interaction as opposed to sharing some of this control with students. The dominant instructional model in most western industrial societies has been termed a *banking* model (Freire, 1985; Freire & Macedo, 1987); this can be contrasted with a *transformative* model of pedagogy. The basic premise of the banking or transmission model is that the teacher's task is to impart knowledge or skills that he or she possesses to students who do not yet have these skills, that is, to deposit knowledge in the students' memory bank. This implies that the teacher initiates and controls the interaction, constantly orienting it toward the achievement of instructional objectives. The instructional content in this type of program derives primarily from the internal structure of the language or subject matter; consequently, it frequently involves a predominant focus on surface features of language or literacy (e.g., handwriting, spelling, decoding, etc.) and emphasizes correct recall of content taught. Content is frequently transmitted by means of highly structured drills and workbook exercises, although in many cases the drills are disguised in order to make them more attractive and motivating to students.

Much of the discourse generated by the Reagan/Bush educational reform movement in the United States is premised on the assumption that schools have deviated from traditional forms of instruction as a result of "progressive" child-centered ideas popular in the 1960s and early 1970s. The recommendations of *A Nation at Risk* and most subsequent reports have focused primarily on raising standards and graduation requirements, eliminating the "curriculum smorgasbord" of "soft" subjects in favor of a common core curriculum for all students and increasing the amount of time that students are expected to spend learning the core academic curriculum. The thrust is toward "getting tough" with students and teachers in order to increase the rigor in curriculum materials and instruction. The focus is on increasing the functional and cultural literacy of students in order to bolster business competitiveness in an era in which knowledge and information constitute primary economic resources.

Several investigators have suggested that the exclusive focus on functional literacy in this educational reform discourse incorporates a sociopolitical agenda designed to limit the development of critical literacy so that students remain unable to deconstruct disinformation and disinclined to challenge structures of control and social injustice (e.g., Freire & Macedo, 1987; Macedo, 1993). For example, the assumption that schools have abandoned traditional forms of instruction is not supported by the empirical data showing that instruction in schools has changed very little over the course of this century (e.g., Goodlad, 1984; Ramirez 1992; Sirotnik, 1983). The process of teaching and learning, according to Sirotnik's (1983; and Goodlad's, 1984) analysis of more than 1,000 elementary and secondary classrooms, "appears to be one of the most consistent and persistent phenomena known in the social and behavioral sciences . . . the 'modus operandi' of the typical classroom is still didactics, practice, and little else" (pp. 16-17). He noted that teacher lecturing or total class work on written assignments continue to emerge as the primary instructional patterns and suggests that "navigating back to the basics should be easy. We never left" (p. 26). Goodlad (1983, p. 106) similarly noted that in the classrooms he observed "traditional not progressive pedagogy dominated."

With respect to the education of culturally diverse students, the major problems with "banking" education and its consolidation in the discourse of educational reform, are:

- It reinforces the cultural ambivalence of subordinated group students by providing no opportunity for students to express and share their experience with peers and teachers; in other words, students are silenced or rendered "voiceless" in the classroom (Giroux, 1991; Walsh, 1991).
- It contravenes central principles of language and literacy acquisition in that it is impossible to learn language or develop literacy in the absence of ample opportunities for communicative interaction in both oral and written modes (Krashen, 1981, 1993; Wong Fillmore, 1991).

Encouragement by the teacher of active use of both written and oral language allows students' experience to be expressed and shared within the classroom context. This expression and sharing of experience has the effect of validating students' identity. By contrast, "banking" approaches usually employ textbooks that reflect the values and priorities of the dominant group, thereby effectively suppressing the experience of culturally diverse students.

By contrast, transformative approaches to pedagogy have three essential characteristics: first, they encourage two-way interaction and active written and oral language use by students; students' language proficiency is developed by providing ample opportunities for students to use language to pursue projects to which they are committed. It is important to note that this in no way implies that explicit instruction of some aspects of language or content is inappropriate. As Delpit (1988) points out, it is important for culturally diverse students to get access to "the rules of the game" or the "codes of power" with respect to how language is used in a wide variety of social contexts. Teachers must learn not only how to "help students to establish their own voices, but to coach those voices to produce notes that will be heard clearly in the larger society" (p. 296). Kalantzis, Cope, Noble, and Poynting (1990) similarly make the point that explicit teaching of "culturally powerful knowledge and culturally powerful ways of knowing" is central to the promotion of critical thinking in a diverse society undergoing rapid change (p. 246).

A second characteristic of transformative approaches is that they build on students' experience, thereby validating and amplifying students' cultural identity. In describing the "personal interpretive" phase of her literacy framework, Ada (1988) points out that this process helps develop students' self-esteem by showing that their experiences and feelings are valued by the teacher and classmates. It also helps students understand that "true learning occurs only when the information received is analyzed in the light of one's own experiences and emotions" (p. 104). An atmosphere of acceptance and trust in the classroom is a prerequisite for students (and teachers) to risk sharing their feelings, emotions, and experiences. It is clear how this process of sharing and critically reflecting on their own and other students' experiences opens up identity options for culturally diverse students. These identity options are typically suppressed within a "banking" approach to pedagogy, in which the interpretation of texts is nonnegotiable and reflective of the dominant group's notions of cultural literacy. The personal interpretive phase deepens students' comprehension of the text or issues being discussed by grounding the knowledge in the personal and collective narratives that make up students' histories. It also develops a genuine cultural literacy in that it integrates students' own experience with "mainstream" curricular content.

The third characteristic of a transformative pedagogy is that it promotes critical thinking about historical and current social realities. In her literacy framework, Ada (1988) terms this the critical phase. She emphasizes that school children of all ages can engage in critical thinking, although the analysis will always reflect children's experiences and level of maturity. Critical dialogue further extends students' comprehension of the text or issues by encouraging them to examine both the internal logical coherence of the information or propositions and their consistency with other knowledge or perspectives. When students pursue guided research and critical reflection, they are clearly engaged in a process of knowledge generation; however, they are equally engaged in a process of self-definition; as they gain the power to think through issues that affect their lives, they simultaneously gain the power to resist external definitions of who they are and to deconstruct the sociopolitical purposes of such external definitions.

Pedagogy that is interactive, experiential, and critical will frequently result in concrete projects designed to further promote comprehension of the issues or to discover what changes individuals can make to improve their lives or resolve the problem that has been presented (Ada's "action" phase). Suppose that students have been researching problems relating to environmental pollution (in the local newspaper or in periodicals such as National Geographic, etc.). After relating the issues to their own experience, critically analyzing causes and possible solutions, they might decide to write letters to congressional/parliamentary representatives, highlight the issue in their class/school newsletter in order to sensitize other students, write and circulate a petition in the neighborhood, write and perform a play that analyzes the issue, and so on. Once again, this action phase can be seen as extending the process of comprehension insofar as when we act to transform aspects of our social realities, we gain a deeper understanding of those realities. In short, a transformative pedagogy will aim to go beyond the sanitized curriculum that is still the norm in most schools. It will attempt to promote students' ability to analyze and understand the social realities of their own lives and of their communities. This inevitably means that educators must be willing to expose and challenge the ways in which dominant groups both historically and currently have maintained their power. Macedo (1993) clearly highlights the challenge of confronting coercive relations of power when he argues: "What we have in the United States is not a system to encourage independent thought and critical thinking. Our colonial literacy model is designed to domesticate so as to enable 'the manufacture of consent'" (p. 204).

ASSESSMENT

Historically, assessment has played the role of legitimizing the instructional disabling of minority students. In some cases, assessment itself may play the primary role, but usually its role has been to locate the "problem" within the student, thereby screening from critical scrutiny the subtractive nature of the school program, the exclusionary orientation of teachers toward subordinated communities, and "banking" models of teaching that inhibit students from active participation in learning.

This process is virtually inevitable when the conceptual base for the assessment process is purely psychoeducational. If the psychologist's task (or role definition) is to discover the causes of a minority student's academic difficulties, and the only tools at his or her disposal are psychological tests (in either L1 or L2), then it is hardly surprising that the child's difficulties will be attributed to psychological dysfunctions. The myth of bilingual handicaps that still influences educational policy was generated in exactly this way during the 1920s and 1930s.

Recent studies suggest that despite the appearance of change with respect to nondiscriminatory assessment, the underlying structure has remained essentially intact. Mehan, Hertweck, and Meihls (1986), for example, reported that psychologists continued to test children until they "found" the disability that could be invoked to "explain" the student's apparent academic difficulties. A similar conclusion emerged from the analysis of more than 400 psychological assessments of minority students conducted by Cummins (1984). Although no diagnostic conclusions were logically possible in the majority of assessments, psychologists were most reluctant to admit this fact to teachers and parents. In short, the data suggest that the structure within which psychological assessment takes place orients the psychologist to locate the cause of the academic problem within culturally diverse students themselves.

The alternative role definition that is required to reverse the traditional "legitimizing" function of assessment can be termed an *advocacy* role. Educators must be prepared to become advocates for the child (Cazden, 1985) by critically scrutinizing the societal and educational context within which the child has developed. This involves locating the pathology within the societal power relations between dominant and subordinated groups, within the reflection of these power relations between school and communities, and within the mental and cultural disabling of subordinated group students that takes place in classrooms.

In most industrialized countries the training of psychologists and special educators does not prepare them for this advocacy role because advocating for minority students in this way frequently will involve a challenge to the societal and educational power structure. Thus, typically, rather than challenging a socio-educational system that tends to disable minority students, educators accept a role definition and an educational structure that makes discriminatory assessment virtually inevitable.

CONCLUSION

Alternative societal visions are expressed in the competing discourses with regard to the education of culturally diverse students that have emerged during the past decade in North America. In particular, there has been a strong resurgence of a neoconservative discourse that articulates a form of intellectualized xenophobia intended to alert the general public to the infiltration of the "other" into the heart and soul of American institutions. Cultural diversity has become the enemy within, far more potent and insidious in its threat than any external enemy. This discourse of "cultural literacy" allies itself with the more general discourse of "functional literacy," which calls for a return to rigorous transmission of basic skills that, it is claimed, characterized traditional teaching prior to the progressive ideas that gained credence during the permissiveness of the 1960s. The envisaged outcome of this discursive alliance is the elimination of bilingual education, multicultural education, and critical literacy in schools, all of which are viewed as threats to "the American way of life."

This discourse envisages an education system in which educators define their roles in such a way that the division of resources and power in the society is not problematized or called into question in any way. As a consequence, educators' interactions with students will simply reflect and reproduce the coercive relations of power in the broader society. The resulting educator-student interactions reflect the typical patterns of interaction that subordinated societal groups have experienced historically in relation to dominant groups. Students' language and cultural values are denied; they are confined to passive ingestion of dominant group cultural literacy within the classroom and their parents are excluded from participation in educational decisions and activities. The failure of culturally diverse students under these conditions has frequently been attributed on the basis of "objective" test scores to deficient cognitive or linguistic abilities..

The alternative "discourse of equity" that is exemplified in the framework elaborated in the present chapter views the neoconservative discourse as an attempt to reinforce the operation of coercive relations of power within the educational system and to ensure that the system continues to serve the interests of the dominant group. The major demographic changes that are occurring in North American society potentially threaten the hegemony of the dominant group and consequently reinforce the necessity of maintaining control of the educational structures that will determine opportunities for economic and social mobility. Hence, there is the insistence on "cultural literacy" and direct instruction of a core curriculum, with teachers' roles limited to the transmission of predetermined content and skills and culturally diverse students' experience and identity actively suppressed.

The societal power structure, however, is not monolithic, and there are opportunities for educators, communities and students to challenge coercive relations of power as they operate in the school system. The proposed framework analyzes underachievement among culturally diverse students as a function of the extent to which schools reflect or alternatively challenge the societal power structure. Specifically, students' educational progress will be strongly influenced by the extent to which educators, individually and collectively, become advocates for the promotion of students' linguistic talents, actively encourage parental participation in developing students' academic and cultural resources and implement pedagogical approaches that encourage students to use oral and written language to reflect critically on and amplify their experience.

The outcome of this process for both educators and students can be described in terms of *empowerment.* Empowerment can be defined as the collaborative creation of power. Conditions of collaborative empowerment are created when educators attempt to orchestrate their interactions with culturally diverse students in such a way that students' options for identity formation and critical inquiry are expanded rather than constricted. Teaching for empowerment, by definition, constitutes a challenge to the societal power structure.

12

Talking Difference: Discourses on Aboriginal Identity in Grade 1 Classrooms*

Allan Luke, Joan Kale, Michael Garbutcheon Singh
with
Tracey Hill and Favardin Daliri
James Cook University of North Queensland

> Cultural imperialism involves the paradox of experiencing oneself as invisible at the same time that one is marked out as different.
> —Iris Marion Young, *Justice and the Politics of Difference* (1990)

How are invisibility and difference established and marked in institutional life? This chapter examines a key element of early schooling for Aboriginal and Torres Strait Islander children: how literacy instruction makes available particular discourses for talking and thinking about cultural identity. It uses critical discourse analysis to describe an array of spoken and written texts generated by students, teachers, and textbooks that position and construct children and children's culture, in ways that both mark and silence cultural difference.

---

*The authors acknowledge the financial support of the Australian Research Council; Martin Nakata, Richard Smith, and Carmen Luke for theoretical and methodological advice; David Corson for editorial assistance; and the teachers and students in the four classrooms for their commitment and assistance.

This is, then, a study of discourse and power at work in the classroom. However, to locate and describe that power we begin by placing these texts and discourses within the broad context of struggles over Aboriginal and Islander education in Australian schools. We then frame an epistemological and methodological position on discourse, subjectivity, and cultural difference, drawing on that position to analyze four school texts.

INTRODUCTION: THE CONTEXT OF ABORIGINAL AND ISLANDER EDUCATION

The education of cultural and linguistic minorities in countries such as the United States, Canada, and the United Kingdom has been the subject of extensive sociological and ethnographic study. Much of this work has documented systemic exclusion and discrimination (e.g., Corson, 1991b, 1993c; Donald & Rattansi, 1992; McCarthy, 1991). The education of Australian indigenous and migrant peoples raises comparable issues: the political and cultural consequences of educational policies; the relationship of such policies to questions of cultural identity, nationhood, and economic productivity; the viability of language planning to sustain multilingualism; and continuing questions about the design, implementation, and effectiveness of antiracist and multicultural curriculum (e.g., Kalantzis, Cope, & Slade, 1989; Singh, 1989).

However, the educational and socioeconomic situation of Australia's first peoples—Aborigines and Torres Strait Islanders—is prima facie far more problematic than that of any other minority ethnic or cultural group in the Australian populace. Aborigines and Islanders constitute almost 2% of the Australian populace, in fact having grown in numbers since 1981 (Castles, Kalantzis, Cope, & Morrissey, 1992). In many urban and rural areas they constitute a significant group within the school-age population. In North Queensland urban schools (on the east coast of Australia, north of the Tropic of Capricorn) this varies from 5-20% of the school population, with much higher percentages in rural, bush schools. In many regions of Queensland, Central Australia, and the Northern Territory, Aborigines and Islanders constitute the single largest ethnic group, outnumbering migrant students and Anglo-Australians. Most recently, the Australian High Court's landmark recognition of indigenous land rights and the government's pursuit of a legal process for Aboriginal conciliation have placed Aboriginal and Islander issues squarely on the table in local and regional, state, and national education.

By almost every social indicator—from unemployment, to per capita income, life-span and infant mortality rate, quality of housing, and so forth—Australia's first peoples are positioned at the social and economic margins. In spite of visible advances of Aborigines and Islanders in the arts, music, sports, and so forth:

It appears that no real effort has been made to incorporate Aborigines into the Australian labour force in the period of postwar expansion. Nor have over twenty years of citizenship brought much improvement in social and economic conditions. . . . [D]espite rhetoric on participation and equal opportunity, official responses to the situation of the Aboriginal population are still defined in terms of welfare and policing. (Castles et al., 1992, p. 23)

Although European migrants became the objects of specialized curriculum development and policy beginning in 1949 (Ozolins, 1993), Aboriginal education did not become a public concern until the early 1970s. The Commonwealth government did not grant Aborigines and Torres Strait Islanders formal citizenship status and rights of personal mobility, franchise, and state education until 1967. That is, although Aborigines and Islanders had been the objects of colonial, missionary education on reserves for a century, their educational achievement and success was not seen as a focal issue in Australian teacher training, educational research, and curriculum development until the last two decades. In many teacher education programs it is still treated as a peripheral, "minority" issue, covered in elective subjects and optional units (Christie et al., 1991).

Since that time there has been a gradual but steady expansion of research and development in Aboriginal education, particularly in the Northern Territory. This work has culminated in the development, funding, and implementation of the National Aboriginal and Torres Strait Islander Education Policy (Commonwealth Department of Employment, Education and Training, 1989), which focuses on equality of access, early intervention, "culturally appropriate" curriculum and schooling, and "two-way" cross-cultural approaches to schooling, albeit within the auspices of an economic rationalist approach to education (Luke, Nakata, Singh, & Smith, 1993). Much of the research drawn on for current policy is ameliorative in orientation, focusing on variables that influence school achievement: learning and communicative style, language variation, cross-cultural miscommunication, inappropriate curricular content, and cultural and subcultural resistance (e.g., M. Christie, 1985; Folds, 1987; Kale, 1990; Malcolm, 1982; Malin, 1990; Osborne, 1991). Reflecting international trends, Australian research generally has moved from deficit explanations to models of mismatch: of communicative styles, pedagogic practices, language, and dialect.[1] More recent work has moved toward explanations that stress the divergence and convergence between home and school discourses, ideologies and "genres" (McKeown & Freebody, 1988; Walton, 1993).

In his wide-ranging review of work on literacy education, Gee (1990) retheorizes the problems of minority children in terms of the transition from what he calls the "primary" discourses of the community to the "secondary" discourses of schooling. In contrast with linguistic and poststructuralist defini-

---

[1]For a contrastive discussion of issues of indigenous education in Maori and Aboriginal contexts, see Corson (1993c).

tions, Gee offers a broad humanist definition of discourse as a "form of life" that entails culture- and discipline-specific ways of seeing, valuing, and acting in the world. His stress on the intrinsic difficulties facing minority students who confront the "secondary discourses" of schooling and mainstream culture recently has been questioned by Delpit (1992). She argues that minority learners require explicit instruction in mainstream codes, registers, and practices in order to have any opportunity of educational achievement. In recent Australian curriculum development by functional linguists, the pedagogic problem is described in terms of the relative inaccessibility of the "Secret English" and "highly valued" genres of mainstream schooling and dominant social institutions (Cope & Kalantzis, 1993).

As this ongoing debate signals, the pivotal question in the schooling of cultural and linguistic minority children concerns the complicity of educational processes in the unequal access to cultural goods, resources, and institutions. How schooling shapes students' textual practice and cultural capital is a central concern, particularly for those minority students whose communities are at the economic margins. But, as Gee's broad approach to discourse suggests, literacy education is also about the formation of cultural and gendered identity. The "selective traditions" of literacy instruction consist of values and ideologies, practices and positions—motivated inclusions and exclusions that act in the interests of particular class and cultural groups (Luke, 1988). In this way, children's introductions to textual practice may entail a universalization of a dominant group's knowledges and culture as natural, necessary and beyond criticism. These selective traditions of school knowledge are constructed materially through the spoken and written texts of schooling. In classrooms, the dynamic work of cultural reproduction and transformation is visibly and audibly "done" through discourse.

EDUCATIONAL DISCOURSE AND THE RACIALIZED SUBJECT

The postwar application of psycholinguistics and sociolinguistics to language and literacy learning set the stage for a move away from behaviorist, mechanistic models of deficit and for a revival of progressive, child-centered pedagogy. In practice this amounted to a reinstatement of the speaking and writing subject—whether through a romantic vision of the child as creative language user or a functionalist model of the child as participant in social norms and rules of "appropriateness." In classroom applications, psycholinguistic and sociolinguistic models continue to offer teachers ways of explaining and analyzing students' text by reference to individuals' intents, competencies, social roles, backgrounds, and so forth.

But such models stop short of explaining how students' subjectivities—their cultural and gendered identities—are themselves produced by discourse.

Poststructuralist analyses of education have broadly followed Foucault's (1972) insistence that discourses "systematically form the objects of which they speak" (p. 49). This work puts child language development and practice in a different perspective, stressing how children's identities are shaped by the web of texts they encounter in everyday institutions such as the family and community organizations, mass media and popular culture, the school and church. By this account, schools and classrooms build contending and competing versions of the child. Particular statements are reiterated across and within texts, forming what Foucault calls a "grid of specification" for officially defining and explaining the human subject to her- or himself and to authoritative others. In pedagogic discourse, then, particular kinds of children are constructed and mapped: from the preoperational child or attention deficit disorder child constructed in the texts of educational psychology, to the culturally deficit, minority or, for that matter, Aboriginal or migrant child constructed in children's literature, staffroom talk, and other texts. These different kinds of children are, in turn, affiliated with differing kinds of power and capital in epistemic and political communities.

This is not to suggest that students are simply compliant subjects. As numerous ethnographies of schooling have shown, they accommodate, resist, and contest available discourses, often building alternate identities and spaces for textual and semiotic work. But this is not the simple, unmediated manifestation of revolutionary spirit or the authentic voice described in the first wave of critical anthropology (cf. Wexler, 1992). They do so by bringing into play various discursive resources with which to read, interpret, and make sense of themselves, others and institutional life, resources which, in turn, have their bases and histories in available cultural discourses and texts.

In this way we could reinterpret Gee's concept of "primary discourses" to describe the multimodal, intertextual community resources that students use to read, write, and speak school texts. All written and spoken texts embody particular lexicogrammatical techniques for defining the social and natural worlds (e.g., lexical choice, transitivity, modality, metaphor) and for positioning readers and hearers within and in relation to those worlds (e.g., pronominalization, mode). That is, in the terms developed by critical language studies, texts both represent and portray the world (via experiential values or in functional linguistic terms, "field"), and they position the reader or hearer to be a particular kind of subject and to read and respond in particular ways (via interpersonal values or "tenor"; Fairclough, 1989).

There are of course continuing debates over whether gendered and racial subjects have essential differences and over the dangers of "false universalism" that tends to "homogenize" difference (West, 1990). But the colonized Other—the person of colored, gendered, different, and "minority" status— is produced through complex and interleaved textual and institutional practices, ranging from scientific description to contemporary fashion, from bureaucratic classifications to face-to-face slurs and degradation (cf. Bhabha, 1990). For the African-American slave, the South Pacific Islander "blackbirded" by the

European master, the eroticized "Oriental" woman as an object of Western male desire, or for the Aboriginal or Native American "savage," each of these historical subjects have a limited number of identity positions available. All tend to be categorical constructions and namings founded on the physicality of race and gender. These historically have been far from benign, but rather have positioned minorities in ways that axiomatically reinforce inferiority or limitation and that encourage the colonized to participate in the representation of their own inferiority and limitation. The effect is what Dubois (1903/1969) called "double consciousness": "this sense of always looking at one's self through the eyes of others, of measuring one's soul by the tape of a world that looks on in amused contempt and pity" (p. 45).

Marginality—this state of existence as "other for the Other"—thus is established in part through discourse. In the case of Aborigines, the historical movement has been from an outright namelessness and invisibility to their inclusion in public discourse as colonized, deficit human subjects (King & McHoul, 1986). The English "renaming" of first peoples was part of what Fesl (1993) describes as a "de-identification" intrinsic to colonialism and slavery. In this way, Aborigines and Torres Strait Islanders have a common experience of domination and exclusion via discourse and institutional practice.

To observers in contemporary Western liberal societies, these may seem like extreme historical examples, particularly to those who work in state institutions governed by laws that ban speech and writing, which propagates racist and sexist "hatred" (Matsuda, Lawrence, Delgado, & Crenshaw, 1993). But they remain relevant examples: What is crucial to our present classroom analysis is that the *racialized subject* is constructed through and in relation to mainstream cultural institutions and discourses.

THE STUDY

The data corpus is drawn from a year-long study of four grade 1 classrooms. Our initial research focus was on what counts as reading and writing for Aborigine and Torres Strait Islander children in their first year of formal schooling. The schools were located in lower socioeconomic areas of an Australian regional urban center. In the four classrooms observed, Aborigines and Islanders constituted between 10-15% of the total student body, with the remainder of the students working-class Anglo-Australians; class size on the day averaged between 23-25 students. Data were collected across the school year: Four days were randomly selected for observation in each classroom. We observed and videotaped over 80 hours of classroom and school interaction, consisting of 452 instructional events ranging from morning news and games to formal lessons. We collected 108 samples of textbooks and school writing from the 115 literacy lessons observed (72 reading, 43 writing).

The teachers were three Anglo-Australian women and a male Torres Strait Islander. All had over 10 years experience with mixed-race classrooms. The teachers had strongly stated commitments to the social justice principles of the Queensland Department of Education and, specifically, to the educational enfranchisement of Aboriginal and Islander children. Although their teaching styles and actual curricular contents varied, three of the four classrooms could be classified as having a traditional skills orientation, with extensive use of worksheets, basal readers, blackboard and flashcard work, and drill activities. One of the classrooms was more oriented toward whole language and featured environmental print, more diverse and generative writing, and reading activities and materials.

The research team consisted of three male Australians of Asian migrant backgrounds (Daliri, Luke, Singh), an Aboriginal woman (Hill), and an Anglo-Australian woman (Kale). Kale has extensive knowledge of Aboriginal and Papuan languages and cultures. All are trained and experienced teachers (in Australia, as well as in India and Canada); all have commitments to state social justice policy and longstanding personal investments in the politics of race and culture. As part of the research program, in two of the three schools we held inservice workshops and acted as consultants on literacy pedagogy, curriculum, and classroom interaction. In one of these schools that involvement led to the continuing implementation of text/context approaches to literacy instruction that attempt to directly address issues of cultural difference and linguistic variation.

This chapter features discourse analyses of four selected texts of identity from these classrooms: (a) a basal reading textbook, (b) a student's oral recount, (c) a classroom writing lesson, and (d) a school administrator's speech to assembled primary classes. The selection of these texts is not random but is an attempt to represent what we viewed as significant issues and patterns that emerged in the coding and classification of classroom events. This process of selection entailed individual and collective reviewing of videotapes and fieldnotes. As we reviewed the data we experimented with different coding and classification schemes. The 452 events were classified by types, using a mixture of conventional formats (e.g., morning news/show and tell; roll call and calendar) and curriculum contents (e.g., mathematics, social studies, reading, and writing). Exemplar lessons have been transcribed for ongoing content and discourse analyses.

At the onset of our study, we had not anticipated that the representation of cultural identity would be central to our analysis. But while working through the data, our readings of the presence and absence of particular contents, discourses, and practices shifted our research foci and questions. The bases for selection of texts here are as follows:

1. The basal reading textbook was typical of the kinds of beginning reading materials used in three of the four classrooms.
2. The student's oral recount is an example of a high frequency instructional event "morning news/show and tell"—and is the single instance in which Aboriginal or Islander culture is mentioned in the 80 hours.

3. The classroom writing lesson is an example of current Australian approaches to the "explicit" teaching of writing.
4. Finally, the assembly event is excerpted from the single "all school" meeting that we witnessed during the data collection period.

Our aim here is to show how each of these texts construct and mark cultural identity differently, engaging students and teachers in differing kinds of agency and textual representation.

BASAL TALK: MAKING CULTURE INVISIBLE

Reading remains a central focus of early primary instruction. In the four classrooms events explicitly dedicated to the teaching of reading constituted 17.48% of all classroom time. The selective traditions of literacy instruction entail the framing of a textual canon and the sanctioning and encouragement of particular reading practices with texts; that is, early reading instruction shapes what will "count" as a valued text, and what will "count" as a valued practice around that text. The selective tradition of children's literature and textbooks has been the subject of a decade of work in the sociology of curriculum, work that has documented the misportrayal, misrepresentation, and outright exclusion of women, ethnic, and cultural minorities (DeCastell, Luke, & Luke, 1989).

In response, most Australian state curricula specify the need for balanced, representative, and inclusive portrayals of cultural diversity, gender roles, and lifestyles. However, unlike in U.S., and Canadian schools, the actual text selection in Australian schools is the local decision of teachers and principals. The four classrooms we observed used a range of resources. However, three of the four reading programs were built almost exclusively around the daily use of basal readers, including *Reading 360 Australia, PM,* and *Endeavour.* The following text was used by the "lower" reading group in one of the classes. Five of the eight students in this group were of Aboriginal and Islander background.

Text 1: Basal Reader Narrative: Ducks.

1   Mother and the children are going to look at the ducks.
2   "Where are the ducks?" said David.
3   "Here they come," said Ann.
4   "Quack quack" said the ducks. "We are hungry."
5   "Here is the bread," said Martin.
6   "Quack quack," said the ducks.
7   "Thank you for the bread. Quack quack quack."
8   Martin looked at the bread.

9   "I'm hungry," he said.
10   Ann shouted, "Martin is a duck. Martin is a du-uck."
11   "Quack quack quack," said Martin the duck."I am a hungry duck."
12   "I am a hungry duck too," said David.
13   "Quack, quack, quack," said Ann.
14   Mother said, "Come on, Martin Duck, and David Duck, and Ann Duck
15   Come on, children."
16   Ann said to the ducks, "We are going away. We are going home."
17   "Quack, quack," said the ducks.

By contemporary benchmarks for reading curriculum, this type of beginning textbook is dated. But these are still used by many skills-oriented teachers because of an emphasis on graded and sequential introduction and repetition of high-frequency words and digraph/diphthong combinations. In this 126-word text several words recur: "said" (11), "duck" (14) and "quack" (15). Each subsequent text in the series incrementally introduces several new words and syntactic structures.

But there is more to this text than its capacity as a skill-inculcating device. The text and its accompanying pictures build a possible world of monocultural, middle-class family life and gender roles. There Mother takes the kids on family outings to the park; the three children, led by the eldest male, play by imitating animals. This is stereotypical, cardboard portrayal, and there is little that is extraordinary here, unless one queries these texts as *cultural representations*, replete with age authority and gender relations and talking ducks that follow politeness protocols (line 7: "Thank you for the bread. Quack quack quack."). Nothing in these texts explicitly names or marks place or time; the setting is a generic, "no-name" UK/North American/English-speaking suburban community. In this way these texts portray an ahistorical, featureless version of culture, void of specificity, locality, and color. In this textual possible world, the total omission of any kind of cultural and ethnic diversity, and the infantalization of children become central features of *the* culture of the literary canon.

It is worth noting that the children in this reading group were moving systematically through the class set of graded texts, which featured similar cultural and linguistic content. Equally significant is the manner in which the text operates as a technology for constructing and positioning its readers. The procedures of the small reading groups we observed involved sequential turns in which each member of the group read aloud a passage nominated by the teacher or teacher aid. Through the use of quotations and pronominalization, the child reader here is positioned to actually become David, Ann, and Martin Duck, to interrogate the world as they do (e.g., line 1: "Where are the ducks?") and to mouth their desires and claims about themselves (e.g., line 4: "We are hungry"; line 10: "I am a hungry duck"; line 15: "We are going home"). This is an exemplary instance of interpellation in early schooling: The text pragmatically inserts the Aboriginal and Islander child into its possible world, a world in which he or she remains invisible.

Regardless of how these texts and others like them portray and hail children as subjects, substantive meanings are constructed and remade in classroom talk, in the lessons and interactions around texts. That is, what counts as an authoritative "reading" or "interpretation" or "response" to *Ducks* and other texts necessarily is mediated in face-to-face interaction. We now turn to examples of two spoken texts in the classroom: lessons in "morning talk" and writing.

IDENTITY TALK: PERSONALIZING CULTURE

All of the classrooms had opening sessions in which children were encouraged to nominate topics and speak extemporaneously. These events, called *morning news* in Australian schools and *show and tell* in Canadian, American, and some Australian schools, are used by many teachers as a way of getting children oriented into the day. At times children are encouraged to speak about an object (e.g., a toy, a piece of work they have done, an artwork or some other artifact); mostly, children are given "free time" to select a topic of choice. Different classrooms establish differing criteria and ways of signaling of what counts as an acceptable topic, but for many recounts of events, TV programs, trips, or vacations suffice. The 17 events we recorded averaged approximately 15 minutes in length each, usually allowing four to seven children to speak (approximately 25% of the class).

The following text contains the only direct reference to ethnicity and cultural background of the children in the entire data corpus. That is, difference and Aboriginality are explicitly marked. Sam, a 6-year-old Torres Strait Islander child, described his weekend.

Text 2: Sam's Story 3:37.

1:	**Teacher**: Scuse me, everybody's feet on the floor. . . . It's Sam's turn.
2:	**Student**: Good morning boys and girls.
3:	**Class/Teacher**: Good morning, Sam.
4:	S: Well, um, when we, we, um in the afternoon time, we went and a

bus and we um we went to our grandad's
and we went on the bus
and then we we jumped off and we had a . . .
and we went inside and then we had a bath
and then we took a long time and I had my GI Joe
and then I had 3 ducks
and I played in there
and then when we came out now and then someone told us to hurry up
and we are, then, we said "OK"
and then we went for the towel and wiped ourselves
and then we went
and then the a . . . a . . . then

and then mmm the man I left it in the cupboard
and I was looking for it
and then I put my then I, I reached into the cupboard to put my clothes
and I was too slow.
So I went outside when trousers on and my buttons open and . . . undone
and my mom have to do them up because I was taking a long time in there.
Then we three went to um, um, um Tom's place
and we practice our dance, our Island dance.
And we made too much noise with our musical im-ple-ments
and we just had to use our hands.
and when we wanted to turn we would just go like that [gestures with
    right hand]
and when we were done we went like that . . .
and, and, and, my Mum, my Big Mum and when they jump, the girls jump,
the girls don't jump real high.
Some of them don't know how to jump real high, so they go like that
    [gestures].
And boys we for.. that, we go like that.

5: T: And you're allowed to jump really high? The girls aren't allowed to
jump really high but you're allowed to jump really high?

6: S: Yeah. Because we've got the short trousers on. And when, when we
came to the end we all went like that [gestures . . . moves] . . . and when
we jumped we turned around first and then we jumped and then we went
down and then we go: "umm, umm, umm" [three gestures to sound]. . .

7: T: Are you really ready to bring this Island dance to the school? Are you
still practicing or are you really ready. Sam, is it ready to come and
show us?

8: S: Yep. We have to arrange with our leader.

9: T: Right . . . and . . . Did you do this over at Tom's place?

10: S: Yep.

11: T: Why didn't you tell me?

12: S: 'Cause we thought you were asleep.

13: T: You thought I was asleep! I live opposite Tom's place and all these
good things were happening at Tom's place and I was not invited.
Everybody sit up for Jason's turn. Jason, would you like to get up for
your turn now. Jason's turn. Big voice, now, Jason.

In his community, Sam is bilingual in Torres Strait Creole and English.
In this event he proceeds in what Michaels and Collins (1984) have described as
an "oral narrative style," and he liberally mixes talk with animated gestures,
jumps, and noises (turn 6). The propositional chunks of his story are joined by
the cohesive tie "and," rather than any of the conventional deictic markers in
written recounts (e.g., "then," "later," "afterwards"). This conjunction is also
used as a marker (in addition to "um") for holding the floor and signaling to the

audience the introduction of each proposition. Sam also marks the end of a proposition with the prosodic cue of rising intonation. As is typical in these morning news events, Sam is allowed to hold the floor for an extended soliloquy (almost 2:30 minutes) until the teacher signals in turn 5 that she wants to take the floor back. During that soliloquy, Sam is able to build for the other students a possible world of his extended family structure (e.g., "Mum" and "Big Mum") and social relations, his toys, play, and community routines.

After returning to a teacher directed Initiate/Response/Evaluate exchange pattern (turns 5 to 13), the teacher signals in turn 13 that the event is over by selecting another child and reorganizing students' attention and bodily postures ("Everyone sit up for Jason's turn"). The generic structure of this teacher's morning news lesson is as follows: selection of speaker (turn 1)—▶formal exchange of greetings (2, 3)—▶ student recount (4)—▶ teacher questioning of details (5 to 13)—▶ selection of next speaker (13). In terms of the social relations set up here, the exclusive use of interrogatives in the "Initiate" moves (turns 5, 7, 9, 11) positions the teacher to direct the event and judge particular kinds of knowledge and detail admissible, but at the same time acknowledges Sam as the knower. In turns 11, 12, 13, the teacher personalizes the exchange, referring to her own omission from the dance practice.

Regardless of its extreme form and content restrictions (F. Christie, 1985), this teacher's morning news session opens up a public space in the classroom for Sam to construct a text of identity. Here Sam quite literally names and describes cultural practices. The importance of this should not be underestimated, especially given the total invisibility of his or many of his classmates' cultural experiences in literature such as *Ducks*. Unfortunately, Sam's mention of "our Island dance" is the only place in the lesson corpus in which Aboriginality, Torres Strait Islander, or any of the students' cultural backgrounds is directly named.[2] This in itself speaks to the issues of "silencing" and "invisibility" of difference in public and pedagogical discourses, standing as a primary school corollary to West's (1990) description of the exclusivity of Anglo-European literary culture in the academy. There are two interesting aspects to this particular "naming" that we take up here: the actual cultural content at issue, and the way that this knowledge is reframed by the teacher.

First, culture here is named by reference to traditional dancing.[3]

---

[2]Like many minority and subcultural groups, Aborigines and Islanders have ways of "naming" themselves that are not commonly available for use by mainstream Anglo/Australians. Aborigines and Islanders in southeast and coastal Queensland often refer to themselves as *Murries*, whereas many in southern states prefer the term *Kooris* (Watego, 1989). However, these terms have recently begun to be appropriated and used by national media. As Fesl (1993) recently has shown, even more ostensibly benign namings—including *indian, native, black,* and *Aborigine*—have been historical acts of appropriation of identity.

[3]Differing Aboriginal and Torres Strait Islander tribal groups and cultures have distinctive dance and musical traditions, practices, and narratives; shared practices emerge between historically, geographically connected groups.

Reform in Australian curriculum toward more culturally inclusive images and portrayals has stressed social studies units, theme days, and projects built around the study and "celebration" of ethnic diversity and culture. Yet, this "first-wave" multiculturalism has been criticized as leading to a trivialization of culture: a reduction of cultural difference, diversity, and even conflict to a matter of clothes and food, music, and dance (Kalantzis et al., 1989). The danger is that such approaches may efface rather than foreground historical and contemporary cultural relations. Although we cannot read intent into this lesson event, the *only* mention of Aboriginal or Islander culture occurs in the context of dance and an impending Aboriginal/ Islander "day," referred to by the teacher in turn 7. Aboriginal and Islander cultures (or Asian, Greek, Italian, or any other cultures) were not named explicitly anywhere in the lesson corpus in relation to history, children's literature study, social studies discussion of the local community, or in relation to students' and teachers' talk of their individual biographies.

Second, the teacher's supportive uptake of the recount encourages Sam to talk further about the dance. But she does not redirect the content to a recognition of the other Islander or Aborigines in the class and their possible interests or knowledges. In other words, the cultural practice represented in this morning talk is personalized, rather than taken up as a substantive issue shared by several of the class members. In this way (collective and communal) cultural difference is recognized in the public sphere of the classroom, but as a variant of individual difference, one to be negotiated between teacher and student. This is not surprising because the very generic structure of morning talk tends to "personalize" knowledge as part of a progressive, child-centered program. "Culture" and "cultural difference" thus are made into individual possessions.

WRITING TALK: LEARNING CULTURAL LOGIC

Our third text is a writing lesson. The teaching of writing was the focus of 43 events, 17.62% of the lesson corpus. Events included handwriting lessons, worksheets requiring short answers and copying, language experience activities combining drawing and transcription, and more directed, "scaffolded" lessons in which teachers provided direct instruction on how to write a particular "genre." This latter style of lesson is encouraged in many Australian states' curriculum documents and inservice materials that stress the need for explicit teaching of "how texts work."

A preferred lesson format for many Australian teachers is collaborative composition. This entails a group composition on an overhead transparency, blackboard, or whiteboard, or, in this case, on large strips of paper mounted on an easel. This approach to "modeled writing" mixes aspects of what are commonly known as "process" approaches (that stress drafting, revision, and publication strategies) with "genre" approaches (that foreground the lexicogrammatical and structural requirements of particular texts types). The year 1 curriculum guides suggest that instruction can begin with personal narratives, such as Sam's recount in Text 1. Here the lesson pivots around the literary conventions and textual features of a specific subgenre: the fairytale. The class group sits on the floor at the teacher's feet while she writes on the easel.

Text 3: Lesson on Writing Fairytales.

1: T: ... Now, when you write a story Alison, there's something very important you gotta do. You gotta keep reading your story as you write it because you might miss out a really important word. So I'm gonna read mine again [points to story script on paper]: "A long, long time ago there lived a princess." I think I can make it a bit better than that.

2: S1:   A dragon too.

3: T: No, no. No. What. How about: when you think about a princess, what'do you think about?

4: S2:   A prince . . .

5: T: No

6: S2:   A prince . . .

7: T: No, what do you think she'd look like?

8: S3:   A . . .

9: T: With long hair? What colour?

10: S3:   Yellow, black . . . [chorus laughter]

11: T: What about long, long golden hair. . . . [reading aloud] "A long long time ago there lived a princess with long long golden hair." Now if she had long hair, what sort of princess do you think she'd be? What would she look like?

12: S1:   Nice

13: T: Nice, Oh yes, wonderful, that's very good. I might put down some of these words . . . [reads aloud] "The princess and the dragon. A long long time ago there lived a beautiful princess with long golden hair. She lived in a big castle with a pink tower. One day the princess was playing outside when she heard a loud growl and out of the bushes rushed a big dragon."

14: S2:   dragon.

15: T: Now I think we could find a better word than big.

16: S2:   Long

17: T: A long dragon, yes. Nadia.

18: S3:   huge . . . and sharp teeth.

19: T: No, we're talking about size, Jake. Another word for big, we're talking about huge, giant.

20: S4:   Enormous.

21: T: Enormous, what a beauty.

While the class writes as a group, the teacher quite literally names the generic parts of the story (e.g., "the title," "the story starter"). Each of these becomes a propositional "slot" to be filled in with (cultural) content. In this instance the class is selecting and describing main characters: princess, prince, dragon, and so forth. At the same time, the teacher provides a "running metatextual commentary" (Luke, DeCastell, & Luke, 1983) on the authorial decisions involved in the "writing process." In this instance, the teacher is modeling drafting: "you gotta keep reading your story as you write it because you might miss out a really important word" (turn 1).

She then proceeds to do so, second-guessing her "word" choices and soliciting from the children possible wordings and contents (turn 3: "When you think about a princess, what do you think about?"). Again, the Initiate/Response/Evaluate structure of talk acts as a selection mechanism, with particular suggestions rejected (turns 2, 4, 6, 10). One child's suggestion of what he "thinks about" in relation to "princess" is rejected twice (turns 5, 7) as inadmissible to the collaborative story (as not what he "thinks about"?). Finally, the teacher provides her preferred distinctive features for the princess, "long, long golden hair" (turn 11). In effect, she is responding to her own initiation in turn 3. A similar routine is used to select terms associated with "dragon" in turns 15 to 21.

This lesson exemplifies the cultural nonneutrality of reading and writing instruction. It could be viewed as a structured introduction to generic structure and the writing process. But the selections of meanings that the teacher here models as preferred authorial choices build a cultural logic. They shape and naturalize a possible world in which human and animal subjects are endowed with particular features (e.g., Princesses = "beautiful, long golden hair"; Dragons = "enormous"), in which particular patterns of action become "typical" and expectable. Narrative entails the sequencing of particular actions, events. In so doing, it represents syntaxes of human action, particular structures of causality and agency. In this instance, the fairy tale represents a culture in which fair-skinned and -haired women (princesses), living in cloistered environments (pink towers), are placed in adversarial relationships with nature (dragons), solved by the intervention of white, aristocratic, armed males (princes). In short, this is how one "does" authorship and the fairytale genre. These are the kinds of lexical and semantic choices that one makes.

Because the students' contributions are pitched into the pool of possible wordings for the story, in a sense they "own" this text far more than *Ducks* or other basal texts. In all of this, the Aboriginal and Islander children's cultural resources, whether their experiences of urban everyday life, their families' and communities' histories, or more traditional tales of land and cultural practice, are not called on. However, they do not give in silently. In turn 10, one of the Islander girls calls out an alternative: that the princess might have "Yellow, black" hair, a claim welcomed by her classmates' chorus of laughter. We take this as an instance in which the student's discursive resources were called into play to mark difference explicitly: that the student was quite deliberately engaged in "playing" with the text in a way that highlighted ethnic/racial/gender difference and, in effect, parodied the genre of the fairytale. What kinds of critical literacy are evidenced in the laughter? Is the image of a princess with black hair forwarded by a student with black curly hair that much of a violation of the regulative cultural logic of the fairytale?

Learning to write—whether by process or by genre, by skills or by whole language—always requires the writing of cultures. The stories one learns to write, like the stories one learns to read, represent and construct gendered and cultural identity. But there are spaces and instances in all classrooms in which other discursive resources and knowledges come into play. Where "minority discourses" (JanMohamed & Lloyd, 1990) are available in these classrooms,[4] it would appear to be possible to "change the subject," to write the fairytale differently and critically. Unfortunately, that opportunity is neither recognized or included in the construction of this class text (turn 11). Consequently, this lesson becomes yet another instance of Aboriginal invisibility, another missed opportunity to develop ways and means for talking about difference and culture.

ASSEMBLY TALK: ENFORCING CULTURE

The school assembly is a public performance, a ritual activity in which particular relations of power and authority are played out and in which narratives of school practice and policy are rehearsed. Lesko's (1988) analyses of administrators' and counselors' speeches in an American Catholic high school illustrate how these school narratives are the material fabric of which school "ethos" is woven and the very sites in which official versions of "ideal" and "successful" students are represented. Many Australian schools still begin the school day with "parade," an organized assembly. One of the schools observed held a fortnightly primary school assembly (grades 1 to 7), in which the principal or deputy principal would address students in several classes collectively.

Before this assembly began, the principal was seen by students and teachers discussing with an Aboriginal girl (about Grade 5, aged 10) her absence from school without a note. His opening comments before the gathered student body were as follows.

---

[4]Minority discourses are those statements, themes, and wordings used to index beliefs, forms of life, patterns, and values of particular marginal groups "in their subjugation and opposition to the dominant culture" (JanMohammed & Lloyd, 1990). Minority discourses entail: (a) identity formation and the assertion of difference, often generated in (b) opposition to and defense against mainstream discourses, and (c) asserted in the gaps and marginal spaces of mainstream institutions. Such discourses are (d) not necessarily unified, coherent, but are as often heteroglossic expressions of intersections of culture and class, gender, and interracial identity.

Text 4: Assembly Speech.

1	A number of children have been absent from school and they haven't
2	brought a note from their parents to say why they were not at school. You
3	know that when you are absent from school, you have to bring a note.
4	These are not my rules, or the school's rules. They are the rules of the
5	Education Department. When children are away from school a lot, and don't
6	bring a note to explain their absence, the Education Department starts to
7	ask questions. I'm not sure what happens to the information—whether it is
8	passed on to the Police, or to the Welfare, or to somewhere else. The
9	Education Department has made education available to all children so that
10	you can learn to read and write. And it is the right of all children to get a
11	good education. If you get a good education, you can get jobs. The
12	Government doesn't like it if people do not get a good education, since they
13	can't get a good job, and the Government has to pay money to support
14	them, which it does not like. Nor do people in jobs, because they have to
15	pay taxes to support the people who are out of work. So if you are away
16	from school, you must bring a note to say why you were away.

After and during the Principal's comments, a few children glanced at the student whom he had spoken to immediately prior to the assembly. By the end of his talk she had dropped her head onto her hands, leaning on a portable blackboard in the room. In this way, the talk constituted an indirect form of punishment and humiliation before the assembled student body. At the same time, that discipline here is transformed into an act of surveillance on the larger student body, an imperative to act within the rules of a bureaucracy beyond most 6- or 7-year-olds' imaginations. Again we can analyze the text in terms of the ways that it constructs Aborigines, Islander (and potentially truant, working-class, Anglo-Australian children), and in terms of the ways that it positions the student addressees.

First, the possible world built up here is one in which particular actions can be traced through a chain of consequences. Two competing narratives are offered as moral equations. Each constructs in "binary opposition . . . the permitted and the forbidden" (Foucault, 1979, p. 183) the "good" child and the "truant" child (who fails to "bring a note to say why you were away"). For the *good* child: good reading and writing—▶ good education—▶jobs. For the *truant* child: no good education—▶ unable to get a job—▶ welfare—▶ anger of government and employed taxpayers. These stories are presented as fact in unqualified declaratives.

At the same time, the actual agency behind these stories is masked. The initial two sentences foreground the anonymous violators as grammatical subjects ("a number of children," "you"). But with the exception of the personal disclaimer in line 7 ("I'm not sure what happens to the information"), the agency rests with faceless bureaucracies: "the Education Department," "the Police," "the Welfare," "the Government." It is a world in which bureaucracies "start . . . to ask questions," "pass . . . on information," "make education available," "don't like it if people do not get a good education," "ha[ve] . . . to pay money to support them." What is interesting is that neither teachers nor administrators are named as having any substantive part to play in this sequence. Their agency is grammatically hidden. This has the panoptic effect of marking out truant (and Aboriginal) children as problematic, as different, as objects of a bureaucratic gaze—whereas those human agents responsible for that surveillance become invisible to its objects. In this way, the talk and discourses of educational administration are local articulations of governmentality. They act as instances of discipline that extend from and construct real and imaginary bureaucratic centers, but that are played out in the (uneven) capillaries of discourse in assemblies, office interviews, staff meetings, and memoranda.

This is a public speech act of power that positions and defines its addressees. Its initial reference to children is indirect and impersonal ("a number of children"). But the use of pronouns and injunctions on proper conduct instructs one to comply: "You know that when you are absent from school you have to bring a note." The text both begins and ends with an injunction, the latter again directly addressed to the collective "you."

For the Aboriginal girl who did not bring a note, this event constitutes a public degradation ceremony. But its broader function is as an act of surveillance, an act of policing. It does so by constructing narrative grids of similarity and difference, then by placing the students within and against those grids. At the same time, its function is to use the exemplar of the Aboriginal girl to establish a "technology of the self" (Foucault, 1988), in which children will internalize the disciplines of school attendance and accountability to authority.

INVISIBILITY AND DIFFERENCE IN THE TEXTS OF SCHOOLING

> It is not difference which immobilizes us, but silence. And there are so
> many silences to be broken.
> —Audre Lorde, *Sister Outsider* (1984)

We have offered here a pastiche of texts from the first year of schooling experienced by urban Aboriginal and Islander children. They are not necessarily generalizable to all year 1 classrooms or to all Aborigines' and Islanders' experiences of schooling. But they amply illustrate the textual presences and absences in the discourses about culture available in early schooling. There is evidence here of what Rattansi (1992) has called "discursive deracialisation," that is, the exclusion and silencing of issues of difference under the auspices of a "color blind" and homogenous approach to curriculum and instruction. We conclude with a discussion of the implications of these silences and exclusions, noting possible alternative directions and challenges for educators.

As described by Young (1990) at the onset of this chapter, cultural imperialism involves a paradoxical state in which the colonized is rendered both invisible and marked as different, at once both absent and present. Although *Ducks* may seem an anachronism, far too many of the texts of early schooling remain, at best, monocultural. But, as we have argued here, the problem is not one of simple imbalance or misportrayal, distortion or archetypal "false consciousness." Both as readers and as writers, Aboriginal and Islander children are inserted pragmatically into these possible worlds—worlds in which middle-class children imitate animals, ducks say "please" and "thank you," and princes rescue blonde princesses. Occasionally, these children attempt to interject statements of their cultural backgrounds and histories into the texts of schooling. When this occurs, it requires that they admit to their identity in the public domain of the school. In some instances, such as Sam's story, these attempts are encouraged, albeit personalized and individualized, and in other instances, like the fairytale lesson, possibilities are missed and ignored altogether. What is missing is any systemic attempt to build on and capitalize on the discourses of Aboriginality in the classroom.

At the same time, the gaze of authority, discipline, and power asserts itself: marking these same children as different, as deficit, as objects of policing, surveillance, and welfare. Events such as the Assembly Speech are quite complementary to the discursive work of the classroom: "Surveillance, defined and regulated, is inscribed at the heart of the practice of teaching, not as an additional or adjacent part, but as the mechanism that is inherent to it and which increases its efficiency" (Foucault, 1979, p. 176). That surveillance works by setting out grids of similarity and difference, at once "imposing homogeneity" (p. 184) and the universalism of a monocultural childhood and possible world and at the same time fixing differences for examination. In this way pedagogic discourse "individualises by making it possible to measure gaps, to determine levels, to fix specialities and to render the differences useful by fitting them one to another" (p. 184). What is entailed in "normalization" is the simultaneous assertion of "the rule of homogeneity" and the mapping of "hierarchies, hyponomic relations" for classifying particular individuals and groups of individuals by race, gender, disability, mental capacity, and so forth (p. 183).

What are the consequences and effects of such texts? Over the last two decades there have been near continual claims that mainstream schooling and curriculum content is culturally unidimensional and exclusionary. As a result, there is a tendency among many teachers and administrators, teacher educators, and researchers to assume that the matter of the equitable representation of culture in the discourses of schooling is something that was effectively dealt with through the activism of the civil rights and feminist movements.[5] How else

---

[5]This is in part attributable to what Apple (1993, p. 22) has described as the conservative "restructuring of common-sense" about social formation and the dynamics of cultural struggle. A great deal of work has gone into the simultaneous appropriation and writing off of the social movements of the 1960s and 1970s—and of their concrete political, leg-

could the cynical claim that inclusive curricula and language in schools is a form of "political correctness" have arisen? In Australia, Canada, and other Western countries, the term is invoked to refer to those sites in which minorities, women, gays, the disabled, and others have claimed a right and place to speak and write within the politics of institutional life and face-to-face relations. But our evidence suggests that in many local sites silences in mainstream curriculum and pedagogy remain (cf. Baker & Davies, 1993). In this context, talk of a "backlash" or "conservative restoration" seems doubly ironic: A "backlash" against curricular reform that never occurred? A "restoration" of silences and exclusions that were never redressed in the first place?

It would be all too easy to explain away this situation as the product of "racism," particularly if we define racism in terms of the attitudes, beliefs, and intentions of community members, teachers, politicians, and others. In the schools we have looked at here, such a conclusion would be absurd. Over the duration of the study and in follow-up in-service workshops, we did not hear one remark from a teacher or administrator that could be construed as overtly "racist." All of the teachers in these classrooms were warm and positive in their interactions with the Aboriginal and Islander children. Three of them went out of their way to establish caring physical contact with the Aboriginal children, gestures well received. Two principals had committed extra personal time and school resources to address these children's achievement. Two of the teachers had extensive experience in outback schools in Aboriginal communities. And the school administrator who spoke at the assembly had extensive community experience with Aboriginal parents and children. Furthermore, all stated their belief that the problem in these classrooms was not an "Aboriginal problem" per se, but rather a home/community literacy transition problem experienced equally by the Anglo-Australian working-class children.

What we might more appropriately call "supremicist practices" (cf. hooks, 1990b)—exclusionary talk and silence—are kinds of *discursive work.* Such practices are not simply attributable to warped mental states, immoral dispositions, or bad attitudes; they are visible, material social practices "done" in speech and writing. Whether in the racist joke or slur, or the textbook passage or lesson—such discourse practices are acts of "symbolic violence" (Bourdieu, 1991), constructing and positioning the targeted subject. These constructions, furthermore, are part of the complex and at times contradictory politics of representation through which identity is shaped and formed. When this is the case, the educational problem is not with "racism" per se, in any conventional or common-sense definition of the word. Rather, the problem rests with an apparent

islative (and educational) gains—as historical anachronisms, as "nostalgia." The attack on the credibility of the gains of women, indigenous peoples, ethnic minorities, and students is thus waged on two fronts: the "backlash" against "political correctness" in universities, the press, and other public forums; and, for example, the popular marketing of "grunge" and "retro" fashions, nostalgia music, and movies as simulations of counterculture sans politics.

lack of discursive resources for talking about race and culture. Our experiences as people of color suggest that many teachers are afraid that to talk about race, culture, and difference is to risk "being racist" or "being seen as racist." Hence, what emerges in early childhood classrooms such as these is a putatively "color blind" curriculum that aims to "universalize" and homogenize children and in so doing unintentionally silences constructive talk and writing about difference.

The matter of how we speak and write with and about people of color and cultural difference is far from closed or dealt with. The imperative for all to develop constructive ways of recognizing and talking about Aboriginality has been placed at center stage in ongoing debates over indigenous land rights. Some educational institutions have taken up the challenge through the publication of autobiographical and expository social analyses by Aborigines and Islanders.[6] Increasing numbers of Australian teachers are now seeing a direct engagement with community languages and discourses, cultures, and forms of life as necessary parts of their work. And in the texts that we have looked at here, there are moments when Torres Strait Islander and Aboriginal children have found places and gaps for "talking back": public "acts of defiant speech" that are "the expression of moving from object to subject" (hooks, 1990a, p. 340).

It is time that the silence is broken. This requires nothing less than that students, teachers, and administrators take up the task of generating spaces, ways, and discourse resources for reading and writing, speaking, and listening about race, culture, and difference explicitly and constructively.

---

[6]See, for example, the journals *Black Voices* (James Cook University of North Queensland, Townsville, Queensland, Australia) and *Ngoonjook: Batchelor Journal of Aboriginal Education* (Batchelor College, Batchelor, Northern Territory).

13

Changing Schools, Teachers, and Curriculum: But What About the Girls?

Jill Blackmore
Jane Kenway
Deakin University

This chapter is about how we came to see feminist poststructuralism as a useful framework for explicating the ways in which a particular set of policy initiatives in Australia sought to produce gender reform and about how these policies were "received" in schools by teachers and students (Willis, Kenway, Rennie, & Blackmore, 1992). We came to this position largely because of the failure of other bodies of theory, critical and otherwise, to adequately theorize the nature of policy and of change. Even the research literature that deals most specifically with educational change (e.g., Fullan, 1991) offered little theoretically. Our concern here is to explain why this was the case. We focus first on that literature that deals most explicitly with educational change because it has largely informed policymakers and has framed gender reform policy in Australia, particularly during the 1980s and 1990s. Then we deal briefly and selectively with "other" critical theoretical frameworks that engage both implicitly and explicitly with theories of change. After developing what constitutes a feminist poststructuralist perspective of change, we conclude with some comments as to its practical implications for professional development, curriculum, and pedagogy.

233

"RATIONALIST" THEORIES OF CHANGE

Schools, teachers, and students are inevitably ignored in the educational policy-making process in England, the United States, and to a lesser extent in Australia, largely because of a dominant rational technicist model of policy (Bowe & Ball, 1992). Although there have been several shifts within this model, in the main researchers and policymakers treat policy generation and implementation as two distinct phases to be carried out by two different groups: policymakers (bureaucrats, researchers, specialist curriculum developers, consultants, and teacher union representatives) and practitioners (the administrators, curriculum coordinators, and the teachers). This occurs in two separate arenas (the center and the school) in a conception-execution model.

Within this "rational" approach to policy, change first became an issue with the disillusionment arising from the failure of the 1960s educational reforms. In this first phase any discrepancy between policy and outcomes was conceptualized as an "implementation problem," which in turn has been variously attributed to teacher resistance, inadequate organizational control, lack of school leadership, and/or lack of accountability (Fullan, 1987). The tendency in the United States was to increase coercion to force individuals to adhere to external policy (McLaughlin, 1987).

The second phase was when attention shifted to teachers as those responsible for implementing change and when the focus was on what actually happens in practice or on what works. Then attention shifted to organizations as contexts in which change is blocked or enabled. Professional development during the 1970s therefore focused on the "traits" of individual change agents and organizations, which led to checklists or taxonomies of change factors and characteristics. This literature tended to concentrate on changing individual teachers and changing individual schools with the assumption that students' educational experience would change accordingly in a positive way. In the meantime, empirical studies in the 1980s indicated that top-down policy imposition aroused teacher resistance or indifference, not because teachers or schools were innately conservative, self-interested, or apathetic, but because of reasoned responses by professionals about whether particular policies addressed the needs of their particular students (McLaughlin & Marsh, 1990). Apart from this, the response by students, who are being viewed as the passive receptacles of expert knowledge, and parents to policy initiatives has been ignored by policymakers, politicians, and researchers. Implicit in all of this is the belief that all policy is "good policy." The policy process has therefore been largely viewed as a linear—either top down or bottom up—relatively centralized process negotiated between representatives of specific interest groups in what could be described as a pluralistic, but state-centric, model.

A third shift within the field of research on educational change occurred toward the end of the 1980s. The unidimensionality of the early literature and the effective schools approach and the messiness of the change process is now recognized (Darling-Hammond, 1990; Fullan, 1994; McLaughlin & Marsh, 1990). School culture becomes the focus in the development of a more holistic account as to why and how schools change. But in drawing from a "corporate" version of culture, the psychology of Schein, and cultural anthropology, culture is narrowly defined in an instrumental manner (Deal & Peterson, 1992; Schein, 1985; Van Maanen & Barley, 1984). Culture is seen to be unitary and monolithic, and individuals are simply enculturated to effect organizational ends and consensual goals. Some cultures, the underground life of organizations, and indeed any cultural difference are seen to be dysfunctional. The power of language, myths, and symbols is recognized but adapted to organizational ends. Principals become change agents, endowed with particular capacities to "shape or manipulate school culture" and implant vision throughout the structures, symbols, language, and rituals of schools (e.g., Deal & Peterson, 1990). In this model the policy process is seen to be cyclical (usually on an annual basis for budgetary purposes), with staff input via collaborative practices and feedback mechanisms (e.g., Caldwell & Spinks, 1992). Yet, the cyclical model assumes short time frames in which the change process can be affected, ignores the micropolitics of schools by oversimplifying the decision-making process, and assumes the neutrality of processes themselves. Essentially, it is an incremental and therefore linear model of change, which suited management purposes in a period of devolved management to schools by linking central budgetary processes to curriculum programs in schools.

This instrumental view of culture is selectively drawn on, as is the effective schools literature, by management-oriented policymakers seeking a "tighter coupling" between schools and the state. It assumes a linear relationship between good leadership, effective schools, and improved student achievement. Curriculum is increasingly important in this context as an area of teachers' work that affects the organizational culture, so principals become instructional or supervisory leaders. It assumes that changing the curriculum will lead to the desired changes in student performance. Indeed, the 1980s is significant for public debates over curriculum (competency-based curriculum, national curriculum, or standards), debates framed by management concerns about selectivity, standardization, comparability, and predictability. The rationalist model of change embedded in the effective schools literature is therefore seductive to politicians seeking quick "technical" solutions to complex educational, social, and political problems.

The final and most recent shift in the rationalist model of policy in the late 1980s is that of the management of change (Bowe & Ball, 1992). This form of strategic management is multifaceted in that it seeks to change systems, organizational structures, curriculum, and teachers' work. At the same time it seeks to more closely target those in need by strategic management. The rhetoric of this particular version of management calls on postmodern claims about the changing nature of work and justifies the strategic approach with the argument that schools must better meet the needs of students and society more quickly. Self-managing

schools are now expected to confront change at the chalkface, in which the work
of autonomous professional "knowledge" workers merely react to the specialist
market needs of individual students (Blackmore, 1993a). This rhetoric draws on
the literature that recognizes that teachers view school knowledge in more fluid
ways, are less "discipline" and more "student" focused, and see subject content as
a vehicle for teaching rather than the substance and aim of teaching. Change is
recognized as being chaotic, uncertain in outcomes, and diffuse (Fullan, 1994).
Yet, this new version of the old rationalist model incorporates this "postmodern"
view of change and builds on earlier phases by still equating "good" schools to
academic achievement. Indeed, curriculum and assessment have increasingly
become the focus by which this change is controlled, as management defines in a
more technicist, nationally ordained, and specifically stated manner the expected
outcomes of schooling. How change actually occurs in schools—the substance
and act of educating people—is of less concern.

　　　School culture is reduced in this structuralist reading of postmodern
society to image making, or as Foucault would say, a *simulacrum*. The language
of managing change and rationality performs as much a symbolic function, in
which policies are symbolic solutions promising order in a society characterized
by disorder. In essence, though, it is still the "brute sanity" approach to change
that believes that sheer argument and authority will produce the desired outcomes, one that tightens control over teachers and students through teacher
appraisal and accountability mechanisms of standardized curriculum and assessment packages (Bowe & Ball, 1992; Fullan, 1991; McLaughlin & Marsh,
1990). The problem now for management is not how to understand change, but
how to manage change in particular ways and how to direct the "knowledge"
workers toward corporate aims within more decentralized systems.

BUT WHAT ABOUT THE STUDENTS?

These technical/managerialist approaches to policy have underlying assumptions about organizations, human motivation, learning, and therefore curriculum. In organizations presumed to be essentially hierarchical, it is necessary
only to change the practices of the school leader or teacher to change classroom
outcomes. Administrative and classroom practices are reduced to matters of
technique. It is a banking view of knowledge. Curriculum also is treated as a
technical issue from the management perspective. It promotes a view of curriculum as content, a transmission view of pedagogy, and a behaviorist view of
learning that casts the teachers as transmitters and students as passive receivers
of agreed on messages. So what are arguably the central and unique features of
schooling—the three message systems of curriculum, pedagogy, and assessment—are rarely mentioned in mainstream/malestream educational administrative and policy texts, except in terms of outcomes as measured by narrow definitions of success (test scores).

The silence about curriculum and pedagogy within this rational/management approach to policy was possible at least until the 1970s, because it reflected the technicist view of curriculum theorizing that drew from a foundationalist view of knowledge derived from the "pure" disciplines (Carr & Kemmis, 1986). It also assumed a particularly narrow positivistic view that claimed educational administration and policy to be value free and instrumental practices (Bates, 1986). And finally, it presumed the technical-empiricist approach to policy described earlier as top down and linear, with a developmental view of change (Codd, 1988). So, on the one hand, schools were treated as discrete decontextualized sites and, on the other, curriculum ideas and policies stating agreed on objectives were seen to be drawn from outside the school.

Although there has been some dispute within the curriculum field between the applied science views of educational theory informed by discourses of developmental psychology and academic disciplines and the philosophical approach that focused on truth and justice with the rise of the new sociology of knowledge in the 1970s, it had little impact on the way in which curriculum policy was produced (Cherryholmes, 1988; Kemmis & Fitzclarence, 1986). Curriculum content was viewed as a given by academic scientists, which would be organized and made sequential by curriculum development specialists (usually experts in psychology) into fixed materials for teachers and students. As Cherryholmes (1988) commented, no one could, with the legitimizing convergence of the powerful discourses of science and administrative theory and their epistemological claims of one truth, ask why racism, sexism, labor history, minority history, social inequality, and injustice were not addressed. Although the feminist movement more than anything else has had the greatest impact on challenging what constitutes school knowledge, it has failed to challenge the manner in which the policy process is conceptualized. This is largely because gender reform policies have to an extent also assumed a linear, developmental, progressive model of change (Kenway, 1990; Yates, 1993).

Within the rationalist model of change, even its more recent culturally holistic perspectives, gender, race, class, and ethnicity are either treated as non-issues or organizational pathologies that cause conflict and therefore are marginalized as disruptive and counterproductive. Equity is only mentioned in antithesis to efficiency or as a means to produce greater efficiencies. Teachers are treated as unified groups with similar interests and, indeed, as unitary, coherent individuals. The principal is at once the instructional leader and instructional supervisor, disregarding the tensions between these roles. Principals are also the initiators of change and the culture builders in ways that position teachers and students as "cultural dupes," incapable of agency.

Issues of power and knowledge and how they are connected and contested in gender-, class-, and race-specific ways in schools are perceived as "problems" rather than legitimate interests that need to be addressed by those seeking to produce change. This is possibly because power, gender, and contested views of knowledge and organization complicate the "mission" of administration and policy and challenge the interests of those in power. It is in management's interests that the notion of the "hidden" curriculum or gender regime in schools remains hidden because it highlights difference when dominant models of management seek consensus, conformity, and compliance. It does not challenge the distribution of power if organizations are decontextualized from their social and political environment, if dichotomies between the public and the private are maintained, and if members of organizations are viewed as abstract, bodiless individuals who have no sexuality, no emotions, and certainly do not procreate. Change from such a perspective can be imposed from above and outside.

Yet, organizations are constructed very much on the gendered identities of workers (Acker, 1990; Hearn, Sheppard, Tancred-Sheriff, & Burrell, 1990; Mills & Tancred, 1992). Indeed, the administration/teaching divide—one of the most overt aspects of the gender regime in schools—specifically naturalizes the association of educational leadership with masculinity and teaching and pastoral work with femininity (Blackmore, 1993b). So at the same time that women's and girl's bodies and voices are either ruled out of order or objectified, male sexual imagery pervades organizational metaphors and language, and the male presence and voices of authority dominate school time and space as both adult males' and boys' positions are naturalized. Now the previously patriarchal forms of management in which sexuality and difference were sublimated within a naturalized gender regime and a discourse of familial (but authoritarian) harmony have been replaced. No less authoritarian are the messages of strategic management in which the individual's energies (intellectual, cultural, and sexual) are molded toward the organizational ends by channeling individual careerism toward a corporate vision (Kerfoot & Knights, 1993).

The dominant model of policy also draws selectively from organizational and management theory in ways that naturalizes the gender order and the gender regime in schools. It also disconnects schools from wider social relationships on the one hand, but seeks to link schools more closely to the economy. It ignores power as a central organizational concept by only talking about authority. It accepts the privileging of particular forms of knowledge (scientific and technical) and authority (male-dominated, hierarchical educational leadership) under the impression that curriculum and organizational structures are neutral. Policy, from this perspective, can therefore be treated abstractly, as intervening in organizations to produce the necessary change without taking into account organizational histories or the ways in which institutional and systemic change produces a specific balance of interests, forces, and perspectives in specific schools sites at any one time. Such a perspective renders individuals, particularly students, incapable of agency, hence, the silence about the reception of policy or about what students do with curriculum policy.

Significantly, although dominant approaches to policy ignore gender, gender reform policies in Australia have been framed since 1975 by managerialist and technicist approaches to policy (Kenway, 1990; Yates, 1993). Equal opportunity policy tends to fall within this rationalist/technicist policy paradigm in that it assumes linearity between policymaking and outcomes; it tends to ignore the differing cultural contexts in which it is to be implemented (with the exception of the *National Policy for Girls* in 1987); and it treats the "reception of policy," for want of a better term, by administrators, teachers, students, and parents unproblematically. It is assumed that policy is "received" uncritically, passively, and in its totality by teachers and girls, with its emphasis on the unitary individual, its uncritical acceptance of the claims as to the neutrality of organizational life, and its neglect of the social context and power relationships in which any social interaction occurs. The emphasis has been on quantitative outcomes, clear linear processes, consultation, and accountability back to the center. In so doing such policies ignored the gender, class, and racial biases embedded in organizational cultures and even the racial and class biases in the very structures and processes of equal opportunity (EO) policy itself. In part this is because gender equity reform, in Australia particularly, has relied on the intervention of the state (and those able to influence the agendas of the state; Yates, 1993).

Even when teachers have actively been seen to produce policy, for example, school-based curriculum development and decision making, it has still been viewed as a linear process. One particular school, unique in the breadth and depth of its gender reform policies, replicated at the school level the top-down linear model to the policy process (writing policy, writing curriculum, implementing) in attempting to integrate gender throughout the whole curriculum of the school. It failed to do so effectively because this process failed to impart a sense of ownership among the staff or indeed the students early in the project, thereby alienating them and marginalizing the gender reform project. Again, changing curriculum, it was assumed, would change girl's attitudes and practices. It was curriculum-centered rather than girl-centered, policy-oriented rather than practice-oriented (Blackmore, 1991).

At the same time, the dominant rationalist-technicist policy perspective, we found, was in direct antithesis to the processes by which much gender reform had occurred in most schools in our study, in which feminist teachers— the gender workers—had largely been the initiators not only of gender reform, but also of curriculum reform since the 1970s (Kenway & Willis, 1993; Weiler, 1988; Weiner, 1989). There has always been teacher activity, predominantly by women, who through their own initiatives, experience, or individual and collective struggle have worked for gender reform in schools in a variety of ways. This school-based activity gained impetus and coherence from the women's movement and since the early 1970s was diverse and widespread. Through EO networks, gender workers cross fertilized ideas and developed strategies and policies, which in turn informed official policymakers. This has led to the increasing recognition of other than liberal feminist approaches and an eclecticism in policy as well as the break down of the policy generation and implementation divide (Kenway, 1990). It also led to a recognition in schools among feminist teachers that change is inconsistent, time-consuming, contradictory, open-ended, and uneven (Blackmore, 1991; Kenway & Evans, 1991).

In summary, therefore, the theories of change described here, which are embedded in current dominant policy frameworks out of which gender reform policies emerged, failed to address how gender reform was received in schools. First, there was a failure to recognize the significance of language in the making of meaning because of the assumption that policy was read as it was written and that there was little room for reinterpretation. Second, there was a failure to recognize agency and the capacity of the objects of policy to act other than how policy intended and with "good" reason. Third, the way in which culture was viewed as integrating the individual into some consensual holistic culture thereby ignored difference and conflict both at the level of the individual and at the collective level. Fourth, the central concept of the disembodied, desexualized yet unitary individual failed to capture the inconsistencies and contradictions of everyday life confronting these feminist teachers and girls.

CRITICAL TRAJECTORIES

Given that issues of agency, resistance, and culture are central to such bodies of critical theory of the Frankfurt schools, cultural studies, and Gramsci, we sought inspiration in these fields. Certainly, critical theory (and critical organizational theory) challenged the neutrality and homogeneity claimed by the "positivistic" and structural functionalist traditions in administration, curriculum, policy, and social theory (e.g., Bates, 1986; Carr & Kemmis, 1986; Codd, 1988; Connell, 1987; Giroux, 1992; Prunty, 1987; Rein 1983). Critical theory in particular focuses on the centrality of the power/knowledge connection and how it mediates through education, the media, popular culture, and language. In particular, the implication from critical theory is that critiquing the ideological underpinnings of curriculum, pedagogy, and evaluation is only a first step in producing radical change. But, at the same time, "theory cannot guide practice." "Change," from this perspective, "comes about as one's awareness of the limitations and constraints upon human potential are clearly perceived" (Prunty, 1987, p. 29). Critical theoretical perspectives, in challenging the means/ends and fact/value dichotomies of the functionalist approach, also redefine policy as being about the allocation of values and the policy process as inevitably political and value-laden as well as being about ethics and justice.

Although critical theory, particularly the work of Habermas, and its attack on foundationalist epistemology has a significant impact on the field of educational administrative and curriculum theory, at the level of the academy, its meaning in terms of practice is as yet unclear with the exception perhaps of the action research (e.g., Biott & Nias, 1992; Elliott, 1992; Sears, 1992). What is clear, at least at the theoretical level, is the seeming convergence between the emancipatory projects of the cultural studies and critical theory traditions with the feminist political project, with their shared focus on culture, power, media, and agency. We explore these relationships briefly now.

Critical theory out of the Frankfurt tradition includes a critique of positivism, a political economic analysis of postliberal capitalism, with its focus on the legitimation crisis of the state, social psychological research and psychoanalysis, and the role of mass culture in cultural domination. As Morrow (1991) suggests, critical theory tends to favor structure in the structure/agency dialectic and does not develop an adequate theory of culture that "demonstrates that socialized subjects are not simply passively subjected to an anonymous steering process but, rather, actively participate in their interpretative performances in the complex process of social integration" (p. 29). Indeed, critical theory, despite influences from cultural studies, tends to have unitary notions of domination that assume all forms of domination are the same, whereas domination or resistance are played out in gender relations differently from other forms of domination (class, race) (e.g., Blackmore, Kenway, Willis, & Rennie, 1993).

Certainly, critical theory usefully conceptualizes policy as increasing the steering capacity of the state and mediating the macro- and microrelations, making connections between the political economy, the state, and social psychology. In particular, critical theory selectively appropriates theories of discourse to produce sound ideology critiques of policy. At the same time, an ideology critique of the curriculum and gender equity discourses either institutionally or at the level of policy does not actually take us far into the realms of teacher practice and how it changes or affects students lives. First, because for teachers there is little strategic advice offered beyond critique, an issue that troubles many critical theorists, critique alone tends to disempower rather than empower due to a sense of paralysis about action. The assumption of ideology critique, in raising critical consciousness and reflection, is that action would somehow automatically ensue. Although the notion of ideology links forms of consciousness to interests that were in a sense external aspects of focusing on lived experience, the notion of discourse (as in Foucault) remains self-consciously skeptical and focuses on the internal features of the practices of communication and language, that is, on the ways in which language discursively constructs subject positions (Purvis & Hunt, 1993). This latter view made more sense about how to understand how individuals read reform initiatives. Second, although the diverse traditions of critical theory (Gramsci, Frankfurt school, Habermas) focus on issues of power and knowledge, the media, subjectivity, and the blatant silences in functionalist approaches to organizational theory, practice, and policy, it fails to distinguish how power or subordination actually works differently for different subordinate groups within specific contexts. Third, critical theory tends to assume a rather negative connotation of power.

Finally, critical theory does not provide an adequate analysis for those concerned with issues of pedagogy. Habermas's theory of communicative action as developed through his notion of asymmetrical relations, although valuable in terms of organizational ways of working through issues of power and language uses, does not provide any way of theorizing pedagogies about change. In classrooms, the implicit asymmetrical power relations of teacher/student cannot be so readily exposed and reformed in more symmetrical ways. Such a context and the student/teacher relationship makes the notion of undistorted communication and the conditions under which it may emerge more problematic.

Indeed, it is Gramsci's theory of hegemony that provides that link between popular culture, social movements (e.g., feminism), and the apparent "passivity" or compliance of agency to domination (Gramsci, 1971). Furthermore, it is his notion of counterhegemony or resistance that makes it more possible to determine the complex and uneven ways of resistance by teachers and students to policy and change in schools and to think about ways in which these responses are mediated by and through popular culture (Blackmore et al., 1993; Kenway, 1992). The Gramscian view of the state also acknowledges the productive, positive aspects of state power (as working for gender reform through policy intervention) working in contradictory ways through diffuse and various locations and sites and not just the state as repressive and negative (by not funding child care, or male dominated) as implied in critical theory. This converges with a poststructuralist Foucaultian notion of power as being situated in various sites and locations rather than centered or totalizing. In turn, this poses a challenge to the theory of emancipation of critical theory as being based largely on a utopian view of power that is ultimately being abolished. Instead, Gramsci provides a conception of the articulation of power that poststructuralism fails to provide (Morrow, 1991).

Cultural theory, although difficult to define, is also attractive because it too is about political practice, structures of domination, experience, reexamining concepts of class or gender, studying questions of pleasure, space, and time, as well as understanding the fabric of social experience and everyday life and the foundations of power. Yet, cultural studies, particularly of the tradition derived from Marxism, although providing explanation of what exists in terms of power relations in organizations, classroom practices, and peer relationships, fail to provide ways of thinking about a strategic politic of change, as all are reduced to particular forms of domination. Such a strategic politic would need to address what many feminist theorists have recognized but have not theorized about adequately. That is, first, that change is messy, intermittent, overlapping, contradictory, and uneven; second, that change cannot be traced back to one particular source or form of power; and third, that change is framed by a network or web of social relations that goes beyond the gender regime of the organization itself.

The issue of how particular policies are translated into pedagogical practices further complicates any theory of change. Here it could be expected that the debates over critical pedagogy would be informative. Yet, the seeming convergence of feminist and critical theory (primarily the strand of Gramscian poststructuralism) has reduced it to more of an internal debate within the academy (Ellsworth, 1989). This debate has not had significant impact on either the pedagogical or curriculum practices in schools or policy. These debates do not particularly inform those working for change in schools first because the debate is largely at the level of the academy or, at best, teacher educators and their students. Therefore, attention is on issues of pedagogy as it relates to adults who attend voluntarily and indeed self-select into particular courses (e.g., women's studies). In schools there is the element of compulsion as well as age-related factors that problematize this particular critical pedagogic focus of curriculum reform discourse (Kenway & Modra, 1992). Second, embedded in much of the concept of empowerment in the critical pedagogy literature is a somewhat patronizing view that some individuals (e.g., teachers) can empower others. It is increasingly clear that the notion of false consciousness is not helpful when considering why girls resist particular feminist reforms and not others. It is no longer tenable to argue that girls do not act in their own interests, that they will act according to their interests as defined by others, or that they do not make "rational" choices within the constraints of their situation, their experience, and their individual histories (Blackmore et al., 1993).

Third, although much of this debate has focused on the issue of critical pedagogy, and therefore one would assume how students receive various curricula and pedagogical forms, it has also been a highly theoretical work rather than practical. This is no more evident in that whereas the debate over curriculum theory has raged sufficiently to produce a new interest in curriculum discourse within the academy, the corporate discourse and all its associated baggage of management approaches to policy has continued to have significant influence on what actually is taught in schools in the United States, Australia, and the United Kingdom (Molnar, 1992). Business has not been so coy about assuming that schools can be engineered to change society, and the economy and indeed curriculum is increasingly being packaged as another form of consumer product, whereas educational policy is being framed from an entirely functionalist view of schooling that lacks any understanding of the complexity of how curricula and pedagogies are received or without any more than gestural tokenism toward equity.

Certainly these debates within critical pedagogy require recognition that both critical and/or feminist pedagogies can be equally tyrannical for particular social groups. These debates lead to greater sensitivity to the politics of the teacher-student relationship and to what can be understood as resistance, compliance, and accommodation of girls to particular curricula forms and pedagogical strategies.

At the same time, certain critical traditions do impact on what happens in schools. The action research and teacher as researcher movements of the previous two decades are still evident in schools and indeed have been major influences in much innovative curriculum development in Australian schools as well as in English schools, particularly with respect to gender reform initiatives (e.g., Kenway & Evans, 1991; Weiler, 1988; Weiner, 1989). But, as argued earlier, these movements had little input into how policy is theorized or received. Second, in England particularly, gender has been ignored as a substantive issue by the mainstream movement leading to different and highly gendered strands

of theory and practice within the movement itself (Weiner, 1989). More specifically, with respect to change, theories of action research and teacher-as-
researcher, by working toward change within the constraints of organizations,
tend to err on the side of the doable and practical rather than on the desirable
and the ideal. Their emphasis on a consensual form of organizational politics
can also submerge difference, whereas the cyclical processes still tend to
assume a linear, incremental, or developmental view of change.

Possibly the major shift in thinking about how policy theorizes change
at the organizational level is the notion of policy as text or discourse (e.g.,
Griffith, 1992). Of interest is the way Ball rethinks policy as text from a poststructuralist perspective, rather than policy as discourse from a critical theoretical perspective (Ball, 1990, 1993; Bowe & Ball, 1992). He does this by considering the rise of the New Right and its impact on educational policymaking in
England (Ball, 1993). Yet, his distinction between policy as text and policy as
discourse is questionable, as text and discourse clearly operate in relation to
each other, rather than in opposition in ways that recognize constraint and
agency (Henry, 1993). The notion of policy as text or discourse does offer new
possibilities in terms of allowing for different readings within institutions and
within individuals. It also collapses the macro/micro distinctions, while allowing it open to analysis, and it does not allow the policy process itself to remain
as a given. It provides a way of thinking about the relationship between policy
intentions, how they are read, and to what effects, while recognizing that the
process is complex and open-ended.

Having reviewed the ways in which particular bodies of literature have
theorized change, we proceed in the following sections to offer some suggestions as to how we found feminist poststructuralism to be a useful framework,
building on the earlier critiques.

FEMINIST POSTSTRUCTURALISM AS A THEORY FOR CHANGE IN SCHOOLS[1]

As we mentioned at the outset, in the process of using a poststructuralist framework to conduct research about gender reform in schools, it became increasingly evident that poststructuralism is also suggestive for the process of gender
reform itself. So, in this third section we share some of our emerging ideas on
this topic. We say, first of all, that we do not believe that poststructuralism provides "The Definitive Answer," but rather that in encouraging feminist workers
for change to see things somewhat differently and to ask some previously
unasked questions, it may help to refine and revitalize their work for change.

---

[1]This chapter arises out of a research project funded by the Australian Council for Research
(1990-1992) on *Gender Reform in Schools: Equal Opportunity Policies, Their Reception and
Effects* involving Jane Kenway, Sue Willis, Jill Blackmore, and Leonie Rennie.

Our view at this stage is that there are two main ways in which post-structuralism might be of practical use to people working for gender justice in and through schools. First, it provokes us to consider some different ways of undertaking the professional development of feminist agents for change in schools. As suggested earlier and as we elaborate further here, it offers teachers and others a way of conceptualizing the gender and other politics of schooling that adequately attends to the complexities of schools and social institutions. In so doing, it is suggestive about the processes and purposes of change. Second, it offers some ideas about new approaches to curriculum and pedagogy that take into account the disorderly ways in which meanings are written, read and rewritten—so to speak. We will consider each in turn.

Professional Development: New Ways for Teachers to Read and Rewrite the Gender Politics of the School

There is a tendency among gender reformers and others in schools to read the gendered aspects of the school in two ways. They most often see the gendered culture of the school as the unfortunate reflection of wider relationships of gender, as elsewhere or out there. And their thinking about gender within the school tends to be structured by the ways in which the practices of schools themselves are structured; so they think of "gender and administration and policy," "gender and teachers," "gender and the curriculum," "gender and the classroom/the playground" and "gender and the students." From here they may move into a problem-solving mode. For example: "What are the problems for girls in the playground?" and "What can we do to prevent these problems from happening?" Or they mobilize a number of dualisms. All of these groups and practices are divided into good/bad, sexist/nonsexist, oppressor/oppressed, on-side/off-side, and so forth. Their task then becomes very daunting. How can we work to shift everyone or everything to the positive side of the binary? And, at this point, an array of beliefs about human motivation, communication, and approaches to change come into play. These have been outlined by one of us at some length elsewhere (Kenway & Evans, 1991). So, suffice it to say here that at one end of the spectrum is a behaviorist viewpoint of motivation and a transmission viewpoint of communication. At the other end is a view that is both voluntaristic and rationalistic. Now, it seems that these ways of thinking are not only unhelpful, but they are quite disabling.

Post-structuralism invokes us to consider the "heterogeneous ensemble of power relations operating at the micro level of society. The practical implication of this model is that resistance must be carried out in local struggles against the many forms of power exercised at the everyday level of social relations" (Sawicki, 1991, p. 23). These comments by Sawicki reiterate a point made earlier, namely, that the gender regime of the school is not simply a reflection of the gender order of society but, rather, that schools participate in the production of gender relations in ways that *make for* their own specificity and that, at the same time, contribute to and are a result of wider social patterns. Furthermore, as Foucault's ideas that we outlined earlier indicate, if we wish to come to grips with the microphysics of power, we would be wise to look beneath conventional institutional ways of structuring our thinking in order to discover the technologies of power that structure and drive *them.*

These technologies of power/knowledge or discourses seek to form "the subjects about which they speak"; their purpose is to regulate, to discipline, to define what is normal and what is deviant, what is desirable, and what is not, so as to divide people from each other and within themselves. They claim the moral and rational high ground; they claim to be telling the truth, and in seeking to discredit other such claims they participate in the politics of truth-telling or discourse.

Now, drawing from these ideas, feminists talk of the politics of gender and of technologies of gender (de Lauretis, 1990) and ask questions such as: How have females become objects and thus subjects of these regimes of truth and dividing practices? How are females defined and organized? Who are the experts that service these technologies? And, in education, they point to such discursive fields as psychology, measurement, and management and to the theories that inform curriculum, pedagogy, and teachers' work and their conceptions of children or students. As they demonstrate, it is these and other school and nonschool discourses, in concert and in contest, that come to define various normal, natural, and preferable ways of being male and female, that construct students', teachers', principals', and parents' identities in gendered ways and in multiple and shifting, yet patterned, relationships of dominance and subordination.

Our research into girls' postschool options certainly showed that girls learn about the future, their futures, and themselves through contradictory and shifting webs of discourses. It showed that these are produced by and through schools and other social and cultural institutions through sets of relationships and representations and through girls themselves as they participate in everyday discourses. Discourses about being female and feminine weave their way through those about being an appropriate and successful student and about what is worthwhile at school. They weave their way through discourses about being social and sexual, about leisure, friendships, romance, image and style, about growing up and "settling down," about dependence and independence, and through those discourses about being in paid work or being a parent, a household member, and a participant in the politics of civic life. Through this discursive tapestry girls are taught about the powers and the pleasures that are suitable for them. They make their futures, and to some extent the future, from the positions made available to them through such discourses and from constrained and often unconscious "selections" from these positions. In other words, and to change the metaphor, they *read* their futures from the gendered and other narratives in which they are immersed, and then they *write* their future's script variously constrained and enabled by the narratives' conventions.

Overall, then, feminist poststructuralism encourages feminists in schools to identify the discourses that are making gendered subjects, the meanings that are being made *from* them by members of the school community, and how these are remade through school members. It also encourages feminists to both work toward remaking meaning and to help others to remake meaning and themselves by participating in the politics of gender. But what really does this rather glib phrase mean?

Is it, as many feminist teachers believe, about becoming another "truthteller" and producing new and feminist technologies of gender? This is a rather tricky question that leads one into epistemological and strategic difficulties, which we briefly attend to shortly (and for a more complete account, see Kenway, 1992). For the moment, let it be said that participating in the politics of gender means, first of all, "not taking established meanings, values and power relations for granted" (Weedon, 1987, p. 175) and recognizing "the political implications of particular ways of fixing identity and meaning" (p. 173). It means asking questions such as: Where do technologies of gender come from? Whose interests do they seem to serve? How do they maintain their supremacy, and in what ways may they be vulnerable to change? It means looking for weak points, contradictions, ruptures, discontinuities, and cracks in systems of representation, and converting them into moments of negotiation and possibility through the use of whatever resources are available. So, for example, when discourses of masculinity are cracking—even if slightly—and when, as a result, men ask "what about the boys?", the possibility arises for the development of feminist pedagogies for boys, for a disarticulation and rearticulation of the meaning of masculinity (see further Kenway, 1991).

Participating in the politics of gender also means, as Weedon (1987, p. 174) said, aiming "to make resistant discourses and subject positions more widely available." Resistant discourses offer new ways of seeing, being, and being seen. So, contesting, subverting, and destabilizing hegemonic gendered discourses is what the politics of gender is about. Bryson and de Castell (1992) turn to postmodernism to find some suggestions about ways of "degendering" "gender" (p. 43). They argue that: "a 'postmodern' conception of gender as [sic] a non-cohesive open textured "pastiche" of characteristics, aptitudes and dispositions whose ongoing construction and reconstruction it is a central task of feminist praxis to enable and encourage" (p. 67).

Accordingly, they suggest that feminist praxis could reconfigure the social relationships and practices that have formed around male/female dichotomies through a politic of pastiche, parody, and mimicry; one in which gendered conventions and codes are exploded and replaced by "novel forms and functions" (p. 43). The suggestion is that a self-conscious playing with gendered positionings parodies their fixity and exposes their truth claims as political. It opens up the possibility for a range of new and more powerful identities for females.

Generally, then, according to this notion of the politics of gender, in rewriting the learning environment, gender reformers should seek—as they do currently do—to make it supportive and inclusive of girls and women, but they should also seek to make it challenging and expansive. This means they should promote and encourage a wide variety of ways of being female, develop and promote new and nonviolent ways of being male, and expect students to try out and take risks with new gender identities.

Curriculum and Pedagogy: What Feminist Poststructuralism Has to Offer

Feminist poststructuralism is immensely suggestive for curriculum and pedagogy. As we have implied throughout, it calls immediately into play a deconstructionist impulse. In part this impulse invokes teachers to consider the gendered positions they make available to students through their teaching (the scripts they write), and it further invokes them to examine their own understanding of gender identity. Among the feminist teachers of our research, there was a range of ways in which teachers viewed girls. They were variously perceived as deficient and as unsung heroines, as highly rational and hence in control of their "choices," and as irrational, governed almost entirely by their feelings and/or by the gendered discourses of their cultures and subcultures. They were viewed as sexual and asexual, as similarly oppressed and differently oppressed, as products of prefeminist and to a much lesser extent feminist and "postfeminist" eras, as victims and as agents. The list goes on. These different views were written into the many teaching and administrative practices that the teachers in our research schools adopted. The point to be made here is that although these perceptions were evident in teaching practices, it was not always the case that teachers were aware of the views of girls that their practices implied or, indeed, of their views of girls per se. Given that such views are the touchstone upon which much else depends, it would seem more than useful that these and other teachers explore both their own perceptions of girlhood (and boyhood) and those implicit in their practices.

Our view is that poststructuralism offers an understanding of girls that is able to accommodate the complex qualities of girlhood. Rather than insisting that girls are one thing or another, it recognizes that they are all of the above at different moments and in different circumstances. It recognizes girls as subjects who are variously "rational" and "irrational" and acknowledges their commonalities and their many differences. It indicates that girls are productions and producers of themselves and their times.

It seems that one fundamental purpose for a feminist pedagogy for girls must be their production both as informed and critical readers of their life worlds and as informed and visionary agents and advocates for a better world. It is therefore quite vital that teachers help them to develop the knowledge and skills that will enable them to be this way. This implies that all school subjects would explicitly teach students about the politics of gender, that is, that gender is not a natural arrangement but rather a social and cultural construction made and changed by people, and that gender relations in the labor force, the home, the school, and elsewhere arise from relationships of power and struggle and that they therefore can be changed—of course, not easily. As our research indicated that starting at girls' starting points was important, such teachings should, of necessity, connect with their lived social and cultural experiences. In this regard, girls would be encouraged to explore the role of gender in shaping their lives and environments and the possibilities of different feminisms for opening their futures in life-enhancing ways. This would involve considerations of the connections between knowledge, power, inequalities, and change and the requirement that students *use* their knowledge and skills; that is, in the school and beyond, they are encouraged to become critical readers and active citizens working for gender justice.

Of course this is easier said than done, particularly if one both accepts a poststructuralist view of communication and therefore acknowledges girls as active readers and rewriters of feminist pedagogies. Nonetheless, at the risk of entering some very slippery epistemological terrain, we do have a few suggestions. Some, again, draw directly from poststructuralism and, others draw from our research on gender reform in schools.

One guiding principle of all curriculum reform should, in our view, be deconstruction—broadly defined.[2] So, pedagogies designed to enhance girls' postschool options would deconstruct the apparently natural organization of work in the paid work force, the home, and in civic life and the apparently natural but deeply political notions of choice and the separation of public and private spheres. Such revisioning of work would involve the use of feminist genealogies[3] and theories about these topics. For example, sexuality education would be discussed in this context, and the historical, symbolic, and concrete connections between sexuality and work, power, value, and violence would be explored. Such a focus would also involve helping students to develop and practice their own genealogical and deconstructive skills so that they could constantly see gendered settlements in the making in a variety of settings, including the school, the workplace, the home, and the media[4]. Of course, seeing, believing, and acting do not necessarily go together. So another question is: How can girls be encouraged both to believe what they see through this process of revisioning and to reenvisage themselves as current and future actors in the processes that they have come to recognize as political? Our research has suggested that

[2]For a practical set of suggestions about "doing deconstruction," see Lather (1991b).

[3]The term *genealogy* is used by Foucault to refer to analyses of the conditions in which discourses have emerged and functioned; they provide "a history of the present." His genealogies of sexuality have been of most interest to feminists.

[4]Davies's recent book *Shards of Glass* (1993) offers an account of the use of deconstruction with primary students and points to some of the benefits and difficulties involved.

assertiveness training, informed negotiation of the curriculum and conscious and active participation in the formal and informal, and contradictory politics of the school are some possibilities. The development and overseeing of action plans by girls and the use of sexual harassment grievance procedures are concrete and powerful examples here.

Having said that, we should also say, again, that this is all easier said than done. Many students—female and male—are, as our research indicated, strongly resistant to denaturing anything at all—particularly matters of gender. We found that, in broad terms, this resistance is associated with matters of identity, investment, pain, and pleasure, and we believe that feminist pedagogies in schools must attend to these. We elaborate with regard, particularly, to the matter of pleasure.

Feminist Pedagogies and Girls' Bodies

As Foucault made eminently clear, the body is a prime site for regulation. And, as Sawicki (1991) pointed out, Foucault calls this "bio-power," and one form it takes is the:

> development of a knowledge of power over the body—its capacities, gestures, movements, location and behaviours. Disciplinary practices . . . aim to render the individual both more powerful productive and useful *and* docile. They are located within institutions . . . but also at the micro level of society in the everyday activities and habits of individuals. They secure their hold not through their use of violence or force but rather by creating desires, attaching individuals to specific identities and establishing norm against which individuals and their behaviours and bodies are judged and against which they police themselves. (pp. 67-68) (emphasis in original)

A number of feminists have picked up the notion of "biopower" and explored it from a feminist angle. For example, Bartky (1988) points out that there is a vast array of institutionalized and noninstitutionalized "disciplines" that "produce a mode of embodiment that is peculiarly feminine" (p. 63). Bartkey offers a stunningly persuasive documentation of the disciplinary regime of femininity and of the forces and experts that produce the female body as a spectacle. Despite the intense interest in the body that feminist scholars have shown, feminists in schools have not particularly recognized the potential of this scholarship for their teaching.[5] Before we proceed to indicate how it might be useful, we explain how some feminist pedagogies in our research schools have dealt with girls' bodies. The following are some examples.

---

[5]In her paper, "Skinned Alive: Towards a Postmodern Pedagogy of the Body," College (1991) develops a number of ideas relating pedagogy to matters of the body "in the institutional order and in popular culture" (p. 72).

An English unit on gender, ethnic, and age stereotyping encouraged students to think "deeply, perceptively and sensitively" about literature generally and the media in particular and the part they play in "constructing perceptions." The teacher who developed this course recognized that "teenage kids are preoccupied with trying to make sense of what it is to be female and what it is to be male." She helped them make sense of their gender by offering them identities as critical and resistant readers of the cultural forces that would shape their lives. Although she herself was not sufficiently critical to be able to recognize the gendered and class forces at play in the systematic devaluing of romance novels, particularly, and popular culture, generally, she positioned them as informed agents in their own self-production and helped them to try to make sense of who they are and might become after school. And, apparently, many girls accepted this position—in the English class at least.

A jewelry-making unit in technical studies in the same school attempted to offer girls similarly expansive positions. By giving them access to the technical skills "that they wouldn't normally get," the course offered them the lesson that being female and being technically competent are perfectly compatible. The teachers who developed this course recognized only too well the ideological power of naming subjects and assigning topics. They knew that to attract girls they had to tap into some aspects of female identity, but they refused to offer them a course that drew on gender stereotypes of women's work in the home and instead that drew on another gendered social construction that was no less problematic: the adolescent girls' preoccupation with self-adornment. In the sense that this attracted girls to the jewelry-making course, it worked; and the girls remained enthusiastic about an expanded identity because the atmosphere was pleasant and because technical success was achieved. Their perceptions of things technical and their relationship to such things changed, and the fact that a significant number wanted an advanced course in jewelry making indicated a willingness to retain an expanded notion of femaleness. On the other hand, the course placed both the girls and the teachers in something of a double bind. The girls were offered old and new identities simultaneously. Becoming technical was framed by femininity's emphasis on adornment and display, and it is possible that the former was only acceptable in the context of the latter. The fact that only a tiny minority of girls contemplated further technical studies without any feminine overlay suggest that this was the case. It seems that even though the teachers were sensitive to some problems associated with some constructions of femininity, they were not so sensitive to others. Although it was certainly useful to tap into girls' concern with their image, the teachers did not take the opportunity to work with, through, and beyond such concerns; ultimately, they offered girls a curriculum that was both expansive *and* constraining.

In comparison with both of the prior examples was the "Looking Good" course from home economics. This course focused almost entirely on the body, its language, and its disguises: teaching girls how best to present themselves by caring for their health and through the use of makeup and clothes.

This unit, along with an equally popular, after-school Grooming and Deportment class run by a fashion model, offered girls ways of capitalizing on their "good points" and minimizing their "bad points." But what it did not do was offer them any sense of themselves beyond their own image and others' gaze. They were implicitly taught that girls (as opposed to boys) must be concerned with managing and constructing others' impressions of them through the way they look. They were offered little or no sense of how the media, the fashion, cosmetic, and even the health industries produce "mass disseminated physical ideal(s)" (Wolf, 1990, p. 14) as commodities; of how women and girls are thus taught how they should look; of how an emphasis on appearances makes women constantly "vulnerable to outside approval"; and ultimately of how "images of beauty are used against women" (p. 14).

In contrast with all of these examples was a physical education unit that offered girls other ways of relating to their bodies. The stress here was on the body, not as a surface for others to look at, or as an object of social control, but as a source of power and pleasure. In single-sex classes, girls were given the opportunity to participate in a range of physical activities that they defined as "fun" to find some new sources of physical fun; at the same time they were expected to explore the full range of their physicality; identifying strengths and capacities they had previously been unaware of.

Clearly girls' postschool options can be enhanced by courses that encourage them to have a productive concern for their health and appearance, and it is highly probable that feeling and looking good are strongly correlated to the sense of well-being that permits girls to act positively and powerfully in and on their social environments. However, a difference exists between offering girls courses that achieve these sorts of effects and offering those that position them firmly and uncritically within certain disabling discourses of femininity. Wolf (1990) has convincingly argued that feminist successes in many social spheres have been accompanied by the intensification of pressure on women to conform to psychologically and medically restrictive, costly, and damaging "beauty myths," which as they have gained power in certain senses, they have lost it in others.

Another of our research schools developed courses about sexual harassment and the use of grievance procedures that helped girls to understand how their bodies are used as sites of oppressive gender relations and encouraged them to employ the "legislative" mechanisms that were available to prevent such oppressive behaviours. This program, like the English class noted earlier, also positioned girls as informed agents and this is important. But where do courses such as these leave them? What new locations do they offer them? A next step might well be courses that, like the physical education class, offer girls new, healthy, positive and expansive ways of relating to their bodies and even to their ornamentation. Such a next step appears necessary in order that they can move beyond the association between their bodies and pain and the ubiquitous gaze to come to associate them with freedom, dignity, pleasure, and power. The pleasures constructed through the Looking Good and the Grooming and

Deportment courses were unfortunately those derived from seeing oneself reflected back in others' eyes. They thus left the girls dependent for their pleasure in their own bodies on the approval of others. Indeed, a mirror metaphor guided these courses. Perhaps, to pick up on the points we made earlier from Bryson and de Castell, a performance metaphor may have been more generative for them. This suggests that femininity is a performance, a drama, or, more light-heartedly, a play that involves lots of temporary roles and costumes. The performance metaphor allows the girls to feel a sense of control over different performance genres, to pick up, discard, play, and take risks with them and even to go beyond them through improvisation, collage, and carnival. Femininity can thus become a source of power and pleasure rather than a source of control.

Another important dimension of a feminist pedagogy for girls therefore is that they are encouraged to play with traditional constraints and to enjoy taking risks with their identities. Overall, then, our reading of poststructuralism would suggest that feminist teachers in school develop curricula and pedagogy for girls that position them as critical and playful agents so as to become, in a sense, what de Lauretis (1990) calls "eccentric subjects," continually and disruptively operating from within and outside of old and new positionings. However, this is only one aspect of a many-sided story. What about the matter of different bodies?

Different Girls and Different Feminisms

Girls are positioned very differently by the discourses of the school and elsewhere. They are positioned by the primary discursive fields of race, class, ethnicity, "disability," and sexuality and by more subordinate discourses to do with, for example, age, competence, and personality. Our research indicated that most, but, we stress, not all, work for change does not address the matter of difference in any adequate way at all. The tendency is to essentialize all girls in terms of the "normal girl" and to assume both that all girls have similar needs, interests, pleasures, and anxieties and that what oppresses one oppresses all, what "empowers" one "empowers" all. Now, although on the one hand there are grains of "truth" in this, on the other hand nothing could be further from "the truth," and of course most of our teachers actually knew this. Their difficulty was what to do about it. Many of those who tried to address this issue inevitably got caught in all sorts of dilemmas associated with either cultural relativism, liberal pluralism, and "anything goes"-isms, or with the cultural prejudices, ignorances, and negativities arising from their own locations around these discursive regimes. In our view, "difference" is one of the most difficult issues facing feminists in schools. Nonetheless, we believe that the sorts of open-ended pedagogies that we have outlined in this section have the potential to support a feminist politic of locations. However, their capacity to do so depends very much on the professional development of teachers, a matter that requires further elaboration but that will not be undertaken here. However, we do want to comment on the dangers and possibilities of pedagogies that recognize the plurality of identity and of femaleness and that make problematic the concept of woman or girl.

Many feminists feel that this spells the end of the identity politics upon which feminism has hitherto been based, and that perhaps it spells the end of the particular feminisms through which they have constructed their feminist identities and upon which they have developed their work for change (see further Kenway, 1992, pp. 137-141). Certainly the emphasis on difference and complexity and on deconstruction generally raises a number of theoretical, political, and pedagogical questions for feminism that many of us are trying to sensitively and cautiously work through (see, for example, Britzman, Santiago-valles, Jimenez-munoz, & Lamash, 1991; Jones, 1991). Now, we do not want to go into detail about all the difficulties that arise here. Rather, what we want to do is note some ways in which thought is proceeding. We have found Martin's work (1988) particularly helpful in this regard, and it is to her thoughts on these matters that we turn to now.

Martin (1988) argues that while acknowledging the limitations of "other" feminisms, they must also be recognized as providing certain conditions of political possibility. She points out that feminism faces something of a paradox that she characterizes as the historical and political necessity "for a fundamentally deconstructive impulse and a need to construct the category woman and to search for truths, authenticity and universals," thus necessitating a "double strategy" (p. 13). In so saying, she asks: "How do feminists participate in struggles over the meaning(s) of woman in ways that do not repress pluralities without losing sight of the political necessity for fiction and unity?" (p. 15). How do we avoid establishing "a new set of experts who will speak the truth of ourselves and our sex in categorical terms, closing our struggle around certain privileged meanings and naturalizing the construct woman?" (p. 18). She concludes by saying: "We cannot afford to refuse to take a political stand 'which pins us to our sex' for the sake of an abstract theoretical correctness, but we can refuse to be content with fixed identities or to universalize ourselves as revolutionary subjects" (pp. 13-18).

Other feminists also emphasize the importance of being practical. They reject the claims by some poststructuralist feminists that negative critique is the best we have to offer and note the importance both of feminist utopias and visions and of political mobilization. However, they also point to the necessity for organizations, strategies, and visions that, as Sawicki (1991, p. 12) put it, are "sensitive to the dangers of authoritarianism, ethnocentricism and political vanguardism."

Drawing from the work of Lorde, Sawicki invites us to explore the many dimensions of difference. She asks us to consider "How power uses difference to fragment opposition and to divide individuals within themselves" (p. 18). But she also insists that we must uncover the distortions in our understandings of each other and, in the process, both redefine what differences mean and seek to preserve them. Furthermore, she says we must search for ways of utilizing difference as a multisource both of resistance to various modes of domination and of change. In this sense, then, feminism becomes a broad-based, diverse struggle that combines an "appreciation of the limits of individual experience" (p. 12) with an appreciation of our commonality. But, of necessity, part of this struggle is to redefine and learn from our differences. In this regard, Sawicki makes the case for radical pluralism and coalition politics built on shifting allegiances and interests, rather than on the ahistorical illusion of stable coalitions.

As we see it, this way of thinking about difference has important implications for curriculum and pedagogy and for the professional development of teachers. Rather than implying the necessity of abandoning certain modernist feminisms, it implies the need for an education in different feminisms, for an exploration of their different weaknesses and strengths in particular circumstances in schools and beyond, and for a view of them as strategies rather than truths for pedagogy. Teachers could help students to see different feminisms as strategies for change to be selectively and judiciously deployed. They could then also help students to see that feminism itself is a discursive field of struggle, not only with different "horses for different courses," but also with different dividends for different punters. However, a recognition of the strategic merits of different feminisms should not blind teachers to their dangers. A feminist politic of difference has alerted other feminisms to their particular dominating tendencies; to their potential dangerousness, as Foucault would say. And, as we noted earlier, poststructuralism's emphasis on interdiscursivity has alerted us all to the ways in which feminism of all hues can be coopted, diverted, and undermined by their "others" and in different sets of circumstances. This points to the necessity for feminist teachers to continually engage in self-critical reflexivity, to "subject feminist categories and concepts to critical historical analysis in a continual effort to expose their limitations and highlight their specificity" (Sawicki, 1991, p. 48). This does not mark the end of feminist history in schools but rather the end of the feminist dogma that abounds.

CONCLUSION

We have covered a lot of ground in this chapter so it may be helpful if we conclude by reminding readers of the path we have taken. We began by pointing to the ways in which dominant models of policy have been informed by theories of change that are not helpful in explaining the gap between policy and practice, particularly as played out in schools among girls. In reviewing this mainstream literature and then more critical approaches, we indicated the need for more sophisticated theories to guide research on educational change, theories that address in particular how students respond to change. From there, we proceeded to offer our interpretation of feminist poststructuralism and to elaborate on the ways in which we developed and deployed this theoretical framework in order to examine the complex and multifaceted process of gender reform in schools. We then suggested that feminist poststructuralism may also be useful for the professional development of teachers and for the production of more powerful curriculum and pedagogy. In the first instance we showed how it offers teachers a different way of reading the gender dynamics of the school, and in the second instance we suggested that teaching or learning proceed in certain ways and that, in the process, it attends much more carefully and sensitively to matters of pleasure and pain. We elaborated on this point with reference to pedagogies addressing girls' bodies and the differences between girls, and we raised a number of matters that warrant further research.

Finally, then, what we have offered here is a number of tentative suggestions about the ways in which feminist poststructuralism can make feminists' hopes for girls practical rather than their despair about girls convincing. Clearly these ideas are, in many cases, rather abstract, and they need to be worked through in dialogue with feminist teachers. We would like to lay stress on the term *dialogue* because there are many institutional practices in education that divide feminists into groups as theorists and practitioners. We think the distinction is dubious and destructive. What is needed in these current hard times are well-theorized practices and practical theories.

14

ideology   force

power

consent   coercion

Critical Language
Awareness and Self-Identity
in Education

Norman Fairclough
University of Lancaster

The issue of language and power in education is just a part of the more general
social problematic of language and power and ought not in my view to be isolated from it. We live in an age in which power is predominantly exercised
through the generation of consent rather than through coercion, through ideology rather than through physical force, through the inculcation of self-disciplin-
ing practices rather than through the breaking of skulls (although there is still
unfortunately no shortage of the latter). It is an age in which the production and
reproduction of the social order depend increasingly on practices and processes
of a broadly cultural nature. Part of this development is an enhanced role for
language in the exercise of power: It is mainly in discourse (by which I mean
use of language conceived of in a socially rich way, as a form of social practice)
that consent is achieved, ideologies are transmitted, and practices, meanings,
values, and identities are taught and learned. This is clear from the generally
acknowledged role of the mass media as probably the single most important
social institution in bringing off these processes in contemporary societies. And
it is recognized in the salience given to language and discourse (the "linguistic
turn") in the work of theorists of modern and contemporary society, including
Heidegger, Foucault, Derrida, Bourdieu, and Habermas.

We also live in an age of great change and instability, in which changing cultural practices are a major constituent of social change, which in many cases means to a significant degree changing discursive practices and changing practices of language use. For example, contemporary society has been widely described as "consumer" or "promotional" society (Featherstone, 1991; Wernick, 1991), pointing to the salient cultural aspects of marketization and commodification, the general reconstruction of social life (including previously protected domains) on a market basis. A significant part of this development has been the generalization of "promotion" as a communicative function—discourse as a vehicle for "selling" goods, services, organizations, ideas, or people—across domains of discursive practice (or what I call "orders of discourse"; Fairclough, 1992a). This has involved, for instance, a colonizing spread of the genre of commodity advertising into professional and public service orders of discourse on a massive scale (see Fairclough, 1993, for an analysis of higher education in these terms).

Another connected dimension of discursively constituted sociocultural change that affects educational institutions among others is, in Giddens' (1991) terms, the shift toward a "post-traditional" society, in which (a) traditions have to be justified against alternative possibilities rather than being taken for granted, (b) relationships in public based automatically on authority are in decline (as are personal relationships based on kinship), and (c) rather than being a function of given positions and roles, people's self-identity is built up through a process of negotiation. One general linguistic consequence with important educational implications is the great increase in demands placed on the dialogical abilities needed for such negotiative processes (witness the new salience of dialogical spoken language "skills" in contemporary language education programs). The posttraditionalization thesis also provides a framework for the process of informalization (Featherstone, 1991; Wouters, 1986), which has been such a prominent feature of contemporary society, and its specifically linguistic facet, which I have referred to as the "conversationalization" of public discourse (Fairclough, 1992a, in press). Conversationalization is, I believe, deeply ambivalent: It can be read in an antielitist way as an opening up of access to public domains, or as an appropriation of private domain practices for the instrumental purposes of dominant forces in public institutions (see the discussion of "synthetic personalization" in Fairclough, 1989).

As a consequence of its increased salience in social reproduction and transformation, discourse (language use) is subjected to attention and intervention on an unprecedented scale. This comes mainly from those in power to sustain the status quo or as part of attempts to engineer change in institutions and organizations in particular wished-for directions. For example, much training in education is oriented to a significant degree toward the use and inculcation of particular discursive practices in educational organizations, more or less explicitly interpreted as an important facet of the inculcation of particular cultural meanings and values, social relationships and identities, and pedagogies. I have suggested in general terms that the "technologization of discourse" is a distinctive characteristic of the contemporary sociolinguistic order (Fairclough, 1992a, in press). This does not amount to a claim that institutional intervention to reshape discursive practices is new per se (which it is not), but that such intervention has assumed distinctive contemporary forms: in its sheer scale, in the systematic way in which it is applied, in its embedding within institutional practices and routines, in its systematic use of academic research, and in the ways in which such research feeds into training.

Educational institutions are involved in many ways in these general developments affecting language in its relation to power. First, educational practices themselves constitute a core domain of linguistic and discursive power and of the engineering of discursive practices. Second, many other domains are mediated and transmitted by educational institutions. Third, educational institutions are to a greater or lesser extent involved in educating people about the sociolinguistic order they live in. In some cases they are aiming to equip them with what has in my view become, because of the enhanced social and cultural role of language and because of the technologization of discourse, an essential prerequisite for effective democratic citizenship: the capacity for the critique of language. No doubt the critique of language is in the best cases already carried out reflexively, that is, it is directed at the practices of the educational institution itself (and even at the practices of the critical classroom) and toward issues of language and power in education.

I believe that the problematic of language and power is fundamentally a question of democracy. Those affected need to take it on board as a political issue, as feminists have about the issue of language and gender. If problems of language and power are to be seriously tackled, they will be tackled by the people who are directly involved, especially the people who are subject to linguistic forms of domination and manipulation. This is as true in educational organizations as it is elsewhere. Struggle and resistance are in any case a constant accompaniment of domination and manipulation: The will to impose discursive practices or engineer shifts in discursive practices from above is one thing, but in actuality the conditions in which such a will to power must take its chance may include a diversity of practices, a resistance to change, and even contrary wills to transform practices in different directions. Of course, struggle against domination has varying degrees of success, and one factor in success is the theoretical and analytical resources an opposition has access to. Critical linguists and discourse analysts have an important auxiliary role to play here in providing analyses and, importantly, in providing critical educators with resources for programs of what my colleagues and I have called *critical language awareness* (Clark, Fairclough, Ivanic, & Martin-Jones, 1990, 1991; Fairclough, 1992a)— programs to develop the capacities of people for language critique.

I describe in this chapter an approach along these lines to the general societal problematic of language and power and indicate its particular applicability to the forms that that problematic takes within educational organizations. The first element in this approach is the development of a critical tradition within language studies, and in the next section of the chapter I sketch my own work on critical language study and critical discourse analysis. The second element that the chapter goes on to describe is the application of this critical theory and method in the development of critical language awareness work within schools and other educational organizations. I conclude the chapter with an example, drawn from analyses carried out by colleagues at Lancaster University, of how critical language awareness work can lead to reflexive analysis of practices of domination implicit in the transmission and learning of academic discourse, and the engagement of learners in struggle to contest and change such practices. I finally use this example for some reflections on the difficulties facing those dealing with issues of language and power, in education and elsewhere, in the complex and often confusing sociocultural circumstances of contemporary societies.

CRITICAL LANGUAGE STUDY[1]

Critical language study (CLS henceforth) is not a branch of language study, but an orientation toward language (and may be a new and more properly social theory of language) with implications for various branches. It highlights how language conventions and language practices are invested with power relations and ideological processes that people are often unaware of. It criticizes mainstream language study for taking conventions and practices at face value, as objects to be described, in a way that obscures their political and ideological investment. CLS is not new, and in fact one important contribution dates from 60 years ago (Voloshinov, 1973, written in the late 1920s), but it has become relatively well known only in the past decade or so (Fairclough, 1989, 1992a; Fowler, Hodge, Kress, & Trew, 1979; Mey, 1985; Pecheux, 1982; van Dijk, in press). Important influences have been social theorists whose work has been relatively language centered (some of whom were mentioned earlier) and theories of discourse that have come to be closely linked with developments in thinking about ideology and the constitution of the social (including the "social subject"; Foucault, 1981; Henriques, Hollway, Urwin, Venn, & Walkerdine, 1984; Pecheux, 1982;). There are various groups and approaches, not all of which identify themselves as "critical." The following account of CLS is a personal one, although I think most of it would attract fairly general agreement from others in the field.

I try to characterize CLS as concisely as possible in terms of five theoretical propositions and a framework for critical analysis of discourse. Needless to say, this account is a highly schematic one, and readers who would like to have a more complete picture should consult some of the material referred to in the last paragraph.

[1]This section and the next section are slightly modified versions of part of my introduction to Fairclough (1992c).

1. Language use—"discourse"—shapes and is shaped by society. It is commonplace that the use of language is socially determined, and that language varies according to the social situation it is used in. What point 1 emphasizes is that discourse has effects on (other dimensions of) society as well as being shaped by it. It is a two-way, dialectical relationship.

2. Discourse helps to constitute (and change) knowledge and its objects, social relations, and social identity. Point 2 details the effects of discourse on society—discourse constitutes the social. Three dimensions of the social are distinguished—knowledge, social relations, and social identity—and these correspond respectively to three major functions of language: the *ideational* function, its function in representing and signifying the world and our experience; the *relational* function, in constituting and changing social relations; and the *identity* function, in constituting and changing social identities. Halliday (1973) collapsed the second and third in his *interpersonal* function. In any discourse, these three functions are simultaneously being served—and in any discourse, knowledge, social relations, and social identities are simultaneously being constituted and/or reconstituted (produced and/or reproduced).

3. Discourse is shaped by relations of power, and invested with ideologies. Point 3 describes the effects of society on discourse. One effect is the way in which particular languages and language varieties are valued or devalued according to the power of their users, with the notion of a "standard" variety legitimizing and naturalizing particular valuations. It is also helpful to think of these effects as shaping conventions for particular discourse types, such as the medical interview genre, that achieve a certain social stability and that are drawn on in discourse. Point 3 suggests that power affects such discourse conventions by "investing" them ideologically in particular ways. We can think of this in terms of the ideational, relational, and identity meanings built into genres such as the medical interview: for example, the way medical interviews tend to be organized, in terms of the distribution of "turns" at talking or in terms of their topics, embodies particular, ideological assumptions about medical knowledge, relations between doctors and patients, and the social identities of doctors and patients. Similarly, the organization of classroom discourse embodies assumptions about educational knowledges, relations, and identities.

4. The shaping of discourse is a stake in power struggles. That is, the processes referred to in point 3 are contested. It is clear from point 2 why this should be the case: If discourse conventions constitute the social in particular ways, then control of these constitutive processes would be a powerful covert mechanism of domination. A particular set of discourse practices and conventions may achieve a high degree of naturalization—they may come to be seen as simply "there" in a common sense way, rather than socially put there. This is a measure of the extent to which powerful social forces and groups dominate a society or a particular institution. But dominant practices and conventions may be confronted with alternative or oppositional ones, with different valuations of languages and varieties or different ideological investments. For example, there are various ways in which medical interviews are conducted these days, including ways favored by those in an oppositional (or "alternative") position within medicine, in which the interview is less tightly controlled by the doctor, and ideological assumptions about medical knowledge, doctor-patient relations, and social identities are different. The same applies for classroom discourse in contemporary educational organizations.

5. *CLS sets out to show how society and discourse shape each other.* In accepting dominant conventions and practices at face value, as just "data" to be described, mainstream language study can be seen as contributing to the naturalization effect referred to earlier—although not, of course, consciously or deliberately. Social sciences are not neutral or innocent; they stand in particular relationships to dominant or dominated groups and forces and contribute correspondingly to social struggles. CLS sees itself as a resource for developing the consciousness of particularly those people who are dominated in a linguistic way (among others). Consciousness is a precondition for the development of new practices and conventions that can contribute to social emancipation—to what one might call *emancipatory discourse practices* (see Clark et al., 1991; Janks & Ivanic, 1992).

The shaping of discourse by society and of society by discourse are on the one hand long-term processes that progressively restructure the sociolinguistic order and its orders of discourse (Fairclough, 1989), but on the other hand they are processes that affect every instance of discourse. I conclude this section with a brief outline of a framework for analyzing specific instances of discourse in a way that highlights these processes—for doing "critical discourse analysis"—and some comments on longer term restructuring of orders of discourse.

Every discoursal instance has three dimensions: It is a spoken or written language *text*; it is an instance of *discourse practice*, involving processes of producing and interpreting the text; and it is (part of) an instance of *social practice*. These dimensions are shown in Figure 14.1.

The relationship between social practice and text is mediated by discourse practice; that is, the nature of the discourse practice—how texts are produced and interpreted—depends on the social practice in which they are embedded; and the nature of the text, its formal and stylistic properties, on the one hand depends on and constitutes "traces" of its process of production, and on the other hand constitutes "cues" for its interpretation. Critical discourse analysis itself also has three dimensions: *description* of the text, *interpretation* of the discourse practice, and its relationship to the text, and *explanation* of how the discourse practice relates to the social practice. Although attention to formal aspects of the language of texts (within "descriptions") is an important element

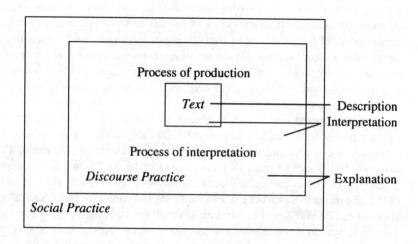

Figure 14.1. A three-dimensional view of discourse analysis
Figure originally published in Clark et al. (1991). Reprinted with permission of
Longman Group UK Limited.

of this framework, so too is its emphasis on the need to "frame" the text and its formal features within the other dimensions of analysis.

In the *interpretation* phase of analysis, the aim is to specify what conventions are being drawn on and how. The repertoire of available conventions includes various genres (interview, advertising, or lecture) and various discourses (medical, scientific, or legal), including both dominant and oppositional/"alternative" conventions organized within orders of discourse. There are standard, normative ways of using and combining these resources, but they can also be used and combined in creative, innovative ways, and interpretational analysis tries to pinpoint how conventions are used. For example, in the "alternative" type of medical interview I referred to earlier, one finds a mixture of conversation, counseling, and a more traditional sort of medical interview—being alternative or oppositional is manifested discoursally in an innovative combination of conventions, which breaks down traditional boundaries between types of discourse practice and between orders of discourse.

In the *explanation* phase of the analysis, one aim is to explain such properties of the discourse practice by referring to its social context—by placing the discourse practice within the matrix of the social action it is a part of. For example, where the social action is conventional and takes places within relatively well-defined social structures, relations, and identities, one might expect discourse conventions to be followed in a relatively normative way (as in a traditional medical interview). It is under conditions of social flux and instability, when the social practice is perhaps oppositional or in some way problematic, that one might expect innovative combinations of conventions, which may in the longer term restructure existing orders of discourse. Explanation is also concerned with assessing the contribution of the discourse to the social practice, the effectiveness of the discourse in constituting or helping to reconstitute the different dimensions of the social referred to in the second of the five propositions described earlier. It also aims to specify the ideological and political investment of conventions and the ideological and political import of particular ways of using and combining them.

This approach to critical discourse analysis is based on a combination of a theory of discourse practice based upon a Bakhtinian view of genre and intertextuality (built into the discourse practice dimension; see Bakhtin, 1986; Kristeva, 1986) and a theory of power based upon the Gramscian concept of hegemony (built into the social practice dimension; see Forgacs, 1988; Gramsci, 1971). The discursive practices within medicine and education that I have alluded to earlier can be interpreted as elements in social practices of hegemonic struggle, struggle to sustain or undermine and transform hegemonies and hegemonic relations. The Bakhtinian view of genre and intertextuality highlights how the social determination of discourse practice is dialectically intertwined with a potentiality for, in principle, endless creativity. It is necessary to combine such a view of discourse practice with a theory of power, of hegemony, that allows one to specify the social conditions and constraints on this creative potential—its dependence on the current state of hegemonic relations and hegemonic struggle. (See Fairclough, 1992a, for a more complete account of this point, and Fairclough, 1989, 1992a, for a detailed exemplification of the overall framework.)

I previously referred to two complementary focuses and time scales in discourse analysis: a focus on specific discourse instances, and a focus on the long-term development of discursive practices and orders of discourse. These microscopic and macroscopic perspectives should not be seen as alternatives; on the contrary, they presuppose each other. On the one hand, the long-term (macroscopic) restructuring of relationships and boundaries between the discursive practices (genres and discourses)[2] within orders of discourse and of the relationships and boundaries between orders of discourse (e.g., between private and public orders of discourse) is the cumulative outcome of restructurings of these relationships and boundaries that are constantly going on (microscopically) in discourse. On the other hand, the current (and potentially unstable and "transitional") states of relationships and boundaries within and between orders of discourse constitute structural conditions of (im)possibility for specific discourse instances.

---

[2] I understand a *genre* to be the discourse conventions associated with a socially ratified type of activity such as interviewing, counseling, or lecturing. And I understand a *discourse* to be the signification of some domain of experience from a particular perspective (so there is a distinction between patriarchal and feminist discourses of sexuality, for instance).

LANGUAGE AWARENESS: CRITICAL AND NONCRITICAL APPROACHES

In recent years, language awareness—knowledge about language—has been widely advocated as an important part of language education in Britain by those associated with the "language awareness" movement (Hawkins, 1984; NCLE, 1985), independently and in some cases earlier (Doughty, Pearce, & Thornton, 1971), and in reports on the teaching of English in schools within the national curriculum (DES, 1988, 1989). Although welcoming this development, I think language awareness work has been insufficiently critical. It has not given sufficient focus to language-related issues of power that ought to be highlighted in language education, given the nature of the contemporary sociolinguistic order. What is needed is an approach based on a critical view of language and language study such as the one described earlier. In this section I contrast such a critical language awareness (henceforth, CLA) with the noncritical conception just referred to (henceforth, LA—I refer mainly to Hawkins, 1984), in terms of the rationale for language awareness work, conceptions of language awareness work, and the relationship envisaged between language awareness and other elements of language education.

A rationale for critical language awareness work emerges from the general contemporary problematic of language and power described at the beginning of the chapter: Given that power relations work increasingly at an implicit level through language, and given that language practices are increasingly targets for intervention and control, a critical awareness of language is a prerequisite for effective citizenship and a democratic entitlement. There is some similarity between this rationale for CLA and part of the rationale for LA, in that the latter attempts like the former to use language education as a resource for tackling social problems that center around language. But the arguments are cast in very different terms. In Hawkins (1984), this dimension of the rationale for LA refers to social aspects of educational failure (which I discuss later), a lack of understanding of language that impedes parents in supporting the language development of their children, and an endemic "linguistic parochialism and prejudice" affecting minority languages and nonstandard varieties. These are indeed problems that language awareness can help to address, but from a CLA perspective, they are just particular points of salience within the much broader contemporary problematization of language I have indicated.

A fundamental difference between LA and CLA is their assumptions about what language awareness can do for such problems. Within LA, schools seem to be credited with a substantial capacity for contributing to social harmony and integration and with smoothing the workings of the social and sociolinguistic orders. Language awareness work is portrayed as making up for and helping to overcome social problems (e.g., making up for a lack of "verbal learning tools" in the home, extending access to standard English to children whose homes do not give it to them). In the case of CLA, the argument is that schools dedicated to a critical pedagogy (Freire, 1985; Giroux, 1983a) ought to provide learners with an understanding of problems that cannot be resolved just in the schools, and with the resources for engaging if they so wish in the long-term, multifaceted struggles in various social domains (including education) that are necessary to resolve them. I suggest later, in discussing the treatment of standard English, that the LA position can in fact have unforeseen detrimental social consequences.

There are a number of other elements in the rationale for LA. I referred earlier to social aspects of educational failure, and Hawkins refers in this connection to evidence that schools have had the effect of "widening the gap" between children who get "verbal learning tools" at home and those who do not (Hawkins, 1984, p.1). Language awareness work can help all children "sharpen the tools of verbal learning" (p. 98). LA is particularly sensitive to the need to improve study skills in the "difficult transition from primary to secondary school language work, especially the start of foreign language studies and the explosion of concepts and language introduced by the specialist secondary school subjects" (p. 4). The poor record of British schools in foreign language learning is part of the rationale; there is an emphasis on developing "insight into pattern" and "learning to listen" as conditions for success in foreign language learning. A related educational problem that LA seeks to address is the absence of a coherent approach to language from the child's perspective, including a lack of coordination between different parts of the language curriculum. There is also reference to the particular linguistic demands arising from rapid social change, in which "many more events require interpretation," especially an interpretation of linguistic signals (NCLE, 1985, p. 23).

Although CLA highlights critical awareness of nontransparent aspects of the social functioning of language, that does not imply a lack of concern with issues such as linguistic dimensions of educational failure or inadequacies in foreign language learning. Nor, turning to a comparison of conceptions of language awareness work, does it imply a lack of concern with formal aspects of language, which take up a large proportion of LA materials. I would see the position of CLA rather as claiming that these important issues and dimensions of language awareness ought to be framed within a critical view of language; for example, in describing a framework for critical discourse analysis earlier I stressed the importance of attending to formal linguistic features of texts, but I also stressed the importance of framing such textual analysis within a critical discourse analysis. Having made these points, I focus my comparison of conceptions of language awareness work on views of linguistic variation, especially on the treatment of standard English.

LA, like the Kingman and Cox Reports (DES, 1988, 1989), takes the position that it is vital for schools to teach pupils standard English, while treating the diversity of languages in the classroom as "a potential resource of great richness," and recognizing that all languages and varieties of languages "have their rightful and proper place" in children's repertories and that "each serves good purposes" (Hawkins, 1984, pp. 171-175). Standard English and other varieties and languages are presented as differing in conditions of appropriateness. Vigorous arguments are advanced for the "entitlement" of children to education in standard English, especially standard written English, as part of the "apprenticeship in autonomy" that schools should provide (Hawkins, 1984, p. 65). Stigmatization of particular varieties or accents is attributed to parochialism or prejudice.

There is no doubt whatsoever that learning standard English does give some learners life chances they would not otherwise have. On the other hand, this view of standard English and language variation misses important issues and can, I think, have detrimental effects. First, there is an assumption that schools can help iron out the effects of social class and equalize the kind of "cultural capital" (Bourdieu, 1984) that access to prestigious varieties of English can confer. I think this assumption needs cautious handling because it is easy to exaggerate the capacity of schools for social engineering: The class system is reproduced in many domains, not just in education. Second, there is no sense in LA work that in passing on prestigious practices and values, such as those of standard English, *without* developing a critical awareness of them, one is implicitly legitimizing them *and* the asymmetrical distribution of high-status cultural capital I have just referred to. Third, portraying standard English and other languages and varieties as differing in conditions of appropriateness is dressing up inequality as diversity: Standard English is "appropriate" in situations that carry social clout, whereas other varieties are "appropriate" at the margins (see Fairclough, 1992b, for a critique of theories of appropriateness). Fourth, attributing the stigmatization of varieties to individual prejudice papers over the systematic socially legitimized stigmatization of varieties. Elevating the standard means demoting other varieties. Again, there is likely to be a mismatch between the liberalism and pluralism of the schools and the children's experience. It is these mismatches, based on well-meaning white lies about language variation, that carry the risk of detrimental effects: Either they will create delusions, or they will create cynicism and a loss of credibility or most probably a sequence of the former followed by the latter. I think a CLA position on the treatment of standard English is that one should teach written standard English for pragmatic reasons, but one should also expose learners to views about standard English, including the critical views I have alluded to here. One should also raise with the learners the question of whether and why and how dominant rules of "appropriateness" might be flouted and challenged (see further discussion later).

I come finally to the relationship envisaged between language awareness and other elements of language education. There is agreement between LA and CLA that, as Hawkins (1984, pp. 73-74) put it, "awareness" affects "competence"—or, as I would prefer to put it, awareness affects language capabilities. LA does not, however, set out to build into language education explicit connections between developing awareness and developing capabilities: Language awareness work is isolated from other parts of language education as a separate element in the curriculum. By contrast, a central theme in a critical approach is that language awareness should be fully integrated with the development of practice and capabilities.

Figure 14.2 (from Clark et al., 1991, p. 16) gives one representation of this integration. This model incorporates the important principle that critical language awareness should be built from the existing language capabilities and experience of the learner. The experience of the learner can, with the help of the teacher, be made explicit and systematic as a body of knowledge that can be used for discussion and reflection, so that social causes for experiences (e.g., of constraint) can be explored. At the same time, links should constantly be made between work on the development of language awareness and the language practice of the learner. This practice must be "purposeful." That is, it must be tied in to the learner's real wishes and needs to communicate with specific real people, because this is the only way for the learner to experience authentically the risks and potential benefits of particular decisions. When critical awareness is linked to such decisions, it broadens their scope to include decisions about whether to flout sociolinguistic conventions or to follow them, whether to conform or not conform (in the use of standard English, for instance, as mentioned earlier). It also allows such decisions to be seen as in certain circumstances, collective rather than individual, associated with the political strategies of groups.

CRITICAL LANGUAGE AWARENESS IN PRACTICE: IDENTITY IN ACADEMIC WRITING

Critical language study and critical language awareness work can of course be reflexively applied within educational organizations to the practices of such organizations. In terms of the concerns of this book, they constitute a resource for investigating and intervening in issues of language and power in education. I

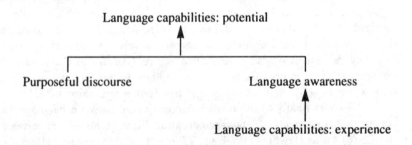

Figure 14.2. A model of language learning
Figure originally published in Clark et al. (1991). Reprinted with permission of Longman Group UK Limited.

have been suggesting that there is an intimate relationship between the development of people's critical awareness of language and the development of their
own language capabilities and practices. Accordingly, such reflexive work
could involve learners and teachers in analysis of and possibly change in their
own practices, as speakers and listeners (and viewers), writers and readers. In
this section I briefly describe one sort of reflexive application of CLA in work
by colleagues at Lancaster (Clark, 1992; Ivanic & Simpson, 1992) and use this
example for some closing reflections on the difficulty of tackling issues of language and power in complex and often opaque contemporary societies.

   The focus of this research is on what I earlier referred to as the identity
function of discourse and specifically the sort of self-identities that are constituted by or for writers in the process of academic writing. Traditional forms of
academic discourse, especially in science and social science, demand an impersonal style, and part of the "apprenticeship" of a student in an academic discipline is the effacing of prior identities in academic writing in order to join the
new "discourse community" (Clark, 1992). This can be an uncomfortable and
alienating process, perhaps especially for older students with extensive experience or established professional backgrounds. The pressure on students to conform is illustrated in an example given by Clark. An academic made the following comment on an essay written by one of Clark's students: "Your arguments
are undermined by the use of the personal pronoun. [Name of student] is not an
established authority . . . or not yet, anyway. Avoid the use of personal pronouns and expressions like 'in my view' in all academic work."

   Both the Clark paper (1992) and the Ivanic and Simpson paper (1992)
describe experiences of working within a CLA framework with students who
are resistant to the constraints of conventional academic writing. In both cases
there are attempts to develop styles of writing that allow students to project self-
identities that they feel more comfortable with. Clark's paper reports her work
on a study skills course for postgraduates taking Diploma or MA degrees in a
department of politics (see also Clark et al., 1990). The focus of the course is
the written assignments that students have to produce for their politics courses
(their practice on the course is thus "purposeful" in the sense of the last section).
The course begins with an exercise designed to raise students' consciousness
about the writing process (more fully described in Clark & Ivanic, 1992), and
the ongoing discussion of the writing process then informs and is fed by collaborative writing workshops and tutorials in which students work on assignments
set for their politics courses. Discussion of the writing process leads to work on
the development of critical awareness of linguistic resources and conventions,
which in turn feeds back into the students' writing. The class used a past student
essay to focus a debate on issues of objectivity and impersonalness in academic
writing, and these issues are then dealt with in more concrete terms by looking
at specific decisions academic writers need to take—whether to use the first
person singular pronoun or not, whether to use modality and tense form that
express strong commitment to propositions or modal forms and hedges that tone

down commitment, and so forth. The objective of the study skills course is to "empower" students by giving them a critical awareness of academic conventions, their social origins, and effects. The course provides students with the means for "emancipation" through the flouting of conventions and the development of nonconventional forms of academic writing, although it is up to students themselves whether they do so (not all do). A major theme of the chapter is that students are faced with the dilemma, which they must resolve for themselves, of whether to conform or not conform, whether to lean in the direction of fulfilling obligations or of claiming rights. (On emancipation as a concept in CLA, see also Janks & Ivanic, 1992.)

The Ivanic and Simpson (1992) paper reports on co-research between an academic (Ivanic) and a mature student (Simpson) who had recently entered higher education, in the latter's development as an academic writer (see also Ivanic & Roach, 1990). This paper also focuses on problems of identity: Given the overwhelming prestige of an "impersonal," "objective" academic style, how can a student—this student—project his or her own identity in his or her writing, "find the 'I,'" or show him- or herself as the sort of person the student wants to be? "Finding the 'I'" is a matter of responsibility to oneself and to one's readership: It is a way toward truthfulness and clarity. The authors suggest that writers may be better able to tackle their dilemmas over identity if they become conscious of the "casts" or "populations" of identities in the texts they read as well as in their own writing. This is a matter of raising their critical awareness of the standard conventions of academic writing and their effects on identities. The paper includes an analysis in these terms of three assignments written by Simpson. The "population" consists of tutors who set the assignments, the people who wrote what the student read, the writer him- or herself, the people the student writes about, and the people who read what he or she writes. What emerges is a tense relationship between the pressures on the student to conform to the norms of traditional academic style and the student's own often cautious and nervous attempts to project his or her own identity and evolve his or her own academic style. One noteworthy feature of the paper is that as well as writing about Simpson's attempts to tackle the problem of identity, the authors explicitly try to tackle it together in the way in which they wrote the paper.

The two papers provide useful practical techniques for using CLA in educational organizations to work on one problematic aspect of the interface of language and power in such organizations: the constraints that organizations and powerholders within them place on the discursively constituted self-identities of learners. Evidently, there is a microscopic emphasis in both papers on how individual students cope with the tension between a will to resist the impositions of conventional academic writing and requirements to conform and how critical language awareness programs can help clarify (if not resolve) such dilemmas. The outcomes of this tension in students' work can be described using the framework for critical discourse analysis introduced earlier. One feature of the student work discussed in the two papers is that its "discourse practice" tends to be complex, involving the mixing of genres and discourses (traditional academic ones and, often, ones drawn from the private domain), and this is realized linguistically in texts that tend to be heterogeneous in style, meanings, and forms. However, I explore a little of how this microscopic focus relates to a more macroscopic view of the state of hegemonic relations and hegemonic struggle in the orders of discourse of educational organizations, in order to raise some issues that have a more general relevance to the problematization of language and power in education.

In my view a microscopic focus on individual calculations of risk and benefit should always be complemented with and contextualized within a macroscopic view. (Recall the discussion of the interdependency of microscopic and macroscopic perspectives earlier.) Student resistance to academic conventions is widespread in contemporary higher education, but the situation is not one of unified academic institutions stolidly defending traditional practices against reluctant students. Traditional practices have already been extensively undermined from within. For instance, as Ivanic and Simpson point out, academic writing is "becoming less segregated from informal speech." There has already been a hegemonic shift that constitutes a favorable environment for the sort of reflexive CLA work that Clark, Ivanic, and Simpson are engaged in: Practices of academic writing that achieve a hybridization of traditional academic styles and colloquial, informal, spoken styles are now well positioned within the order of discourse. Personalized writing, space to project identities that academic writers feel comfortable with, are part of this evolution. This shift is often construed in terms of a suspect contrast between one's "real self" and the artificial identities taken on in academic writing—suspect because there is no "real self," only various socially constituted selves, some of which may however feel more real than others. What is I think actually at issue is pressure for specialized academic identities to give way to private domain or "lifeworld" identities. It would be a mistake to overstate the hegemonic shift or underestimate the continuing power of traditional forms within certain types of institution and particular disciplines. Nevertheless, the shift is clear.

But this shift in educational discursive practices and orders of discourse needs to be explained, that is, it needs to be situated within wider sociocultural changes that it is a part of. At this point I strike a cautionary note: It is often difficult to assess the full social and cultural import of a change in discursive practices and therefore its effect upon power relations and power struggle in the institution concerned. This underlines for me the importance of avoiding directive, top-down interventions designed (perhaps by well-intentioned theorists like myself) to shift practices in a particular emancipatory direction: Such decisions must be left to the people directly involved, "on the ground," who are generally better able to weigh the complex odds and interpret the sometimes ambivalent, complex, and contradictory values, risks, and benefits.

Consider for instance the case in point, in light of my earlier comments on the ambivalence of the "conversationalization" of public discourse. The impetus in educational organizations to break down barriers between academic discourse and the more informal and personal practices of the private sphere is not isolated: It is part of a general rejection in contemporary societies of elite, professional, bureaucratic, and other practices and a valorization of ordinariness, naturalness, "being oneself," and so forth, in discourse and more generally. It is what I referred to in the first part of the paper as the "conversationalization" of public discourse, and it ties in with the "informalization" of contemporary society and its "posttraditional" properties. Seen in these terms, it can be interpreted positively as a democratizing development.

But the push for democracy is not the only source of attacks on tradition, and it is not the only impetus for the breaking down of barriers. Education like other institutions has been and is being "marketized," incorporated into the consumer society and culture. This entails a standardization of practices across institutions on the model of the market. One obvious and indeed notorious surface example of this standardization is the generalization of the persona and the vocabulary of the "consumer" (or "customer") across institutions, including the reconstruction of students as consumers. The difficulty is that it is not always easy to distinguish between attacks on and attempts to reconstruct traditional academic practices that are democratically rooted and those that are rooted in marketization. How, for instance, might one decide whether a student who is resisting the impersonalness of academic writing is operating from a democratic rejection of elitism, or as someone who wishes to assert his or her authority as a consumer? (On the "authority of the consumer," see Abercrombie, Keat, & Whitely, 1994; Fairclough, 1994.) One way of reading the difficulty in this case is in terms of appropriation: One could see the impetus toward marketization of education as having appropriated some of the themes and values and discursive practices of the historically earlier impetus toward antielitism. The 1960s being appropriated by the 1980s so to speak.

The point is not in any way to retreat from reflexive critical language awareness work, still less to defend traditional practices. It is to highlight the difficulty in contemporary society in being entirely confident about the target, in the sense of what needs changing and what it needs changing to. People on the ground must make up their minds about these complex issues, as they will whether critical language work is in progress or not. We need CLA work of a sensitive, nondogmatic, and nondirective sort. We also need, in support of it, critical discourse analysis research into the complex and ambivalent interdependencies between discursive practices and sociocultural systems and transformations in education.

15

Dancing, Seducing, or Loving

Robert Young
University of Sydney

It is too easy to theorize oppression in politically unhelpful ways; it is too easy to theorize oppression in ways that rob victims of counteroppressive agency. Of course, circumstances may sometimes do that. It is possible to be helpless. But I am talking of theory that diminishes the *probability* of effective resistance and liberating action. Functional Marxism can serve as an example of this kind of theory. If one inflates capitalism and the *system* to an all-powerful, all-seeing *pervasive* world, one has little theoretical room for resistance and politically created, therefore, "historical" change (as contrasted with blind change, which is merely a change of fashions or customs). One of the results of this was a tendency for theorists of this ilk to argue that political change in the wider society must precede changes in schooling, thus discouraging politically relevant activity by those whose work was primarily within some dimension of publicly provided education (Castles & Wustenberg, 1979).

Some versions of poststructural ideas get rather close to this difficulty. It is useful to recognize that the private sphere is not entirely insulated from the wider public society. But it is not useful to deny the existence of any boundary between the two. The danger is in the inflation of the systematicity of the system, so everything is seen to be equally linked with everything else. During the Cold War, similar emphases emerged in conservative accounts of the Soviet Union.

273

The Communist party was seen as an all-powerful, omniscient, worldwide conspiracy, when, in reality, it was an inept, bungling, compartmentalized bureaucracy. The speed with which the Soviet Union broke up testifies to the presence all along of other forces—ethnicity, class aspirations of professional groups, regionalism, and religion. Societies are loosely coupled systems, with islands of tighter coupling here and there. If Foucault's distopian vision could be applied to any society, it could be applied to the Soviet Union, where, officially at any rate, rational planning, governmentalization, and professional (pastoral) power were developed to a greater degree than in the more anarchical "market" societies of the West. Clearly, there were margins (Foucault, 1980, p. 85) in that society, and those who operated within them were not without historical influence.

But this criticism does not mean that Foucault's distopia is of no use in our theorizing, on the contrary. Distopias are as useful as Utopias—they are useful to think with. They postulate particular "mechanisms" of oppression or liberation. In both cases these are woven more tightly, in more simple systems, peopled by persons more malleable and less cussed than reality inconveniently presents us with. Nevertheless, a useful distopia is defined by the usefulness of the mechanisms depicted in it. Foucault's "dispositifs" alert us to linkages among typical discursive resources and practices, institutional structures, and patterns of social management. This has implications for educators because they are depicted as being among the key operatives in the distopia.

But Foucault was not the first to assert that ideology is something people do to themselves. The problem is that a too literal reading of his distopia as *history* can blind us to the fact that resistance, critique, and praxis are things people do for themselves. Since the linguistic turn (Hiley, *for* Bohman & Schusterman, 1991) in social theory, it has been recognized that the reality that people inhabit is a constructed one—a web of meaningful situations, actions and utterances that are brought into being by human powers of creating significance. Since Hegel (or, arguably, Plato), it has been recognized that this creativity is often blind, and the things created are capable of taking on an obdurate "objectivity" in which they face their creators as bland, sometimes oppressive, fact.

Where contemporary social theory breaks up into contending accounts is in the differing stories that are told about the ways in which this creativity may be understood and related to the lives of categories and classes of people and to the physical and technological apparatuses, bodies, and territories of concrete experience. Theories differ too in their accounts of human capacities for "seeing through" this process and the ways, even methods, by which communities can enter into critical engagement with the stories with which they tell out their lives. They also differ consequentially in their account of the roles of public schooling and of educational professionals. In most theories, since the linguistic turn, the critical process is seen in some way to involve "discourse" or dialogue, so it is often around differences in the account of educational talk that educational applications of social theory differ. Even conservative social theory has had to come to terms with this linguistification of social theory.

Conservative stories provide narratives in which life is a struggle to approximate an underlying order, perhaps once possessed, but now lost. Convergence on a "best" set of meanings is enhanced by taking great care not to depart from past discoveries of this lost essence, or at least to continue the pursuit of it within the preservation of a tradition. In traditional religious cosmologies this narrative displays a certain integrity because it provides a holistic and many-sided account of the good life, but in the modern, secular versions of conservatism it is reduced to a thin account of "progress" within some limited set of criteria that is focused on the preservation of a particular political and social order. Conservativism of this kind is lacking in the kind of conviction or richness that particular religious traditions provide. Critique is a matter of correct application of method. Dialogue fine-tunes criticism at the stage when practitioners of recognized disciplines have mastered them.

Liberal stories (in the John Stuart Mill sense) are more open to the celebration of change, although it is sometimes difficult to separate liberal from conservative stories because a certain version of liberal values has become a tradition. The liberal tradition is expressed in some of our existing social institutions and is already an aspect of the social order of liberal-democratic societies. Its focus is on the "individual" and "rights" within a contractual account of the state and a rationalistic account of the progress of knowledge. Liberal accounts of discourse and meaning celebrate the progress of human knowledge and the possibility of progressive enlightenment through critical inquiry in which the hero is the skeptical, individualistic intellectual rebel who speaks at first with a lone voice, but is eventually heard. Dialogue is appropriate because only through the contending of all individual voices can we be sure of not missing out on some of the data we need to reach true conclusions. The crucial connection between liberation and dialogue occurs through the educational ideal of individual rational autonomy—speaking for oneself. This liberal ideal is not absurd, considered as a goal—the problem lies in the difficulties that liberal views gloss over.

Radical stories are of various kinds, but most noticeably of late of a kind that wears labels such as *postmodern* or *poststructuralist* (which is not to be taken to mean that these accounts wear such labels with justification). Postmodern accounts acknowledge the constructed character of our "reality," but tend to underplay or even deny our ability to engage in constructive as opposed to deconstructive critique. Strangely enough, they still share, in their own flamboyant way, the romanticism of the liberal/individualist intellectual protagonist, while denying the very possibility of having a self that could be a candidate for authorship of critique. The very possibility of dialogue is called into question because the very possibility of response and question is denied (Derrida, 1992, p. 13). In Foucault's case this possibility is undermined by a denial of the existence of margins where oppositionary talk could find play. In Derrida's case it is undermined by a direct denial of the possibility of unequivocally speaking for oneself. In both writers, the account of the educational relationship, or of the role of educational professionals is decidedly obscure and ambiguous.

Critical approaches recognize the tension between the individual and their cultural formation, between the hero who makes or unmakes culture and the culture that makes and unmakes particular individuals. They try to connect this with an acceptance of some aspects of the liberal vision of the possibility of progress through critique, while recognizing that any standards against which critique might be judged are a moving horizon that reforms itself even as it comes into view. Conservatism is left behind, and liberal views are subjected to the corrective of a recognition that critical agency is not something to be taken for granted but something to be won and defended in a dialectical relationship with the cultural horizon against which it appears as well as in an internal dialogue with the many forms of otherness within the "self." Issues of method have the same ambivalent, passing reality and validity. Critical educators must come to terms with these difficulties and can be said to be learning by teaching in a quite old-fashioned way—learning about their own ambivalence, about their choices, about their own formation as persons, and about the otherness of those they relate to as teacher/learner.

Attacks by postmodern thinkers on earlier attempts to develop a critical theory of education have been useful because they have compelled critical theorists to be more explicit about issues of *misplaced* essentialism, *mistaken* auteurship, Eurocentrism, and theological-ontological views masquerading as the spaces between the lines. However, the legacy of Foucault and the continuing work of Derrida leave little basis for a positive or constructive moment in critique. Postmodern critique is at best minimalist when it comes to positive guidance—and this is a quality that can hardly have continuing appeal to educators, particularly to educators of the young. However, poststructuralist thought may provide valuable resources for critique, and even a kind of hidden affirmation, if it is treated with due respect for the rhetorical character of its expression, rather than perversely, as if it were secretly intended to achieve modernist theoretical and explanatory goals (Rorty, 1992). Certainly, Foucault approached this affirmation in his last interviews when he spoke of a "critical principle" (in Rabinow, 1984, p. 379) of open dialogue, and Derrida clearly wants his work to have a positive impact when he declares that it "intervenes" politically, and when he recently renamed deconstruction "affirmative interpretation" (Derrida, 1981, p. 93, cited in Bernstein, 1991). But the young require more. They have a certain optimism of the body. In any case, it is nothing more than temerity in their teachers if they would seek to deny the young the destiny of righting the wrongs of the world inscribed by the failing and too fearful imaginations of older generations. Critical theory was also accused of negativity, at least in Adorno's version of it, and it was one of Habermas' self-chosen tasks to overcome this negativity, finding in the nature of linguistic communication itself a source of positive value.

It is in speech that Habermas finds the fundamental grounds of positive critique, whereas it is in language (or in Foucault's case, something like culture in the sense in which that term is used by American cultural anthropologists) that postmodern thought finds the basis for its negative critique. The tension between the two remains. Language is about structure, speech about events and unfoldings. Poststructuralism is still clearly structuralist, focused as it is on system, webs, and networks. It can be demonstrated that Derrida's analysis of Saussure is one-sided; the constraints of structure in language are only a part of the story. Speech is always at war with language. Language enables speech, but speech disables language—at least, language as a fixed *archi-écriture*. Critical theory is very much a theory of action-in-time, a theory of communicative action and of speech's escape from language, speakers' escape from culture, and learners' escape from the curriculum, hidden or otherwise. Of course, it is not a theory about absolute escape; only relative escape is possible. A critical theory of classroom discourse theorizes both the oppressive moment and escape from it, both how learners ideologize themselves and how they resist ideology, even how, more positively, they create new realities. It is not a theory about the structure of classroom communication, or rather, not solely about structure, but about process and emergence, about turning points and opportunities. However, the limitations of the presentation of data and of analysis presented in sequential written form constantly undercut this dimension. Short of showing a videotape, this dimension of emergence can only be represented analytically, through the identification of possible alternatives, through the employment of conceptions of structure over time, such as "genre," and through signaling notions of flow and choice in the discussion.

IDEOLOGY AS ONTOGENETIC DANCE AND SEDUCTION

The point of the term *metaphysics* was that a fixed state of affairs was believed to underly the flux of "physical" events that presented itself to our eyes. In a postmetaphysical (Habermas, 1987; Young, 1995) perspective this flux is seen to be a reality, whose underlying nature is to change, reform, shift, and form again. Plastic reality, like the reality of large biological systems, is still real enough, but it is constantly in motion from one reality to another—it can be studied by a kind of "ecological ontology." Nowhere is this plasticity more evident than in the information-dependent processes of cultural reality. There, the computer game of life continually reveals changes in the state of play, at the same time as the rules of the game, even the object of the game, may change. Changes in the macroculture reciprocally require changes in the microculture of self-image or identity, although the two are in tension. This is a metaphor familiar to us in another guise. Von Neurath saw scientific theory as being like a ship, sailing on a limitless ocean toward a constantly moving horizon, the very substance of which the ship was being torn apart and rebuilt even as it sailed on. Derrida writes of this process as a kind of emergent teleology, differing from essentialist teleology because it is open ended, yet still guided by a human, future orientation, so it is still teleological (see Johnson, 1993).

The same images are helpful in talking about learning. Learning is not a process of simple puzzle solving or addition, such as Kuhn's "normal science," it is also a process of "paradigm shift" or, in Piagetian terms, schema shift.

Liberal views of classroom dialogue recognize the formative power of the teacher's views and focus their defense against ideology on attempts to prevent "indoctrination." Avoidance of indoctrination is generally defined with reference to learners coming to believe statements, views, and so on, on the basis of their own reasoning, rather than on the teacher's authority, peer pressure, or heteronymous pressures of any kind. Where liberal views fail is in failing to give sufficient recognition to the paradoxes and problems of this model of dialogic process.

To the extent that individual statements, facts, experiences, and so on, are meaningful only within some wider framework, it is necessary to first acquire the framework for the new information to be meaningful. That is, it is necessary to be indoctrinated in order to reason for oneself because it is necessary to learn a framework in order to learn at all. Much the same implications follow from a strict theoretical holism in theories of scientific knowing (such as the early Quine).

Of course, this notion of the all-powerful framework is just another form of the overestimation of the systematicity of social reality. Scientific theories are not all of a piece; some bits are more central than others, as Lakatos and Musgrove (1971) showed. But there is one thing that is worse than the "myth of the framework" (as Popper, 1972, called it) and that is the liberal failure to recognize the constraints of frameworks at all.

Orderly talk in typical structures of observed classroom communication do not display the transparent self-representation, unequivocal agency, and openness of ontogenetic opportunity that liberal theories of nonindoctrinatory learning celebrate. Nor is the attainment of these things likely, unless we theorize the processes that rob us of some progress toward these things. Moreover, the failure to achieve these things is not simply a failure of goodwill or intention, nor will it yield to exhortations to new teachers to open up their classroom communication. The ideology producing processes of our classrooms are sociocultural in origin, imbedded in the generic structure of classroom exchanges, which in turn are imbedded in the situation definitions of lesson occasions, which in turn are constrained by curricular expressions of social expectations of schooling, and physical, legal, and institutional/managerial processes.

Radical views of these constraints, although sometimes falling into the myth of the framework, help us recognize the nonauthored, systemic character of the structural constraints on the meanings we can inscribe in each other in our classrooms—the "set" toward the ontogenesis of categories of persons, of hierarchies of categories, and of the constrained writing of ourselves that results often in a writing of our identity in a shaky hand with words we would not freely have chosen.

Critical views, learning from radical critique, give rather more recognition to the "wild magic" of resistance, creative deviance, and the resistive displacement of ideology, which results in hybrid ontology. Willis's (1981) working-class school resisters did not create an entirely "free" identity, but neither did they fall into the identity thrust on them. Unable to entirely deny the constraints of their situation, but able to displace the meanings being tailored for them, they created a new, unofficial set of meanings and their own hierarchies and categories. They entered into a strategic dance of resistance, a struggle with the teachers, for meaning, for "having a laugh" and rejecting the school's value categories, which privileged academic achievement.

For their part, in situations like this, teachers may coerce, creating a kind of armed truce, or they may seduce. (Or they may struggle with *their* constraints, of which more later.) The structure of seduction is so familiar that we call it simply the pattern of classroom communication. It is characterized by a persistent strategic deception or deformation of language and speech. The presence of this deformation can be theorized in a number of ways. In earlier work (Young, 1988) I employed Habermas's model of strategic distortion of communication to do this. In that approach the perlocutionary function of the talk structure (or genre) is contrasted with the microforms of speech, which call for an illocutionary attitude on the part of speakers.

The most common structure in classroom official speech is the teacher question, student answer, teacher reaction to student answer structure (sometimes called the IRF, the Question/Answer Cycle, or, simply, The Teaching Exchange). Teachers' questions, and lines of questioning, have been called pseudo-questions because it is most often the case that they are not being asked in order for teachers to find out the answers—they already know them. All this is familiar enough and ubiquitous enough to seem harmless. The problem emerges in the relationship between the question/answer part of the sequence and its closing move—the teachers' reactions to the students' answers, for example:

T: So what happens to the air?
P1:   It gets warm.
T: Yes (evaluation), it gets warm. And what happens to it then?
P2:   It rises.
T: So what happens?
ALL: Hot air rises!
T: Right. So *our* conclusion is that hot air rises.
        (emphasis added).

Typically, student answers are not simply evaluated, they are reworked in the teacher's reaction in ways that formulate them as:

1. something the student actually believes
2. a part of the teacher's line of thought
3. a part of a line of thought shared by all who have not openly dissented.

But talk moves that would permit students to disconfirm these formulations are not available to them. There is simply not a talk slot for a student move at this point, unless signaled by a teacher invitation to enter into negotiation about what has been formulated, and such invitations are extremely rare in available data.

In this way the talk task, or communicative role of students, which is to provide the answer the teacher wants or to provide an answer that will please the teacher, is formulated as autonomous participation in an argument. Student identity is formulated as that of a liberal, rational agent. Now, the point is not that this would not be a valuable, if incomplete, goal for schools to aim at, but that the formulation of what is going on in teaching a predecided curriculum to students whose economic opportunities may be powerfully influenced by school assessments, as if it were a process of open debate among (potential) equals, is precisely an ideological seduction.

In this way, the necessary complement to important meanings in the outcomes of schooling are constructed in classroom discourse (and outside the schools too, of course). For instance, the necessary complement of the idea of mathematics as a high, hard, intellectual accomplishment is the mathophobic student identity. Deconstruction of what systemic analysis would call the "register" of classroom speech can show that the generic constraints of situation, person category tasks, and functional speaking roles are reinforced by the semiotic linkages in the set of signifiers brought into play by the legislation of the teacher. In this way, teachers can control the terminology of outcomes. Many restatements of student answers are done simply to replace "incorrect" terminology, often with technical terms, but sometimes with terms or turns of phrase with wider implications for identity categories, such as gender, race, or belief/allegiance.

TOWARD A COMMUNICATIVE ETHICS FOR TEACHING

But this process is not without opposition, as anyone who has taught knows. No doubt a certain amount of classroom restlessness is a product of children's animal high spirits, and a certain amount of boredom or lack of interest is a product of the gap between children's existential concerns and a curriculum focused on their adult future. But one of the main sources of a lack of interest is a lack of interests—that is, if the task of the classroom, as controlled by the teacher, and the roles and moves for students in it are unconnected with the problems and concerns—the existential *interests*—of the students, we cannot expect that students will be interested (Young, 1992). It is a basic fact of human motivation that we are interested in what touches our interests. The level of involvement of interests varies, but at its very least we have an interest in expressing ourselves, in coming to understand the world around us, in relationships, and in exercising our powers and skills, and finally, we have an interest in play and playing. The dominant structure of classroom roles provides little room for these things.

The result is the appearance of various kinds of resistance, subversion, and the wresting of opportunities for play and power from the unpromising terrain of the teacher-dominated classroom. In Australia this is called *mucking up.*

In an analysis I have presented elsewhere (Young, 1992), the structural locations within generic sequences of opportunities for resistance are identified. These are also the most likely sites for teacher repairs and controlling moves.

But it is possible for teachers to learn enough about the relationship between task structures as represented in talk structures and the student role represented by those structures to change them. Change can move the role of the learner toward making real the liberal appeal to his or her own agency and experience or, at least, to exploring this agency and experience. Change can move the learner toward the exploration of the self that can lead to its integration despite oppression, to the extent that this is possible at any given time.

When the students' role is really to express their own reasoning, the teacher must show respect for this by employing talk structures in which there is an additional slot for student talk after the teacher's reaction to the students' answers. There must also be a freer exchange of the questioning role. At present, more than 90% of questions are asked by the teacher, but tapes of peer tutoring show that this asymmetry is not a necessary part of the teaching role, because peer learners ask 30-40% of questions in such data. The task of evaluating answers must be farmed out to other students and to each student.

But this is not a free-for-all. The teacher can still take all sorts of responsibility. Nor is it a prescription for a perfect classroom—for the utopia of complete communicative freedom. Teachers may still ask more questions than students, certainly many more than any one student. But students' views will not be formulated as views of any kind by the teacher without students' opportunity to reject a particular formulation and to restate their views. Teachers can provide this by using a confirmation/disconfirmation invitation every time they formulate student answers or expressed views as views of a certain kind, as related to other views in a certain way, and so on.

In turn, teachers can set tasks of a different kind, requiring students to take more responsibility for the direction of inquiry and for its quality. If students are asked to evaluate particular moves, including the teacher's, to sum lines of argument to a particular point, and to connect inquiry with their own experience, they will take responsibility for their own learning because it is in their interests to do so. Even in a set of curriculum constraints in which students could not have a great deal of input into selecting the main problems about which inquiry was to center, the adoption of these reforms to the task structure would have benefits. In any case, the reasons curriculum decision makers have given for a particular set curriculum could be the subject of some discussion.

However, I do not mean to suggest that the rehearsal by students of "speaking for themselves" necessarily and automatically leads to anything more than deepening personal ownerships of the common shibboleths of society, although it is a first and necessary step toward genuine critique. It is necessary to go further, by opening up genuine differences of experience and situation and encouraging these to emerge into argument in such a way that students pass beyond archetypes of common experience celebrated by the mainstream culture and come into some awareness of the "otherness" of experience around them, undercutting the false common ground. This is a difficult process and must be founded on a real sensibility of difference and deep respect for others.

The sensitivity and restraint this calls for from teachers is great. Teachers have to learn the limits of their own agency and claim back their educative selves from their present levels of immersion in heteronymy. This is a lifelong task. Gradually they may discover the extent to which they have been what Freire (Freire & Shor, 1987, p. 160) calls the "manipulating, *domesticating* educator [who] always keeps in his or her *own* hands" both the process of classroom talk and the conclusions of classroom argument.

Teachers must learn, as Shor stated, to distribute ownership of the learning task to students (Freire & Shor, 1987). This is a delicate thing, and poststructuralist critique has enhanced awareness of its delicacy and of the need to go beyond a kind of shallow ownership that is really just a subtler form of being owned. However, with critical theory, and against some absolutist/relativist readings of poststructuralism, teachers need to make the pragmatic political affirmation that even small steps toward this are worth taking.

16

Experience-Near Classroom Examples as Commodities *

Stanton E.F. Wortham
Bates College

Teachers often provide or solicit examples from students' own experience. Both teachers and students consider this technique pedagogically powerful. Careful examination of such examples, however, shows that teachers often accept an experience-near example as a token of understanding—without exploring either the general point or the experience. Sizer (1984), Woods (1983), and others have given functional explanations of such apparently productive, but superficial classroom routines. This chapter argues that functionalist explanations do not suffice. To explain the particular character of experience-near examples as an apparently productive teaching technique, we need more powerful theories.

In his analysis of cultural commodities, Adorno (1938/1978) builds on Marx's account of capitalism to explain the peculiar character of contemporary cultural products. This chapter applies his account to experience-near classroom examples. To explore the similarities between this type of classroom event and cultural commodities, the chapter draws on ethnographic observations, inter-

*Originally presented at the 1993 Ethnography in Education Research Forum at the University of Pennsylvania. I thank Fred Erickson for encouraging me to write the paper and present it at that event. I also acknowledge Andy Hargreaves, Jay Lemke, Bud Mehan, and Michael Silverstein, for their useful comments and criticisms of an earlier draft. I particularly thank Moishe Postone for his indispensable help with this project.

views, and analyses of transcripts taken from a 3-year study of high school English and history classes. The chapter ends by considering a disturbing prospect: The commodification of classroom discourse may be leading schools to produce passive, rather than reflective, students.

Sizer (1984) and Woods (1983) have described how teachers and students sometimes compromise the pedagogical quality of their conversation. In some classrooms teachers settle for superficial discussion of the material in exchange for students' participation. Sizer and Woods describe various techniques used in such discussions: digressions about popular music or sports, entertaining demonstrations, and so on. Despite its intellectual shallowness, this sort of classroom discussion often appears lively and engaging to the casual observer.

This chapter describes another pedagogical technique that can lead to apparently productive, but actually shallow, classroom discussion. "Experience-near examples" present an object or event from students' own experience to illuminate the subject matter. This pedagogical technique *can* lead students to reflect deeply, both on their own experience and on the content. Teachers and students, however, often accept the example alone as sufficient evidence of understanding. Instead of exploring the general point and the experience in light of each other, they simply go on—as if the example itself sufficed.

Sizer and Woods give functional explanations for this type of superficiality. Teachers want students to participate in discussion. Students do not want to be challenged too much or put on the spot in public. So they compromise. Teachers tacitly agree to keep their questions simple, and students tacitly agree to participate in an orderly way. On this type of account, superficial experience-near examples serve a function: Their familiarity keeps students involved, while their superficiality keeps students from being challenged too much.

This theory, however, cannot fully explain the character of classroom experience-near examples. In particular, it cannot explain teachers' and students' vigorous praise for this pedagogical technique. To explain their misperception as well as other peculiar characteristics of experience-near examples, the functionalist account must be supplemented.

This chapter sketches a more complete explanation, drawing on Adorno's (1938/1978) account of cultural commodities. The analyses point out similarities between standardized, reified cultural products and experience-near examples. These similarities support arguments made by Apple (1982a) and others, who suggest that the peculiar character of products and social relations in capitalist society has spread into classrooms. The superficiality of many experience-near examples may reflect larger sociohistorical ways of speaking and thinking, not just compromises made by particular teachers and students.

EXPERIENCE-NEAR EXAMPLES

I have gathered data on experience-near examples in a larger study of classroom example use. For this study I observed eight English and history classes, led by six different teachers, over three years. All classes were in one inner-city public high school, with an ethnically mixed student body (about 50% black, 25% Hispanic, 15% white, and 10% Asian). I spent 128 hours in the school, observing classes and interviewing teachers, students, and administrators. In the final year I observed and audiotaped 81 class sessions, in one ninth-grade English class, one ninth-grade history class, and one twelfth-grade English class. The statistics and examples described here come from eight hours of transcribed conversation selected from these 81 classes.

Teachers and students give examples often. Exactly how often depends on what counts as an example: Are analogies examples? Should brief examples given in a series be counted separately? When does new information added to an old example count as a separate example? Using strict criteria, I found an average of one example every five minutes in my data—eight per 40-minute class. Using broad criteria, I observed one example every two and a half minutes—16 per class (cf. Wortham [in press] for a description of the larger project).

Fully half of the examples in my transcribed data lasted for only one speaking turn. That is, half the examples given were not discussed by any subsequent speaker. One-third of these one-turn examples (17% of all the examples given, roughly two per 40-minute class) explicitly included students' or teachers' experiences. This provides a rough estimate of brief "experience-near" examples.

Not all brief examples are superficial, however. In some cases sufficient context has been established such that a brief example illuminates the subject matter. I coded each one-turn, experience-near example in my transcripts as either superficial or merely brief. About one-half of them are "superficial," as described earlier, in which teachers and students accept the example without exploring the subject matter or the experience reported.

Conservatively, then, I found one superficial experience-near example per 40-minute class. This underestimates the actual incidence because examples discussed for more than one turn can still be superficial, and because examples that do not explicitly involve participants can still be experience-near. One or two other examples per class probably also involved some superficiality, without taking the canonical form. The rough estimate suffices, however, to establish that superficial experience-near examples occur regularly in classrooms.

This type of example occurred in all three classes I audiotaped, with roughly equal frequency. I did not expect this because the three teachers varied sharply in their classroom styles. One demanded precise answers and strictly enforced classroom discipline. One allowed constant digression and let students break classroom rules. The third fell in between. The regular occurrence of superficial experience-near examples across these three classes suggests that my conclusions do not depend on the style of one teacher or one group of students.

To explore the character of experience-near examples, we must go beyond summary statistics to actual language use. The following example comes from a ninth-grade history class. The class is discussing the myth of Theseus. They have been talking about the power that King Minos of Crete had over the Greeks and about his evil demand for human victims to feed to the Minotaur.

The teacher has been controlling this class firmly. He is leading the students through the myth, scene by scene, highlighting one main point in each scene, then going on. At this point, they have reached the scene in which Theseus—who has volunteered himself as a sacrifice, with the goal of overcoming Minos's power over the Greeks—reaches Crete in the slave ship. The teacher (Mr. Smith—T/S) highlights Theseus's impertinence in demanding an audience with King Minos:[1]

```
      T/S:    Now- He gets to Crete, what's the first thing he does.
      STS: [6 seconds overlapping, unintelligible comments]
      T/S:    He- the ship docks in Crete. They're here. What
              happens next.
5     JAS:    He meets the king.
      STS:    [2 seconds overlapping, unintelligible comments]
      GER:    He- he ordered to see the king uh privately, before he
              knew uh=                      =yeah
      T/S:            =He the prisoner    =demands to see the king
10    privately?
      GER:    Yeah, before he would leave the ship.=
      T/S:    Bo:y what nerve. That would be like uh: uh got a
              younger sister? Anyone have a younger sister?=    Your=
      STS:                                          =yeah.
15    T/S:    =younger sister comes up and sends you a message that
              she demands you come to her room so she can tell you
              when to get off.=
      MRC:    No.
      STS:    hnh hnh
20    T/S:    OK?
      MRC:    Mr. Smith.
      T/S:    Yeah.
      MRC:    The king sent for him=not the
      T/S:                          =Did the king send for him before
25    or after he demanded.
      CAN:    After
      MRC:    After
      T/S:    After. OK the- did- the king then did see him.
              Correct?
30    STS:    Right. Yeah.
```

At line 9, note that Mr. Smith breaks into the student's speech. He does not do so to correct her, because she has the right answer. Instead, his eagerness reveals that he has reached the point he wants to raise about this scene: He wants the students to understand Theseus the slave's impertinence in demanding something from King Minos.

To help them understand this point, Mr. Smith gives an example at lines 12ff. He presents a younger sister's hypothetical demand as analogous to that of Theseus. Without any discussion of this example, in line 20 he asks "OK?"—as if the example alone suffices to explicate Theseus's action. Then at lines 28ff. He goes on to the next scene in the myth.

Because he goes right on to the next scene without discussing the example, Mr. Smith apparently considered the example sufficient explication of the issue. Theseus's impertinence was the point he was aiming toward in this scene, so if he thought the example had not worked, he would have stopped to elaborate. In their discussion of other scenes, when he did not think students understood his point, Mr. Smith took time to explain further. Here he treats the example as unproblematic.

Note, however, that the class does not reflect on the example at all. The example might illuminate Theseus's inappropriate behavior toward a superior because it does involve a power relationship students could reflect on. But the class does not focus on some aspect of the younger sister's demand in order to examine Theseus's character or his action. Nor do they examine the students' experiences with their younger sisters in light of the myth. Could the example really be illuminating for the students if all these issues remain undiscussed?

In this case, as in all others, alternative explanations could be given for the failure to reflect on the example. The teacher may have been rushing to get to another point, or he may have run from the topic because sisters are for some reason a sensitive issue. Language use in classrooms certainly serves various interactional functions. As I have argued elsewhere (Wortham, 1992, in press), examples themselves often play a role in classroom interactional events. But the regular occurrence of superficial experience-near examples suggests that a more general pattern remains to be explained.

Consider another example. Here a ninth-grade English class is discussing whether a group sealed in a bomb shelter for three months should have an armed policeman as one of its members. The students have split into two groups on this issue. One group thinks that the gun would be dangerous and lead to conflict. The other thinks it would provide protection.

Students have been engaged by this issue, and they speak for almost the entire 10-minute discussion of it. Aside from a bit of turn management, the teacher makes only four substantial comments in these 10 minutes. Each utterance reveals her own belief that the gun would be dangerous. Although she does not impose her view on the students, the teacher's role in this segment is to support the students who oppose the gun.

The teacher's (T/B) first substantial contribution takes the form of an example, in the following excerpt:

```
        JAS:                 I mean what you- what you going to do
                    with a gu:n down there. That's the last thing you
                    nee:d really. 'Cause I know everybody going to start
                    a:rguing and everything. And they probably going to
  5                 say some stuff.   I want to kill him.   And=if he have=
        STS:                                              =hahahaha
        JAS:        =a gu:n he could do it.
        T/B:        Three mon- can you imagine this group if we had to
                    spend three =months in this room together.
  10    JAS:                     =Yeah        yes         exactly right.
        STS:        oh uh =hahahahahaha
        TYI:               =Howcome we don- that we need somebody else going
                    to protect ou- u:h our system. But that's why we got
                    police now to help protect us.=
  15    MAR:        But ain't nobody going to be around but you so=
        TYI:        But when you produce these-
        STS:        [3 seconds overlapping, unintelligible comments]
        T/B:        OK.  She made her point.  Maurice.
```

The teacher, Mrs. Bailey, gives the example at lines 8-9. The student immediately responds as if the example demonstrates the teacher's understanding. After a brief interlude, at line 18 the teacher goes on as if the point has been established. The example goes by unproblematically.

Neither in this excerpt, nor anywhere else, does Mrs. Bailey take the opportunity to elaborate the example. She acts as if the example establishes the argument against the gun. Her participation on this point, here and elsewhere, shows that she feels strongly about the issue, and that she is motivated to show her position to the students. So if she thought the example had not adequately made the antigun argument, she would have explained it further. Nonetheless, the class does not explore details of the example to illuminate either the general point or the hypothetical experience.

This example seems less compelling, however. Everyone has experienced an apt example in this way, as if it really indicates a connection among speakers. Surely the point was clear in this case without elaboration.

It is precisely this sense of clarity and connection that needs to be explained. The example did not get elaborated. The class did not explore how and why conflicts might arise if they were confined together, or how they would deal with conflicts in such a case. Nor did they use reflection on their own reactions to explore the general claim that people living in close quarters may well get frustrated and resort to violence. Despite this, we as analysts imagine, and the teacher and student act as if, the example clearly established the point.

Of course, teachers and students could further reflect on any issue, no matter how extensively they have discussed it. A class could not explore all aspects of every example. The existence of undiscussed but relevant issues does not in itself require explanation. But superficial experience-near examples do demand such explanation because teachers and students often treat the example as if it represents substantial reflection when it in fact does not.

Teachers' and students' misperceptions allow a critique of some examples as "superficial." Any critique presupposes some set of standards, against which the object comes up short. In this case the teachers themselves articulate the standards that I use to critique pedagogical practice. With this sort of "immanent critique," there need be no Archimedean point. It suffices to show that people violate standards they themselves espouse.

The standards here concern reflective practice. These teachers conceive education, in large part, as a process of introducing children to reflection. As they describe it, their students come to ninth grade full of creative ideas, but without the skills or the discipline to reflect systematically on them. In their classes the teachers encourage systematic reflection on students' ideas and on the subject matter, in order to give students practice in reflective activity.

In interviews with them I found further evidence of teachers' and students' misperceptions of examples' value. I spent about 25 hours interviewing seven teachers and eight students, and I asked each of them about examples as a teaching technique. Both teachers and students recognize examples as a type of speech event, and they have theories about examples' value. In general, they claim that experience-near examples help students learn to reflect.

Teachers and students' ethnotheories of examples build on our culture's view of examples. I take Hall's (1985) handbook on writing, in its fifth edition in 1985, as representative of our folk theory of examples. Hall claims that "we say something general, and then we make it clear by locating it in one or more examples" (p. 71). A generalization "needs a location in the particular world" to be understood. On this theory examples function, first, to bring intellectual clarity. Second, examples provide motivation or relevance: "Examples are necessary to clarify and also to keep the reader from falling asleep" (p. 72). Abstractions supposedly cannot connect with whatever motivates people to think, whereas examples can.

These two crucial aspects—clarity and relevance—recur in teachers' and students' ethnotheories. Teachers consider examples essential pedagogical devices because they make material both clear and relevant to students. Without examples, teachers claim that they would "lose" the students.

When I asked teachers why examples provide clarity and relevance, they fell back on various metaphors for knowledge and learning. An example brings the general issue closer to students' own experience and thus provides a "basis" for knowledge. An example "translates" the issue into something the students already understand. An example gives students a "reference point" from something they know. Examples give students "something to tap into" in exploring a general issue.

Giving good examples was important to the teachers I spoke with. They recognized and admired particular teachers' ability to give examples.

Several people at the school singled out one teacher for his skillful use of this pedagogical device. The students I interviewed agreed about examples' pedagogical usefulness. They claimed that examples often help explain things, and they appreciated teachers with particular skill at this. One student fondly remembered an example that had helped her get a question right on an exam. She still remembered the example, but not the general point.

All the teachers and students I interviewed gave experience-near examples particularly positive reviews. Several expressed surprise that I would ask about the value of such an obviously useful technique. Two teachers articulated theories that made this type of example central to their view of teaching. One history teacher described his pedagogical aim as "teaching students to give good examples," because this forces them to connect the particulars of history and their lives to the larger truths that the discipline has to offer. An English teacher made a similar claim about teaching literature. He said that giving experience-near examples leads students to reflect on their lives by forcing them to make connections between their experience and the universal truths embodied in great literature.

In addition to such theoretical praise for examples, teachers got excited when they presented an example that "worked." In both interviews and observations I found that a good example generated enthusiasm and a sense of success. One teacher felt so strongly about it that she spent more than half of a 1-hour interview giving glowing praise for experience-near examples in particular.

When asked, however, all the teachers I interviewed agreed that experience-near examples involve risk. Discussions of examples can drift away from the subject matter toward telling stories about the example itself. The teachers presented this as a dilemma: One needs examples to make the material relevant, but once the class starts discussing something more relevant, no one wants to go back to the subject matter. The teachers had intuitions about which examples would be prone to digressions. One teacher told me, for instance, that one must not let students start discussing dogs' intelligence because this topic will eat up the rest of the class time.

Two teachers in particular had thought deeply about the uses and dangers of experience-near examples. They recognized the danger of simply valorizing students' experience, without getting them to reflect on it. One teacher estimated that genuine reflection occurs in only about 10% of all examples. He explained this low rate in functional terms: Both teachers and students are often bored, tired, or discouraged, and they find it easier to "coast" in superficial discussions of familiar topics.

Educational researchers have also noticed examples' potential to serve simply as placeholders instead of tools for reflection. Bruner (1971, p. 65) warns teachers against simply linking subject matter to the familiar. Connecting the subject matter to "everyday banalities" trivializes it. Sizer (1984) points out both the commonness and the poverty of brief student-teacher exchanges in which ideas are not probed systematically.

Despite the widespread praise for experience-near examples, then, at least some teachers and educational researchers recognize that such examples are often used superficially. There needs to be an explanation as to why—despite such recognition—some of these same teachers continue to use experience-near examples superficially, and why they continue to act as if these examples enhance student understanding and encourage reflection.

FUNCTIONALIST ACCOUNTS

Both educational researchers and teachers give functional explanations for the superficial use of experience-near examples. Such functional accounts describe how teachers and students often reach a "negotiated truce" to overcome the "mismatch between teacher and pupil aims" (Woods, 1983, p. 133).

According to Sizer (1984) and Woods (1983), students often worry about being humiliated in classroom discussion. To get the focus off themselves, students develop strategies such as simply rearranging the teacher's words to give an acceptable answer. In general, students find it easier and less dangerous to remain passive and to depend on the teacher to provide information.

Teachers, on the other hand, want students to participate. They want the material to be relevant enough so that students will say something. But teachers worry about control. They often maintain control by determining the right answers in advance and by guiding the discussion in familiar directions.

To overcome this mismatch between their goals, teachers and students compromise. In the process, however, they sacrifice intellectual substance. Sizer (1984) describes this as an "agreement between teacher and students to exhibit a facade of orderly purposefulness" (p. 156). Teachers implicitly agree not to demand too much of students, and students implicitly agree to participate on topics the teacher chooses. Teachers maintain control, and students avoid humiliation, but their discussions become vacuous.

Techniques like superficial experience-near examples function in such teacher-student compromises, as "a way to fill time with neither strain nor untoward effort" (Sizer, 1984, p. 154). Neither Sizer nor Woods mentions experience-near examples, but they do analyze similar routines. By analogy, they would argue that experience-near examples get students talking by giving them something safe to talk about. But deep reflection on examples would challenge students and threaten teachers' control, so many classes simply accept the example and move on without considering it.

Such a functional account of superficial experience-near examples cannot suffice, for two reasons. The first problem is conceptual. Functionalism cannot explain the particular character of the object. The second problem is empirical. The functionalist accounts given here cannot explain two important aspects of superficial experience-near examples—their standardized character and the distinctive misperception that teachers and students have of such examples' value.

To explain a phenomenon through the function it serves in some larger system cannot explain why that phenomenon "has the specific content it does" (Postone, 1986, p. 315). Religion, for instance, is sometimes explained as a soporific for the masses. That is, religious belief systems function to keep the masses docile—with their eyes fixed on otherworldly rewards—and distract their attention from the exploitation going on in this world. Religion may indeed function this way, but such an explanation does not explain the content of religious belief systems. On this sort of account any belief would suffice, as long as it distracted the masses.

How then does one explain the shift from polytheism to monotheism? How does one explain the emergence of Protestantism in the Reformation? These various sorts of religion could all function to distract the masses. Along with the functionalist account, there needs to be an account of the sociohistorical context that explains the specific character of these belief systems.

Similarly, a functionalist account of experience-near examples cannot suffice. These examples may indeed keep students and teachers from working too hard, but this does not explain why this particular type of speech event occurs regularly. Many types of classroom routines could detract from reflection. A theory that could account for the particular characteristics of experience-near examples would be more powerful.

In particular, the functionalist accounts cannot explain two aspects of experience-near examples. First, superficial experience-near examples involve an abstraction or flattening. Because they claim to represent someone's experience, their particularity appears important. But in fact their particularity does not get considered at all. Speakers simply slot the example into place and go on, such that the particular characteristics of the example do not matter much.

Second, despite this flattening, teachers and students claim that such examples do connect with students' unique experiences. If experience-near examples were simply a device to slide through class without working too hard, teachers would not be proud of this technique. But in fact even brief experience-near examples give teachers and students a sense of success, and they are often proud of them. Through such examples teachers and students get a sense of connection with students' experiential knowledge—even though they slide right by the particularity of the experience.

This sense of direct, unmediated connection represents a particular type of misperception. In the next two sections I suggest that both this misperception and the flattening of particulars in experience-near examples can be explained by Adorno's theory of cultural commodities. If this is so, the functionalist account can be supplemented with an explanation of experience-near examples' particular character.

CULTURAL COMMODITIES

Contemporary Marxism often relies on functionalist explanations. Such theories emphasize the exploitation of one class by another and the ideologies that function to distract the exploited. One tradition, however—running from Lukács's (1922/1971) seminal reading of Marx through Horkheimer and Adorno (1944/1991) and their colleagues in the Frankfurt School (cf. Held, 1980, for an overview)—has elaborated a nonfunctionalist core to Marx's theory of capitalism. On this account, Marx (1867/1978)—particularly his analysis of the commodity in *Capital*—analyzes the specific character of objects and consciousness in capitalist societies. My description and use of Marx and the Frankfurt School owes much to Postone's (1993) rethinking of the tradition.

In *Capital*, Marx describes the distinctive characteristics of societies in which goods are produced primarily for exchange. Products are no longer primarily mediated by overt social relations, but through a quasi-objective exchange system that supersedes those overt social relations as the dominant form of social mediation. Marx describes the particular type of abstraction that this mediation introduces, when products come to be valued on a universal scale and exchanged for a universal equivalent (i.e., money).

Producers and consumers, however, do not see the abstract mediation that shapes the value of their products and their relationships. Instead, they see only the physical, qualitatively specific aspects of those products. Marx called this form of misperception—whereby products and relationships appear either natural or contingently conventional—the "fetishism of commodities." To producers and consumers, the value of their products and their relations appears concrete and immediate, or contingent.

In capitalist societies, then, products of labor become *commodities*. Commodities are constituted in part through abstract mediated processes, but people perceive them only in terms of their immediate properties. What is socially constituted and historically specific appears decontextualized, either as natural and quasi-objective or as contingent.

Following Lukács, who provided the seminal reading of Marx on this issue, I use *reification* to refer to the distinctive sort of misperception that Marx analyzes as the fetishism of commodities. Reification must be distinguished from *objectification*. All societies objectify, in that language requires society to conceive categories of objects independent of its involvement with them. The reification described by Marx, in contrast, appears only at a specific historical point—with the emergence of capitalism.

Note that Marx's theory of the reification of commodities is not the typical Marxist theory of class exploitation and functional ideology. Marx analyzes the basic type of economic relation in capitalist societies, and argues that both practice and consciousness are shaped by this commodity-based relation. At its core, capitalism involves not just objective processes, but also a particular form of thought—the reification of commodities (cf. Postone, 1993). So Marx himself does not rely on the typical, functionalist Marxist analysis of ideology, in which distorted consciousness simply protects the interests of the dominant class by masking exploitation. A simple functionalist analysis gives no account of the particular misperception. Marx provides a more specific account of the content of distorted consciousness in capitalist societies.

As Marx himself predicted, capitalist societies have changed since his time. His basic analysis must be supplemented to deal with contemporary capitalism. Horkheimer and Adorno's (1944/1991) analysis of the "culture industry" builds on Marx's analysis of the commodity and tailors it to 20th-century America. They describe how intellectual and artistic products have become consumer goods. Cultural goods have become "commodities" not only in that they are produced for profit, but also in their distinctive form. Both the nature of "cultural commodities" and people's perceptions of them have a particular character that Adorno and his colleagues have analyzed.[2] I summarize their analyses using three central concepts—standardization, passivity, and reification.

Commodities in this century have a distinctive, *standardized* form that Marx did not fully foresee. He did argue that commodities' universal exchangeability gave them an abstract equivalence, in which their qualitative differences get flattened out. But he did not live to see the extreme form of standardization brought by Henry Ford and mass production. Adorno goes beyond Marx to describe the form of cultural commodities in the age of mass production.

Popular literature, music, film, and television are highly standardized. In the middle of the story, song, or show an attentive reader, listener, or viewer can predict what will come. Adorno argues that contemporary stories, songs, and shows are constructed using commonplace formulae into which different content is slotted. The particular contents of a popular story—the conniving wife manipulating her husband out of her own ambition, the young man coming of age and taking his place in the adult world, and so on—are "ready-made clichés to be slotted in anywhere; they never do anything more than fulfill the purpose allotted them in the overall plan. Their whole *raison d'être* is to confirm it by being its constituent parts" (Horkheimer & Adorno, 1944/1991, p. 125). The story's particulars fit into the prefabricated frame, without enhancing or challenging it.

Adorno contrasts this type of static part-whole relationship with the dynamic one found in great art and music. In great art the particulars that compose the piece force observers to rethink their prior conception of the meaning of the whole. Serious art disrupts everyday life. It resists dominant forms by

[2]In what follows I focus on Adorno's analyses of cultural commodities. This is not the place to trace in detail the contributions of the various members of the Frankfurt Institute for Social Research—Adorno, Horkheimer, and Marcuse being the central figures (cf. Held, 1980, for an overview). In his writings on music, Adorno (1938/1978) gives detailed analyses of cultural commodities. These have provided a model for my analysis of experience-near examples.

portraying a discrepancy between the vision of the artist and the reality that artist and viewer live in.[3]

Mass, commodified art has little part-whole tension and thus little critical power. The particulars do not provoke reflection on the whole, because they fit into prefabricated slots. The particular content drawn from life becomes irrelevant because it has few implications for the larger frame. The villain in a drama can be insane, sadistic, greedy, and so on, but his particular character—insofar as it is worked out—does not change the overall structure and message of the story. The good guys still get him in the end.

Such standardized cultural commodities both invite and create *passive* consumers. Watching television becomes like buying toothpaste: A certain range of products is presented, and consumers simply pick one. Consumers cannot engage with the standardized products, intellectually or creatively. They must simply adjust. Popular art does not provoke consumers to understand their world in a new way. It just distracts them.

Because of the formulaic character of cultural commodities, consumers do not have to reflect on the whole work. Instead of putting together meaning from various components, consumers can accept the predigested forms uncritically. Consumers attend to cultural commodities in a way Adorno (1938/1978) called "quotational listening." They listen, read, or watch for the isolated moments of enjoyment provided by the unrelated but catchy pieces of the work. Consumers also listen, read, or watch by formula—looking for familiar patterns—and they often enjoy a work just because they recognize pieces of it. Recognition substitutes for thought.

This analysis of cultural commodities has disturbing implications for those who regularly consume them. Because they are exposed, from an early age, to media that encourage docility and inattentiveness, such individuals never develop the ability to criticize and to reflect. They are socialized into "the passive status of compulsory consumers" (Adorno, 1938/1978, p. 292).

Because they are commodities, however, popular cultural goods invite *reification*. Consumers often do not perceive contemporary cultural products as standardized. In fact, many cultural commodities appear unique and spontaneous. Consumers often claim that songs or stories carry genuine immediacy and intimacy. Adorno argues that this impression is engineered using tricks and special effects that "strive to create the appearance of being the outburst or cari-

---

[3]One should not read Adorno's praise for "great art" as a cultural elitist condemning the masses' lack of taste. Popular art movements tried to overcome the privileged classes' monopoly on art appreciation, and Adorno sympathizes with this project. But popular art is no longer of the people. It is mass produced like any other industrial product, and in this commodified form it subdues the masses rather than enlightens them. Adorno does not criticize the people, but the commercialization that masquerades as "popular." (As Jay Lemke has pointed out to me, in his praise for disruption and reflection Adorno is defending a Western aesthetic. But it is one I would defend as well. It also provides a reasonable standard against which to judge Western educational practices.)

cature of untrammelled subjectivity." These tricks fail to deliver what they promise: "The method becomes trapped in its own net. For while it must constantly promise its listeners something different, excite their attention and keep itself from becoming run-of-the-mill, it is not allowed to leave the beaten path; it must be always new and always the same" (Adorno, 1955/1981, p. 126). Standardized cultural products are always the same, because they are composed of formulae and clichés. But consumers, encouraged by advertising, perceive commodities as distinctive.

Such reification—the misconstrual of formulae and canned tricks as unique and spontaneous—helps explain the great irony of American culture: *individualism*. Many standardized goods, from songs to films to automobiles, are advertised and consumed as if they express the individuality of the producer who makes them or the consumer who buys them. A car that 100,000 other people are driving cannot match its owner's distinctive qualities, but this is how consumers perceive many products.

Adorno (1955/1981) calls this aspect of contemporary commodities "pseudo-uniqueness":

> As the mass-production and centrally organized distribution of goods which are all basically similar advances, and as the technological and economic framework of life increasingly excludes the individuation of the here and now based on hand-production, the appearance of the here and now, that which cannot be replaced by countless other objects, becomes an imposture. It is as if in claiming something to be special and unique—and this claim must be constantly exaggerated in the interest of sales—each object were mocking a condition in which all men are subjugated to an order whose principle is more of the same. (p. 78)

Because of their formulaic character, cultural commodities are actually just "more of the same." But through reification, the value of standardized commodities appears to come from their "natural" attributes. Consumers often misperceive cultural goods as spontaneous expressions of subjectivity—when in fact they are prefabricated.

Following Marx, Adorno does not give a primarily functionalist analysis of reification. Producers' and consumers' misperceptions of commodities' value do, in part, function to distract the masses. But this is not Adorno's primary explanation for the misperception of abstract, mediated value as natural and immediate. This misperception comes from the basic form of social mediation in capitalist society, not from one class' need to deceive another. Marx and Adorno claim to explain the form of the misperception, not just its function.

EXPERIENCE-NEAR EXAMPLES AS COMMODITIES

Apple and his colleagues (Apple, 1982a; Beyer & Apple, 1988) have begun to describe the commodification of classroom practices. In particular, they have analyzed the standardization of curriculum materials and the "deskilling," or passivity, that such standardized materials encourage. This section begins a parallel analysis for classroom discourse, by describing similarities between superficial experience-near examples and cultural commodities.

Given the space limitations, this section can only be suggestive. It cannot definitively link abstract social theory with the details of classroom talk. In the three volumes of *Capital* it takes Marx 3,000 pages to describe how the "commodity form"—the basic way in which people relate to each other and to their products in capitalist society—molds various aspects of life. And he does not move down to the microanalysis necessary to study discourse.

Young (1992), however, begins to show how social theory and classroom discourse analysis can be productively combined. Marx's social theory fundamentally concerns human relationships—how people interact and communicate. Young argues that educational practice, too, contains an implicit view of human relationships. Thus we can use the insights of critical theory to reflect on the details of classroom activities, by asking: What view of humanity is implicit in these interactions, and what type of social system does it fit with? In this spirit we can consider the parallels between some classroom experience-near examples and Adorno's account of cultural commodities.

Superficial experience-near examples are standardized. Their use encourages passivity. And we often reify them. This suggests that Adorno's theory might explain the particular character of experience-near examples in today's classrooms.

At first glance, experience-near examples seem the opposite of standardized. A description of someone's experience reports a unique event. Experience-near classroom examples claim to connect with students' unique experiences in order to make some general issue relevant or vivid to them.

Nonetheless, many experience-near examples are standardized. As illustrated and described earlier, teachers and students do not discuss superficial experience-near examples. They simply accept such examples as tokens of understanding, without exploring the experience or the general point in light of each other. In doing so they effectively standardize the experience, because none of its uniqueness gets explored.

Because teachers and students do not treat the experience as a unique event to be explored, any similar experience would have sufficed. This makes the particular content of the example irrelevant. Like the pieces of contemporary cultural commodities, the example simply fits into a slot in the formula. Teachers and students expect and accept experience-near examples at certain points in verbal routines, without reflecting on the experience or on the larger point being discussed. In this way, discussion of superficial experience-near examples resembles the formulaic classroom routines discussed by Mehan (1979).

Because of their quasi-standardized character, superficial experience-near examples encourage passivity among classroom discussants. This does not mean that they lead to silence. In fact, experience-near examples often get students to participate. But the conversation generated by superficial experience-near examples does not require active engagement with either the subject matter or the experience reported.

This lack of engagement seems analogous to the passivity encouraged by cultural commodities. Because of the poverty of the songs, consumers of popular music have no opportunity to reflect on the relation between a particular refrain and the whole work. They simply recognize the fragments and get pleasure from that. With superficial experience-near examples, recognition also gets substituted for thought. Teachers and students recognize the experience and go on, without reflecting.

Because of this passivity, students often remember examples but not the general point they were meant to illustrate. In this way students, as "consumers" of experience-near examples, resemble the consumers of popular music. They both remember the catchy refrain, but not the larger conceptual or musical context that the refrain might have contributed to.

As described earlier, teachers and students often misperceive the poverty of superficial experience-near examples. They claim that such examples can genuinely connect with students by making the subject matter meaningful and intellectually immediate. This misperception resembles the reification of cultural commodities described by Adorno.

Consumers often think that standardized cultural products express the artist's subjectivity. Similarly, teachers and students say that experience-near examples connect with students' experience so as to make the subject matter immediate. In both cases people have a sense of unmediated connection with another through the expression of the other's unique experience. Consumers of popular music feel grabbed by the expression of the musician's experience. With experience-near examples, teachers often feel as if they have "gotten through" to students. In both cases people misperceive a standardized product as a unique, genuine experiential connection.

The reification of experience in particular lends itself to explanation in terms of cultural commodities. Adorno (1964/1973) describes the peculiar modern misperception of immediacy, in which people claim to achieve unmediated connection with another through "authentic" reports of experience. Against this misperception, Adorno argues that all experience is mediated. Instead of searching in vain for unmediated connection, one should examine the social conditions that provide the mediating categories for one's experience. In the classroom this would mean examining the contextual factors that shape experience in this society. This requires reflection on students' experience, not simply valorization of it.[4]

---

[4]This line of argument suggests that another type of reification also operates in experience-near examples. Such examples promise more than access to learners' minds. They

Note that a such a theory of reification promises to explain particular misperceptions about superficial experience-near examples. That which is standardized and mediated gets perceived as genuine and immediate. For reasons described earlier, such forms of thought should be expected at this point in the historical development of capitalism. Functionalist theories, in contrast, cannot explain the particular character of the misperceptions.

CONCLUSION

Several salient features of superficial experience-near examples can be explained by considering them as cultural commodities. The standardized character of such examples, and the particular type of misperception teachers and students often have of them, make sense on Adorno's account.

The analysis given here remains suggestive, not conclusive, however. Certain observed aspects of superficial experience-near examples do correlate with Adorno's predictions. But further work needs to be done on this type of speech event. In particular, it would be nice to know the history of experience-near examples in the classroom. If they have become more common and more superficial over the last century or so, this would further support an account of them in terms of cultural commodities.

If classroom discourse has become commodified, this has disturbing implications for schools as educational institutions. As described earlier, commodities encourage passive consumption. Commodified classroom conversational routines discourage the active reflection that teachers try to help students develop. Others have noticed the docility that students develop in dysfunctional classrooms (e.g., Dewey, 1938; Sizer, 1984). A more complete analysis in terms of cultural commodities would more specifically explain the origins and character of such docility.

Such an analysis would agree with contemporary sociologists of education—such as Apple (1982a), Mehan, Hertweck, and Meihls (1986), and Sizer (1984)—that social-level constructs are needed to explain educational pathology. Pointing to lazy or unskilled teachers and students does not suffice. Aspects of the larger social context reach into the classroom and distort activities there. This chapter has suggested that one aspect of the social context in particular influences interaction and learning in the classroom: commodified ways of thinking and speaking shaped by the dominant type of economic relationship in our society.

---

also promise a more authentic *relationship* between teacher and student. In this culture society often shares personal experiences as a way to connect with others. But if sharing personal experiences has become commodified, this relational connection may often be illusory. This line of thinking requires another research project on the commodification of relationships.

Just because dysfunctional classroom patterns are embedded in larger social processes, however, does not mean that they cannot change. It does mean that they resist change. Reification, in particular, makes the commodification of classroom discourse hard to change. If teachers and students continue to believe that superficial experience-near examples establish intellectual connections, they will see no need to stop speaking this way. But if one can break through this belief in unmediated connection with experience, one may come to recognize the intellectual poverty of commodified teaching techniques.

For large numbers of people to escape reification in general, large scale social change must occur. Such change can happen because social systems contain internal contradictions, and societies develop through history. In the meantime—and as their own small part in bringing change —students of education can reflect critically on the details of educational practices, and act on these reflections.

APPENDIX A: TRANSCRIPTION CONVENTIONS

'-'	for abrupt breaks, stops (if several, stammering)
'?'	for rising intonation
'.'	for falling intonation
'_'	(underline) for stress
'CAPS'	for heavy stress
(1.0)	for silences, to the nearest second
'['	indicates simultaneous talk by two speakers
'='	interruption or next utterance following immediately, or continuous talk represented on separate lines because of need to represent overlapping comment on intervening line
'[...]'	doubtful transcription or conjecture
'((*...*))'	transcriber comment
':'	elongated vowel
'o...o'	segment quieter than surrounding talk
','	pause, breath without marked intonation
'(hh)'	laughter breaking into words while speaking

Conclusion

David Corson
Ontario Institute for Studies in Education

These latter chapters from Stanton Wortham and Bob Young trace the impact of wider processes and structures operating through classroom discourses and onto the subjectivities of children. Along with earlier chapters in Part II, they focus discussion on the *function* of educational organizations, as distinct from their *purpose*. In other words, they address the way that modern schooling typically positions children so that they are prepared for uncritical admission into socio-cultural conditions discursively constructed well in advance of that admission. Rather than preparing children for "initiation into a worthwhile form of life," schools offer them filtered immersion in the discursive practices in which schools themselves are positioned; they reflect onto children a sanitized version of the social formations that surround them; and by doing all this, they represent *sectional* sociocultural, political, and economic interests to children as though they were *universal*.

In the face of such a dire, disturbing, and uncomfortable description, this book is very short on solutions, as the real work has only just begun. The social sciences in general are only beginning to stumble onto this problem, helped now by the discursive turn, mentioned in my Foreword to this book, and by the obsolescence of what the new direction replaces. Taken together, this book's chapters raise and focus aspects of the problem in challenging and direct ways. Although the book presents a disconnected narrative, it does illustrate how wider discursive structures and processes filter into school organizations, and then into classrooms, to recreate: (a) ideology-producing classroom processes; (b) instructional rather than educational action; (c) a commodification of classroom discourse; and (d) a reproduction of unjust sociocultural arrangements. In all this, there are obvious winners and losers, as many chapters illustrate. The fact that the losers are almost always the same people who start out from behind is a startling indictment of the institution of education itself and of its management in the broadest sense.

As part of its purpose, this book tries to show how links can be made between the researcher's interests and the interests of practitioners. The ideas found in many of these chapters suggest that we need a new research and policy agenda. It must be an agenda that involves practitioners and researchers as co-participants at every point. It must encourage students of education to reflect critically on the good practices of critical practitioners and then use evidence of those good practices not as data to be copied, but as insights to be learned from. Above all, it must attempt to trace the seamless links between the discourses of wider social formations, the discourses of educational policy and administration, and the discourses of classrooms.

What we need are more wide-ranging critical ethnographies like Stephen May's study of Richmond Road School (1994). We also need more conventional ethnographies comparing community and school discursive practices such as Shirley Heath's *Ways With Words* (1983). But following the discursive turn, future ethnographies need to be broadened to connect political, economic, and organizational discourses with the discourses of home, community, and classroom. We also need critical discourse analyses that try to improve on those presented in the chapters of this book. Mixed with the ever-present need for high quality studies is the demand that research look outward in every direction because discursive practices permeate every "closed" context and every "closed" system.

The postmodern condition is emancipatory in one respect above all others: It reveals a world where orthodoxies, ideologies, disciplinary boundaries, and closed contexts exist only in the minds of those positioned by them. Awareness of this fact allows us to begin to "reclaim reality" at last. Freed by this knowledge, researchers can begin to enlarge their aims and scope considerably. Future emancipatory studies in education will link the administration of schools with wider social processes and policies, but also with what really happens in classrooms. There is much to be done, but the discursive turn in the social sciences is at last pointing us in genuinely emancipatory directions.

References

Abbott, M., & Caracheo, F. (1988). Power, authority and bureaucracy. In N.J. Boyan (Ed.), *Handbook of research on educational administration* (pp. 239-257). London: Longman.

Abercrombie, N., Keat, R., & Whiteley, N. (1994). *The authority of the consumer*. London: Routledge.

Acker, J. (1990). Hierarchies, jobs and bodies: A theory of gendered organizations. *Gender and Society, 4*(2), 139-158.

Ada, A.F. (1988). The Pajaro Valley experience: Working with Spanish-speaking parents to develop children's reading and writing skills in the home through the use of children's literature. In T. Skutnabb-Kangas & J. Cummins (Eds.), *Minority education: From shame to struggle*. Clevedon, Avon: Multilingual Matters.

Adorno, T. (1973). *The jargon of authenticity*. Evanston, IL: Northwestern. (Original work published in 1964)

Adorno, T. (1978). On the fetish-character in music and the regression of listening. In A. Arato & E. Gebhardt, *The essential Frankfurt School reader*. Oxford: Basil Blackwell. (Original work published in 1938)

Adorno, T. (1981). *Prisms*. Cambridge, MA: MIT Press. (Original work published in 1955)

Agar, M.H. (1986). *Speaking of ethnography*. Beverly Hills: Sage.

Ahlgren, I. (1990). Sign language in deaf education. In S. Prillwitz & T.

Vollhaber (Eds.), *Sign language research and application: Proceedings of the International Congress*. Hamburg: Signum Press.

Andraschko, E., & Ecker, A. (1982). Frauen im Lehrberuf. *Erziehung und Uterricht, 4*, 295-308.

Apple, M. (1982a). *Cultural and economic reproduction in education*. Boston: Routledge and Kegan Paul.

Apple, M. (1982b). *Education and power*. London: Routledge.

Apple, M. (1992). The text and cultural politics. *Educational Researcher, 21*(7), 4-11, 19.

Apple, M. (1993). *Official knowledge: Democratic education in a conservative age*. New York: Routledge.

Argyris, C. (1982). *Reasoning, learning and action*. San Francisco: Jossey-Bass.

Argyris, C. (1985). *Strategy, change and defensive routines*. Boston: Pitman.

Argyris, C., & Schön, D. (1974). *Theory in practice: Increasing leadership effectiveness*. San Francisco: Jossey-Bass.

Baker, C.D., & Davies, B. (1993). Literacy and gender in early childhood. In A. Luke & P.H. Gilbert (Eds.), *Literacy in contexts: Australian perspectives and issues*. Sydney, Australia: Allen & Unwin.

Bakhtin, M. (1981). *The dialogic imagination: Four essays*. Austin: University of Texas Press.

Bakhtin, M. (1986). *Speech genres and other late essays*. Austin: University of Texas Press. (Original work published in 1975)

Ball, S.J. (1987). *The micro-politics of the school: Towards a theory of school organization*. New York: Routledge.

Ball, S. (1990). *Politics and policy making in education: Explorations in policy sociology*. London, Routledge.

Ball, S. (1993). What is policy? Texts, trajectories and toolboxes. *Discourse, 13*(2).

Barry, B. (1989). *A treatise on social justice: Vol. 1—Theories of justice*. Berkeley: University of California Press.

Bartky, S.L. (1988). Foucault, femininity and the modernization of patriarchal power. In I. Diamond & L. Quinby (Eds.), *Feminism and Foucault: Reflections on resistance*. Boston: Northeastern University Press.

Bates, R. (1984). Toward a critical practice of educational administration. In T. Sergiovanni & J. Corbally (Eds.), *Leadership and organizational culture* (pp. 240-259). Urbana and Chicago: University of Illinois Press.

Bates, R. (1986). *The management of knowledge and culture*. Geelong, Australia: Deakin University Press.

Bauman, Z. (1988/89). Strangers: The social construction of universality and particularity. *Telos, 78*, 7-42.

BBC. (1988). *Pictures in the mind* [Video]. Bristol: BBC.

Berger, P.L., & Luckmann, A. (1967). *The social construction of reality: A treatise on the sociology of knowledge*. Garden City, NY: Doubleday.

Berkowitz, L. (1986). *A survey of social psychology*. New York: Academic Press.

Berlin, I. (1990, September 27). Joseph de Maistre and the origins of Fascism. *New York Review of Books, 37*(14), 57-64.

Berman, P., Chambers, J., Gadaura, P., & et al. (1992). *Meeting the challenge of linguistic diversity: An evaluation of programs for pupils with limited proficiency in English.* Berkeley: BW Associates.

Bernstein, R. (1989) in cherryholmes.

Bernstein, R. (1991). *The new constellation.* Cambridge: Polity Press.

Beyer, L., & Apple, M. (1988). *The curriculum.* Albany: State University of New York.

Bhabha, H.K. (1990). The other question: Difference, discrimination and the discourse on colonialism. In R. Ferguson, M. Gever, T.T. Minh-ha, & C. West (Eds.), *Out there: Marginalization and contemporary cultures* (pp. 71-88). New York & Cambridge, MA: New Museum of Contemporary Art & The MIT Press.

Bhaskar, R. (1986). *Scientific realism and human emancipation.* London: Verso.

Bhaskar, R. (1989). *Reclaiming reality: A critical introduction to contemporary philosophy.* London: Verso.

Bifano, S.L. (1989). Researching the professional practice of elementary principals. Combining qualitative methods and case study. *Journal of Educational Administration, 27*(1), 58-70.

Biott, C., & Nias, J. (1992). *Working and learning together for change.* Buckingham, UK: Open University Press.

Blackmore, J. (1991). *The ironies of whole school gender reform.* Geelong, Australia: Deakin University Press.

Blackmore, J. (1993a). *Women and educational leadership in the new hard times of educational restructuring. Proceedings of the Women and Leadership Conference.* Perth, UK: Edith Cowan University.

Blackmore, J. (1993b). The historical construction of administration as a masculinist enterprise. In J. Blackmore & J. Kenway (Eds.), *Gender matters in educational administration and policy.* Sussex, UK: Falmer Press.

Blackmore, J., Kenway, J., Willis, S., & Rennie, L. (1993). What's working for girls? In C. Marshall (Ed.), *Race and gender in the politics of education.* Sussex, UK: Falmer Press.

Blase, J. (1988a). The everyday political perspectives of teachers: Vulnerability and conservatism. *Qualitative Studies in Education, 1*(2), 125-142.

Blase, J. (1988b). The politics of favoritism: A qualitative analysis of the teacher's perspective. *Educational Administration Quarterly, 24*(2), 152-177.

Blase, J. (1988c). The teachers' political orientation vis-à-vis the principal: The micropolitics of the school. In J. Hannaway & R. Crowson (Eds.), *The politics of reforming school administration: The 1988 yearbook of the politics of education association* (pp. 113-126). New York: Falmer.

Blase, J. (1991a). Analysis and discussion: Some concluding remarks. In J. Blase (Ed.), *The politics of life in schools* (pp. 237-255). Newbury Park, CA: Sage.

Blase, J. (1991b). The micropolitical perspective. In J. Blase (Ed.), *The politics of life in schools* (pp. 1-18). Newbury Park, CA: Sage.

Blauner, R. (1969). Internal colonialism and ghetto revolt. *Social Problems, 16,* 393-408.

Blumberg, A., & Amidon, E. (1965). Teacher perceptions of supervisor-teacher interactions. *Administrator's Notebook, 14*(1), 1-4.

Blumberg, A., & Cusick, P. (1970). Supervisor-teacher interaction: An analysis of verbal behavior. *Education, 91*(2), 126-134.

Blumberg, A., & Jonas, R.S. (1987). Permitting access: Teacher's control over supervision. *Educational Leadership, 44*(8), 58-62.

Bogdan, R., & Biklen, S. (1992). *Qualitative research for education: An introduction to theory and methods.* Boston: Allyn & Bacon.

Bogdan, R., & Taylor, S. (1975). *Introduction to qualitative research methods: A phenomenological approach to the social sciences.* New York: Wiley.

Bolin, F.S., & Panaritis, P. (1992). Searching for a common purpose: A perspective on the history of supervision. In C.D. Glickman (Ed.), *Supervision in transition* (pp. 30-43). Alexandria, VA: Association for Supervision and Curriculum Development.

Bolinger, D. (1980). *Language—the loaded weapon: The use and abuse of language today.* London: Longman.

Borisoff, D., & Merrill, L. (1985). *The power to communicate: Gender differences as barriers.* Prospect Heights, IL: Waveland Press.

Bourdieu, P. (1977a). *Outline of a theory of practice.* London: Cambridge University Press.

Bourdieu, P. (1977b). Cultural reproduction and social reproduction. In J. Karabel & A.H. Halsey (Eds.), *Power and ideology in education.* New York: Oxford University Press.

Bourdieu, P. (1984). *Distinction: A social critique of the judgement of taste* (R. Nice, Trans.). London: Routledge.

Bourdieu, P. (1987). *Die kritik der feinen Unterschiede.* Frankfurt/Main: Suhrkamp.

Bourdieu, P. (1988). *Homo academicus.* Cambridge: Polity Press.

Bourdieu, P. (1991). *Language and symbolic power.* London: Polity Press.

Bowe, R., & Ball, S. (1992). *Reforming education and changing schools.* London: Routledge.

Branson, J. (1988). Gender, education and work. In D. Corson (Ed.), *Education for work: Background to policy and curriculum.* Palmerston North, Australia: The Dunmore Press.

Branson, J., & Miller, D. (1979). *Class, sex and education in capitalist society: Culture, ideology and the reproduction of inequality in Australia.* Melbourne: Longman-Sorrett.

Branson, J., & Miller, D. (1989). Beyond integration policy: The deconstruction of disability. In L. Barton (Ed.), *Integration: Myth or reality?* London: Falmer Press.

Branson, J., & Miller, D. (1991a). Normalization and the socio-cultural construction of "disabilities": Towards an understanding of schooling, discipline and the integration programme. In M. Lovegrove & R. Lewis (Eds.), *Classroom discipline.* Melbourne: Longman Cheshire.

Branson, J., & Miller, D. (1991b). Language and identity in the Australian deaf community: Australian sign language and language policy. An issue of social justice. *Australian Review of Applied Linguistics, Series S*(8), 135-176.

Branson, J., & Miller, D. (1993, Summer). Normalization, community care and the politics of difference. *Australian Disability Review.*

Branson, J., Miller, D., & Branson, K. (1988). An obstacle race: A case study of a child's schooling in Australia and England. *Disability, Handicap and Society, 3*(2), 101-118.

Branson, J., Miller, D., & McLeod, J. (1989). The integration of the so-called "disabled" into mainstream education: Beyond the add-on principle. In C. Szaday (Ed.), *Addressing behaviour problems in Australian schools.* Melbourne: Australian Council for Educational Research.

Briggs, C.L. (1986). *Learning how to ask: A sociolinguistic appraisal of the role of the interview in social science research.* Cambridge: Cambridge University Press.

Britzman, D., Santiago-valles, K., Jimenez-munoz, G., & Lamash, L. (1991). Dusting off the erasures: Race, gender and pedagogy. *Education and Society, 9*(2), 88-89.

Bruner, J. (1971). *The relevance of education.* London: George Allen and Unwin.

Bryson, M., & de Castell, S. (1992). *So we've got a chip on our shoulder: Sexing the texts of educational technologies* (Draft, Gender Enriches Curriculum Conference). Vancouver, British Columbia: University of British Columbia.

Bullough, R.V., Jr., & Gitlin, A.D. (1985). Beyond control: Rethinking teacher resistance. *Education and Society, 3*(1), 65-73.

Burbules, N. (1986). A theory of power in education. *Educational Theory, 36*(2), 95-114.

Burbules, N. (1992). Forms of ideology-critique: A pedagogical perspective. *International Journal of Qualitative Studies in Education, 5*(1) 7-17.

Burbules, N., & Rice, S. (1991). Dialogue across differences: Continuing the conversation. *Harvard Educational Review, 61*(4), 393-416.

Caldwell, B., & Spinks, J. (1992). *The self-managing school.* London: Falmer Press.

Cameron, D. (1984). Sexism and semantics. *Radical Philosophy, 36,* 14-16.

Cameron, D. (1985). *Feminism and linguistic theory.* London: Macmillan.

Campos, S.J., & Keatinge, H.R. (1988). The Carpinteria language minority student experience: From theory, to practice, to success. In T. Skutnabb-Kangas & J. Cummins (Eds.), *Minority education: From shame to struggle* (pp. 299-307). Clevedon, Avon: Multilingual Matters.

Carr, W., & Kemmis, S. (1986). *Becoming critical: Education, knowledge and action research.* Geelong, Australia: Deakin University Press.

Castles, S., Kalantzis, M., Cope, B., & Morrissey, M. (1992). *Mistaken identity: Multiculturalism and the demise of nationalism in Australia* (3rd ed.). Sydney, Australia: Pluto Press.

Castles, S., & Wustenberg, W. (1979). *The education of the future.* London: Pluto Press.

Cazden, C.B. (1985, April). *The ESL teacher as advocate.* Plenary presentation to the TESOL conference, New York.

Cherryholmes, C. (1988). *Power and criticism: Poststructural investigations in education*. New York: Teachers College Press.

Chomsky, N. (1987). The manufacture of consent. In J. Peck (Ed.), *The Chomsky reader* (pp. 121-136). New York: Pantheon Books.

Christie, F. (1985). *Language education*. Geelong, Australia: Deakin University Press.

Christie, F., Devlin, B., Freebody, P., Luke, A., Martin, J.R., Threadgold, T., & Walton, C. (1991). *Teaching English literacy: A project of national significance on the preservice preparation of teachers for teaching English literacy* (Vols. 1-3). Canberra, Australia: Department of Employment, Education and Training.

Christie, M.J. (1985). *Aboriginal perspectives on experience and learning: The role of language in Aboriginal education*. Geelong, Australia: Deakin University Press.

Cicourel, A.V. (1992). The interpenetration of communicative contexts: Examples from medical encounters. In A. Duranti & C. Goodwin (Eds.), *Rethinking context: Language as an interactive phenomenon* (pp. 291-310). Cambridge: Cambridge University Press.

Clark, R. (1992). Principles and practice of CLA in the classroom. In N. Fairclough (Ed.), *Critical language awareness*. London: Longman.

Clark, R., Fairclough, N., Ivanic, R., & Martin-Jones, M. (1990). Critical language awareness part 1: A critical review of three current approaches to language awareness. *Language and Education, 4*(4), 249-260.

Clark, R., Fairclough, N., Ivanic, R., & Martin-Jones, M. (1991). Critical language awareness part 2: Towards critical alternatives. *Language and Education, 5*(1), 41-54.

Clark, R., & Ivanic, R. (1992). Consciousness-raising about the writing process. In P. Garrett & C. James (Eds.), *Language awareness*. London: Longman.

Codd, J. (1988). The construction and deconstruction of educational policy documents. *Journal of Educational Policy, 3*(3), 235-47.

Cogan, M.L. (1973). *Clinical supervision*. Boston: Houghton Mifflin.

College, M. (1991). Skinned alive: towards a postmodern pedagogy of the body. *Education and Society, 9*(1), 61-72.

Comer, J.P. (1984). Home/school relationships as they affect the academic success of children. *Education and Urban Society, 16*, 323-337.

Commonwealth Department of Employment, Education and Training. (1989). *National Aboriginal and Torres Strait Islander education policy: Joint policy statement*. Canberra, Australia: Commonwealth of Australia.

Connell, R.W. (1987). *Gender and power*. Sydney, Australia: Allen & Unwin.

Cope, W., & Kalantzis, M. (Eds.). (1993). *The powers of literacy: A genre approach to teaching writing*. London: Falmer Press.

Corson, D. (1986a). Primitive semantic notions about hierarchy: Implications for educational organizations and educational knowledge. *Journal of Educational Administration, 24*, 173-186.

Corson, D. (1986b). Policy in social context: A collapse of holistic planning in education. *Journal of Education Policy, 1*, 5-22.

Corson, D. (1987). *Oral language across the curriculum*. Clevedon, Avon:

Multilingual Matters.

Corson, D. (1990). *Language policy across the curriculum*. Clevedon, Avon: Multilingual Matters.

Corson, D. (1991a). Educational research and Bhaskar's conception of discovery. *Educational Theory, 41*(2), 189-98.

Corson, D. (1991b). Language, power and minority schooling. *Language and Education, 5*(4), 231-253.

Corson, D. (1991c). Bhaskar's critical realism and educational knowledge. *British Journal of Sociology of Education, 12*(2), 223-241.

Corson, D. (1992a). Social justice and minority language policy. *Educational Theory, 42*(2), 181-200.

Corson, D. (1992b). Language, gender and education: A critical review linking social justice and power. *Gender and Education, 4*(2), 229-254.

Corson, D. (1993a). Discursive bias and ideology in the administration of minority group interests. *Language in Society, 22*(2), 165-192.

Corson, D. (1993b). *Language, minority education and gender: Linking social justice and power*. Toronto: OISE Press/Clevedon, Avon: Multilingual Matters.

Corson, D. (1993c). Restructuring minority schooling. *Australian Journal of Education, 37*(1), 46-68.

Corson, D., (1995). *The lexical bar* (2nd ed.). New York: Kluwer Academic.

Crickmore, B.L. (1990). *Education of the deaf and hearing impaired: A brief history*. Mayfield, NSW: Education Management Systems.

Cummins, J. (1984). *Bilingualism and special education: Issues in assessment and pedagogy*. Cleveden, Avon: Multilingual Matters.

Cummins, J. (1986). Empowering minority students: A framework for intervention. *Harvard Educational Review, 56*, 18-36.

Cummins, J. (1988). From multicultural to anti-racist education: An analysis of programs and policies in Ontario. In T. Skutnabb-Kangas & J. Cummins (Eds.), *Minority education: From shame to struggle*. Clevedon, Avon: Multilingual Matters.

Cummins, J. (1989). *Empowering minority students*. Sacramento: California Association for Bilingual Education.

Cummins, J. (1993). Bilingualism and second language learning. In W. Grabe (Ed.), *Annual review of applied linguistics* (Vol. 13, pp. 51-70). Cambridge: Cambridge University Press.

Cummins, J., & Danesi, M. (1990). *Heritage languages: The development and denial of Canada's linguistic resources*. Toronto: Garamond/Our Schools Our Selves.

Cummins, J., & Swain, M. (1986). *Bilingualism in education*. New York: Longman.

Darling-Hammond, L. (1990). Instructional policy into practice: "The power of the bottom over the top." *Educational Evaluation and Policy Analysis, 12*(3), 233-241.

Davies, B. (1993). *Shards of glass: Children reading and writing beyond gendered identities*. Sydney, Australia: Allen and Unwin.

Davis, H.E. (1992). The tyranny of resistance, or the compulsion to be a "good feminist." *Philosophy of Education, 1991 Proceedings of the Forty-Seventh annual meeting of the Philosophy of Education Society* (pp. 76-86). Normal, IL: Philosophy of Education Society.

Deal, T., & Peterson, K. (1990). *The principal's role in shaping school culture.* Washington, DC: U.S. Department of Education.

De Castell, S.C., Luke, A., & Luke, C. (Eds.). (1989). *Language, authority and criticism: Readings of the school textbook.* London: Falmer Press.

De Lauretis, T. (1990). Eccentric subjects: Feminist theory and historical consciousness. *Feminist Studies, 16*(1).

Delpit, L. (1988). The silenced dialogue: Power and pedagogy in educating other people's children. *Harvard Educational Review, 58* 280-298.

Delpit, L. (1992). Acquisition of literate discourses: Bowing before the master? *Theory into Practice, 31*(4), 296-302.

Department of Education and Science (DES). (1988). Report of the committee of inquiry into the teaching of English language (Kingman Rep.). London: HMSO.

Department of Education and Science (DES). (1989). *English for ages 5 to 16* (Cox Rep.). London: HMSO.

Derrida, J. (1981). *Positions.* Chicago: The University of Chicago Press.

Derrida, J. (1992). Passions: An oblique offering. In D. Woods (Ed.), *Derrida: A critical reader* (pp. 5-35). Oxford: Blackwell.

Dewey, J. (1938). *Experience and education.* New York: Macmillan.

Dewey, J. (1980). *Art as experience.* New York: Putnam. (Original work published in 1934)

Dewey, J. (1989). The development of American pragmatism. In J.J. McDermott (Ed.), *The philosophy of John Dewey* (pp. 41-57). Indianapolis, IN: Hackett. (Original work published in 1925)

Donald, J., & Rattansi, A. (Eds.). (1992). *"Race," culture and difference.* London: Sage.

Doughty, P., Pearce, J., & Thornton, G. (1971). *Language in use.* London: Edward Arnold.

Driver, K. (1990, December). *United Kingdom: Quality matters, an initiative in developing school leadership from the secondary heads association.* Paper presented at the Equal Advances in Education Management Conference. Council of Europe, Vienna, Austria.

Dubois, W.E.B. (1969). *The souls of black folk.* New York: New American Library. (Original work published in 1903)

Dumont, L. (1980). *Homo hierarchicus: The caste system and its implications.* Chicago: University of Chicago Press.

Dunlap, D.M., & Goldman, P. (1991). Rethinking power in schools. *Educational Administration Quarterly, 27*(1), 5-29.

Dunn, L. (1987). *Bilingual Hispanic children on the U.S. mainland: A review of research on their cognitive, linguistic, and scholastic development.* Circle Pines, MN: American Guidance Service.

Edelman, M. (1984). The political language of the helping professions. In M. Shapiro (Ed.), *Language and politics.* Oxford: Basil Blackwell.

Eisner, E. (1982). An artistic approach to supervision. In T. J. Sergiovanni

(Ed.), *Supervision of teaching* (pp. 53-66). Alexandria, VA: Association for Supervision and Curriculum Development.

Elliott, J. (1992). *Action research for educational change*. Buckingham, UK: Open University Press.

Ellsworth, E. (1989). "Why doesn't this feel empowering?" Working through the repressive myths of critical pedagogy. *Harvard Educational Review, 39*(3), 297-325.

Ewoldt, C. (1979). *Mainstreaming the hearing impaired child: Process not goal*. ERIC Report No. ED 168 275; ED 114 148.

Fairclough, N. (1985). Critical and descriptive goals in discourse analysis. *Journal of Pragmatics, 9*, 739-763.

Fairclough, N. (1989). *Language and power*. London: Longman.

Fairclough, N. (1992a). *Discourse and social change*. Cambridge: Polity Press.

Fairclough, N. (1992b). The appropriacy of "appropriateness." In N. Fairclough (Ed.), *Critical language awareness*. London: Longman.

Fairclough, N. (1992c). *Critical language awareness*. London: Longman.

Fairclough, N. (1993). Critical discourse analysis and the marketization of public discourse: The universities. *Discourse and Society*.

Fairclough, N. (1994). Conversationalization of discourse and the authority of the consumer. In N. Abercrombie, R. Keat, & N. Whiteley (Eds.), *The authority of the consumer*. London: Routledge.

Fairclough, N. (in press). Discourse, change and hegemony. In N. Fairclough (Ed.), *Critical language studies*. London: Longman.

Fay, B. (1987). *Critical social science: Liberation and its limits*. Ithaca, NY: Cornell University Press.

Featherstone, M. (1991). *Consumer culture and postmodernism*. London: Sage.

Fesl, E.M.D. (1993). *Conned*. Brisbane, Australia: University of Queensland Press.

Fletcher, L. (1991). Deafness: The treatment. In G. Taylor & J. Bishop (Eds.), *Being deaf: The experience of deafness*. London: Pinter Publishers.

Folds, R. (1987). *Whitefella School: Education and aboriginal resistance*. Sydney, Australia: Allen & Unwin.

Fordham, S. (1990). Racelessness as a factor in Black students' school success: Pragmatic strategy or Pyrrhic victory? In N.M. Hidalgo, C.L. McDowell, & E.V. Siddle (Eds.), *Facing racism in education* (pp. 232-262, Reprint series No. 21, Harvard Educational Review).

Forgacs, D. (1988). *A Gramsci reader*. London: Lawrence and Wishart.

Foster, W. (1984). *Paradigms and promises: New approaches to educational administration*. Buffalo, NY: Prometheus.

Foucault, M. (1972). *The archaeology of knowledge*. New York: Harper & Row.

Foucault, M. (1977). *Die Ordnung des Diskurses*. München: Fink.

Foucault, M. (1979). *Discipline and punish: The birth of the prison*. New York: Vintage Books.

Foucault, M. (1980). Power/knowledge. In C. Gordon (Ed.), *Power/knowledge: Selected interviews and other writings, 1971-1977*. New York: Pantheon.

Foucault, M. (1981). The order of discourse. In R. Young (Ed.), *Untying the text: A post-structuralist reader* (pp. 48-78). Boston: Routledge & Kegan Paul.

Foucault, M. (1988). Technologies of the self. In L.H. Martin, H. Gutman, & P.H. Hutton (Eds.), *Technologies of the self* (pp. 16-49). London: Tavistock.

Fowler, R., Hodge, R., Kress G., & Trew, T. (1979). *Language and control.* London: Routledge.

Freire, P. (1985). Banking education. In H. Giroux & D. Purpel (Eds.), *The hidden curriculum and moral education: Deception or discovery?* Berkeley, CA: McCutcheon.

Freire, P., & Macedo, D. (1987). *Literacy: Reading the word and the world.* South Hadley, MA: Bergin & Garvey.

Freire, P., & Shor, I. (1987). *A pedagogy for liberation.* London: Macmillan.

Friedrich, P. (1989). Language, ideology, and political economy. *American Anthropologist, 91*(2), 295-312.

Fulcher, G. (1986). Australian policies on special education: Towards a sociological account. *Disability, Handicap and Society, 1*(1).

Fullan, M. (1987). *Implementing educational change: What we know.* In World bank, planning for the implementation of educational change.

Fullan, M. (1991). *The new meaning of educational change.* New York: Teachers College Press.

Fullan, M. (1994). *Change forces. Probing the depths of educational reform.* London: Falmer Press.

Garcia, O., & Otheguy, R. (1987). The bilingual education of Cuban-American children in Dade County's ethnic schools. *Language and Education, 1,* 83-95.

Garfinkel, E. (1988). *Ways men and women in school administration conceptualize the administrative team.* Unpublished doctoral dissertation, Hofstra University, Hempstead, NY.

Garman, N.B. (1982). The clinical approach to supervision. In T.J. Sergiovanni (Ed.), *Supervision of teaching* (pp. 35-52). Alexandria, VA: Association for Supervision and Curriculum Development.

Garman, N.B. (1990). Theories embedded in the events of clinical supervision: A hermeneutic approach. *Journal of Curriculum and Supervision, 5*(3), 201-213.

Gatens, M. (1992). Power, bodies and difference. In M. Barrett & A. Phillips (Eds.), *Destabilizing theory: Contemporary feminist debates.* Cambridge, UK: Polity Press.

Gee, L. (1990). *Social linguistics and literacies.* London: Falmer Press.

Giddens, A. (1979). *Central problems in social theory.* Berkeley: University of California Press.

Giddens, A. (1984). *The constitution of society.* Cambridge: Polity Press.

Giddens, A. (1991). *Modernity and self-identity.* Cambridge: Polity Press.

Giroux, H.A. (1981). Hegemony, resistance, and the paradox of educational reform. *Interchange, 12*(2-3), 3-26.

Giroux, H.A. (1983a). *Theory and resistance in education: A pedagogy for the opposition.* New York: Heinemann.

Giroux, H.A. (1983b). Theories of reproduction and resistance in the new sociology of education: A critical analysis. *Harvard Educational Review, 53*(3), 257-293.

Giroux, H.A. (1991). Series introduction. Rethinking the pedagogy of voice, difference and cultural struggle. In C.E. Walsh (Ed.), *Pedagogy and the struggle for voice: Issues of language, power and schooling for Puerto Ricans* (pp. xv-xxvii). Toronto: OISE Press.

Giroux, H.A. (1992). *Border crossings: Cultural workers and the politics of education.* New York: Routledge.

Gitlin, A.D. (1990). Educative research, voice and school change. Harvard *Educational Review, 60*(4), 443-466.

Gitlin, A.D., Ogawa, R.T., & Rose, E. (1984). Supervision, reflection, and understanding: A case for horizontal evaluation. *Journal of Teacher Education, 35*(3), 46-52.

Gitlin, A.D., & Smyth, J. (1989). *Teacher evaluation: educative alternatives.* New York: Falmer Press.

Glickman, C.D. (1990). *Supervision of instruction: A developmental approach* (2nd ed.). Boston: Allyn & Bacon.

Goldhammer, R. (1969). *Clinical supervision: Special methods for the supervision of teachers.* New York: Holt, Rinehart & Winston.

Goodlad, J.I. (1984). *A place called school: Prospects for the future.* New York: McGraw-Hill.

Goodman, J. (1988). The disenfranchisement of elementary teachers and strategies for resistance. *Journal of Curriculum and Supervision, 3*(3), 201-220.

Goodwin, C., & Heritage, J. (1990). Conversation analysis. In B.J. Siegel (Ed.), *Annual review of anthropology* (Vol. 19, pp. 283-307). Palo Alto, CA: Annual Reviews.

Grässel, U. (1991). *Sprachverhlaten uind Geschlecht.* Stuttgart: Pfaffenweiler-Centaurus.

Gramsci, A. (1948). *Opere di Antonio Gramsci* (Quaderni del Carcere). Torino, Italy: Einaudi.

Gramsci, A. (1971). *Selections from prison notebooks.* London: Lawrence & Wishart.

Greenberg, P. (1989). Parents as partners in young children's development and education: A new American fad? Why does it matter? *Young Children, 44,* 61-75.

Griffith, A. (1992). Educational policy as text and action. *Educational Policy, 6*(4), 415-28.

Gronn, P.C. (1983). Talk as the work: The accomplishment of school administration. *Administrative Science Quarterly, 28,*(1), 1-21.

Gronn, P.C. (1984). "I have a solution . . .": Administrative power in a school meeting. *Educational Administration Quarterly, 20*(2), 65-92.

Gumperz, J.J. (1992). Contextualization and understanding. In A. Duranti & C. Goodwin (Eds.), *Rethinking context: Language as an interactive phenomenon* (pp. 229-252). Cambridge: Cambridge University Press.

Gunn, G. (1992). *Thinking across the American grain: Ideology, intellect, and the new pragmatism.* Chicago: University of Chicago Press.

Habermas, J. (1970). Towards a theory of communicative competence. *Inquiry, 13,* 360-375.

Habermas, J. (1971). *Knowledge and human interests*. Boston: Beacon Press.
Habermas, J. (1979). *Communication and the evolution of society*. Boston: Beacon Press.
Habermas, J. (1982). *Theorie des kommunikativen Handelns*. Frankfurt/Main: Suhrkamp.
Habermas, J. (1984). *The theory of communicative action: Vol. 1, Reason and the rationalization of society*. Boston: Beacon Press.
Habermas, J. (1985). *The philosophical discourse of modernity*. Cambridge: MIT Press.
Habermas, J. (1987). *Nachmetaphysisches Denken*. Frankfurt: Suhrkamp.
Habermas, J. (1990). Discourse ethics: A proposal for a program of philosophical justification. In S. Benhabib (Ed.), *The communicative ethics controversy*. Cambridge: MIT Press.
Hall, D. (1985). *Writing well* (5th ed.). Boston: Little Brown.
Hall, E.T. (1959). *The silent language*. Greenwich, CT: Fawcett.
Halliday, M. (1973). *Language as social semiotic*. London: Edward Arnold.
Hansen, B. (1989). *Trends in the progress towards bilingual education for deaf children in Denmark*. København, Denmark: Doves Center for Total Kommunikation.
Hansen, B. (1991). *The development towards acceptance of sign language in Denmark*. København, Denmark: Doves Center for Total Kommunikation.
Hargreaves, A. (1981). Contrastive rhetoric and extremist talk. In A. Hargreaves & P. Woods (Eds.), *Classrooms and staffrooms: The sociology of teachers and teaching*. London: Open University Press.
Hargreaves, A. (1985). The micro-macro problem in the sociology of education. In R.G. Burgess (Ed.), *Issues in educational research: Qualitative methods* (pp. 21-47). London, UK: The Falmer Press.
Hargreaves, A. (1990). Teachers' work and the politics of time and space. *Qualitative Studies in Education, 3*(4), 303-320.
Hargreaves, A. (1994). Development and desire: A postmodern perspective. In T. Guskey & M. Huberman (Eds.), *New paradigms and practices in professional development*. New York: Teachers College Press.
Havel, V. (1992, March 1). *The end of the modern era*. The New York Times, p. 15.
Hawkins, E. (1984). *Awareness of language: An introduction*. Cambridge: Cambridge University Press.
Haynes, N.M., Comer, J.P., & Hamilton-Lee, M. (1989). School climate enhancement through parental involvement. *Journal of School Psychology, 27*, 87-90.
Hearn, J., Sheppard, D., Tancred-Sheriff, P., & Burrell, G. (Eds.). (1990). *The sexuality of organization*. London: Sage.
Heath, S.B. (1983). *Ways with words: Ethnography of communication in communities and classrooms*. Cambridge: Cambridge University Press.
Held, D. (1980). *Introduction to critical theory*. Berkeley: University of California Press.
Helgesen, S. (1990). *Fraen führen anders*. Frankfurt/Main: Campus.
Hempel, C. (1965). *Aspects of scientific explanation: And other essays in the philosophy of science*. New York: Free Press.

Henriques, J., Hollway, W., Urwin, C., Venn, C., & Walkerdine, V. (1984). *Changing the subject: Psychology, social regulation and subjectivity.* London: Methuen.

Henry, M. (1993). What is policy? A response to Stephen Ball. *Discourse, 14*(1).

Hiley, D., & Bohman, J., & Schusterman, R. (Eds.). (1991). *The interpretive turn.* Ithaca, NY: Cornell University Press.

Hirsch, E.D., Jr. (1987). *Cultural literacy: What every American needs to know.* Boston: Houghton Mifflin.

Holland, P.E. (1989). Implicit assumptions about the supervisory conference: A review and analysis of literature. *Journal of Curriculum and Supervision, 4*(4), 362-379.

hooks, b. (1990a). Talking back. In R. Ferguson, M. Gever, T.T. Minh-ha, & C. West (Eds.), *Out there: Marginalization and contemporary cultures* (pp. 337-341). New York & Cambridge, MA: New Museum of Contemporary Art & MIT Press.

hooks, b. (1990b). *Yearning: Race, gender and cultural politics.* Boston: South End Press.

hooks, b. (1990c). Marginality as a site of resistance. In R. Ferguson, M. Gever, T.T. Minh-ha, & C. West (Eds.), *Out there: Marginalization and contemporary cultures* (pp. 341-343). Cambridge, MA: MIT Press.

Horkheimer, M., & Adorno, T. (1991). *Dialectic of enlightenment.* New York: Continuum. (Original work published in 1944)

Hoyle, E. (1986). *The politics of school management.* London: Hodder and Stoughton.

Huberman, A.M. (1984). *Innovation up close: How school improvement works.* New York: Plenum Press.

Hughes, J. (1990). *The philosophy of social research.* London: Longman.

Hunter, M. (1984). Knowing, teaching, and supervising. In P.L. Hosford (Ed.), *Using what we know about teaching.* Alexandria, VA: Association for Supervision and Curriculum Development.

Huspek, J. (1991). Review of language and power. *Language in Society, 20*(1), 131-137.

Hymes, D.H. (1966). Two types of linguistic relativity. In W. Bright (Ed.), *Sociolinguistics.* The Hague: Mouton.

Iannacone, L. (1975). *Education policy systems: A study guide for educational administrators.* Fort Lauderdale, FL: Nova University.

Ivanic, R., & Roach, D. (1990). Academic writing, power and disguise. In N. Fairclough et al. (Eds.), *Language and power: Proceedings of the BAAL Annual Meeting.* London: CILT.

Ivanic, R., & Simpson, J. (1992). Who's who in academic writing? In N. Fairclough (Ed.), *Critical language awareness.* London: Longman.

James. W. (1981). *Pragmatism.* Indaianapolis, IN: Hackett. (Original work published in 1907)

Janks, H., & Ivanic, R. (1992). Critical language awareness and emancipatory discourse. In N. Fairclough (Ed.), *Critical language awareness.* London: Longman.

JanMohamed, A.R., & Lloyd, D. (1990). Toward a theory of minority discourse: What is to be done? In A.R. JanMohamed & D. Lloyd (Eds.), *The nature and context of minority discourse* (pp.1-16). Oxford: Oxford University Press.

Johnson, C. (1993). *System and writing in the philosophy of Jacques Derrida.* Cambridge: Cambridge University Press.

Johnson, R.E., & Erting, C.J. (1990). Ethnicity and socialization in a classroom for deaf children. In C. Lucas (Ed.), *The sociolinguistics of the deaf community.* New York: Academic Press.

Jones, A. (1991). Is Madonna a feminist folk hero, is Ruth Richardson a woman? Postmodern feminism and dilemmas of difference. *Sites, 23,* 84-100.

Kagan, S. (1986). Cooperative learning and sociocultural factors in schooling. In California State Department of Education (Ed.), *Social and cultural factors in schooling language minority students.* Los Angeles: Evaluation, Dissemination, and Assessment Center, California State University.

Kalantzis, J., Cope, B., Noble, G., & Poynting, S. (1990). *Cultures of schooling: Pedagogies for cultural difference and social access.* London: The Falmer Press.

Kalantzis, M., Cope, W., & Slade, D. (1989). *Dominant culture and minority languages.* London: Falmer Press.

Kale, J. (1990). Controllers and victims: Language and education in the Torres Strait. In R. Baldauf & A. Luke (Eds.), *Language, planning and education in Australasia and the South Pacific* (pp. 106-126). Clevedon & Philadelphia: Multilingual Matters.

Kanpol, B. (1988). Teacher work tasks as forms of resistance and accommodation to structural factors of schooling. *Urban Education, 23*(2), 173-187.

Kanpol, B. (1991). Teacher group formation as emancipatory critique: Necessary conditions for teacher resistance. *The Journal of Educational Thought, 25*(2), 134-149.

Kemmis, S., & Fitzclarence, L. (1986). *Curriculum theorizing: Beyond reproduction theory.* Geelong, Australia: Deakin University Press.

Kenway, J. (1990). *Gender and education policy.* Geelong, Australia: Deakin University Press.

Kenway, J. (1991). *Masculinity: Under siege, on the defensive and under reconstruction?* Paper presented at the Bergamo Curriculum Conference, Dayton, OH.

Kenway, J. (1992). Feminist theories of the state: To be or not to be? In M. Muetzelfeldt (Ed.), *Society, state and politics in Australia.* Sydney, Australia: Pluto Press.

Kenway, J., & Evans, M. (1992). *Working for gender justice in schools.* Victoria: Victorian Ministry of Education, Ministerial Advisory Committee on Women and Girls.

Kenway, J., & Modra, H. (1992). Feminist pedagogies and emancipatory possibilities. In C. Luke & J. Gore (Eds.), *Feminism and critical pedagogy* (pp.). New York: Routledge.

Kenway, J., & Willis, S. (1993). *Telling tales: Girls and schools changing their ways.* Department of Employment, Education and Training, Canberra.

Kerfoot, D., & Knights, D. (1993). Management, masculinity and manipulation:

From paternalism to corporate strategy in financial services in Britain. *Journal of Management Studies, 30*(4).

King, D., & McHoul, A.W. (1986). The discursive production of the Queensland Aborigine as subject: Meston's proposal. *Social Analysis, 19*(1), 22-39.

Knight, J., Smith, R., & Sachs, J. (1990). Deconstructing hegemony: Multicultural policy and a populist response. In S.J. Ball (Ed.), *Foucault and education: Disciplines and knowledge* (pp. 133-152). London: Routledge.

Kozol, J. (1991). *Savage inequalities: Children in American schools.* New York: Crown Publishers.

Kraft, R.E. (1991, April). *Gender differences in the supervisory process.* Paper presented at the annual meeting of the American Educational Research Association, Chicago, IL.

Krashen, S. (1981). *Second language acquisition and second language learning.* London: Pergamon Press.

Krashen, S. (1993). *The power of reading.* Englewood, CO: Libraries Unlimited.

Kristeva, J. (1986). Word, dialogue and novel. In T. Moi (Ed.), *The Kristeva reader.* Oxford: Basil Blackwell.

Kuhn, T.S. (1972). *The structure of scientific revolutions.* Chicago: The University of Chicago Press.

Labaree, D. (1992a). Doing good, doing science: The Holmes Group Reports and the rhetorics of educational reform. *Teachers College Record. 93*(4), 628-640.

Labaree, D. (1992b). Power, knowledge, and the rationalization of teaching: A genealogy of the movement to professionalize teaching. *Harvard Educational Review, 62*(2), 123-154.

Labov, W. (1972). *Language in the inner city.* Philadelphia: University of Pennsylvania Press.

Ladd, P. (1991). Making plans for Nigel: The erosion of identity by mainstreaming. In G. Taylor & J. Bishop (Eds.), *Being deaf: The experience of deafness.* London: Pinter Publishers.

Lakatos, I., & Musgrove, A. (Eds.). (1971). *Criticism and growth of knowledge.* Cambridge: Cambridge University Press.

Lakoff, R. (1985, Fall). *The politics of language.* Paper #11 presented to the California Association of Teachers of English to Speakers of Other Languages, San Diego, CA.

Lalouschek, J., Menz, F., & Wodak, R. (1990). *Alltag in der Ambulanz.* Tübingen: Narr.

Lane, H. (1988). *When the mind hears: A history of the deaf.* Harmondsworth, UK: Penguin Books.

Lane, H. (1992). *The mask of benevolence.* New York: Knopf.

Lather, P. (1991a). Deconstructing/deconstructive inquiry: The politics of knowing and being known. *Educational Theory, 41*(2), 153-173.

Lather, P. (1991b). *Feminist research in education: Within/against.* Geelong, Australia: Deakin University Press.

Lesko, N. (1988). *Symbolizing society*. London: Falmer Press.
Lindstrom, L. (1992). Context contests: Debatable truth statements on Tanna (Vanuatu). In A. Duranti & C. Goodwin (Eds.), *Rethinking context: Language as an interactive phenomenon* (pp. 101-124). Cambridge: Cambridge University Press.
Lorde, A. (1984). *Sister outsider*. New York: Crossing Press.
Luetke-Stahlman, B. (1983). Using bilingual instructional models in teaching hearing-impaired students. *American Annals of the Deaf, 128*(7), 873-877.
Lukács, G. (1971). Reification and the consciousness of the proletariat. In G. Lukács (Ed.), *History and class consciousness*. Cambridge, MA: MIT Press. (Original work published in 1922)
Luke, A. (1988). *Literacy, textbooks and ideology*. London: Falmer Press.
Luke, A., Nakata, M., Singh, M.G., & Smith, R. (1993). Policy and the politics of representation: Torres Strait Islanders and Aborigines at the margins. In B. Lingard, J. Knight, & P. Porter (Eds.), *Schooling reform in hard times* (pp. 139-152). London: Falmer Press.
Luke, C., DeCastell, S.C., & Luke, A. (1983). Beyond criticism: The authority of the school textbook. *Curriculum Inquiry, 11*(2), 111-128.
Lukes, S. (1974). *Power: A radical view*. London: Macmillan.
Macedo, D. (1993). Literacy for stupidification: The pedagogy of big lies. *Harvard Educational Review, 63*, 193-206.
Malcolm, I. (1982). Speech events of the Aboriginal classroom. *International Journal of the Sociology of Language, 36*, 115-134.
Malin, M. (1990). The visibility and invisibility of Aboriginal students in an urban classroom. *Australian Journal of Education, 34*(3), 312-329.
Marris, P. (1975). *Loss and change*. New York: Anchor Press/Doubleday.
Marshall, C., & Scribner, J. (1991). "It's all political!": Inquiry into the micropolitics of education. *Education and Urban Society, 23*(4), 347-355.
Martin, B. (1988). Feminism, criticism and Foucault. In I. Diamond & L. Quinby (Eds.), *Feminism and Foucault: Reflections on resistance*. Boston: North Eastern University Press.
Marx, K. (1978). Capital (Vol. 1, S. Moore & E. Aveling, Trans.). In R. Tucker (Ed.), *The Marx-Engels reader* (2nd ed.). New York: Norton. (Original work published in 1867)
Marx, K., & Engels, F. (1976). *The German ideology*. Moscow: Progress Publishers. (Original work published in 1846)
Mason, C. (1991). School experiences. In G. Taylor & J. Bishop (Eds.), *Being deaf: The experience of deafness*. London: Pinter Publishers.
Matsuda, M.J., Lawrence, C.R., Delgado, R., & Crenshaw, K.W. (1993). *Words that wound: Critical race theory, assaultive speech and the First Amendment*. Boulder, CO: Westview Press.
Maxcy, S. (1991). *Educational leadership: A critical pragmatic perspective*. New York: Bergin & Garvey.
May, S. (1994). *Making multicultural education work*. Clevedon, Avon: Multilingual Matters.
May, W.T., & Zimpher, N.L. (1986). An examination of three theoretical perspectives on supervision: Perceptions of preservice field supervision.

Journal of Curriculum and Supervision, 1(2), 83-99.

McCaleb, S.P. (1994). *Building communities of learners: A collaboration among teachers, students, families and community.* New York: St. Martin's Press.

McCarthy, C. (1991). *Race and curriculum.* London: Falmer Press.

McDermott, R.P. (1977). Social relations as contexts for learning in schools. *Harvard Educational Review, 47,* 198-213.

McDermott, R.P., Godspodinoff, K., & Aron, J. (1978). Criteria for an ethnographically adequate description of concerted activities and their contexts. *Semiotica, 24*(3/4), 245-275.

McDermott, R.P., & Tylbor, H. (1983). On the necessity of collusion in conversation. *Text, 3*(3), 277-297.

McKeown, G., & Freebody, P. (1988). The language of Aboriginal and non-Aboriginal children and the texts they encounter in school. *Australian Journal of Reading, 11*(2), 115-120.

McLaren, P. (1985). The ritual dimensions of resistance: Clowning and symbolic inversion. *Journal of Education, 167*(2), 84-97.

McLaughlin, M. (1987). Learning from experience: Lessons from policy implementation. *Educational Evaluation and Policy Analysis, 9*(2), 171-178.

McLaughlin, M., & Marsh, M. (1990). Staff development and school change. In (Eds.), *Schools as collaborative cultures: Creating the future now.* Lewes, UK: Falmer Press.

Mehan, H. (1979). *Learning lessons.* Cambridge, MA: Harvard University.

Mehan, H., Hertwick, A., & Meihls, J.L. (1986). *Handicapping the handicapped: Decision making in students' educational careers.* Palo Alto: Stanford University Press.

Menand, L. (1992, June). Teh real Johe Dewey. The New York Review of Books, XXXIX(12), 50-55.

Merrill, E.C. (1975, Fall). *Universal rights and progress in education of the deaf.* Gallaudet Today.

Mey, J. (1985). *Whose language? A study of linguistic pragmatics.* Amsterdam: John Benjamins.

Michaels, S., & Collins, J. (1984). Oral discourse styles: Classroom interaction and the acquisition of literacy. In D. Tannen (Ed.), *Coherence in spoken and written discourse* (pp. 219-224). Norwood, NJ: Ablex.

Miller, D. (1991). Louis Dumont. In P. Beilharz (Ed.), *Social theory: A guide to central thinkers.* North Sydney: Allen & Unwin.

Miller, D., & Branson, J. (1987). Pierre Bourdieu: Culture and praxis. In D.J. Austin-Broos (Ed.), *Creating culture.* North Sydney, Australia: Allen & Unwin.

Miller, D., & Branson, J. (1991). Pierre Bourdieu. In P. Beilharz (Ed.), *Social theory: A guide to central thinkers.* North Sydney, Australia: Allen & Unwin.

Mills, A., & Tancred, P. (Eds.). (1992). *Gendering organizational analysis.* New York: Sage.

Minh-ha, T.T. (1986/87). Introduction. *Discourse, 8,* 3-9.

Ministerial Review of Educational Services for the Disabled. (1984).

Integration in Victorian education: Report of the Ministerial Review of Educational Services for the Disabled. Melbourne, Office of the Director-General, Education Department.

Moerman, M. (1988). *Talking culture: Ethnography and conversation analysis.* Philadelphia: University of Pennsylvania Press.

Molnar, A. (1992). Contemporary curriculum discourse: Too much ado about nothing. *Theory into Practice, 31*(3), 198-203.

Morrow, R. (1991). Critical theory, Gramsci and cultural studies: From Structuralism to Post-structuralism. In G. Whitty (Ed.), *Critical theory now.* London: Falmer Press.

Munro, P.M. (1991). Supervision: What's imposition got to do with it? *Journal of Curriculum and Supervision, 7*(1), 77-89.

Muth, R. (1984). Toward an integrative theory of power and educational organizations. *Educational Administration Quarterly, 20*(2), 25-42.

Nairn, R., & McCreanor, T. (1991). Race talk and common sense: Patterns in Pakeha discourse on Maori-Pakeha relations in New Zealand. *Journal of Language and Social Psychology, 10*(4), 245-262.

National Commission on Excellence in Education. (1983). *A nation at risk: The imperative for educational reform.* Washington, DC: U.S. Government Printing Office.

National Congress on Languages in Education (NCLE). (1985). *Language awareness.* London: CILT.

O'Barr, W. (1982). *Linguistic evidence: Language, power and strategy in the courtroom.* New York: Academic Press.

Oakes, J. (1985). *Keeping track: How schools structure inequality.* New Haven, CT: Yale University Press.

Ogbu, J. (1978). *Minority education and caste.* New York: Academic Press.

Ogbu, J. (1992). Understanding cultural diversity and learning. *Educational Researcher, 21*(8), 5-14, 24.

Ong, W. (1982). *Orality and literacy.* London: Methuen.

Ortiz, F.I., & Marshall, C. (1988). Women in educational administration. In N. Boyan (Ed.), *Handbook of research on educational administration* (pp. 123-141). New York: Longman.

Osborne, A.B. (1991). Towards an ethnology of culturally responsive pedagogy in small scale communities: Native American and Torres Strait Islanders. *Qualitative Studies in Education, 4*(1), 1-17.

Ozolins, U. (1993). *The politics of language in Australia.* Melbourne, Australia: Cambridge University Press.

Patterson, J., Purkey, S., & Parker, J. (1986). *Productive school systems for a nonrational world.* Alexandria, VA: Association for Supervision and Curriculum Development.

Pecheux, M. (1982). *Language, semantics, and ideology: Stating the obvious.* London: Macmillan.

Peirce, C. (1905). Review of Nichols' A treatise on cosmology. In H.S. Thayer (Ed.), *Meaning and action: A critical history of pragmatism.* Indianapolis, IN: Hackett.

Perry, A. (1992). *A comparison of the ways that women and men principals supervise teachers*. Unpublished doctoral dissertation, Hofstra University, Hempstead, NY.

Popper, K. (1972). *Objective knowledge*. Oxford: The Clarendon Press.

Popper, K.R. (1976). The logic of the social sciences. In T.W. Adorno (Eds.), The positivist dispute in German sociology (pp. 87-104). London: Heinemann.

Postone, M. (1986). Anti-semitism and national socialism. In A. Rabinach & J. Zipes (Eds.), *Germans and Jews since the holocaust.* New York: Holmes and Meier.

Postone, M. (1993). *Time, labor, and social domination*. New York: Cambridge University.

Potter, J., & Wetherell, M. (1987). *Discourse and social psychology: Beyond attitudes and behavior.* London: Sage.

Prunty, J. (1987). *A critical reformulation of educational policy analysis.* Geelong, Australia: Deakin University Press.

Purvis, T., & Hunt, A. (1993). Discourse, ideology, discourse, ideology, discourse, ideology. *British Journal of Sociology, 44*(3), 473-499.

Rabinow, P. (Ed.). (1984). *The Foucault reader*. London: Penguin.

Rado, M. (1989). *Bilingualism and the school community.* Paper prepared for the Australian Advisory Council on Languages and Multicultural Education, Australian Second Language Program-Bilingualism Project.

Ramirez, J.D. (1992). Executive summary. *Bilingual Research Journal, 16,* 1-62.

Rasinski, T.V., & Fredericks, A.D. (1989). Dimensions of parent involvement. *Reading Teacher, 43,* 180-182.

Rattansi, A. (1992). Changing the subject? Racism, culture and education. In J. Donald & A. Rattansi (Eds.), *"Race," culture and difference* (pp. 11-48). London: Sage.

Rawls, J. (1972). *A theory of justice.* London: Oxford University Press.

Reid, E., & Reich, H. (1992). *Breaking the boundaries: Migrant workers' children in the EC.* Clevedon, Avon: Multilingual Matters.

Rein, M. (1983). *From policy to practice.* London: Macmillan.

Retallick, J.A. (1990, April). *Clinical supervision and the structure of communication.* Paper presented at the annual meeting of the American Educational Research Association, Boston.

Roberts, J. (1991). Administrator training: The instructional conference component. *Journal of Educational Administration, 29*(2), 38-49.

Roberts, J. (1992a). Face-threatening acts and politeness theory: Contrasting speeches from supervisory conferences. *Journal of Curriculum and Supervision, 7*(3), 287-301.

Roberts, J. (1992b, April). *The relationship of power and involvement to experience in supervisory conference: Discourse analysis of supervisor style.* Paper presented at the annual meeting of the American Educational Research Association, San Francisco.

Robinson, K. (1991). *Children of silence.* Harmondsworth, UK: Penguin.

Robinson, V.M.J. (1989). The nature and conduct of a critical dialogue. *New Zealand Journal of Educational Studies, 24*(2), 175-187.

Robinson, V.M.J. (1992). Doing critical social science: Dilemmas of control.

International Journal of Qualitative Studies in Education, 5(4), 360-375.

Robinson, V.M.J. (1993). *Problem-based methodology: Educational research for the improvement of practice.* Oxford: Pergamon Press.

Rorty, R. (1980). *Philosophy and the mirror of nature.* Princeton, NJ: Princeton University Press.

Rorty, R. (1990). Introduction. In J.P. Murphy (Ed.), *Pragmatism: From Peirce to Davidson.* Boulder, CO: Westview Press.

Rorty, R. (1991). *Objectivity, relativism and truth: Philosophical papers* (Vol. 1). Cambridge: Cambridge University Press.

Rorty, R. (1992). Is Derrida a transcendental philosopher? In D. Woods (Ed.), *Derrida: A critical reader* (pp. 235-246). Oxford: Blackwell.

Sacks, H., Schegloff, E., & Jefferson, G. (1978). A simplest systematics for the organization of turn taking for conversation. In J.N. Schenkein (Ed.), *Studies in the organization of conversational interaction* (pp. 7-55). New York: Academic Press.

Sadker, M., & Sadker, D. (1986). Sexism in the classroom: From grade school to graduate school. *Phi Delta Kappan, 67*(7), 512-515.

Sarason, S. (1990). *The predictable failure of educational reform.* San Francisco: Jossey-Bass.

Sawicki, J. (1991). *Disciplining Foucault: Feminism, power and the body.* New York: Routledge.

Sayers, D. (1991). Cross-cultural exchanges between students from the same culture: A portrait of an emerging relationship mediated by technology. *Canadian Modern Language Review, 47,* 678-696.

Schein, E. (1985). *Organizational culture and leadership.* San Francisco: Jossey-Bass.

Schlesinger, A., Jr. (1991). *The disuniting of America.* New York: Norton.

Schneider, H.D. (1977). *Sozialpsychologie der Machtbeziehungen.* Stuttgart: Klett.

Schön, D. (1983). *The reflective practitioner.* New York: Basic Books.

Sears, J. (1992). The second wave of curriculum theorizing: Labyrinths, orthodoxies and other legacies of the glass bead game. *Theory into Practice, 31*(3), 210-217.

Sergiovanni, T.J. (1982). Toward a theory of supervisory practice: Integrating scientific, clinical, and artistic views. In T.J. Sergiovanni (Ed.), *Supervision of teaching* (pp. 67-78). Alexandria, VA: Association for Supervision and Curriculum Development.

Shakeshaft, C. (1987). *Women in educational administration.* Newbury Park, CA: Sage.

Shakeshaft, C. (1989). The gender gap in research in educational administration. *Educational Administration Quarterly, 25*(4), 324-337.

Shakeshaft, C., Nowell, I., & Perry, A. (1991). Gender and supervision. *Theory into Practice. 30*(2), 134-139.

Shilling, C. (1991). Educating the body: Physical capital and the production of social inequalities. *Sociology, 25*(4), 653-672.

Shilling, C. (1992). Reconceptualising structure and agency in the sociology of education: Structuration theory and schooling. *British Journal of*

Sociology of Education, 13(1), 69-87.

Singh, M.G. (1989). A counter-hegemonic orientation to literacy in Australia. *Journal of Education, 151*(1), 34-56.

Sirotnik, K.A. (1983). What you see is what you get—consistency, persistency, and mediocrity in classrooms. *Harvard Educational Review, 53*, 16-31.

Sizer, T. (1984). *Horace's compromise.* Boston: Houghton Mifflin.

Skeggs, B. (1991). Postmodernism: What is all the fuss about? *British Journal of Sociology of Education, 12*, 255-267.

Skrtic, T. (1991). *Behind special education: A critical analysis of professional culture and school organization.* Denver, CO: Love.

Skutnabb-Kangas, T. (1984). *Bilingualism or not: Education of minorities.* Clevedon, Avon: Multilingual Matters.

Skutnabb-Kangas, T. (1988). Resource power and autonomy through discourse in conflict—a Finnish migrant school strike in Sweden. In T. Skutnabb-Kangas & J. Cummins (Eds.), *Minority education: From shame to struggle* (pp. 251-277). Clevedon, Avon: Multilingual Matters.

Slavin, R. (1983). *Cooperative learning.* New York: Longman.

Smolicz, J. (1984). Multiculturalism and an overarching framework of values. *European Journal of Education, 19*, 11-24.

Smyth, J. (1985). Developing a critical practice of clinical supervision. *Journal of Curriculum Studies, 17*(1), 1-15.

Smyth, J. (1988). A critical perspective for clinical supervision. *Journal of Curriculum and Supervision, 3*(2), 136-156.

Smyth, J. (1990, April). *Problematising teaching through a "critical approach" to clinical supervision.* Paper presented at the annual conference of the American Educational Research Association, Boston.

Smyth, J. (1991). *Teachers as collaborative learners: Challenging dominant forms of supervision.* Buckingham, UK: Open University Press.

Spivak, G.C. (1987). *In other worlds.* London: Methuen.

Spolsky, B. (1986). *Language and education in multilingual settings.* Clevedon, Avon: Multilingual Matters.

Stanley, W. (1992). *Curriculum for utopia: Social reconstruction and critical pedagogy in the postmodern era.* Albany: State University of New York Press.

Stanworth, M. (1983). *Gender and schooling: A study of sexual divisions in the classroom.* London: Hutchinson.

St. Maurice, H. (1987). Clinical supervision and power: Regimes of instructional management. In T.S. Popkewitz (Ed.), *Critical studies in teacher education: Its folklore, theory and practice* (pp. 242-264). London: Falmer Press.

Strong, M., & Chaarlson, E. (1987). Simultaneous communication: Are teachers attempting an impossible task? *American Annals of the Deaf, 132*(6).

Strotzka, H. (1985). *Macht: Ein psychoanalytischer Essay.* Wien: Europa Verlag.

Swanton, C.H.M., Robinson, V.M.J., & Crosthwaite, J. (1989). Treating women as sex objects. *Journal of Social Philosophy, 20*(3), 5-20.

Tannen, D. (1990). *You just don't understand.* New York: Ballantine.

Taylor, G., & Bishop, J. (Eds.). (1991). *Being deaf: The experience of deafness.* London: Pinter Publishers.

Terdiman, R. (1985). *Discourse/counter-discourse: The theory and practice of symbolic resistance in nineteenth-century France.* Ithaca, NY: Cornell University Press.

Thayer, H. (1984). *Meaning and action: A critical history of pragmatism.* Indianapolis, IN: Hackett.

Thompson, J. (1984). *Studies in the theory of ideology.* Cambridge: Polity Press.

Tizard, J., Schofield, W.N., & Hewison, J. (1982). Collaboration between teachers and parents in assisting children's reading. *British Journal of Educational Psychology, 52,* 1-15.

Toulmin, S. (1990). *Cosmopolis: The hidden agenda of modernity.* New York: The Free Press.

van Dijk, T. (Ed.). (1985). *Handbook of discourse analysis* (Vol. 4). London: Academic Press, Inc.

van Dijk, T. (1989). Structure of discourse and structures of power. In J. Anderson (Ed.), *Communication yearbook 12* (pp. 18-59). Los Angeles: Sage.

van Dijk, T. (in press). Foundations of critical discourse analysis. *Discourse and Society.*

van Maanen, J., & Barley, R. (1984). Occupational communities: Culture and control in organizations. In J. Van Maanen & R. Barley (Eds.), *Research in organizational behavior.* Greenwich, CT: JAI Press.

van Maanen, M.J. (1977). Linking ways of knowing with ways of being practical. *Curriculum Inquiry, 6*(3), 205-228.

Voloshinov, V. (1986). *Marxism and the philosophy of language.* New York: Seminar Press. (Original work published in 1973)

Waite, D. (1990). *Behind the other set of eyes: An ethnographic study of instructional supervision.* Unpublished doctoral dissertation, University of Oregon.

Waite, D. (1992a). Instructional supervision from a situational perspective. *Teaching and Teacher Education, 8*(4), 319-332.

Waite, D. (1992b). Supervisors' talk: Making sense of conferences from an anthropological linguistic perspective. *Journal of Curriculum and Supervision, 7*(4), 349-371.

Waite, D. (1992c). *Teachers in conference: A qualitative study of teachers' behavior in conferences with supervisors.* Paper presented to the annual meeting of the American Educational Research Association, San Francisco.

Waite, D. (1994). Understanding supervision: An exploration of aspiring supervisors' definitions. *Journal of Curriculum and Supervision, 10*(1), 60-76.

Walker, J.C. (1985). Rebels with our applause? A critique of resistance theory in Paul Willis's ethnography of schooling. *Journal of Education, 167*(2), 63-83.

Walsh, C.E. (1991). Pedagogy and the struggle for voice. Issues of language, power and schooling for Puerto Rican. Toronto: OISE Press.

Walton, C. (1993). Aboriginal education in Northern Australia: A case study of literacy policies and practices. In P. Freebody & A. Welch (Eds.),

References   325

Knowledge, culture and power: International perspectives on literacy as policy and practice (pp. 55-81). London: Falmer Press.

Watego, C. (1989). Institutional racism: Economics and education. *Black Voices, 5*(1), 9-21.

Weedon, C. (1987). *Feminist practice and post-structuralist theory.* Oxford: Basil Blackwell.

Weiler, K. (1988). *Women teaching for change: Gender, class and power.* Boston: Bergin and Garvey.

Weiner, G. (1989). Professional self-knowledge versus social justice: A critical analysis of the teacher-researcher movement. *British Educational Research Journal, 15*(1), 41-51.

Weller, R. (1971). *Verbal communication in instructional supervision.* New York: Teachers College Press.

Wernick, A., (1991). *Promotional culture.* London: Sage.

West, C. (1989). The American evasion of philosophy: A genealogy of pragmatism. Madison: The University of Wisconsin Press.

West, C. (1990). The new cultural politics of difference. In R. Ferguson, M. Gever, T.T. Minh-ha, & C. West (Eds.), *Out there: Marginalization and contemporary cultures* (pp.19-38). New York & Cambridge, MA: New Museum of Contemporary Art & MIT Press.

Westbrook, R.B. (1991). John Dewey and American democracy. Ithaca, NY: Cornell University Press.

Wexler, P. (1992). *Becoming somebody: Toward a social psychology of school.* London: Falmer Press.

Willis, P. (1977). Learning to labor: How working class kids get working class jobs. Lexington: D.C. Heath.

Willis, P. (1981). *Learning to labour: How working class kids get working class jobs.* London: Methuen.

Willis, S., Kenway, J., Rennie, L., & Blackmore, J. (1992, June). Studies of reception of gender reform in schools. *Curriculum Perspectives, Newsletter Edition,* pp. 3-12.

Wilson, T.P. (1991). Social structures and the sequential organization of interaction. In D. Boden & D.H. Zimmerman (Eds.), *Talk and social structure: Studies in ethnomethodology and conversation analysis* (pp. 22-43). Berkeley: University of California Press.

Wise, A. (1977). Why educational policies often fail: The hyperrationalization hypothesis. *Curriculum Studies, 9*(1), 43-57.

Wodak, R. (1986). *Language behavior in therapy groups.* Los Angeles: University of California Press.

Wodak, R. (1989). The irrationality of power. In P. Anderson (Ed.), *Communication yearbook* (pp. 79-94). Los Angeles: Sage.

Wodak, R. (1992a). Communication in institutions. In P. Stevenson (Ed.), *Sociolinguistics in the German-speaking countries.* Oxford: Oxford Press.

Wodak, R. (1992b). Discourse-sociolinguistics and doctor-patient interaction. In P. Linell & B.L. Gunnarson (Eds.), *Discourse and the professions.* London: Longmans.

Wodak, R., & Andraschko, E. (1992). Frauen führen anders? Eine diskurssoziolinguistische Untersuchung. *Erziehung und Unterricht.*

Wodak, R., Andraschko, E., Lalouschek, J., & Schrodt, H. (1992). *Scholpartnershaft: Kommunikation in der Schule.* Wien: Institut für Sprachwissenschaft, Projectreport.

Wodak, R., Menz, F., & Lalouschek, J. (1989). *Sprachbarrieren.* Wien: Edition Atelier.

Wolcott, H.F. (1988). "Problem finding" in qualitative research. In H.T. Trueba & C. Delgado-Gaitan (Eds.), *School & society: Learning content through culture* (pp. 11-35). New York: Praeger.

Wolf, N. (1990). *The beauty myth: How images of beauty are used against women.* London: Vintage.

Wong Fillmore, L. (1991). Second-language learning in children: A model of language learning in social context. In E. Bialystok (Ed.), *Language processing in bilingual children* (pp. 49-69). Cambridge: Cambridge University Press.

Woods, P. (1983). *Sociology and the school.* Boston: Routledge and Kegan Paul.

Wortham, S. (1992). Participant examples and classroom interaction. *Linguistics and Education, 4,* 195-217.

Wortham, S. (in press). *Acting out participant examples in the classroom.* Amsterdam: John Benjamins.

Wouters, C. (1986). Formalization and informalization: Changing tension balances in civilizing processes. *Theory, Culture and Society, 3*(2), 1-8.

Wrong, D. (1979). *Power: Its forms, bases and uses.* Oxford: Basil Blackwell.

Yates, L. (1987a). *Curriculum theory and non-sexist education: A discussion of curriculum theory, feminist theory and Victorian education policy and practice 1975-1985.* Unpublished doctoral dissertation, La Trobe University, Australia.

Yates, L. (1987b). Australian research on gender and education 1975-1985. In J. Keeves (Ed.), *Australian education: A review of recent research.* North Sydney, Australia: Allen & Unwin.

Yates, L. (1993). Feminism and Australian state policy: Some questions for the 1990s. In M. Arnot & K. Weiler (Eds.), *Feminism and social justice in education.* London: Falmer Press.

Young, I.M. (1981). Towards a critical theory of justice. *Social Theory and Practice, 7,* 279-302.

Young, I.M. (1990). *Justice and the politics of difference.* Princeton, NJ: Princeton University Press.

Young, R. (1988). Critical teaching and learning. *Educational Theory, 38*(1), 47-59.

Young, R. (1992). *Critical theory and classroom talk.* Philadelphia: Multilingual Matters.

Young, R. (1995). Postmetaphysical discourse and pedagogy. In P. Atkinson, B. Davies & S. Delamont (Eds.), *Discourse and reproduction: Essays for Basil Bernstein.* Cresskill, NJ: Hampton Press.

Zanger, V.V. (1994). "Not joined in": Intergroup relations and access to English literacy for Hispanic youth. In B.M. Ferdman, R-M. Weber, & A. Ramirez (Eds.), *Literacy across languages and cultures.* Albany: State

University of New York Press.

Zeichner, K.M., & Liston, D. (1985). Varieties of discourse in supervisory conferences. *Teaching and Teacher Education, 1*(2), 155-174.

Zimpher, N.L., deVoss, G.G., & Nott, D.L. (1980). A closer look at university student teacher supervision. *Journal of Teacher Education, 31*(4), 11-15.

Author Index

Subject Index

between sign languages and, 177-
178
Speech
ideal situation for, 136
language and, 277
Standardized cultural commodities,
294
Structure, as intractability of social
world, 8-9
Student(s)
in Canada, 193
culturally diverse, 191-193
deaf
in Australia, 181-182
bilingual/bicultural education for,
185-186
denigration of sign language and,
175-177
mainstreaming and, 170-173,
183-185
oralism and, 174-175
professionalism and, 180-181
sign language and, 173-174
signed English and, 178-180
in Sweden, 187
educational change and, 236-240
existential interests of, 280
minority, instructional disabling of,
207-208
relationship between teacher and,
299n
Subjective meaning of change, 156-157
Superintendent, 139
Supervision
description of, 72
teacher resistance and, 86
Supervision conference, teacher resistance in, 71, 85-86
Supervision literature, definition of,
72
Supervisors, inexperienced versus
experienced, 67-68
Supervisor-teacher interaction, 69-70
at conferences, 58-68

reflecting personal orientation,
59-63
at instructional conferences, 68-69
at supervisory conferences, 55-57
Supervisory conferences
gender differences in, 21-24
investigation of, 57-58
supervisor-teacher interaction at,
55-57
technical proficiency at, 56
Sweden, schools for the Deaf in, 187
Symbolic violence
professionalism as, 180-181
signed English as, 178-180
Symbols
prosodic analysis and, 87-88
transcript, 102-110

T

Talk
extremist, 13
orderly, in classroom communication, 278
Teacher(s); *see also* Supervisor-
teacher interaction
interaction styles of, 142
relationship between student and,
299n
Teacher evaluations, gender differences in, 24-25
Teacher reflection, supervisory con -
ferences and, 56
Teacher resistance
to communicative hegemony, 76-
77
activation of counterdiscourse,
80-81
breaking frame of conference, 77-
80
from resistance to hegemony, 81-
85
in supervision conference
methodology and researcher perspective, 74-76